Building
SPSS Graphs
to Understand Data

*I dedicate this textbook to my children, Sally, James (1965-1996),
and Wendy, and to my grandchildren, Tawny, James, Mitch,
Tyler, Jared, Jade, Lydia, and Elena—God bless them all.*

And to my students:
We are born
We live for a while
Then we all die
The living part is about education
The pinnacle of education is research

—James O. Aldrich

*With all my love to Ines, Hilda, Berta, Marta, Marilu, Blanca, Roberto, Ulices, Esmeralda,
Veronica, Luis, Dalila, Carlos, Edward, Edgar, Marlon, Genesis, Alexander, Andrew,
Leslie, Stephanie, José, Axel, Emely, Cynthia, Melanie, Orlando, Taylor, Jeannette,
Luis Jr., Ariel, Adrienne, Jhosselyn, Anthony, Joshua, James, Francisco, Fausto and
children, Abraham and children, and to all my other family members
who have been my motivation for happiness and success in life.*

*An extended family is like a graph built from the data points of a spread sheet,
its members may be many and different, but together, they form a beautiful picture.*

—Hilda M. Rodríguez

Building
SPSS Graphs
to Understand Data

James O. Aldrich
Hilda M. Rodríguez

California State University, Northridge

Los Angeles | London | New Delhi
Singapore | Washington DC

Los Angeles | London | New Delhi
Singapore | Washington DC

FOR INFORMATION:

SAGE Publications, Inc.
2455 Teller Road
Thousand Oaks, California 91320
E-mail: order@sagepub.com

SAGE Publications Ltd.
1 Oliver's Yard
55 City Road
London EC1Y 1SP
United Kingdom

SAGE Publications India Pvt. Ltd.
B 1/I 1 Mohan Cooperative Industrial Area
Mathura Road, New Delhi 110 044
India

SAGE Publications Asia-Pacific Pte. Ltd.
3 Church Street
#10-04 Samsung Hub
Singapore 049483

Acquisitions Editor: Vicki Knight
Associate Editor: Lauren Habib
Editorial Assistant: Kalie Koscielak
Production Editor: Brittany Bauhaus
Copy Editor: QuADS Prepress (P) Ltd.
Typesetter: C&M Digitals (P) Ltd.
Proofreader: Laura Webb
Indexer: Rick Hurd
Cover Designer: Anupama Krishnan
Marketing Manager: Nicole Elliott
Permissions Editor: Adele Hutchinson

Figures: Reprint Courtesy of International Business Machines Corporation, © SPSS, Inc., an IBM Company. SPSS was acquired by IBM in October, 2009.

Printed in the United States of America

Library of Congress Cataloging-in-Publication Data

Aldrich, James O.

Building SPSS graphs to understand data / James O. Aldrich, Hilda M. Rodriguez.

p. cm.

ISBN 978-1-4522-1684-3 (pbk.)

1. SPSS (Computer file) 2. Social sciences—Statistical methods—Computer programs. I. Rodriguez, Hilda M. II. Title.

HA29.A495 2013
005.5'5—dc23   2011050600

This book is printed on acid-free paper.

12 13 14 15 16 10 9 8 7 6 5 4 3 2 1

BRIEF CONTENTS

DETAILED CONTENTS

About the Authors

James O. Aldrich (Doctor of Public Administration, University of Laverne) is a retired lecturer on statistics and research methods at California State University, Northridge. He has served as principal investigator and codirector of a National Cancer Institute research project. He held the appointment of instructor in the Department of Pathology at the University of Southern California School of Medicine. He has served on various committees for the Los Angeles chapter of the American Statistical Association and has taught biostatistics, epidemiology, social statistics, and research methods courses for 20 years. The primary statistical software used for his coursework has been SPSS. Aldrich has recently coauthored the book *Using SPSS: An Interactive and Hands-on Approach*, which was published in July 2011 by Sage.

Hilda M. Rodríguez (Bachelor's of Arts in Sociology, California State University at Northridge) was a teaching assistant in statistics and the laboratory using the Statistical Package for the Social Sciences. She edited the original manuscript for the book *Using SPSS: An Interactive and Hands-on Approach* published by Sage in July 2011. Her work included a review of all SPSS instructions given in this publication. She came to the United States from El Salvador speaking only Spanish but soon learned English and began her pursuit of higher education. Hilda is active at her church, St. Joseph the Worker, in Winnetka, California, where she teaches religious doctrine to children, young adults, and seniors. It is in this work that her bilingual and bicultural capabilities benefit her students.

PREFACE

★ **INTENDED AUDIENCE**

This book was written for anyone needing to understand large or small amounts of data. More specifically, it describes how to build and interpret graphs to answer questions about databases. In this book, "understanding data" specifically means that the graph must clearly and succinctly answer questions about the database.

The text is primarily designed for students at all levels. This includes lower- and upper-division students studying statistics and/or research methods for the first time. However, you will find that the book sometimes assumes that the reader has some knowledge of statistics. A background that includes an introductory statistics class will make the text easier to understand and more comfortable to read. Most graduate and doctoral-level students will appreciate the graph-making instructions presented in this book. Anyone who needs to graph data—faculty, student, or business professional—will find useful information in this book.

★ **PURPOSE OF WRITING THE BOOK**

For many years, the authors have taught students how to use the Statistical Package for the Social Sciences (SPSS) (SPSS was acquired by IBM in October 2009 and is an IBM company) graphs as a way to better understand a mass of numbers. Often the information manuals, provided by SPSS and others, either contained too much information or not enough. The authors have attempted to reach a "golden mean" regarding the amount of information needed to build effective SPSS graphs.

This book is intended to encourage the use of graphing as a way to understand data. When one seeks to understand data, it usually means answering questions. If the data were collected under scientific circumstances, then these questions are usually research questions. Therefore, our graphs are not only intended to answer general questions but detailed research questions worthy of scientific presentation.

Our intent in writing this book is to empower and encourage the SPSS user to build graphs that effectively describe data. Such skills can be extremely useful, and often required, when attempting to conduct research or to communicate to others the information contained in the data.

The authors believe that graphs can be beautiful, even elegant, and perhaps considered as works of art, which convey useful information in a truthful manner. Graphs can and should be pleasing to look at—they do not, in our opinion, have to be "all work and not pleasing to the eye." However, if the cosmetic (artistic) construction of the graph hides or conceals the true meaning of the data, then, of course, this is unacceptable. That being said, we have made the *communication of information* as the most important consideration in building the graphs used in this book. We have attempted to make the graphs pleasing to the eye and "easy to look at," but we do not claim that they are works of art. We leave the creation of artistic graphs up to the reader of this book.

Our hope is that the reader proceeds through the chapters constantly accumulating useful information—information designed to impart the skills needed to answer questions concerning large (or small) databases. The answers provided through the interpretation of the graphs will then guide the user in making informed (educated) decisions.

STATISTICAL PACKAGE FOR THE SOCIAL SCIENCES (SPSS)   ★

The graphing methods described in this book are found in the Statistical Package for the Social Sciences (SPSS). Therefore, the reader should have the SPSS program available to build the graphs as described in the chapters of this book. Basic information regarding the operation of SPSS is provided in Appendix A, although familiarity with the software would be helpful.

SPSS Versions 18, 19, and 20 were used to build the graphs in this book. Most of the graphs shown in this book can be built using any of these three versions. However, there are few instances where Version 20 will not perform certain functions as it did in Versions 18 and 19. Most of these instances are cosmetic and can be worked around. If the reader is using Version 20, then some of the graphs described in Chapter 9 (Population Pyramid) will not be exactly reproducible. For instance, you will not be able insert unique patterns when splitting a continuous distribution. There are also similar problems when paneling graphs on one dimension (Chapter 16) and two dimensions (Chapter 17). Wherever there was a conflict, we chose to have the reader build the graph using SPSS Version 20. However, we do show the reader what the graphs look like when building the graphs using the other versions. SPSS is aware of most of the problems and will likely fix the defects in the next version. The minor differences between the versions will permit the user to follow the bullet points when using Version 18, 19, or 20.

Although SPSS offers different methods for building graphs, this book uses the feature known as the *Chart Builder*. We found the *Chart Builder* to be, by far, the most efficient and user-friendly way to build accurate and beautiful graphical depictions of data.

★   BOOK'S STRUCTURE

The following sections give a brief description of the chapters and appendices contained in this textbook.

Chapter 1

The first chapter has multiple intentions. First, it discusses the purpose and intent of making graphs and how they can be used to answer questions about databases. It also informs the reader how to choose the appropriate graph for the type of data one is trying to understand. It explains how to identify whether the variables are considered as discrete of continuous.

This first chapter also discusses those databases used to give the reader direct graph-building experience. It tells where they can be found in SPSS and how to open the needed databases. A major portion of the chapter is devoted to the *Chart Builder* in SPSS. This is done to familiarize the reader with the *Chart Builder*'s various windows and key control features. The level of detail does not approach that seen in later chapters but is intended to give the SPSS user a solid grounding in the basics of building a graph while using the *Chart Builder*. The chapter concludes by defining key terms and concepts used throughout the book.

Chapters 2 Through 17

After the first chapter, you find that Chapters 2 through 17 follow the same basic format. A more detailed description of these chapters is provided in the "How to Use the Book," which immediately follows this section.

Chapter 18

This chapter differs from earlier ones in that it covers deceptive graphing methods. It is also worthy to note that some book users may wish to read Chapter 18 on finishing Chapter 1. Chapter 18 is where ethical considerations are brought into focus by illustrating graphs built with the intention of deceiving graph readers.

This chapter on deception is not limited to a single graph type, as are earlier chapters, but presents several types to illustrate deceptive practices for each. Examples of graphs that distort the meaning of the underlying data are first shown. Then a graph portraying an honest picture of the data is given. This chapter also posses questions about a database and shows how the dishonest graph can provide false answers to the graph reader.

Chapters 19

This final chapter summarizes the book.

Appendix A: SPSS Basic Information

This appendix presents some basic commands for SPSS for the first time user. There are some screen shots that will get the new user started on using the SPSS software.

Appendix B: Answers to Chapter Exercises

This appendix contains the answers to the questions posed in the Review Exercises section of Chapters 2 through 17. The graphs that provide the information needed to answer these questions are shown at the end of each chapter. The reader should build these graphs and then make sure they answer the questions correctly by using this Appendix.

Appendix C: Chapters and SPSS Databases Used

This appendix lists all the SPSS databases that are used in each chapter. Therefore, you will see databases that are repeated in the table provided. This list will make it easy for those readers choosing to save the databases in their computer.

Appendix D: Graph Selection: Type and Purpose

This appendix provides additional guidance in the selection of the appropriate graph to answer questions about databases not found in this book. This appendix is especially important when the reader is ready to build graphs based on data of their own choosing.

The table in this appendix begins with a description of the types and number of variables that you may need to graph. It, then, names the various graphs that are appropriate. It finally, succinctly states the purpose of that particular graph type.

★   HOW TO USE THE BOOK

We recommend that the reader pay careful attention to the basic principles of graphing presented in the first chapter. It is in this first chapter that the reader is introduced to the basics concerning the use of the *Chart Builder* in SPSS.

As discussed in the above section that describes Chapter 18, some readers may wish to read Chapter 18 following Chapter 1. Doing so will not interrupt the continuity of the book.

Chapters 2 through 17 are formatted in an identical manner. They all have five major sections as presented below:

- *Section 1* of each of these chapters provides an introduction that describes the uses of the graphs while also showing examples of the graphs that are covered.
- *Section 2* covers the databases and questions that will be used in the chapter.
- *Section 3* is where you actually follow step-by-step instructions to build those graphs that will provide the information needed to answer the questions about the database.
- *Section 4* is where you interpret the graphs just built. The interpretation means that you will answer the questions about the database.
- *Section 5* provides Review Exercises presenting questions about a database and the graph that you are to build. Answers are found in Appendix C.

Proceed at Your Own Pace

The book is designed to be used in an "as needed" basis. By that we mean that the book's reader should proceed at his or her own pace. For example, we may give two graphing examples—you may grasp the information in one. Do not hesitate to move forward in the book toward building and interpretation of your graph. Once the reader has finished the first 3 to 4 chapters, they will be sufficiently familiar with the *Chart Builder* to jump ahead to any particular chapter that may be of special interest. You may also think of this book as a reference guide that helps you answer questions about databases by the building and interpretation of graphs.

BULLETED POINTS FOR SPSS ★

In the SPSS bulleted sections, we **bold** those things that require some reader/user action. The names of the SPSS databases used are also in **bold**. Other important location names, tabs, panels, and so on are in *italics*. You will find that each graph you build will repeat various techniques, such as changing patterns in the bars of a graph. These steps are repeated since the book is designed to make each graph-building exercise totally independent. You will very quickly develop skills that will permit you to proceed without carefully looking at many of the individual bullet points.

ACKNOWLEDGMENTS

I first thank my coauthor who would exercise more than enough calmness during periods of my frustration with either words or the computer. She also frequently exceeded what would normally be expected of a coauthor, small things, like adding several chapters to our "little" book on graphs.

I also thank my research and statistics professors and in particular Bernard Hanes. Bernard was one of those special professors whom we can all recall. He continually nurtured my interest in research and statistics and the importance of the valid and reliable measurement of our observations. I also thank James Cunningham who shared his ideas about what a book on graphs should look like early in this enterprise. Helen Dosik reviewed the early chapters and offered many thoughtful suggestions about the structure and content of the book. Wendy Thompson (my daughter) and Tawny Aldrich (my granddaughter) also carefully read our early chapters and offered valuable suggestions and words of encouragement. Dominic Little was a tremendous help with technical questions regarding the SPSS software. I also thank Esmeralda Rodríguez for her careful pre-production review of the entire manuscript.

—James O. Aldrich

I want to thank my coauthor and former professor for inviting me to be part of this book. His encouragement in the classroom and in every step of the writing process inspired me to do my very best. He made the journey an exciting and enlightening experience. I also thank Esmeralda Rodríguez for her detailed review of the entire work. Her support during this writing project is truly cherished. The computer technical assistance provided by Dominic Little is greatly appreciated. I am grateful for the early assistance provided by Helen Dosik, Wendy Thompson, and Tawny Aldrich. My family and friends exhibited a great deal of patience, support, and understanding during the many hours I spent at the computer. I thank God for blessing me with the capability to coauthor this rather technical book on the building and interpretation of graphs.

—Hilda M. Rodríguez

We both thank the professionals at Sage Publications for their valuable contributions from the very beginning to the marketing of this writing project. Vicki Knight, Publisher encouraged us through the early changes in the content and direction of this book of graphs. Vicki always had a word of encouragement as we sometimes struggled over difficult terrain. Lauren Habib, Associate Editor; Kalie Koscielak, Editorial Assistant; and Brittany Bauhaus, Production Editor, always kept us on track during the editorial and production processes. Thanks to Anupama Krishnan for the cover design and to Rajasree Ghosh and Shankaran Srinivasan of QuADS Prepress for copyediting. Many thanks to Helen Salmon, Marketing Manager, and Adele Hutchinson, Permissions Editor, for their assistance during this project.

Early contacts at IBM SPSS included Jewan Park who guided us through the maze of IBM employees and put us in contact with the appropriate people. Karen Gonda smoothed the road leading to the use of IBM copyrighted materials. Other IBM professionals providing assistance were DeJay Leang (Support Analyst), Jay Fischer (Client Care), Monica Young (Author's Program), and Beth Narrish (Marketing Manager). We thank these IBM employees for their assistance during the early days of this writing project.

The authors and Sage Publications also acknowledge the following reviewers for their contributions to this text:

Clifton C. Addison, *Jackson State University*

James P. Donnelly, *University at Buffalo/State University of New York*

Camille L. Lawrence, *Columbus State University*

Christopher N. Lawrence, *Virginia Tech*

Rosemary McCaslin, *California State University, San Bernardino*

David P. Nalbone, *Purdue University Calumet*

Thomas H. Short, *John Carroll University*

Brian C. Smith, *Graceland University*

Susan Swayze, *George Washington University*

1

INTRODUCTION

GRAPHICAL PRESENTATION OF DATA

The principal purpose of a graph is to answer questions about data. Answers to the questions may then provide direction for additional analysis or convey information about the data to colleagues or students. The old adage "a picture is worth a thousand words" is especially applicable when working with large amounts of data. A graph summarizes a mass of data and is an excellent way to "make visible" answers to questions that may be hidden in the data. We may even say that graphs give "life" to the data.

The purpose of all statistical procedures is to make data understandable. Properly constructed graphs can do this in a very direct and straightforward way. In this book, each chapter presents questions concerning variables from many different databases. The proper SPSS graph is selected, built, and interpreted in a manner that answers those questions. Following this process you have made the data more understandable.

Whether you are reading a data report at work or conducting a cancer research project, it is a good idea to be able to interpret large amounts of numerical data. The interpretation of data can mean different things to different people. For this book, "interpretation of data" means that anyone reading the data is able to recognize and understand the *information* contained in the data. This information is then used to answer questions. Answering such questions will then assist one in making a decision. One way to extract this information and make the data usable is to build a graph. A well-built graph will provide a clear visual representation of the data.

Numbers by themselves have meaning. But when they are used to measure and/or count something, they have more meaning. Throughout this book, the "meaning" may be thought of as information. The ultimate purpose of a graph is to make a "bunch of numbers" (the data) understandable. One way the graph accomplishes this is to extract *information* that is often hidden in the data. This information is then used to assist one in making a decision. Making an informed (educated) decision involves answering questions.

For example, a new professor designs her first statistics course so that her 90 students can each earn between 0 and 500 total points. At the end of her first semester of teaching, she questions the amount of material she attempted to cover in the class lectures. She wonders if she attempted to cover too much or perhaps too little material. One way to answer her question would be to analyze the data and determine the proportion of students scoring in various intervals that make up 0 to 500 points.

Let's say that she produces a graph known as a cumulative histogram. The graph reveals that 70 (78%) of the students earned between 200 and 240 total points. In other words, the graph revealed that more than three fourths of her students earned less than half of the possible points. Such a finding provides evidence that she might consider reducing the amount of material for the second semester of her teaching career. Perhaps, she might make a decision to present less material and to slow down, just a bit, with the intention that the students will increase their learning and therefore earn more total points.

The professor could have relied on basic descriptive statistical analysis to "interpret" or to extract this information from the data. As there are many statistical approaches designed to make data more understandable, for instance, she may have elected to organize the data into a table, determine percentile ranks, and calculate the mean and standard deviation.

This book is about graphs and how to use the graphing features found in the Statistical Package for the Social Sciences (SPSS) to make sense of data. This book is not about building tables or the calculation of numerous descriptive statistics. It is about the *how* and *when* to produce the appropriate graphical representation as a way to better understand data and answer pertinent questions. The actual "production" of the graph will be done by utilizing the power of the SPSS software. Much of this book is devoted to step-by-step procedures needed to build SPSS graphs. You are introduced to this aspect of our book in Section 1.5 of this chapter.

1.2 PROPORTIONAL THINKING AND GRAPH MAKING ★

It should be obvious that data are usually collected with some purpose in mind. The purpose is that the data will possess the information needed to answer specific questions that will assist us in making a decision. Thus, one should always have a clear idea about the questions that we seek to answer by our graph making.

Often such questions revolve around the idea of percentages, proportions, and probability.[1] Let's use an example that places an emphasis on this aspect of a database. A young woman is trying to decide if she wants to attend a campus party. She hopes to meet a nice young man as a potential boyfriend. A basic question for this young lady is as follows: Given the gender makeup of the party, what is the probability of meeting a potential boyfriend?

She is able to look at the list of 100 names of those attending. She wants to use these data (the 100 names) to help decide whether to attend the party. Just looking at the list of names gives her some information about the proportion of males that will be at the party. She may have an intuitive feeling about the party's gender makeup but little understandable information.

Since the data are discrete (having the two categories of male and female), we could produce a bar graph to give us a clear picture of the proportion of males and females. Most would agree that the proportion of males attending the party would be something for this young woman to consider when deciding whether to go or not. For instance, the bar graph might show that there are 80 females and 20 males on the party list; therefore, there is a .80 probability that any encountered person would be female. We could also say that 80% of those people encountered at this party would be female. We could all agree that such information would be useful when one considers her purpose in attending the party. If her purpose is to meet a young man as a potential boyfriend, then perhaps, she should forget the party, stay at home, and study statistics.

Being able to visualize proportions (hence probabilities) as demonstrated in the party example represents only one of many graphing purposes. Another purpose for a graph might be that we wish to determine if a

---

[1]Percentages, proportions, and probabilities may, in a general sense, be thought of as possessing the same type of information. Percentages use a base of 100, and therefore, any observed value represents a portion of 100 and can be expressed as a percentage of the total (100%). Probability uses a base of 1, and therefore, any observed value represents a portion of 1 and can be expressed as a decimal or fraction. The words proportion and probability actually convey the same information. Therefore, we say the proportion of females may be .80 or that the probability of a female is .80. Expressed as a percentage, we would say that 80% of the group is female.

distribution of continuous values are approximately normally distributed.[2] Or perhaps, we wish to see how two variables change together. We could also determine if the values of a variable change in some systematic manner over a period of time. These are only a few of the many uses of graphs. Later chapters will inform the reader as to the purpose of the graph and the type of graph required to answer the question at hand.

Proportional-type thinking is also related to inferential statistical concepts. When proportions are calculated on samples that were obtained through random techniques, another dimension is opened. In looking at the above party example, that new dimension is whether similar parties would be expected to have approximately the same proportion of females and males. If proper research practices were followed, then we can use the sample proportions to estimate the *likelihood* that those same proportions would exist at a similar party.

There are several considerations for the graph maker when deciding the best way to use the power of SPSS to answer questions about a database. This is the topic of the following section.

★   **1.3 DECISIONS FOR THE GRAPH MAKER**

What is the best approach when seeking to extract useful information from a large mass of data? What type of graph should be built to answer specific questions about the data? How can the extracted information be used to assist one in making decisions? What is the best way to organize data so as to answer specific questions? These are the types of questions about data answered in this section.

Since this book uses SPSS, the first step in understanding data is to make sure that its format is compatible with SPSS.[3] Once this is accomplished, we can let SPSS do the difficult and time-consuming work involved in producing a graph. Once SPSS has been selected as the software, there are other considerations before one attempts to produce a specific graph.

1.3.1 First Consideration: How Were the Variables Measured?

The first consideration when attempting to graph data is whether the measurement of the variable was discrete or continuous. When using SPSS, you

---

[2]More details regarding the normal distribution are provided in Chapter 8 on histograms.

[3]For information on how data are inputted into the SPSS format (not required in this textbook) consult *Using SPSS: An Interactive Hands-On Approach* by Cunningham and Aldrich, 2011, Sage.

will *not* see data classified as discrete or continuous, but you will see a column heading called "Measure" in the "Variable View" Screen. Measure is short for "level of measurement." It is here that the person entering the data indicates how the data were measured. If you are entering the data into the SPSS software yourself, you must understand the meaning of "level of measurement" as it relates to the numerical values associated with your observations. The data used in this textbook already have these levels of measurement specified, so this point becomes academic.[4] When using this text, you will only have to decide if the data are discrete or continuous. The SPSS databases used in this text will have already specified the data as being measured at one of three levels of measurement (scale, ordinal, and nominal).[5] Those variables measured at the *scale* level are considered as continuous data. Variables specified as being measured at the *nominal* or *ordinal* level should be considered as discrete.

Variables measured at the continuous level are not based on distinct categories. Such variables can be recognized when an infinite number of points between each interval are possible. To understand the concept of infinite points, think of the variable of weight. If it was observed that an individual weighs 165 pounds, we can see that there are an infinite number of points between 165 and say 166. One could weigh 165.25 pounds or a more sensitive scale could record 165.2567 pounds and so on. One of the common methods used to understand a large database of continuous variables is to construct a histogram. SPSS constructs intervals for the continuous data and records these on the *x*-axis. Next it counts the number of observations within these intervals, which are read from the *y*-axis. Such graphs are distinct from the bar graph in that the intervals are connected on the *x*-axis and are not separate categories as with the bar graph.

Discrete variables are made up of separate and distinct categories. An example of a discrete variable is *gender* (nominal), where all observations must fall into one of two unique categories, male or female. Another example could be responses on a survey where one has several choices such as military ranks of general, colonel, captain, sergeant, and private. In this example, the respondent must fall in one of the five categories, which measure the level (amount) of military rank (ordinal). At this point, it is instructive to

---

[4]If you wish to refresh yourself on the meaning of "levels of measurement," we refer you to *Using SPSS: An Interactive Hands-On Approach* by Cunningham and Aldrich.

[5]One note of caution is that the levels of measurement specified in the databases found in SPSS Sample files are not always correct. We will only use such databases when absolutely necessary and when it does not affect the graph building procedure. You should be alert to incorrect levels of measurement as you continue to develop your graph making skills and you explore other databases in the SPSS Sample files.

think in terms of a bar or pie graph when attempting to understand the distributions of discrete variables. With discrete data, each distinct bar or pie slice represents a category. Each category is represented either by a rectangular box or a slice of the pie. It must be mentioned that it is sometimes desirable to use a bar graph to represent continuous data. SPSS accomplishes this by organizing the continuous data into separate categories by specifying ranges. A bar graph can also be used to compare the means (continuous data) of a number of groups. An example would be to compare two university classes on the mean number of points earned on an exam. In spite of these exceptions, the primary use of the bar graph is to represent discrete data.

In many of the later chapters, you will learn to build graphs that use a combination of discrete and continuous data. At this time, we do not attempt to describe all the various combinations of discrete and continuous data and the appropriate graphs for these situations. You will learn these procedures when we describe the types of graphs and how they are used. Additional guidance in choosing the correct graph for various levels of measurement and to provide answers for specific questions is provided in Appendix D (Graph Selection: Type and Purpose).

To summarize this section: When one wishes to make a graph to discover information contained in a mass of data, it is necessary to first establish whether the data are discrete or continuous.

1.3.2 Second Consideration: What Are We Trying to Understand About the Data? What Is the Question? What Information Must the Graph Communicate?

When confronted with a large amount of data, we might be seeking information about a single variable. In this case, we are not concerned with how the values of one variable may relate to the values of other variables. In other words, we are concerned with what the distribution of values "looks like." If we have a discrete variable, such as the previously discussed gender variable, then "looks like" can refer to the number (or percentages) of males and females in the database. A bar graph would encourage thinking in a proportional way by drawing a graph, making it easy to visualize the relationship between the two categories for the single variable of gender. Another method might be to construct a pie graph. The pie graph is especially useful with more than two categories in that it makes it easier to see the proportions between the distinct categories and the whole. We will address such issues in greater detail when they are discussed in later chapters that describe how to produce such graphs.

If we are investigating a single continuous variable, we might choose to build a graph known as a histogram to see what the data "looks like."

The histogram could provide evidence as to whether the data approximates the normal distribution.[6] Such graphing of continuous data could also discover extreme values (outliers) that should be dealt with before additional statistical analysis is undertaken.

If the question we are seeking to answer involves two or more variables, we need a graph that depicts their relationship. With two variables, we need to display a bivariate relationship.[7] A scatter plot–type graph will enable the graph maker to display the relationship between two variables. In this application, the x-axis and y-axis both represent a value for each variable. Another example of graphing two variables would be putting the results of a 2×2 crosstab analysis into a stacked bar chart, making it easier, for most people, to visualize the proportions.

Another question might be the interpretation of the results of a multivariate analysis, where it is necessary to graph three or more variables. You will soon learn how to build a graph representing, say, two continuous and single discrete variables. Another use would be to use a line graph to display an interaction or lack of interaction between two independent variables.

Later chapters discuss all the above graphing possibilities (and more) with detailed guidelines as to which graphs answer specific questions about the data.

1.3.3 Third Consideration: Who Will Use the Information and What Is Their Level of Statistical Knowledge?

Another consideration would be the type of audience. By this we mean that graphs prepared for a meeting of members of the American Statistical Association might take on a different appearance than graphs prepared for an introductory course in statistics. Whoever the audience, graphs should always be clear and concise representations of the data and should be readily understandable.

1.3.4 Fourth Consideration: Is the Graph Intended to Guide Further Research or Will It Be Used for Presentation to Others?

If the intention of the graph builder is to use the graph to guide students or other users in the selection of further statistical approaches, then the use of

---

[6]The normality aspect of continuous data is discussed in more detail in Chapter 8 on histograms.

[7]When graphing a bivariate relationship, we have a single point on the graph that represents two values, one for x and one for y.

the SPSS *Chart Editor* is not required. The basic graph produced by SPSS will usually provide the information required to answer their questions. On the other hand, a graph intended as part of a larger presentation to students and/ or colleagues would require one to "edit" the graph using the SPSS *Chart Editor*. The editing process, which uses the *Chart Editor*, is covered in detail in the later chapters.

★   **1.4 DATABASES USED IN THIS BOOK**

In all cases, the databases you will use to build the graphs are found in the SPSS Sample file that was downloaded with the software. In general, each database selected for use is briefly described when it is introduced. However additional information on specific databases is available by using the SPSS *Help* menu as follows:

- Open **SPSS**.
- Click **Help**, then click **Topics**, and type **sample files**.
- Click **list topics**, then click **sample files**.
- Click **Display**.

The data used to illustrate various graphs at the beginning of each chapter were obtained from the authors' years of teaching intermediate-level statistics classes. You are not required to have access to these data.

1.4.1 Access to Databases Used to Build Graphs

Before we can examine the major features of the *Chart Builder* in the next section, we must open a database. The procedure shown below will open one of the databases (**accidents.sav**) that was included with the SPSS software. You will use many of the databases that are found in the SPSS Sample files location. You should make a note to mark this page since you will use these procedures in almost every chapter.[8]

- Start **SPSS** if it is not already running.
- On the SPSS Menu, click **File**, select **Open**, and then click **Data**.

---

[8]As you proceed through the chapters, you will be required to repeatedly use the same databases from the SPSS Sample files. You may wish to save the most used databases to your computer, making access much quicker. A chapter-by-chapter listing of all SPSS databases used in this book is given in Appendix C.

- In the *Open data* window, click the **down arrow** in the *Look in* box and scroll to and click the **C drive**.
- Double click **Program Files**.
- Scroll to **SPSSInc**, then double click **SPSSInc**.
- Double click **PASW Statistics 18** (currently Version 20 shows 18, and you may see other version numbers as well).
- Double click **Samples**.
- Double click **English**.
- A window opens in which you will see a long list of available files.
- Click **accidents.sav**.
- Click **Open** (*Data Editor* opens). We now have the required database and may open the *Chart Builder*.
- Click **Graphs**, and then click **Chart Builder**.
- *Chart Builder* window opens as shown in Figure 1.2. Make sure that **Gallery** is selected—if not, click **Gallery**.

Following the above procedures can sometimes be tricky. It may become necessary to exercise some patience, but we assure you that the procedure is the correct way to access SPSS Sample files. Be sure to double click on the files as specified.

1.5 SPSS Graph Production: Using the *Chart Builder*   ★

The *Chart Builder* feature available in SPSS plays a major role in this book. Detailed procedures on building simple to complex graphs while using the *Chart Builder* are provided throughout this textbook. The purpose of this section is to provide you with a *basic* understanding about how to use the SPSS *Chart Builder*. Don't worry, you won't have to memorize everything in this section, as you are given step-by-step procedures when building graphs in the later chapters. We do, however, highly recommend that you take this time to become familiar with the *Chart Builder*. It won't be long before you will easily produce graphs to better understand large amounts of data. Let's proceed with the assumption that you have never used the SPSS *Chart Builder* feature.

When you click **Graphs** on the SPSS *Main Menu*, you are given three options for building a graph: (1) *Legacy Dialogs*, (2) *Graphboard Template Chooser*, and (3) *Chart Builder*. The *Legacy Dialogs* option is one of the first methods developed by SPSS, some people feel comfortable in using this earlier method. There is nothing wrong with the *Legacy* approach; however, it does take more statistical knowledge (and time) to use it correctly. The next option *Graphboard Template Chooser* came along a few years later and offered more automatic steps in building a graph. The final option *Chart Builder* is the most recent version, and in the opinion of the authors, it is the most efficient. Therefore, we have chosen the *Chart Builder* as the option described in this book. Therefore, all step-by-step instructions in this book begin and end with the *Chart Builder*.

   Chart Builder is the first available option when clicking **Graphs** on the SPSS *Main Menu* (Figure 1.1). This is the option used in all chapters of this textbook.

Figure 1.1   SPSS *Main Menu* Showing How to Open the *Chart Builder*

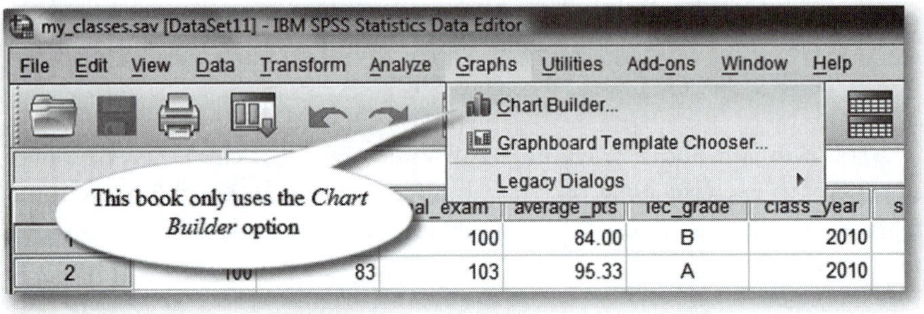

   The following section provides details on the *Chart Builder* window that opens once you click on *Chart Builder* in the drop-down menu as shown in Figure 1.1.

1.5.1 A Description of the *Chart Builder* Window

Figure 1.2 shows the basic *Chart Builder* window that opens once *Chart Builder* is clicked. If the window you see is slightly different from the one shown in Figure 1.2, then look at the horizontal row of buttons in the middle of the window to make sure that *Gallery* is highlighted, which means it is active and does not need to be clicked. If one of the other buttons (*Basic Elements*, *Groups/Point ID*, and *Titles/Footnotes*) is highlighted, the window's appearance will not match the one shown in Figure 1.2, and you must then click the *Gallery* button.

   Let's go through some of the features and options available when you open the *Chart Builder* window. At this time, our intention is to only familiarize you with the major features available in the *Chart Builder* window. You will learn to build graphs, using the *Chart Builder* window, starting with the next chapter.

Figure 1.2 *Chart Builder* Window Showing Key Features and Control Points

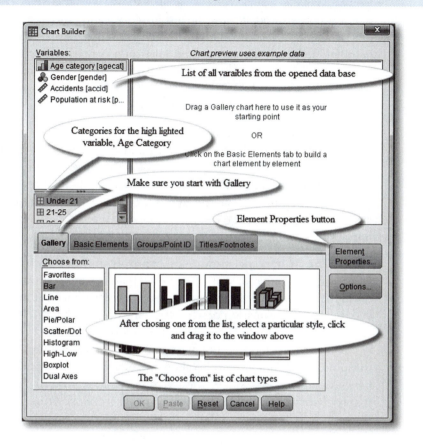

1.5.2 Panels in the *Chart Builder* Window

There are three major panels in the *Chart Builder* window titled as follows: (1) *Variables*, (2) *Chart preview uses example data*, and (3) *Choose from*. Let's examine each of these panels.

1. **The "Variables:" Panel:** The *Variables* panel provides a list of all the variables in the opened database. The level of measurement is also specified by the icon that precedes the variable's name. The first icon shown in the *Variables* panel is for *Age category*, and it represents data measured at the ordinal level. Therefore, if you select this variable for graphing you will only use graphing procedures appropriate for discrete data. The next variable, *Gender*, is represented by an icon resembling three balloons that denotes nominal data. Once again, for graphing procedures, one must consider this

as discrete data. The third variable in this panel, *Accidents*, is preceded by an icon looking like a small ruler. A variable shown with this SPSS icon indicates that it was measured at the scale level (interval and ratio). Data measured in this manner and accompanied by this icon are treated as continuous data for graphing purposes. We summarize our icon descriptions as follows:

- Icons for *discrete* variables are and
- Icon for a *continuous* variable is

The lower portion of the *Variables:* panel also provides a brief description of the categories for discrete (nominal and ordinal) data. You obtain these descriptions by clicking on each variable. This feature can be very useful when deciding on variables to include in your graph-building projects.

Figure 1.2 shows that the **accidents.sav** database has four variables available for graphing, two discrete (*Age category* and *Gender*) and two continuous (*Accidents* and *Population at risk*).

2. **The "Chart preview uses example data" Panel:** SPSS uses the words "uses example data" to emphasize that the graph shown in the panel, during the graph-building process, does not represent your data. It is only a very rough approximation of what your finished graph will look like. In later chapters, we shorten this panel's name to "*Chart preview.*"

It is in this panel that much of your basic chart building takes place. At this time, we do not attempt to show the many different appearances of this panel. Basically, this panel provides a template for various types and styles of graphs that are selected from the third panel ("*Choose from:*" panel). Briefly, the procedure is to select a graph and style from the *Choose from* panel, drag it to the *Chart preview* panel, then drag appropriate variables onto the shown graph. The procedures for using this panel, as they relate to specific graph-building projects, are detailed in all the later chapters.

3. **The "Choose from:" Panel:** Direct your attention to the *Choose from:* panel in Figure 1.2. Notice that "Bar" has been highlighted; this was accomplished by clicking on "Bar." When the word "Bar" is clicked, a specific set of bar styles appears to the right. If a different graph type had been clicked (highlighted), then you would see different set of graph styles to choose from. Clicking the Bar graph gives you eight style choices. Notice that some are hidden by our informational balloon. It is from these eight different styles that you choose one and then click and drag it to the *Chart preview* panel directly above. Later chapters will show styles appropriate for answering specific questions about a particular database. Once the style has been moved to the *Chart preview* panel, you will then drag variables onto various places on the graph to continue the graph-building process.

1.5.3 *Element Properties* Window

The *Element Properties* button is located in the center-right portion of the window shown in Figure 1.2. Clicking this button opens the *Elements Properties* window (Figure 1.3), which provides many ways to make changes during the graph-building process. The use of the features accessed through the *Element Properties* window will be illustrated as the need arises. In most cases, this window opens automatically when performing operations in the *Chart Builder* window. If it does not open automatically, then clicking the *Element Properties* button in the *Chart Builder* window offers an alternative way to gain access to its features.

Once you have made changes to your graph from the *Element Properties* window, remember to click the **Apply** button as shown in Figure 1.3. Clicking the **Apply** button takes you back to the *Chart preview* panel that incorporates your changes.

Figure 1.3   *Element Properties Window*

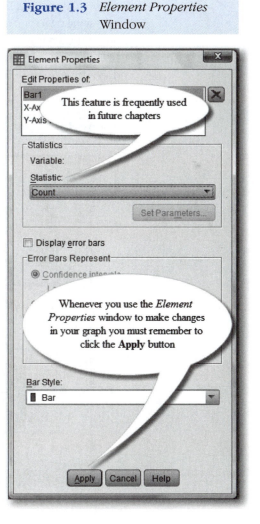

1.5.4 Final Stages When Using the *Chart Builder*

In the row of buttons at the bottom of the *Chart Builder* window, you will most frequently use **OK** and **Reset**. Clicking **OK** causes all previous instructions to be incorporated into the graph and immediately produces the finished basic graph that appears in the *Output Viewer* of SPSS. If the *Output Viewer* does not appear on the screen after clicking **OK**, then click **Output** found on the *Task* bar at the bottom of your computer screen.

Once your graph appears in the *Output Viewer*, there is an opportunity to further modify this basic graph. We refer to this graph as "basic" since there are many ways it can be embellished and improved by using the *Chart Editor* as described in the following section.

Before leaving the *Chart Builder*, we describe the use of the *Reset* button found at the bottom of the *Chart Builder* window. This handy feature clears all prior work from the *Chart preview* panel

(Figure 1.2). We recommend this, unless you are building another graph of the same type and style as the one you may have just built.

1.5.5 *Chart Editor* and *Properties* Window

The *Chart Editor* window is key when building clear and concise graphs that effectively communicate the information needed to understand the data. The *Chart Editor* window (see Figure 1.4) opens when you double click the basic graph in the *Output Viewer*.

In this section, our intention is to briefly introduce you to some of the editing features made possible by using the *Chart Editor*. Specific instructions on how to use the *Chart Editor* are provided in later graph-building exercises. You will utilize features of the *Chart Editor* and its associated *Properties* window (see Figure 1.5) to make changes that you see immediately as you continue with your graph-building project.

Figure 1.4 shows the *Chart Editor* window with a few of the key features and control points emphasized with information bubbles. As before, our

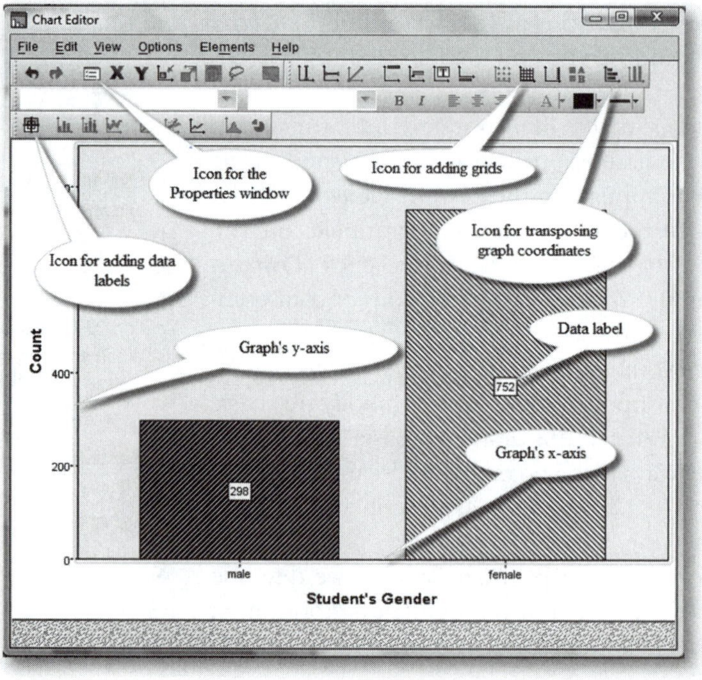

Figure 1.4   *Chart Editor* Window With Some Useful Points Tagged

intention here is to only familiarize you with the *Chart Editor* window. You will learn much more about its use as you progress through various graph-building procedures.

Figure 1.5 shows the *Properties* window (not to be confused with the *Element Properties* window shown in Figure 1.3). Normally the *Properties* window opens with the *Chart Editor*. If it does not, then click the *Properties* icon as shown in Figure 1.4. Depending on the particular graph-building project and the request you make by clicking items in the *Chart Editor*, the

Figure 1.5 *Properties* Window Showing the *Categories* Tab Clicked

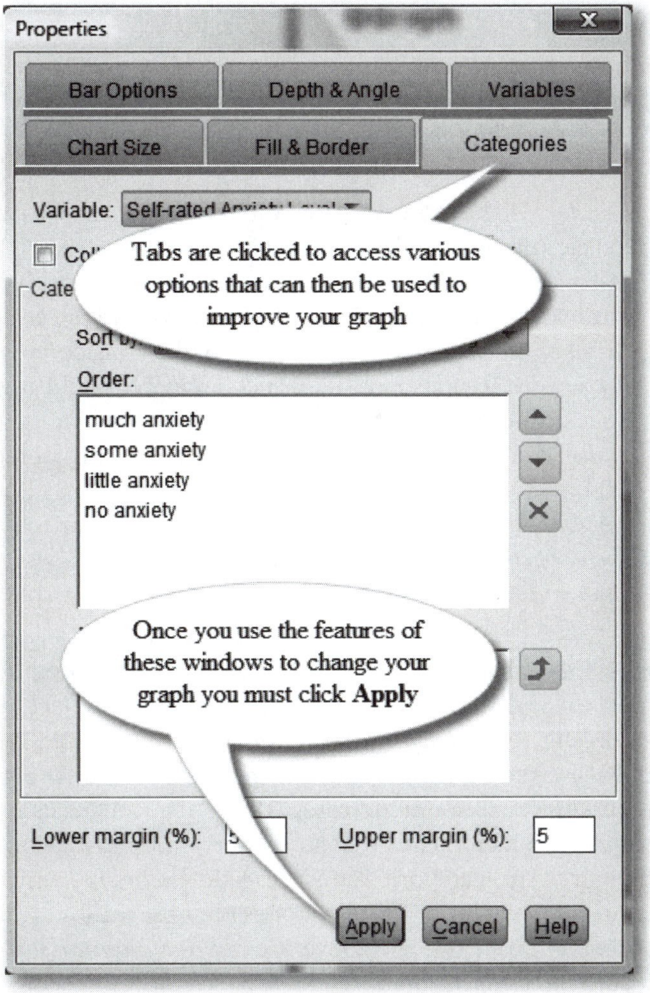

Properties window takes on many different appearances. You will be directed on a case-by-case basis to click various tabs, which then provide access to the features needed to make the desired changes.

At this point, you may feel a little overwhelmed by the many details associated with graph building. However, we assure you that after making a few graphs as described in the following chapters, the process becomes very natural and intuitive—SPSS has done an excellent job in this regard.

★   1.6 DEFINITION OF KEY TERMS AND CONCEPTS

Variable—A characteristic that describes some physical or mental aspect of the individual, group, or inanimate object. The key point is that variables can *vary* and can be expressed as a particular numerical value or as falling in a unique category. The following are some examples:

- *Gender* as the observed variable could vary in two ways: male or female (discrete).
- *Mental state* could be a variable and vary in five ways: very anxious, anxious, neutral, relaxed, and very relaxed (discrete).
- *Number of errors* on a written test can be considered as a variable. If there were 10 questions, then such a variable could vary from 0 to 10 errors (discrete).
- *Make of automobile* owned or leased can be considered as a variable (discrete).
- *Weight of an individual* can be considered as a variable (continuous).
- *Speed of an airplane* can be considered as a variable (continuous).
- *How high one can jump* can be considered as a variable (continuous).

Discrete Variable—A characteristic that describes some physical or mental aspect of the individual, group, or inanimate object that has been observed. The term *discrete* describes how the variable is measured or counted. Discrete variables vary in a manner so that the characteristics being measured fall in unique categories. Such categories must be *mutually exclusive*, which means that any observation must fall in one and only one category. The categories must also be *inclusive*, which means that there must be a category for every possible observation. Examples of discrete variables from the list above are *gender*, *mental state*, *number of errors*, and *make of automobile*.

Continuous Variable—A characteristic that describes some physical or mental aspect of the individual, group, or inanimate object that has been observed. The term *continuous* describes how the variable is measured. Continuous variables vary by taking on any one of a large number of measures (often infinite). Examples of continuous variables from the list above are *weight*, *speed*, and *how high one can jump*.

Category—A natural grouping of the characteristics of a discrete variable. Think of the type of automobile as a variable having categories such as Porsche, Ferrari, and Maserati. The automobile possessing "Porsche" characteristics is counted or placed in a category titled Porsche.

Continuous Distribution—Plainly speaking, a continuous distribution is just a "bunch of numbers" that resulted when something was measured at the continuous level. We use various types of statistical analysis, including graphs, to make sense of such distributions. Histogram and line graphs are the most commonly used graphing techniques to describe continuous distributions.

Discrete Distribution—Could also consist of a bunch of numbers, but the numbers take on a different meaning. Using the gender variable as an example, we could assign the value label of 1 to the male category and 2 to the female category. This being the case, you now have a column of numbers consisting of 1s and 2s that you are trying to understand. You could use SPSS to produce a bar graph.

Levels of Measurement—A classification method used to define how variables are measured. For most statistical work, there are four possible ways to measure variables: (1) nominal, (2) ordinal, (3) interval, and (4) ratio. When using SPSS, you will find that interval and ratio have been combined and are referred to as *scale*. For purposes of graph making, only two methods of measurement need to be distinguished: (1) continuous, which includes interval and ratio (SPSS's scale) and (2) discrete, which includes SPSS's nominal and ordinal levels of measurement.

Independent Variable—The independent variable is manipulated and has the freedom to take on different values. It is the presumed cause of change in the dependent variable in experimental work. In observational-type studies, it is often referred to as the predictor variable. This definition hinges on the idea that knowledge of the predictor variable will facilitate the successful estimation of the value for the dependent variable.

Dependent Variable—This variable can take on different values; however, these values are said to "depend" on the value of the independent variable. In experimental work, we test whether the manipulation of the independent variable results in a significant change in the dependent variable. In observational studies, the value of the dependent variable can be better predicted by knowledge of the value of the independent variable.

Horizontal Axis—In this book, the term horizontal axis is used infrequently, as the preferred terminology is the x-axis. Both these terms will always refer to the horizontal axis of the chart you are building. During certain SPSS operations, you will find that the vertical axis is referred to as the x-axis. When this happens, we revert to the term *horizontal axis* so as to avoid confusion.

Vertical Axis—The vertical axis rises perpendicular to the x-axis (horizontal) and is most frequently referred to as the y-axis.

2

SIMPLE BAR GRAPH

PURPOSE OF GRAPHS YOU ARE ABOUT TO BUILD

- To describe the number of observations in each category of the discrete variable
- To visualize estimated error for discrete variables

2.1 INTRODUCTION TO THE SIMPLE BAR GRAPH ★

In the first chapter, we presented an overview about *how* and *why* graphs might be used when attempting to understand large amounts of data. We discussed decisions required of the graph maker and provided a brief primer on the *Chart Builder* feature of SPSS. The present chapter, and all that follow, may be thought of as a direct application of the principles presented in the first chapter—this is where the "rubber meets the road."

The simple bar graph consists of horizontal or vertical rectangular boxes. The lengths for horizontal graphs and heights for vertical graphs represent the number or percentage of observations in each category of the variable being measured (see Figures 2.1 and 2.2).[1] While the lengths and heights may vary, the width of each box must be the same for all categories. SPSS automatically determines both these dimensions, which depend on the number of categories and the number of observations in each. The vertical box style is the most used and is the style chosen for this chapter.[2]

The bar graph is not always the best choice when seeking to answer questions about the distribution of a discrete variable. There are certain situations when a pie graph provides more useful information. Whenever you seek to describe the proportion of observations in each category *and* its relationship to the *whole*, then the pie graph should be the choice. We discuss this aspect in more detail in Chapter 5 on pie graphs.

The reader should also be aware that the simple bar graph can be built with the intention of deceiving the graph reader. For examples of the simple bar graph used for deception, one should turn to Chapter 18 on deceptive graphing examples.

2.1.1 Simple Bar Graph (Horizontal Orientation)

Figure 2.1 is an example of a simple bar graph showing bars with a horizontal orientation. This graph displays data that resulted from a survey of 37 statistics students at a major university. One of the items on this survey asked the students to self-rate their level of anxiety about taking the class. Figure 2.1 presents the information obtained for this anxiety level variable as a simple horizontally oriented bar graph.

While reading the simple bar graph shown in Figure 2.1, one of the first things to notice is that the collected data were classified as *discrete*. We know this because there are observations in each of the four discrete categories: (1) much anxiety, (2) some anxiety, (3) little anxiety, and (4) no anxiety. One way to display such discrete data is to use a simple bar graph. In SPSS, the level of measurement was specified as ordinal. Recall from Chapter 1 that data measured at the nominal or ordinal level are both considered as *discrete* data.

---

[1]The bar graph is principally used with discrete data; however, there are occasions when the heights or lengths of the category boxes may represent a summary statistic of a continuous variable. SPSS gives the *Chart Builder* many choices of summary statistics, such as the mean or median. The list of choices for the summary statistic is found in the *Element Properties* window. These types of applications will be demonstrated in later chapters.

[2]On some occasions, you may wish to build a horizontal bar graph. This is easily accomplished in the *Chart Editor* by simply clicking the "transpose chart coordinate system" icon, which is found as the next to last icon in the *Chart Editor's* menu bar.

Figure 2.1   Simple Bar Graph for Self-Rated Anxiety Level (Horizontal Orientation)

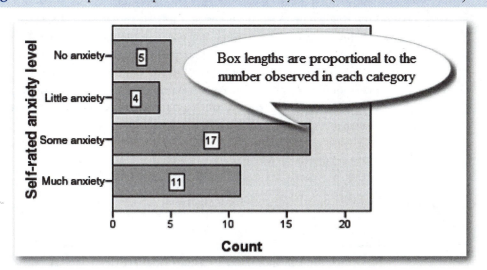

Recall that in Chapter 1, we stated that understanding a database was the major reason for building a graph. Such an understanding usually means answering questions about the data. Let's speculate about one possible question concerning the above-graphed student database.

Begin with the assumption that the data were collected with the belief that the information obtained from the effort would offer insight into ways to improve teaching. One obvious question about this group of students would be the number (or percentage) of students in each of the four levels of categorized anxiety. This information could be helpful when the professor prepares for future classes. For instance, it would be useful information when deciding on the type of lecture material and the approach used at the first class meeting. Let's say that the data had revealed that most students, say 35 of 37, expressed much anxiety about the class. If this were the case, then the professor might attempt to alleviate student anxiety with the hope that this would increase learning.

2.1.2 Simple Bar Graph (Vertical Orientation)

The "picture" of the classes' level of anxiety is easily visualized by producing the simple bar graph. Figure 2.2 shows the same data used above, but this time using the simple bar graph with a vertical orientation.

One might legitimately argue that a data table would provide much the same information as provided by either of these bar graphs. However, one should remember that an important purpose of a graph is to provide the *maximum* amount of useful information. In this regard, we see that the bar graph (a picture) makes it easier for the human mind to recognize and understand the relative proportions between the four categories. This is something that very few people see when reading a data table filled with numbers.

One look at Figure 2.1 or 2.2, and you immediately see the number of observations (and the proportional size) in each of the four anxiety categories. The horizontal and vertical boxes record the number of students reporting various levels of anxiety. It is obvious that most students (17) reported that they had "some anxiety" about taking the statistics class. We assume that "some anxiety" is considered a normal student response and not anything for the teacher to be overly concerned about when designing course requirements.

Figure 2.2   Simple Bar Graph for Self-Rated Anxiety Level (Vertical Orientation)

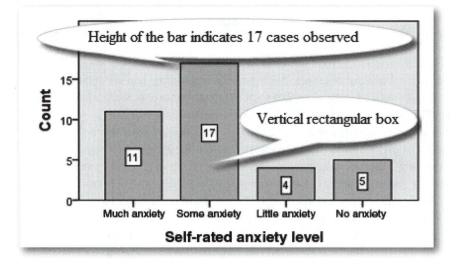

2.1.3 Simple Bar Graph (Percentage)

Let's see if we can improve on the graph shown in Figure 2.2 with the idea of making the data more easily understood by encouraging proportional thinking. One method to accomplish this is to express the *y*-axis, now titled "Count" as a percentage of the total. We use the same data to build the simple bar graph shown in Figure 2.3; however, the *y*-axis now gives the percentage.

Proportional thinking is encouraged when visualizing data in terms of percentages. Thus, Figure 2.3 now shows individual bars as a percentage of those students participating in the survey.

Figure 2.3   Simple Bar Graph for Self-Rated Anxiety Level (Percentage)

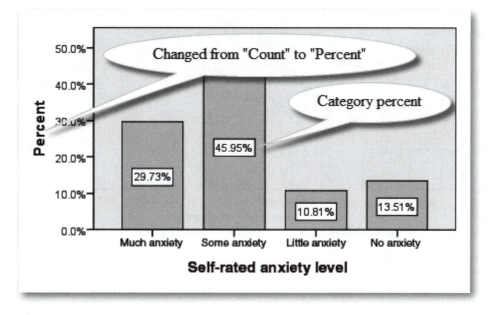

2.1.4 Simple Bar Graph With Error Bars

One final example represents data collected on 1,050 statistics students over an 11-year period. The purpose of the graph shown in Figure 2.4 is to demonstrate the use of *Error Bars*. Error bars are used to permit the visualization of an important concept in inferential statistics—the range of potential error when using a sample to estimate unknown values in a population.

It is important to understand that to use the error bar feature in its intended capacity, the data must be obtained by random sampling and must approximate a normal distribution. The data presented in Figure 2.4 show the number of students enrolled in one professor's classes over a period of 11 years. We are going to assume that this professor was selected at random from a much larger population of statistics professors and that the number of students follows the normal curve. Based on these important assumptions, the graph will serve two purposes, one descriptive and the other inferential. The descriptive aspect shows the actual number of students enrolled in the professor's classes for each of the 11 years. These numbers are given by the heights of the rectangular bars of the graph. The inferential aspect of the graph is to use the error bars to show the range of error when using this professor's enrollment to estimate enrollment for the much larger population of professors. This

Figure 2.4   Bar Graph With Error Bars: 1,050 Statistics Students for One Professor

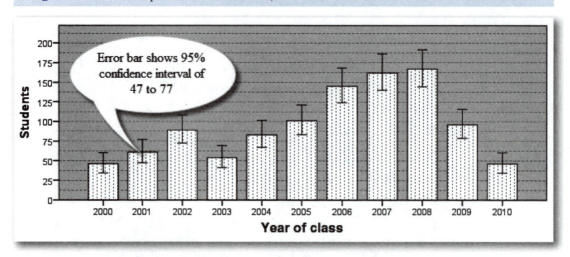

information is obtained by reading the top and bottom horizontal lines of the "I beam"–shapes at the top of each rectangular bar.

Let's look at the year 2001 for an example of the type of questions answered by this simple bar graph. By looking at the height of the rectangular bar, we read from the y-axis (students) and determine that the professor had 62 students in the year 2001. This is the descriptive use of the graph. Used for its inferential purpose, we direct our attention to the error bar as shown by the information bubble in Figure 2.4. We once again read the y-axis to determine the values at the lower and upper ends of the error bar. These values, the lower and upper confidence limits, are found to be 47 and 77. Notice also that this has been designated as the 95% confidence interval. This simply means that repeated sampling from the population would result in enrollment numbers between 47 and 77 students in 95% of the samples.

The following section introduces the specific databases used to demonstrate how SPSS can produce various bar graphs such as those in Figures 2.1 through 2.4. We also present questions that we seek to answer by graphing variables from the selected database.

★   **2.2 DATABASES AND QUESTIONS**

The database used to make the first three bar graphs is found in the SPSS Sample files. The file name is **credit_card.sav**. This database consists of 26,280 cases that are measured on 11 variables. To open the SPSS Sample file and the **credit_card.sav** database follow the procedures given next.

- Start SPSS if it is not already running.
- On the SPSS Menu, click **File**, select **Open**, and then click **Data**.
- In the *Open data* window, click the **down arrow** in the *Look in* box and scroll to and click the **C drive**.
- Double click **Program files**.
- Click the **right arrow** and scroll to **SPSSInc**. Double click **SPSSInc**.
- Double click **PASW Statistics 18**.
- Double click **Samples**.
- Double click **English**.
- A window opens in which you will see a long list of available files.
- Click **credit_card.sav**.
- Click **Open**.

Once **credit_card.sav** is open, click the **Variable View** tab (at the bottom of the screen), then examine the variable list and their specifications. The single variable, number 4, is used to demonstrate the production of a simple bar graph. This variable is named *card* and labeled *Primary credit card*.[3] In SPSS terminology, *card* is the variable's name while *Primary credit card* is its label. Be sure to look at the *measure* column in the *Variable View*, which identifies the level of measurement (nominal). The level of measurement specified in the measure column for the *card* variable tells you that you must select a graph designed to display discrete data. Next click the **Data View** tab and scroll through the data for the *card* variable to give you some idea of the numerical values you are trying to understand.

The purpose of graphing data is to learn something about the measured variable. You wish to answer questions about the data. Stated another way, we wish to make sense out of all those numbers that were written down when the observations were counted or measured. The database used in this chapter is hypothetical, so the assumptions about the research questions and their answers are based on conjecture. Something to keep in mind is that the first step when designing a data collection instrument is to clearly state the questions you are attempting to answer.

The discrete variable *card* consists of five nominal categories: (1) American Express, (2) Visa, (3) MasterCard, (4) Discover, and (5) Other. To demonstrate

---

[3]SPSS provides for the naming and labeling of variables. The variable list that you use when building graphs can be set to provide one or the other. The SPSS user can also right click (directly on the variable list) back and forth between names and labels. A database having hundreds of variables can challenge a person's patience (may we say sanity) when looking through the many variables for the one you wish to select. We have included both designations (names and labels) in the hope of making the task of finding variables less daunting.

the usefulness of the bar graph, we pose four questions concerning this one variable in Section 2.2.1.

The fourth bar graph built in this chapter adds error bars. This graph is similar to the one shown in Figure 2.4. For building this graph, you have to once again open SPSS Sample file. This database has 582 cases and 18 variables. Follow the process outlined above, but this time, you will locate the database named **Satisf.sav**. For this graph-building experience, select the variable named *dept*, which has seven categories (Automotive, Sporting, Clothing, Appliances, Electronics, Tools, and Other). Remember that to use error bars, it is necessary to consider these data as obtained through random sampling and that their distribution approximates the normal curve.

2.2.1 Questions for the Simple Bar Graph

The major purpose of this subsection, and the one that immediately follows, is to present those questions that can be answered by the graphs that you will soon build.

1. How many individuals are in each of the five different credit card categories?

2. What proportion of the 26,280 individuals are in each of the five categories?

3. Which of the five categories of credit card types is the most popular?

4. Rank the popularity of the five credit card categories from the least to the most?

2.2.2 Questions for the Simple Bar Graph With Error Bars

1. Which of the seven store departments had the most customer visits and what was this number?

2. If the 146 customer visits is used to estimate the number of appliance department visits for the larger store population, what are the lower and upper limits of this estimate?

3. Given the information in the previous two answers, what can be said about the expected number of visits for the larger population of retail stores?

4. What are the lower and upper 95% confidence limits for the electronics department and what was the samples' observed number of customers?

2.3 USING SPSS TO BUILD THE SIMPLE BAR GRAPH   ★

In the following two sections, you will build two simple bar graphs—one without error bars and the other showing error bars.

2.3.1 Building the Simple Bar Graph

If the **credit_card.sav** database is not opened, follow the procedures described in the previous section and open it at this time. We next present the step-by-step SPSS procedures to make a simple bar graph using one variable from the **credit_card.sav** database.

- Open **credit_card.sav** (found in the SPSS Sample file).
- Click **Graphs** and then click **Chart Builder** (sometimes a smaller *Chart Builder* window opens, this window permits the definition of variable properties, which is rarely needed. We advise you to click the box that says **Don't show this dialog again**, then click **OK**).
- With the larger *Chart Builder* window open, make certain that **Gallery** is selected—if not, then click the **Gallery button** (the *Gallery* button is located in the middle-left portion of the window).
- Click **Bar** and then drag the first **graph icon** to the panel at the top right of the window, which is called the *Chart preview* panel.
- Click **Primary credit card** in the *Variables* panel and drag it to the *x*-axis.
- Click **OK** (*Output Viewer* opens showing the basic simple bar graph as shown in Figure 2.5).

Figure 2.5   Simple Bar Graph for 26,280 Primary Credit Card Users

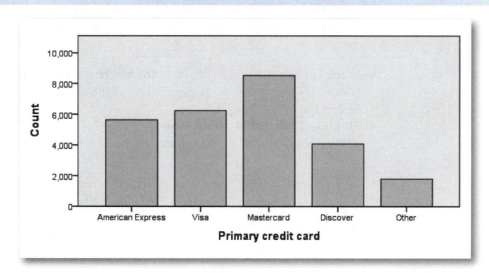

Figure 2.5 is the basic graph produced (shown in the *Output Viewer*) by the SPSS commands just given.[4] You might notice that the graph shown in Figure 2.5 is smaller than the graph depicted in the *Output Viewer*. The size of any graph can be easily changed either in the *Output Viewer* or once it is copied/ pasted into a new document. We highly recommend that changing the graph's size be done in the *Output Viewer* since SPSS automatically preserves the vertical and horizontal proportions. Changing the size of the graph once it is in the document should be for minor adjustments only, as the font and other graphics are easily distorted. To change the graph size in the SPSS *Output Viewer*, just click the **graph** (a frame appears around the graph) and then click and grab the lower right corner of the frame (marked by a small black box), hover the mouse pointer until you see a double-headed arrow, and move it diagonally up and to the left to reach the desired size. You may also adjust the graph's size by moving the vertical and/or horizontal sides of the frame separately.

2.3.2 Using the Chart Editor to Improve Interpretation

The basic graph in Figure 2.5 answers the first question regarding the number of individuals in each category. However, you do have to read the numbers from the *y*-axis to get this information. The second question about percentages in each category would require some calculations. We can improve this basic graph and answer both questions more directly by following some SPSS steps. These improvements can be accomplished by using the *Chart Editor*. We could make the graph easier to interpret by placing numerical values (known as *data labels*) in each rectangular box. Thus, the graph reader will not have to interpret the *y*-axis. The procedures given below show the steps required to open the *Chart Editor* and add data labels to your graph.

With the *Output Viewer* showing the graph depicted in Figure 2.5 follow the procedures, given next, to add numbers (data labels) to each rectangular box in the graph.

- In the *Output Viewer*, double click **anywhere** on the **graph** (*Chart Editor* window opens, the upper portion of this window is shown in Figure 2.6).
- Click the **Data Label Mode icon** shown in Figure 2.6 (the mouse pointer now takes on the appearance of the icon itself).

---

[4]We describe this graph as "basic," since it was produced without using the *Chart Editor* function of SPSS. It is often necessary to utilize the *Chart Editor* feature to add clarity to your graph. We frequently demonstrate the use of the *Chart Editor* as the need arises in this and later chapters.

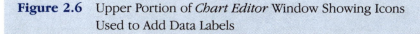

Figure 2.6   Upper Portion of *Chart Editor* Window Showing Icons Used to Add Data Labels

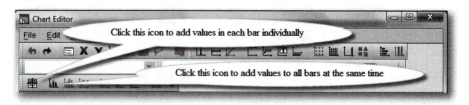

- Place the mouse pointer (the pointer now looks like the *Data Label Mode* icon) over the first bar, then click the **mouse** (the number of observations for that category appears in a small window), repeat this step for each individual bar, after clicking the **last** bar, click the **Data Label Mode icon** to turn it off (an alternative method is to click the **second icon** from the left, shown in Figure 2.6, which adds all data labels at the same time).

The following four bullet points illustrate how to directly insert a title in your graph by using SPSS. In all chapters that follow, we use a different procedure consistent with our book publisher's requirement. In your personal graph-building projects, you may not always have this option; therefore, the next few bullet points should be useful. In any graph, the title is an important, if not critical, component of the graph-building procedure. You should also notice that the *x*-axis title is deleted as it becomes redundant when adding the SPSS title for this type of graph.

- Click the **Insert a title icon** (the 10th icon from right to left). A faint yellow box with the word *Title* appears above the graph. (Note: If the *tools bar* with the *Insert a title* icon is not present, click **Options**, then click **Title**.)
- Click the **yellow box** and type **Primary Credit Card Used by the Customers**, delete the word **Title**.
- Click the **x-axis title** one time (this activates a box with the *x*-axis title).
- Click the **x-axis title** once more, and delete **Primary credit card**.
- Click the **X** in the top right-hand corner as shown in Figure 2.6 to close the *Chart Editor* (Figure 2.7 appears in the *Output Viewer*)

Figure 2.7   Bar Graph Showing Inserted Title and Data Labels

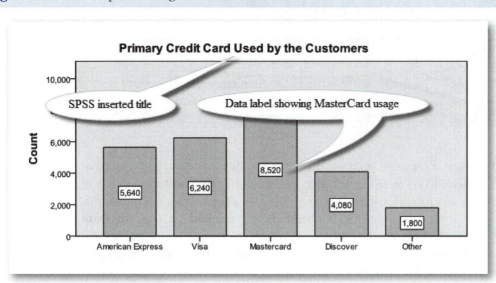

2.3.3 Building the Graph Showing Percentages and Other Embellishments

Figure 2.7 depicts a useful and informative graph, but we can make further improvements. Proportional thinking can be encouraged by changing the numbers in the rectangular boxes to percentages by the following procedures.

- Click **Graphs**, and then click **Chart Builder**. When the *Chart Builder* window opens, make certain that **Gallery** is selected (located middle-left of the window). If not selected, then click the **Gallery button**.
- If work from a previous graph shows in the *Chart preview* panel, click **Reset**.
- Click **Bar** (from the *Choose from:* list), then click and drag the first **graph** icon to the large panel on the top right of the window (*Chart preview* panel).
- Click **Primary credit card** in the *Variables* panel, and drag it to the *x*-axis.
- If the *Element Properties* window is not open, then click the **Element Properties button** (located in the middle-right portion of the *Chart Builder* window).
- In the *Statistics* panel of the *Element Properties* window, click the **black arrow** beneath the word *Statistic* and to the right of *Count*.

- Click **Percentage (?)** in the drop-down menu.
- Click **Apply**.
- Click **OK** in the *Chart Builder* window.

At this point, the *Output Viewer* opens with the graph now showing percentage on the *y*-axis. The following procedures result in each category showing its individual percentage of the total. We also give procedures to enhance the appearance of the graph by adding a three-dimensional (3-D) effect. If you are producing the graph for your own personal use, say to examine further research approaches, you will likely find the 3-D steps unnecessary. If you are preparing it for a presentation and/or publication, you may wish to consider this option.[5]

- Double click the **graph** (*Chart Editor* window opens).
- Click the **Show Data Labels icon** (second one from the right as shown in Figure 2.7).
- Click **any one** of the **bars** that represent categories (a faint frame should appear around all bars, and *Properties* window opens or changes its appearance if already open. Remember to avoid clicking on the data labels).
- Click **Depth and Angle** tab in the *Properties* window, then click **3-D**.
- Click **Apply**.
- Click the **X** in the top right-hand corner to close the *Chart Editor*, and the graph appears in the *Output Viewer*.
- Click the **graph** (a frame appears around the graph), and place the mouse pointer over the **small black square** at the lower right-hand corner of the frame, and when the double-headed arrow appears, drag it upward to approximate the size of the graph shown in Figure 2.8.

At this point in your graph-building experience, you can choose to save the output or not—it is up to you. The graphs you build in this textbook are not used in subsequent chapters. If you wish to save your work, follow the procedures given next.

- Click **File**, then click **Save As** (the *Save Output As* window opens).
- In the *File name box* type **Figure 2.8** (actually you may name it as you please).
- Click **Save** (unless you specified another location, the graph is saved in the *Documents* folder).

---

[5]The 3-D bar graph can be used by the dishonest (or unknowing) individual to mislead the graph reader. Section 18.2.6 shows one way that the three-dimensional bar graph can result in deception.

Figure 2.8   Final Simple Bar Graph With Percentages and Three-
Dimensional Embellishment

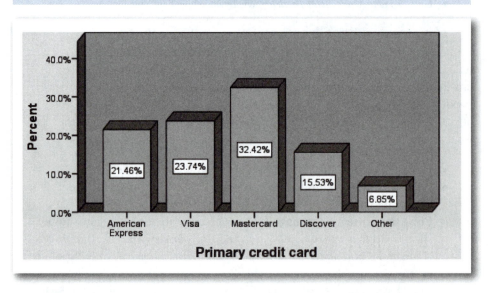

The bar graph in Figure 2.8 depicts the distribution of the primary credit card categories succinctly and makes it easy to identify proportions in each category. Section 2.4 presents interpretations of the information extracted from the data by building this simple bar graph.

2.3.4 Building the Simple Bar Graph With Error Bars

Follow the process given below to build a simple bar graph with error bars.

- Open **Satisf.sav** (found in the SPSS Sample file).
- Click **Graphs**, and then click **Chart Builder** (make certain that **Gallery** is selected—if not, then click the **Gallery button**).
- Click **Bar** and drag the first **graph icon** to the panel at the top right of the window that is called *Chart preview*.
- Click **Primary department** in the *Variables* panel and drag it to the *x*-axis.
- In the *Element Properties* window, click the **small square** to the left of *Display error bars*.
- Click **Apply**.
- Click **OK** in the *Chart Builder* window (*Output Viewer* opens with the basic graph).

- Double click the **graph** (*Chart Editor* opens).
- Click the **x-axis title**, then click the **title** a second time and replace the existing title with the following: **Primary department with error bars at the 95% confidence interval**.
- Click the **title below the one just added**, which reads "Error Bar: 95% CI" (a faint frame appears around the title), and delete this title.
- Click any of the error bars (all bars should be highlighted).
- In the *Properties* window (with the *Fill & Border* tab highlighted), click the **black arrow** beneath *Weight* found in the *Border Style* panel, and then click **1.5**.
- Click **Apply**.
- In the *Properties* window, click the **Bar Options tab**, and in the *Width* panel, drag the **slider** beneath *Bars* to the point where it reads **30** or directly type **30** in the box to the right of %.
- Click **Apply**.
- Click any of the **rectangular bars** (all bars are highlighted).
- In the *Properties* window (with the *Fill & Border* tab highlighted) and in the *Color* panel, click the **square** to the left of *Fill*, then click the **white rectangular box** to the right. Next click the **black arrow** beneath *Pattern* and click the **first pattern** in the **second** row.
- Click **Apply**.
- Click **any number** on the *y*-axis.
- In the *Properties* window, click the **Scale tab**, and in the *Range* panel, change *Major Increment* to **20**.
- Click **Apply**.
- Click the **Show Grid Lines icon** (the fifth icon from the right), and in the *Properties* window (with the *Grid Lines* tab highlighted), click the **small circle** to the left of *Both major and minor ticks*.
- Click **Apply**.
- Click **any of the grid lines** (all grid lines are highlighted), and in the *Properties* window, click the **Lines tab**, and in the *Lines* panel, click the **black arrow** beneath *Weight*, and click **0.25**, then click the **black arrow** beneath *Style*, and click the **first dotted line**.
- Click **Apply**.
- Click the **X** in the top right-hand corner to close the *Chart Editor*, and the graph appears in the *Output Viewer*.
- Click the **graph** (a frame appears around the graph), and place the mouse pointer over the **small black square** at the lower right corner of the frame, and when the double-headed arrow appears, drag it upward to approximate the size of the graph shown in Figure 2.9.

Figure 2.9   Simple Bar Graph With Error Bars

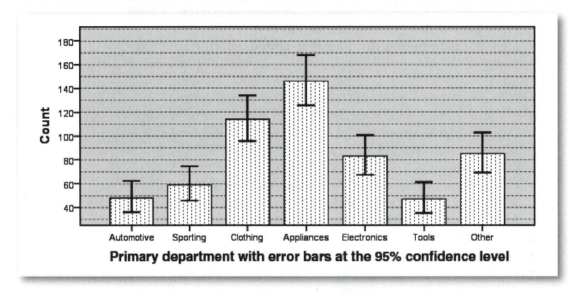

★   2.4 INTERPRETATION OF THE SIMPLE BAR GRAPH

The purpose of a graph is to make the data more understandable by answering specific questions about selected variables in the database. At this point, we may ask—did we succeed? When building the three graphs for the first database, what we sought to learn was very modest as we only looked at the values of one discrete variable called *Primary credit card*. There were 10 other variables that were ignored in our analysis. At the beginning of Section 2.2 of this chapter, you looked at the raw data for the *Primary credit card* variable and only saw a bunch of numbers. Specifically, there were 26,280 numbers that were 1, 2, 3, 4, or 5. These numbers were the labels for the five unique credit card categories of the variable. Looking at these 26,280 numbers provided little (if any) information to answer the questions.

In building the graph shown in Figure 2.9, we sought answers to questions of a descriptive and inferential nature. We first sought answers about the distribution values that were directly observed. Following this, we looked for answers concerning unknown values in the population from which the sample was obtained. In the following two subsections, we revisit our original questions and see if the graphs just built provide us with the information needed to answer our questions.

2.4.1 Questions and Answers for the Simple Bar Graph

Information leading to answers to the following questions can be found in Figures 2.7 and 2.8.

1. How many individuals are in each of the five different credit card categories?

We can look at Figure 2.8 and see that the *Primary credit card* variable consists of five discrete categories. The graph also presents the following number of people having each of the five credit card types as follows: American Express (5,640), Visa (6,240), MasterCard (8,520), Discover (4,080), and Other (1,800).

2. What proportion of the 26,280 individuals are in each of the five categories?

Figure 2.9 does an excellent job of answering this question while also encouraging the user to think in a proportional manner. The percentages for each of the five categories are as follows: American Express (21.46%), Visa (23.74%), MasterCard (32.42%), Discover (15.53%), and Other (6.85%).

3. Which of the five categories of credit card types is the most popular?

The MasterCard is the most popular as it has the tallest bar in the graph as shown in Figures 2.6 and 2.8.

4. Rank the popularity of the five credit card categories from the least to the most.

The least used credit card is the "Other" category, next is "Discover," then "American Express," "Visa," and finally the "MasterCard."

Such proportional thinking will often assist the graph reader when attempting to make an informed (educated) decision. What kind of decision might benefit from the data description provided in these simple bar graphs?

To describe how the bar graphs shown in Figures 2.8 and 2.9 might assist one in making various decisions, we must engage in some speculation. Let's assume that a Visa executive had been given the job of increasing the number of people using the Visa credit card. To understand and make comparisons with the competition, the graphs depicted in Figures 2.8 and 2.9 would be critical. They would be used in making a decision as to where one's efforts should be focused. The information communicated by these graphs would be essential in tracking any progress toward the goal of increasing Visa usage.

You can begin to see that the number of questions that might be asked and answered to better understand this database is almost limitless. Actually, there are many questions that could be asked and answered about the single variable used to make the bar graph. Some of these questions might seek information as to how credit card choice is related to other variables in the study. You explore such questions in future chapters when building graphs that will help answer these questions.

2.4.2 Questions and Answers for the Simple Bar Graph With Error Bars

Information leading to answers to the following questions can be found in Figure 2.9.

1. Which of the seven store departments had the most customer visits, and what was this number?

The sample store indicated that the appliance department had 146 customer visits, which was the largest of all departments.

2. If the 146 customer visits is used to estimate the number of appliance department visits at the larger store population, what are the lower and upper limits of this estimate?

The lower error bar value is 126 (read this on the y-axis) and the upper bar value is 168.

3. Given the information in the previous two answers, what can be said about the expected number of visits at the larger population of retail stores?

We can say that if repeated sampling of the larger population of retail stores was performed, then 95% of the samples would show that the appliance departments had between 126 and 168 customer visits.

4. What are the lower and upper 95% confidence limits for the electronics department and what was the samples observed number of customers?

The electronics department had 83 customer visits, with the error bar showing a lower estimate of 67 with an upper limit of 101 customers.

★ 2.5 Review Exercises

1. Open **customer_dbase.sav** database and build a simple bar graph as in Figure 2.10, using the *Job satisfaction* variable on the x-axis. Use the vertical orientation for this graph.

Question: What are the numbers of observations in each of the five categories that rate the respondent's level of job satisfaction?

Figure 2.10 Review Exercise: Simple Bar for Job Satisfaction (Numbers)

2. Open the **customer_dbase.sav** database and build a simple bar graph as in Figure 2.11, using the *Job satisfaction* variable on the *x*-axis. Use the vertical orientation for this graph.

Question: What are the percentages of observations in each of the five job satisfaction categories?

Figure 2.11 Review Exercise: Simple Bar Graph for Job Satisfaction (Percentages)

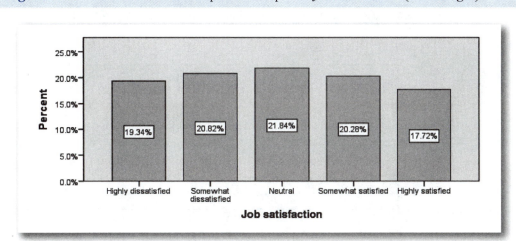

3. Open the **customer_dbase.sav** database and build a simple bar graph as in Figure 2.12, using the *Marital status* variable. Use the horizontal orientation for this graph.

Question: What are the numbers of observations in each of the two categories of marital status?

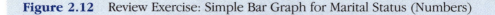

Figure 2.12   Review Exercise: Simple Bar Graph for Marital Status (Numbers)

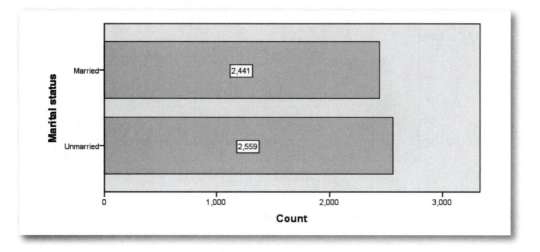

4. Open the **customer-dbase.sav** database and build a simple bar graph as in Figure 2.13, using the *Marital status* variable. Use the horizontal orientation for this graph.

Question: What are the percentages of observations in each of the two categories?

Figure 2.13   Review Exercise: Simple Bar Graph for Marital Status (Percentages)

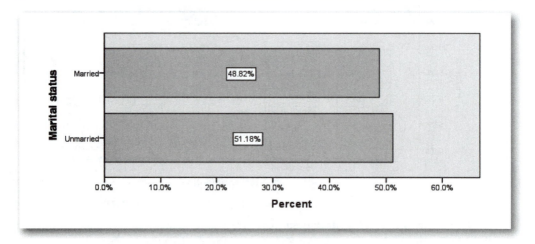

5. Open the **customer_dbase.sav** database and build a simple bar graph as in Figure 2.14, using the *Building type* variable. Use the vertical orientation for this graph.

Question: What are the numbers of observations in each of the four building type categories?

Figure 2.14   Review Exercises: Simple Bar Graph for Building Type (Numbers)

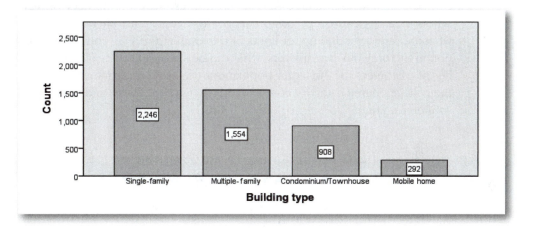

6. Open the **customer_dbase.sav** database and build a simple bar graph as in Figure 2.15, using the *Building type* variable. Use the vertical orientation for this graph.

Question: What are the percentages of observations in each of the four building type categories?

Figure 2.15   Review Exercises: Simple Bar Graph for Building Type (Percentages)

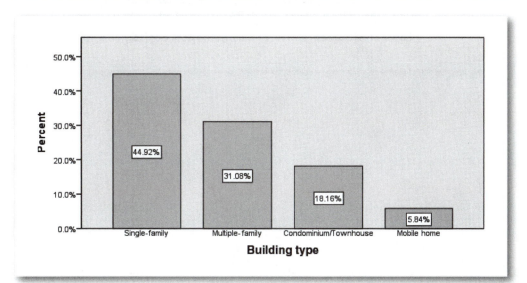

7. Open the **telco.sav** database and build a simple bar graph showing error bars as in Figure 2.16, using the variable *Level of education*. Use the vertical orientation for this graph.

Questions: (a) Which of the five levels of education has the most individuals and what is this number? (b) If the sample of telco's customers that earned a high school degree (287) is used to estimate the number of high school degrees earned by customers for the larger customer population, what are the lower and upper limits of this estimate? (c) Given the information in the previous two answers, what can be said about the expected number of customers for the larger population? (d) How many individuals does the college degree category contain, and what are the lower and upper 95% confidence limits?

Figure 2.16   Review Exercise: Simple Bar Graph With Error Bars

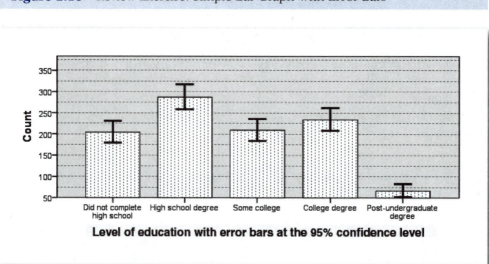

3

STACKED BAR GRAPH

PURPOSE OF GRAPHS YOU ARE ABOUT TO BUILD

- To explore for a relationship between the categories of two discrete variables

3.1 INTRODUCTION TO THE STACKED BAR GRAPH ★

As with the simple bar graph, the stacked bar graph uses rectangular boxes to represent categories of a variable. The variable located on the *x*-axis is known as the *stacked* variable. The stacked bar graph differs from the simple bar graph in that each rectangular box on the *x*-axis is made up of smaller individual boxes that SPSS calls *segments*. The *segments* are stacked on top of one another and could also be called the *y*-axis variable. The height of each segment represents the percentage of cases in a category of the *stacked* variable and a category of the *segment* variable. The stacked bar graph depicts the relationship between the categories of the *stacked* and *segment* variables. The stacked bar graph provides a convenient way to discover and then visualize relationships between two discrete variables. Another use of the stacked bar is when you wish to describe the relationship between two discrete and a single continuous variable. We have elected not to demonstrate this particular graph, as you can provide the same description by building a clustered bar graph as shown in the next chapter.

The reader should also be aware that the stacked bar graph can be used to mislead someone using a graph to understand data. Some readers may wish to view an example of a deceptive stacked bar graph at this time. An example may be found in Chapter 18 on deceptive uses of graphs, see Figure 18.3.

The appearance of the stacked bar can vary greatly depending on how the percentages are calculated. In the next two examples, we use the same data to demonstrate two ways to calculate percentages. The first is where you instruct SPSS to calculate percentages with each stack representing 100% of the observations within that stacked category. With this approach, certain questions can be answered, which are soon discussed. The second approach is to have SPSS calculate the percentage of the total across the segments, which results in answers to another set of questions. We next take a closer look at these two approaches.

3.1.1 Stacked Bar Graph (Percentage of Stack's Total)

To build the stacked bar, as shown in Figure 3.1, you must instruct SPSS to calculate percentages so that each *stack* represents 100% of the observations in that stack. You will soon learn how to accomplish this when building the stacked bar.

The stacked bar graph in Figure 3.1 summarizes data for students in statistics classes collected over an 11-year period. The intention of this current analysis is to compare gender and earned grade for 1,050 students in these statistics classes.[1] The *stacked* variable in Figure 3.1 is *gender*, having two categories—male and female. The *segment* variable is the *grade* earned and has five categories—A, B, C, D, and F.

In this example, the major question we are trying to answer is whether there is a difference in the performance for the males and females. For instance, is the percentage of A's the same for males and females taking the class? This question may be repeated for each of the four remaining grades. We may also examine how the grades are distributed within each category of the stacked variable, in this case *gender*. Are the distributions of grades for the males and females similar?

The stacked bar is especially useful when seeking to discover relationships between two variables. In our example, the variable gender was chosen for the *x*-axis, having the two categories of male and female. Each segment within the rectangular boxes for male and female represents the percentage of students earning a specific grade (second variable) *within* their gender category. For an example, look at Figure 3.1 and notice that

[1]These data were obtained from records of 1,050 students taking an intermediate level social statistics class with the authors.

19.13% of males earned A, while 18.48% of females earned this same grade—very close to identical.

The stacked bar graph shown in Figure 3.1 answers the major question that sought to determine if grade earned was related to gender. Do males and females differ in the proportion of the various grades that were earned? Stated another way, we could seek to discover if the distributions of grades for males and females were approximately the same. One quick glance at the graph shows that there is very little gender difference in the proportion of grades earned, and hence, the shapes of the distributions are approximately identical.[2] In the following section, the database used to build a stacked bar graph and the questions we seek to answer are presented.

Figure 3.1   Stacked Bar Graph (Percentage of Stack's Total) for Gender and Grade

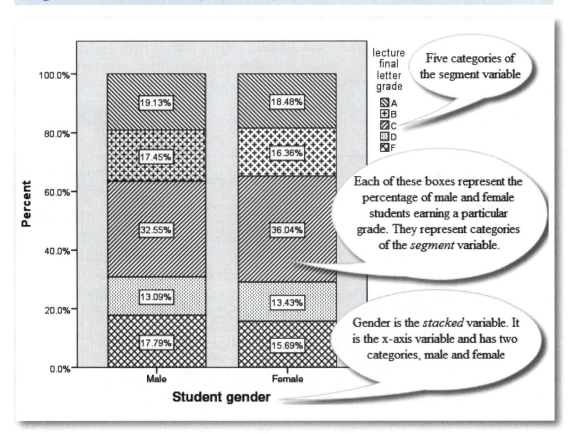

_____

[2]Although there appears to be little difference in values, it would be appropriate to test for significance using chi-square analysis to confirm your visual interpretation.

3.1.2 Stacked Bar Graph
(Percentage of Segment's Total)

To build the stacked bar shown in Figure 3.2, you must instruct SPSS to calculate percentages so that each *segment* represents 100% of the observations. You will soon use a few clicks of the mouse button to accomplish this calculation.

Figure 3.2 uses the identical data used in Figure 3.1 except that the *x*-axis or *stacked* variable is now *grade* and the *segment* variable is *gender*. The percentages shown in each bar now represent the percentage of the total observations in all segments. Go ahead; add the segment percentages' together to confirm this fact.

In this example, it is acceptable to directly look at each bar (grade) and determine the correct percentage of males and females earning that grade. As in the previous graph, 19.13% represents the percentage of males who earned the grade A. The first segment of the "A" stack shows 18.48%, which is the percent of all female students earning that grade. By reading each segment horizontally, we can see the percentage of males earning the various grades. The same can be done for the females.

Figure 3.2   Stacked Bar Graph (Percentage of Segment's Total) for Gender and Grade

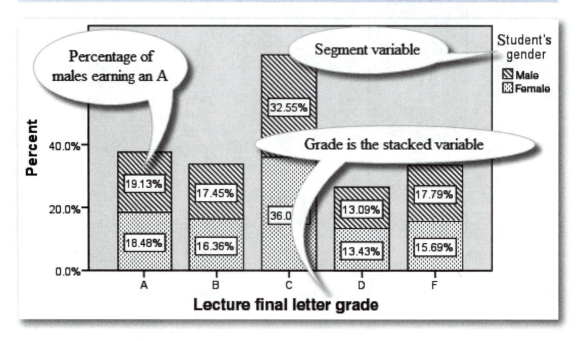

There are many variations in how to place your variables (*x-axis* or *legend*) as well as ways in which to calculate percentages (total, total of segment, or total of stacked variable). Each of the variations will produce unique graphs that may be tailored to answer different sets of questions about the data.

The reader will soon have the knowledge to experiment with the various possibilities of this versatile graph.

3.2 Database and Questions   ★

The data used to build a stacked bar graph is found in the SPSS Sample files and is named **1991 U.S. General Social Survey.sav**.[3] You should open this database now. If you need to review the opening procedure, refer to Section 2.2 of Chapter 2.

The General Social Survey (GSS) has been conducted by the National Opinion Research Center every year since 1972. There are 43 variables and 1,517 cases in the current SPSS version of a small portion of this database. We use two discrete variables to produce a stacked bar graph. One variable is named *race* and labeled *Race of the respondent*, which will be the *x*-axis variable (*stacked* variable). The *segment* variable is named *region* and labeled *Region of the United States*.

3.2.1 Questions for the Stacked Bar Graph (Percentage of Stack's Total)

1. How are the three races (White, Black, and Other) distributed between the three regions of North East, South East, and West.

2. What region do those in the White race category prefer?

3. What are the first, second, and third choices of those in the Black category?

---

[3]Some readers may feel that this database is just a little outdated. However, there are a couple of reasons we have chosen to use this database dating back to the 1991 census. First of all, it was included with SPSS and contained useful data that was measured at the levels of measurement needed for our graph-making demonstrations. On a more serious note, one should remember that to measure any change in society, one must have a starting point. Thus, the data presented in 1991 are extremely important in many situations where the amount of change is important.

3.2.2 Questions for the Stacked Bar
Graph (Percentage of Segment's Total)

1. Which region had the highest percentage of those categorized as White?

2. Rank the regions, in order from the least chosen to the most chosen by those respondents who were classified as "Other."

3. Which region is the least desirable for the White category?

In the next section, you produce stacked bar graphs to answer these questions about the GSS database.

★   3.3 USING SPSS TO BUILD THE STACKED BAR GRAPH

In this section, you build a stacked bar graph that requires the use of the *Chart Builder*, the *Element Properties* feature, and finally the *Chart Editor* to embellish the graph. The finished stacked bar graph will then answer the questions concerning a possible relationship between race and region of residence.

3.3.1 Building the Stacked Bar Graph
(Percentage of Stack's Total)

- Open **1991 U.S. General Social Survey.sav** (found in the SPSS Sample file).
- Click **Graphs**, and then click **Chart Builder**. When the *Chart Builder* window opens, make certain that **Gallery** is selected—if not, then click **Gallery**.
- Click **Bar** (found in the *Choose from:* list in the lower left portion of the window), and drag the third **graph icon** (*Stacked Bar*) to the large panel on the top right of the *Chart Builder* window.
- Click **Race of Respondent** in the *Variables* panel, and drag it to the *X-Axis* box.
- Click **Region of the United States**, and drag it to *stack: set color* box.
- If *Elements Properties* window is not open, then click **Element Properties button** to open.
- In the *Statistics* panel, click the **down arrow** and click **percentage (?)**.
- Click **Set Parameters** (*Element Properties: Set Parameters* window opens) (see Figure 3.3).

Figure 3.3 *Element Properties: Set Parameters* Window

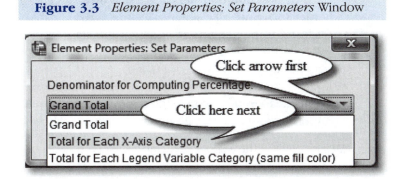

- Click the **black arrow** to the right of *Grand Total* and click **Total for Each X-Axis Category** (doing this calculates the percentage of each category of the *segment* variable within the *stacked* variable category).
- Click **Continue.**
- Click **Apply**, then Click **OK.**

Once **OK** is clicked, a basic draft of the stacked bar graph appears in the SPSS *Output Viewer*. The following procedures will enhance this graph and make it easier to answer our questions.

- Double click the **graph** in the *Output Viewer* (*Chart Editor* window opens).
- Click the **Data Label Mode icon** as shown in Figure 3.4, and then click on each **segment**, which inserts a percentage amount for each category within the *stacked* variable.
- Click the **Data Label Mode icon**, which turns it off.

Figure 3.4 *Chart Editor* Window and *Show Properties Window* and *Data Label Mode* Icons

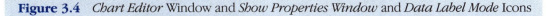

- Click the **rectangular box** for the **White** category (a faint yellow border surrounds all categories for the *x-axis* variable.
- Click the **upper segment** of any of the stacked categories (a faint yellow border appears on all the upper segments of your *stacked* variable categories).
- If *Element Properties* window is not open, you must click the **Show Properties Window icon** in the *Chart Editor* menu as shown in Figure 3.4 (once clicked the *Properties* window opens as shown in Figure 3.4.

We next utilize the *Properties* window (shown in Figure 3.5) to make some improvements to the stacked bar graph. These improvements will enhance the question answering ability of the graph.

- In the *Color* panel, click the **small box** to the left of *Fill*, then click the **white rectangular box** to the right (Figure 3.5).
- Click the **black arrow** beneath *Pattern* in the *Properties* window, then click the **third pattern** in the **top** row.

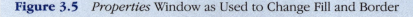

Figure 3.5   *Properties* Window as Used to Change Fill and Border

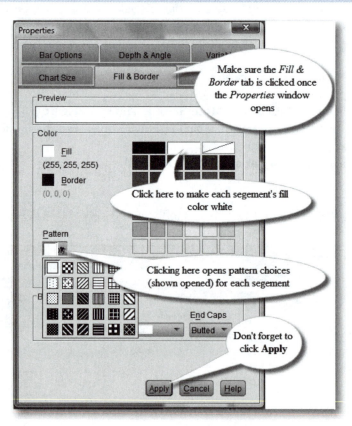

- Click **Apply** (next we repeat this pattern selection process for each of the segments).
- Click the **middle segment** (all these segments are now framed with a yellow border).
- In the *Color* panel, click the **small box** to the left of *Fill*, then click the **white rectangular box** to the right (Figure 3.5).
- Click the **black arrow** beneath *Pattern*, and click the **first pattern** in the **second** row.
- Click **Apply**.
- Click the **lowest segment** (all these final segments are framed in yellow).
- In the *Color* panel click the **small box** to the left of *Fill*, then click the **white rectangular box** to the right (Figure 3.5).
- Click the **black arrow** beneath *Pattern*, and click the **second pattern** in the **second** row.
- Click **Apply**.
- Click the **X** in the box in the top-right portion of the *Chart Editor* (the finished graph now appears in the *Output Viewer* as shown in Figure 3.6).

Figure 3.6   Stacked Bar Graph (Percentage of Stack's Total) for Race and Region

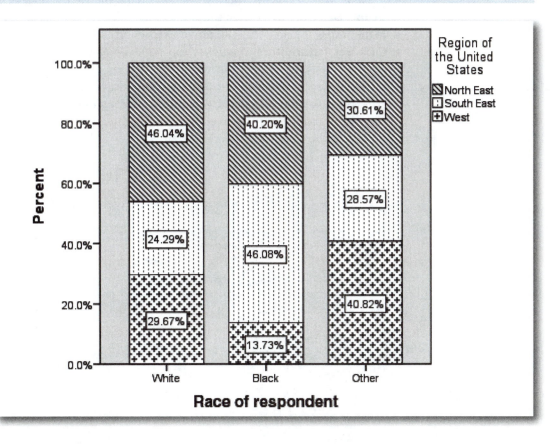

The stacked bar graph in Figure 3.6 depicts the relationship of race of respondents and the region in which they reside.

3.3.2 Building the Stacked Bar Graph (Percentage of Segment's Total)

- Open **1991 U.S. General Social Survey.sav** (found in the SPSS Sample file).
- Click **Graphs**, and then click **Chart Builder**. When the *Chart Builder* window opens, make certain that **Gallery** is selected—if not, then click **Gallery**.
- Click **Reset button** (clears previous work from *Chart preview* window).
- Click **Bar** (found in the *Choose from:* list in the lower left portion of the window), and drag the third **graph icon** (*Stacked Bar*) to the large panel on the top right of the *Chart Builder* window.
- Click **Race of respondent** in the *Variables* panel, and drag it to the *stack: set color* box.
- Click **Region of the United States**, and drag it to *X-Axis* box.
- If *Elements Properties* window is not open, then click **Element Properties button** to open the window.
- In the *Statistics* panel, click the **down arrow** and click **percentage (?)**.
- Click **Set Parameters** (*Element Properties: Set Parameters* window opens) (see Figure 3.7 for this window).
- Click the **down arrow** to the right of where it says *Grand Total*, and click **Total for Each Legend Variable Category (same fill color)** (doing this calculates the percentage of each category of the *segment* variable within the *stacked* variable category)

Figure 3.7 *Element Properties: Set Parameters* Window

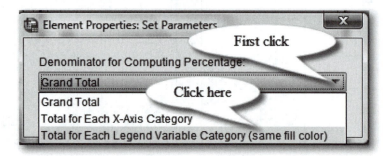

- Click **Continue**.
- Click **Apply**, then Click **OK**.
- Double click the **graph** in the *Output Viewer* (*Chart Editor* window opens).
- Click the **Show Data Labels icon** as shown in Figure 3.8 (data labels, as percentages, are added to all segments).
- Click the **upper segment** of any of the stacked categories (a faint yellow border appears on all bars for the *stacked* variable categories), click the **same segment** a second time, and only the horizontal segment remains framed.
- If *Element Properties* window is not open, you must click the **Show Properties Window icon** in the *Chart Editor* menu as shown in Figure 3.8.

Figure 3.8 *Chart Editor* (Upper Portion) Indicating the *Show Data Labels* icon

- In the *Properties* window, click the **Fill & Border tab** (once clicked, the *Properties* window should appear as shown in Figure 3.5).
- In the *Color* panel, click the **small box** to the left of *Fill*, then click the **white rectangular box** to the right (see Figure 3.5 and be sure to avoid clicking the white rectangular box with the **red** line through it).
- Click the **black arrow** beneath *Pattern* in the *Properties* window, then click the **first pattern** in the **third** row.
- Click **Apply** (we next repeat this pattern selection process for each of the segments).
- Click the **middle segment** (all these segments are now framed with a faint border).
- In the *Color* panel, click the **small box** to the left of *Fill*, then click the **white rectangular box** to the right (Figure 3.5).
- Click the **black arrow** beneath *Pattern*, and click the **third pattern** in the **first** row.

- Click **Apply**.
- Click the **lowest segment** (all these final segments are framed in yellow).
- In the *Color* panel, click the **small box** to the left of *Fill*, then click the **white rectangular box** to the right (Figure 3.5).
- Click the **black arrow** beneath *Pattern*, then click the **second pattern** in the **fifth** row.
- Click **Apply**.
- Click the **X** in the box in the top-right portion of the *Chart Editor* (the finished graph now appears in the *Output Viewer* as shown in Figure 3.9).

Figure 3.9   Stacked Bar Graph (Percentage of Segment's Total) for Region and Race

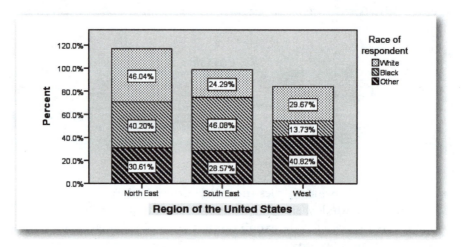

★   **3.4 INTERPRETATION OF THE STACKED BAR GRAPH**

Let's examine the graphs in Figures 3.6 and 3.9 to see if they answer our questions about the data. Remember that the graph in Figure 3.6 shows the segment variable as the region of residence, while the stacked variable is race. For the graph in Figure 3.9, the segment variable is race and the stacked variable is the region of residence.

One of the first things to note is that the appearance of both graphs differs from the examples we presented in Figures 3.1 and 3.2, when gender and grade were compared. In the "gender and grade" graphs, the segments are approximately the same size sending the message that males and females performed equally. The graphs just produced for "race and region" show segments that are not equal. The message here is that those in the three race categories choose different regions of the United States in which to reside. Let's examine this more closely by revisiting our original questions.

3.4.1 Questions and Answers for the Stacked Bar (Percentage of Stack's Total)

The answers to the following questions are provided by the graph in Figure 3.6.

1. How are the three races (White, Black, and Other) distributed between the three regions of North East, South East, and West?

The graph shown in Figure 3.6 clearly indicates that the race categories are not evenly distributed between the regions of residence. It is the proportional sizes of the segments in the various stacks that tell us that the race categories are *not* evenly distributed. It is also informative to note the percentages of the race categories (Whites, Blacks, and Other) choosing one of three regions (North East, South East, and West) to reside.[4]

2. What region do those in the White race category prefer?

Forty-six percent of those in the White category choose the North East as a place to live.

3. What are the first, second, and third choices for those in the Black category?

The first, second, and third choices for those in the Black category are shown in the Black stack. Those in the Black category have selected their Number 1 region of choice as the South East (46.08%), the second choice was the North East (40.20%), and the third was the West (13.73%).

The stacked bar graph is a useful tool when attempting to describe the relationship between two variables. In the following chapter, we discuss another form of bar graph—clustered bar.

3.4.2 Questions and Answers for the Stacked Bar (Percentage of Segment's Total)

The answers to the following questions are provided by the graph in Figure 3.9.

---

[4]You could at this point, under certain conditions, conduct a statistical test and determine the likelihood that the observed differences are statistically significant.

1. Which region had the highest percentage of those categorized as White?

The highest percentage recorded for whites was the North East at 46.04%.

2. Rank the regions, in order from the least chosen to the most chosen by those respondents who were classified as "Other."

The smallest percentage of the "Other" category chose the South East (28.57%), next was the North East at 30.61%, and the most preferred choice of residency was the West at 40.82%.

3. Which region is the least desirable for the White category?

The respondents of the South East region represent 24.29%, making it the least desirable choice of residency by those categorized as White.

★   3.5 REVIEW EXERCISES

1. Open the SPSS Sample file **1991 U.S. General Social Survey.sav**. Select the two discrete variables of *Sex* (Variable 1) and *occcat80* (Variable 14) to construct a stacked bar graph as in Figure 3.10. Place the *occcat80* variable on the *x*-axis, change the *y*-axis to percent, and make the *segment (color)* variable the *Respondent's sex*. Use a horizontal orientation as one way to accommodate the long category names.

Question: What are the proportions of males and females in each of the six occupational categories?

Figure 3.10   Review Exercise: Stacked Bar Graph for Occupation and Sex

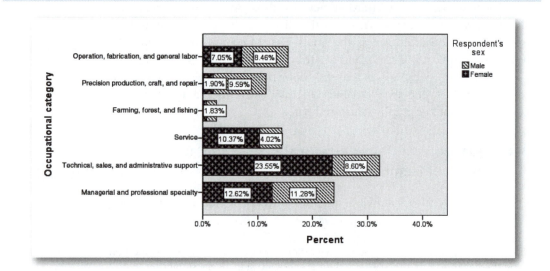

2. Open the SPSS Sample file **1991 U.S. General Social Survey.sav**. Select the two discrete variables of *Sex* (Variable 1) and *life* (Variable 5) to construct a stacked bar graph as in Figure 3.11. Place the *life* variable on the *x*-axis, change the *y*-axis to percent, and make the *segment (color)* variable the *Respondent's sex*.

Questions: You want to explore the database seeking to discover any relationship between gender and outlook on life. (a) What are the gender differences for each category? (b) Which of the three life outlook categories has the greatest gender difference? (c) Which has the least difference?

Figure 3.11   Review Exercise: Stacked Bar Graph for Sex and Outlook on Life

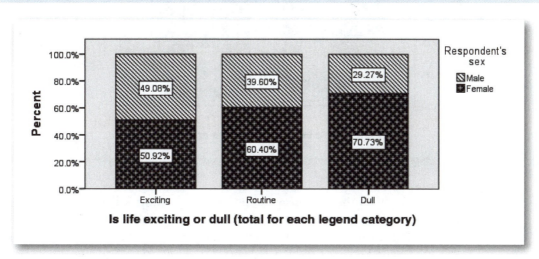

3. Open SPSS Sample file **1991 U.S. General Social Survey.sav**. Select the two discrete variables of *Sex* (labeled *Respondent's sex*) and *life* (labeled *Is life exciting or dull*) to construct a stacked bar graph as in Figure 3.12. Place the *Sex* variable on the *x*-axis, the *segment (color)* variable is *life*, and change the *y*-axis to percent.

Questions: You want to explore the database seeking to discover any relationship between gender and outlook on life. (a) What percentage of males think that life is Exciting? (b) What percentage of females think that life is Exciting? (c) What percentage of males think that life is Routine? (d) What percentage of females think that life is Routine (e) What percentage of males think that life is Dull? (f) What percentage of females think that life is Dull? (g) Do males and females have the same outlook on life in this study?

Figure 3.12   Review Exercise: Stacked Bar Graph for Sex and Outlook on Life

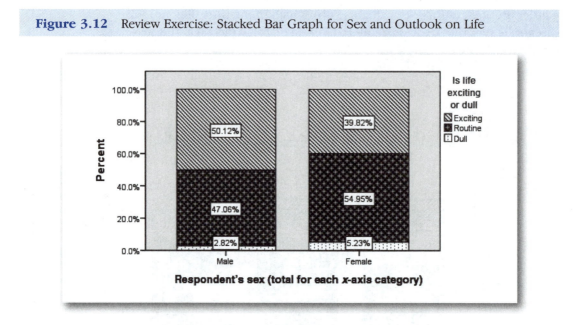

4. Open the SPSS Sample file **poll_cs_sample.sav** to build a stacked bar graph as in Figure 3.13. Select the discrete variable named *county* and labeled *County* (Variable 4) and place it on the *x*-axis. Select the discrete variable named *votelast* and labeled *Voted in last election* (Variable 7) and place it on the *stack: set color* box. Change the *y*-axis to percent.

Questions: (a) What percentage of individuals who live in the *Eastern* county voted in the last election? (b) What percentage of individuals who live in the *Northern* county did not vote in the last election? (c) What percentage of individuals who live in the *Central* county voted in the last election? (d) What percentage of individuals who live in the *Southern* county did not vote in the last election? (e) What percentage of individuals who live in the *Western* county voted in the last elections? (f) Which county region has the largest percentage of individuals who voted in the last election?

Figure 3.13   Review Exercise: Stacked Bar Graph for County Region and Voting Behavior

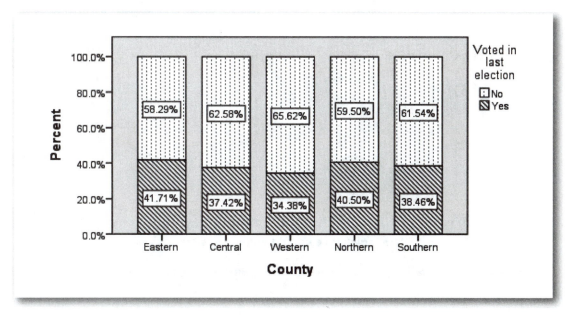

5. Open the SPSS Sample file **poll_cs_sample.sav** and build a stacked bar graph as in Figure 3.14. Select the discrete variable named *opinion_gastax* and labeled *The legislature should enact a gas tax* (Variable 9) and place it on the *x*-axis. Select the discrete variable named *agecat* and labeled *Age category* (Variable 5) and place it on the *stack: set color* box. Change the *y*-axis to percent.

Questions: (a) What percentage of individuals who strongly disagree that there should be a gas tax are older than 60? (b) What percentage of individuals who agree that there should be a new gas tax are aged 18 to 30? (c) What percentage of individuals who strongly agree that there should be a new gas tax are aged 46 to 60? (d) What percentage of individuals who strongly disagree that there should be a new gas tax are aged 18 to 30 years? (e) Which of the age categories, within the strongly agree that there should be a new tax group, contains the highest percentage of individuals? (f) Which of the age categories have the lowest percentage of individuals who disagree that the legislature should enact a gas tax?

Figure 3.14 Review Exercise: Stacked Bar Graph for Gas Tax and Age Category

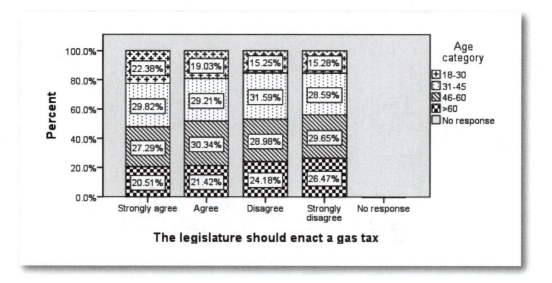

4

CLUSTERED BAR GRAPH

PURPOSE OF GRAPHS YOU ARE ABOUT TO BUILD

- To explore for a relationship between the categories of two discrete variables
- To categorize an individual or object on two discrete variables and a statistic of a continuous variable and then compare the groups

4.1 INTRODUCTION TO THE CLUSTERED BAR GRAPH ★

The clustered bar graph has the same basic purpose as the stacked bar graph that was presented in the previous chapter. You will recall that the stacked bar graph was used to discover and interpret relationships between the categories of two discrete variables. The clustered bar graph as shown in Figure 4.1 will accomplish this same task. We also demonstrate how the clustered bar graph in Figure 4.2 can be used to show the relationship between two discrete and a single continuous variable.

The person building the graph should choose between the stacked or clustered type graphs, depending on which best answers the questions about the data. Often, this involves the graph maker's personal preference. The authors recommend that both be produced and then you make the judgment as to which one best answers the questions about your database.

4.1.1 Clustered Bar Graph for Two Discrete Variables

The clustered bar graph uses rectangular boxes to represent the number (count) or percentage of cases in the categories of two variables. It accomplishes this by "clustering" the categories of an *x*-axis variable. We use data from 1,050 statistics students to illustrate the clustered bar graph (Figure 4.1). The information bubbles in this figure were inserted to show how variables are entered in the SPSS *Chart Builder*. This information will assist you when you actually build a clustered bar graph using SPSS Sample file data in Section 4.3. In Figure 4.1, the *x*-axis variable represents the grade earned by the students (A, B, C, D, or F). The *Cluster on X: set color* variable is whether the students attended a day or an evening class. How to use *Cluster on X: set color* will be further explained when you build the clustered bar later in this chapter.

As you might expect, there are many interesting questions about a database containing the records of 1,050 statistics students. We selected one such question to demonstrate the clustered bar graph: Is there a difference in grade performance for those students taking day and evening

Figure 4.1 Cluster Bar Graph Example Showing Data for 1,050 Statistics Students

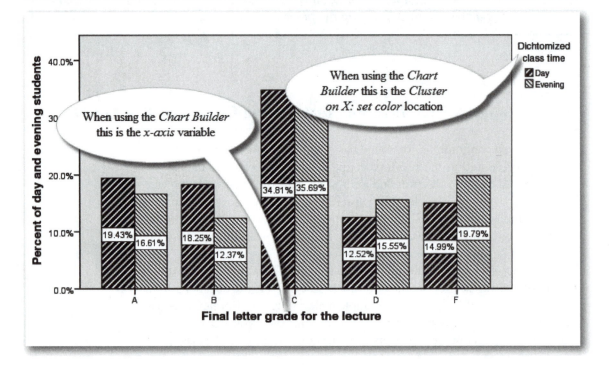

classes? Take a close look at Figure 4.1 to see how this question might be answered.

The percentages in each bar of the graph in Figure 4.1 represent the percentages of day and evening students earning the particular grade shown on the *x*-axis. For instance, 19.43% of *all day* students earned an A, while 16.61% of *all evening* students earned the same grade. To further understand what the percentages in each bar represent, it may be instructive for the reader to add the percentages for all day students (19.43% + 18.25% + 34.81% + 12.52% + 14.99% = 100%) and then repeat the process for the evening students.

The graph suggests that there are some differences in the grade categories. An additional question is whether these differences are greater than one would expect by chance? One might look at the graph and reach the conclusion that the pictured differences are not significant. Further testing of the data using chi-square analysis would indicate that the assumption of nonsignificance is correct.

4.1.2 Clustered Bar Graph for Two Discrete and One Continuous Variable

In the preceding example, we used two discrete variables. There are occasions when you may wish to investigate a continuous variable and its relationship to discrete variables. Let's use the same database (1,050 statistics students) to show a clustered bar graph, using the *mean* score on the final exam (a continuous variable) on the *y*-axis. We use the *Dichotomized class time* as the *x*-axis variable and the *Student's gender* as the variable moved to the *Cluster on X: set color* box in the *Chart Builder*. This clustered graph is shown in Figure 4.2.

For this example, the question is whether gender is related to the average score on the final exam *and* whether the student is taking a day or an evening class. We may ask whether males score differently for the day and evening classes. Are there differences between females for the day and evening classes? Are there differences in male and female performance in the day class?

How does the clustered bar graph shown in Figure 4.2 answer these questions? A quick look at the graph informs us that, on average, females performed slightly better than males in both day and evening classes. You can determine this by observing that the bars marked with plus signs (females) are taller than the bars with diagonal lines (males). You might also observe that the average test scores, presented in the windows of each

Figure 4.2   Clustered Bar Graph Showing One Continuous and Two Discrete Variables

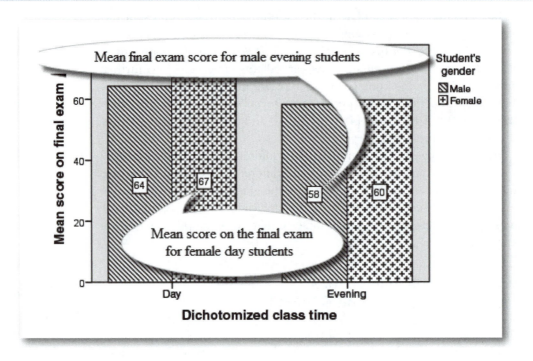

rectangular box, convey this same information. Since each cluster (day and evening) compares males and females, we see that the average score for daytime males is 64, while the average test score for females attending these day classes is 67. The same pattern (females scoring slightly higher) holds true for the evening students, with males averaging 58 points and females 60.

Each rectangular bar represents three observations concerning a group of students. Given the proper instructions, the SPSS *Chart Builder* places all female students (first observation) attending day classes (second observation) in a category and then calculates the mean points earned on the final exam (third observation) for all students so categorized. The mean points earned by these students are the values displayed in each of the rectangular bars in Figure 4.2.

In the following section, we describe the database you will use to build cluster graphs similar to those shown above. Also, this section gives a set of questions that will be answered by graphs that you will soon build.

4.2 DATABASE AND QUESTIONS   ★

For your graph-building experience, in this chapter you will use **customer_dbase.sav** from the SPSS Sample files. This database consists of 5,000 cases and 132 variables. SPSS describes it as being hypothetical data collected by a company with the intended use of making special sales offers to only those most likely to be interested. We use three of the 132 variables to build two different clustered bar graphs.

In Section 4.3, you produce two clustered bar graphs using data contained in the **customer_dbase.sav** Sample file. Open this database and examine the *Data View* and *Variable View*. You will build a clustered bar graph using the two discrete variables. The first is named *jobcat* and labeled *Job category*, the second is named *gender* and labeled *Gender*. You will produce a second graph using the discrete variables of *Job category* and *Gender* and a third measure named *income* and labeled *Household income in thousands*—a value calculated from a continuous variable.

4.2.1 Questions for the Clustered Bar Graph (Two Discrete Variables)

The following three questions are concerned with situations involving the two discrete variables of *Gender* and *Job category*.

1. For each of the six job categories, are males and females equally represented?

2. Which job category attracts the most and least females?

3. Which job category attracts the most and least males?

4.2.2 Questions for the Clustered Bar Graph (Two Discrete and One Continuous Variable)

The following five questions use the discrete variables of *Job category* and *Gender* and the mean of the continuous variable of *Household income in thousands*.

1. What is the mean household income for males in the Managerial and Professional category?

2. What is the mean household income for females working in the Service category?

3. Which job category represents the highest household income for males?

4. Which job category represents the lowest household income for females?

5. In which job category are males and females most likely to have the same household income?

Of course, there are many additional questions, and we will leave it up to the reader to hypothesize other things we could learn from these three variables. We next proceed to build graphs that will provide answers to these and many similar questions.

★ 4.3 USING SPSS TO BUILD THE CLUSTERED BAR GRAPH

With **customer_dbase.sav** open, follow the procedures below to build the graph that will answer our questions about the data.

4.3.1 Building the Clustered Bar Graph for Two Discrete Variables

Follow the procedures below and build a clustered bar graph having two discrete variables. This graph will be similar to the example provided in Figure 4.1.

- Open **customer_dbase.sav** (found in the SPSS Sample file).
- Click **Graphs**, then click **Chart Builder**.
- Click **Bar** in the *Choose from* list.
- Click and drag the **Clustered Bar icon** (the second icon in the first row of icons) to the *Chart preview* panel.
- Click and drag **Gender** to the *X-Axis* (found in the *Variables:* panel).
- Click and drag **Job category** to the *Cluster on X: set color* box in the *Chart preview* panel.
- Click **Count** found on the *Y-Axis*.
- In the *Statistics Section* of the *Element Properties* window click the **black arrow** to the right of *Count*, then click **Percentage (?)**.
- Click **Set Parameters** (*Element Properties: Set parameters* window opens).
- Click **black arrow** to the right of *Grand Total*.

- Click **Total for Each X-Axis Category**, click **Continue**.
- Click **Apply**, then click **OK** (*Output Viewer* opens showing Figure 4.3).

The clustered bar graph appears, and SPSS automatically assigns different colors to each of the bars that represent job categories. This book is not printed in color, so you only see different shades of grey. Since most scientific articles and student papers are not published in color, you next delete the colors and insert unique patterns for each of the six job categories by using certain features of the *Chart Editor*. This process will then enable you to associate each of the bars with the legend (found in the upper right-hand portion of the finished graph) when the graph is printed in black and white only.

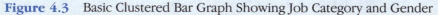

Figure 4.3   Basic Clustered Bar Graph Showing Job Category and Gender

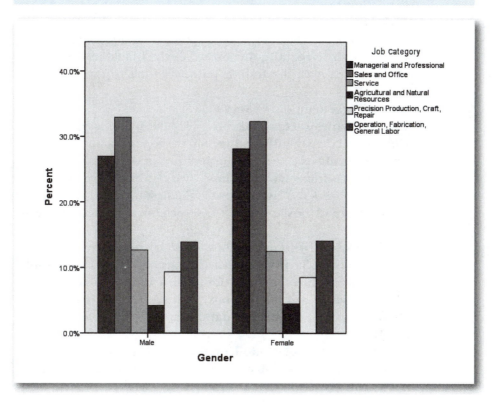

Next, we use the *Chart Editor* to demonstrate how the clustered bar can be improved to more directly and clearly answer the questions about the data.

4.3.2 Using the Chart Editor to Embellish the Clustered Bar Graph Just Built

- Double click the **graph** as it appears in the *Output Viewer* (The *Chart Editor* opens).
- Click the **small box** to the left of the *Job category* of **Management and Professional** (a faint frame appears around the box and the corresponding rectangular boxes in the graph).
- In the *Properties* window, click the **Fill & Border tab**.
- In the *Color* section, click the **white rectangular box** in the top row of available colors.
- Click the **black arrow** beneath *Pattern*, then click the **third pattern** in the **first** row.
- Click **Apply**.
- Click the **box** to the left of the **Sales and Office** job category.
- Click the **white rectangular box**, click the **black arrow** beneath *Pattern*, then click the **fourth pattern** in the **top** row and click **Apply**.
- Click the **box** to the left of **Service**.
- Click the **white rectangular box**, click the **black arrow** beneath *Pattern*, and then the **fifth pattern** in the **top** row and click **Apply**.
- Click the **small box** to the left of **Agricultural and Natural Resources**.
- Click the **white rectangular box**, click the **black arrow** beneath *Pattern*, and click the **last pattern** in the **first** row and click **Apply**.
- Click the **small box** to the left of **Precision Production, Craft, Repair**.
- Click the **white rectangular box**, click the **black arrow** beneath *Pattern*, and click the **first pattern** in the **second** row and click **Apply**.
- Click the **small box** for **Operation, Fabrication, General Labor**.
- Click the **white rectangular box**, click the **black arrow** beneath *Pattern*, and click the **second pattern** in the **second** row and click **Apply**.
- Click the **Data Label Mode icon** (the one that resembles a target), then click **each rectangular bar** in the graph inserting the percentage.

- Click the **Data Label Mode icon** to turn it off.
- Click the *x-axis* label **Male**.
- In the *Properties* window, click the **Labels and Ticks tab**.
- In the *Major Ticks* panel, click the **box** to the left of **Display Ticks** and click **Apply** (this removes all ticks from the *x*-axis).
- Click **X** in the box in the **top right corner** of the *Chart Editor* (Figure 4.4 appears in the *Output Viewer* although not the same size).

4.3.3 Adjusting the Size of the Clustered Bar Graph

The finished graph now appears in the *Output Viewer* and is shown in Figure 4.4. You may notice that the size of the graph is different from the basic graph that was automatically produced by SPSS. There are occasions when you may find it desirable to alter the size of your graph. One example is when you increase the width of a graph to accommodate percentage or numerical values placed as data labels within the individual bars (see Figure 4.4). We next change the size of the graph showing in the *Output Viewer*.

Figure 4.4   Clustered Bar Graph Example Showing Job Category and Gender

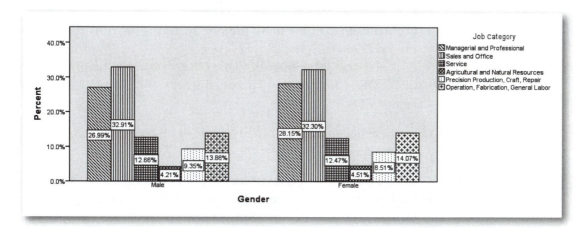

- Click the **graph** (a frame appears around the graph with small black squares at the corners and midpoints of the horizontal and vertical lines).
- Hover the mouse pointer over the lower right black square until you see a double-headed arrow, then click and **drag the blinking line** to increase or decrease the width or the height of the graph (experiment with the process and try to match the size and appearance of the clustered bar graph shown in Figure 4.4).

You just produced a clustered bar graph that displays the relationship between the two discrete variables of *Job category* and *Gender*.

4.3.4 Building the Clustered Bar Graph for Two Discrete and One Continuous Variable

Follow the procedures given below to build a clustered bar graph that shows the relationship between *Gender*, *Job category*, and *Household income*.

- Open **customer_dbase.sav** (found in the SPSS Sample file).
- Click **Graphs**, then click **Chart Builder**.
- In the *Chart Builder* window, click **Reset**.
- Click **Bar** in the *Choose from:* panel.
- Click and drag the **Clustered Bar icon** (second one in the first row) to the top panel in the *Chart Builder* window.
- Click and drag **Gender** to the *X-Axis*.
- Click and drag **Household income** to the *Y-Axis* (this is the box labeled *Count*).
- Click and drag **Job category** to the *Cluster on X: set color* box.
- Click **OK** (the *Output Viewer* displays the graph shown in Figure 4.5).

Using the procedures given below will embellish the basic graph so as to more directly and explicitly answer the questions.

- Double click the **graph** in the *Output Viewer* (the *Chart Editor* opens).
- Click the **Data Label Mode icon**, then click each **rectangular bar** in the graph (be sure to click on each bar even though all data

Figure 4.5   Basic Clustered Bar Using Two Discrete and the Mean of One Continuous Variable

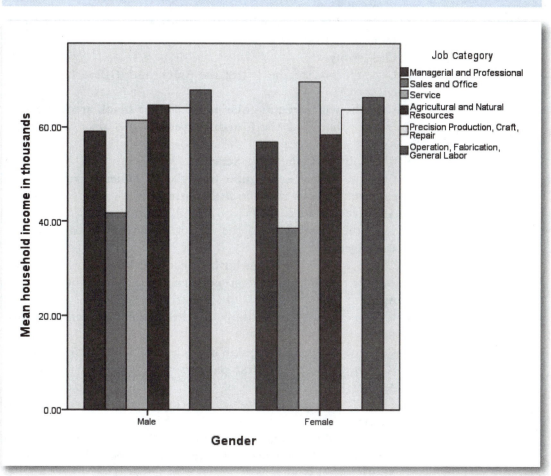

labels may not appear, once the graph is stretched horizontally they will appear).

- Click the **Data Label Mode icon** to turn it off.
- Click the **small box** beneath *Job category* and to the left of **Management and Professional** (a faint frame appears around the box and the corresponding rectangular bars in the graph).

- In the *Properties window*, click the **Fill & Border tab**.
- In the *Color* section, click the **white rectangular box** in the top row of available colors.
- Click the **black arrow** beneath *Pattern*, then click the **third pattern** in the **first** row.
- Click **Apply**.
- Click the **box** to the left of the **Sales and Office** beneath *Job category*.
- Click the **white rectangular box**, click the **black arrow** beneath *Pattern*, then click the **fourth pattern** in the **top** row and click **Apply**.
- Click the **box** to the left of **Service**.
- Click the **white rectangular box**, click the **black arrow** beneath *Pattern*, and then click the **fifth pattern** in the **top** row and click **Apply**.
- Click the **small box** to the left of **Agricultural and Natural Resources**.
- Click the **white rectangular box**, click the **black arrow** beneath *Pattern*, and click the **last pattern** in the **first** row and click **Apply**.
- Click the **small box** to the left of **Precision Production, Craft, Repair**.
- Click the **white rectangular box**, click the **black arrow** beneath *Pattern*, and click the **first pattern** in the **second** row and click **Apply**.
- Click the **small box** for **Operation, Fabrication, General Labor**.
- Click the **white rectangular box**, click the **black arrow** beneath *Pattern*, and click the **second pattern** in the **second** row and click **Apply**.
- Click on the **Male or Female** label found on the *X-Axis*.
- In the *Properties* window, click the **Labels and Ticks tab**.
- In the *Major Ticks* panel, click the **box** to the left of **Display Ticks** and click **Apply** (this removes all ticks from the *X-Axis*).
- Click **X** in the box in the **top right corner** of the *Chart Editor*, and Figure 4.6 appears in the *Output Viewer*.
- Adjust the graphs size as described in Section 4.3.3 above, except that you must be sure to stretch the graph horizontally until all data labels appear in the bars.

Figure 4.6   Clustered Bar Graph Using Two Discrete and the Mean of One
Continuous Variable

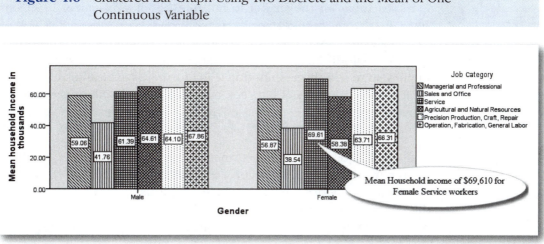

You have now built two clustered bar graphs, one designed for two discrete variables (Figure 4.4) and the other for two discrete and one continuous variable (Figure 4.6). In the following section, we examine how these graphs answered the questions about this database.

4.4 INTERPRETATION OF THE CLUSTERED BAR GRAPH   ★

We now show how the individual graphs answer the questions. For convenience, the questions stated earlier in the chapter are repeated, and then the answers are discussed. Let's begin with an interpretation of the graph in Figure 4.4, which was built to answer questions concerning two discrete variables.

4.4.1 Questions and Answers (Two Discrete Variables)

The answers to the following questions are provided by the graph in Figure 4.4.

1. For each of the six job categories, are males and females equally represented?

Yes, one quick look at Figure 4.4 informs the viewer that males and females are approximately equal in all six categories of employment. We can easily compare the height of the bars or look at the percentages imbedded in each bar for the answer to this question. For instance, 26.99% of the male customers held Managerial and Professional jobs and 28.15% of the females did also. The interpretation just by looking at the graph is that the small difference is of no practical importance. Of course, one might wish to test this assumption using further statistical-testing procedures. Further analysis could seek evidence that the differences shown in our graphical representation of the data are the result of chance or gender preferences.

2. Which job category attracts the most and the least females?

The most popular job category for females is Sales and Office and the least popular is Agricultural and Natural Resources as shown in Figure 4.4. This one is easy to see, just look for the tallest and shortest rectangular boxes in the female category. You could also simply find the highest (32.30%) and the lowest (4.51%) percentages in the female category.

3. Which job category attracts the most and least males?

The answer to this question is identical to the previous one. For the males, we see that Sales and Office attract the most (32.91%) while Agricultural and Natural Resources attracts the least (4.21%) males. You might also look at the tallest and shortest rectangles that communicate the highest and the lowest values for employment attractiveness for males.

4.4.2 Questions and Answers
(Discrete and Continuous Variables)

The answers to the following questions are provided by the graph in Figure 4.6.

The following questions and answers address the variables of *Gender*, *Job category*, and *Household income*.

1. What is the mean household income for males in the Managerial and Professional category?

Don't let the fact that the mean income amounts displayed in each rectangular box are given in thousands of dollars confuse you. Just move the decimal three places to the right and you have the answer. Therefore, we find that the mean household income for males in the Managerial and Professional category is 59.06 or $59,060.

2. What is the mean household income for females working in the Service category?

Look at the Female category on the *x*-axis and the bar representing the *Service* job category to answer this question. The mean household income for females in the *Service* category is 69.61 or $69,610.

3. Which job category represents the highest household income for males?

To answer this question, direct your attention to the male category and look for the tallest bar then read the dollar amount in its window (Data Label). The male job category of Operation, Fabrication, and General Labor indicates a mean household income of $67,860 (67.86). This finding indicates that males working in this occupation have an average household income of $67,860.

4. Which job category represents the lowest household income for females?

This question is answered in the same manner as the previous one, except that you now look for the shortest bar in the female category. The female job category of Sales and Office indicates a mean household income of $38,540 (38.54). This finding indicates that females working in the Sales and Office category have an average household income of $36,540.

5. In which job category are males and females most likely to have the same household income?

To answer this question, focus on the male and female categories and look for bars that are approximately the same height and in the same job category. A less visual method is to directly compare the values appearing in each rectangular bar for all categories. This method is sometimes required when the differences are minor as is the case with these data. Let's use both of these methods to answer the question. Looking at the graph, we can see that the job category of Precision Production, Craft, Repair has approximately the same height for males and females. Further inspection reveals the mean household incomes of $64,100 for males and $63,710 for females. If we carefully compare the heights and numerical values for all job categories, we discover that males and females working in the Precision Production, Craft, Repair category report the closest household income.

★   **4.5 REVIEW EXERCISES**

1. Open SPSS Sample file **verd1985.sav**. Select the two discrete variables labeled as *Neighborhood preference* (named *live*) and *Marital status* (named *marital*). Use *Neighborhood preference* as the *legend/color* variable and *Marital status* on the *x*-axis to build a clustered bar graph as in Figure 4.7.

Questions: (a) What percentage of single individuals choose to live in towns, villages, and the country? (b) What percentage of married individuals choose to live in towns, villages, and the country? (c) What percent of individuals classified in the "other" category choose to live in towns, villages, and the country?

Figure 4.7   Review Exercise: Clustered Bar Graph for Marital Status and Neighborhood Preference

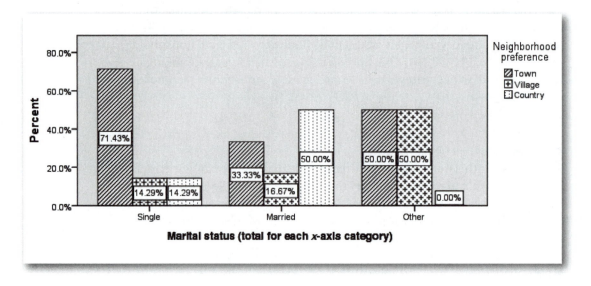

2. Open SPSS Sample file **University of Florida graduate salaries .sav**. Select the two discrete variables of *Gender* and *College* and the continuous variable of *Starting salary* (*salary*) and construct a clustered bar graph. Place the mean starting salary on the *y*-axis and college on the

x-axis, gender is the *color* variable. You may have to transpose the axis in the *Chart Editor* to make the graph easier to read as was done in Figure 4.8.

Questions: (a) Which college has the greatest difference in starting salaries? (b) Which college has the highest starting salary for females? (c) Which college has the highest starting salary for males? (d) Which colleges start females with higher salaries than males?

Figure 4.8   Review Exercise: Clustered Bar Graph for College Department and Salary

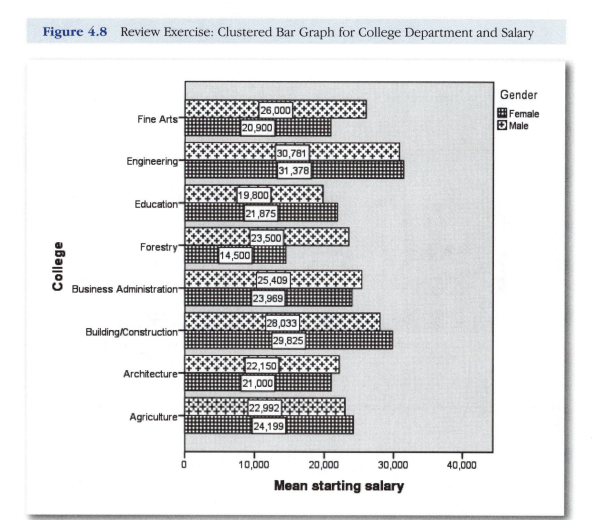

3. Open SPSS Sample file **workprog.sav**. Select the two discrete variables of *Level of education* (*ed*) and *Gender*, and build the clustered bar graph as in Figure 4.9. Use *Level of education* (*ed*) on the *x*-axis and *Gender* as the *legend/color* variable, and change the *y*-axis to percent.

Questions: (a) What percentage of those not completing high school were females? (b) What percentage of those not completing high school were males? (c) What percentage of those completing high school were females? (d) What percentage of those completing high school were males? (e) Without conducting further analysis, would you estimate that there was a significant difference between males and females in any of the four educational categories?

Figure 4.9   Review Exercise: Clustered Bar Graph for Level of Education and Gender

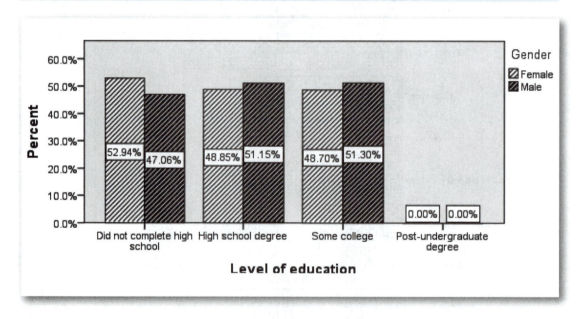

4. Open **customer_dbase.sav**, and select the continuous variable named *creddebt* and labeled *Credit card debt in thousands* for the *y*-axis variable. For the *x*-axis, select the variable named *townsize* and labeled *Size of hometown*. For the *Cluster on X* variable, select the discrete variable

named *marital* and labeled *Marital status*. Build a clustered bar graph as in Figure 4.10 to answer the following questions.

Questions: (a) Which of the 10 groups has the highest credit card debt and what is the amount? (b) Which of the groups has the least amount of credit card debt? (c) Can you identify any pattern between married and unmarried that appears to be related to size of hometown and credit card debt? (d) Marital status shows the least effect on which group?

Figure 4.10   Review Exercise: Clustered Bar Graph for Marital Status and Size of Hometown

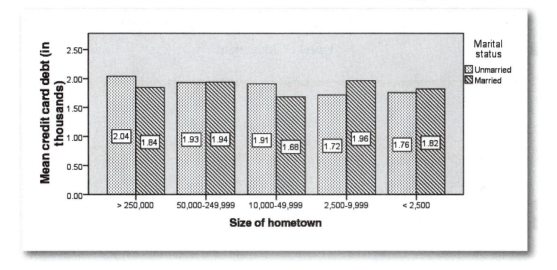

5. Open **customer_dbase.sav** and select the discrete variable named *edcat* and labeled *Level of education* for the *x*-axis variable. For the second discrete variable, select the one named *gender* and labeled *Gender*. Build a clustered bar graph as in Figure 4.11 to answer the following questions.

Questions: (a) How many of male respondents in this study had some college degree? (b) How would you describe the largest group of respondents? (c) What could be stated about the differences between male and female in the various age categories? (d) How many were total respondents in this study?

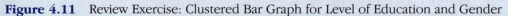

Figure 4.11   Review Exercise: Clustered Bar Graph for Level of Education and Gender

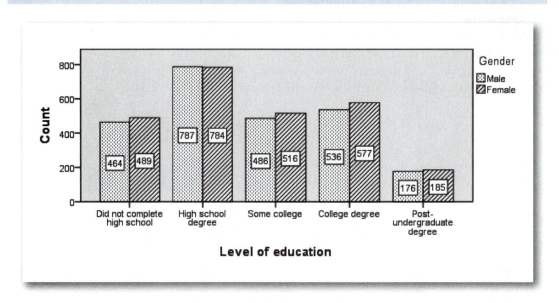

5

PIE GRAPH

PURPOSE OF GRAPHS YOU ARE ABOUT TO BUILD

- To describe the number and/or percentage of observations in each category of the discrete variable and compare each part (pie slice) to the whole

5.1 INTRODUCTION TO THE PIE GRAPH ★

In the previous three chapters, we explained the use of simple, stacked, and clustered bar graphs. The simple bar graph is used to analyze a single variable, and the stacked and clustered bar graphs are used to analyze the relationship between two variables and, occasionally, a third measure.

In this chapter, we describe and explain the pie graph. The pie graph is similar to the simple bar graph in that both are used to analyze a single discrete variable. The advantage of using a pie graph over a simple bar graph is that the pie makes it easier to visualize how each slice relates to the entire pie. Think of each slice of the pie as a container into which observations are placed. The larger slices must be bigger to hold more observations. Hence, larger slices represent larger proportions of the entire pie. Using the pie makes it easier to visualize the relationship between the *parts* and the *whole*. Perhaps, it is because all the parts are enclosed by a well-defined boundary—a circle.

The slices represent the categories of the observed variable. An example would be the variable *gender* that has two categories, male and female. Hence, the pie would be divided into two slices, one for males and one for females. Each of the slices represents the counts and/or percentages of males and females who were observed. Because the slices represent the counts and/or percentage of cases observed in each category of the variable, the size of the slices vary according to the values they represent. The largest slice simply tells us that the category it represents contains more observations than smaller slices.

There are some writers who say that pie graphs are dumb—we disagree. In our opinion, pie graphs are powerful in that they convey numerical information in a straightforward and concise manner. These critics seem to be saying that pie graphs are easily used to mislead the graph reader. They suggest that the orientation of various slices and the angle of the 3-D pie can be manipulated so as to deceive the graph user.[1] While this is true, it is also true of the other graph types as well. The pie graph is no more susceptible to misuse than any other graph type. At the same time, these pie critics profess that data points are more efficiently interpreted by a simple table. In contrast to this view, we see that the most valuable aspect of the pie is to enhance the graph reader's ability to visualize proportions. More specifically, it informs the reader exactly what proportion of the whole each pie slice represents.

In the following two sections, we show the appearance of two different styles of pie graphs. The first presents a pie having labels that show percentages only, although counts could have been presented. This style requires a legend to tell the reader what each slice represents. The second style is presented without a legend since labels are presented directly on the graph. This style gives the reader the name of the slice (category), the number of observations in that slice, and the percentage of the total that the slice represents—all in one label per slice. The choice is based on the questions you have about those variables being investigated. You will build both styles later in the chapter.

The reader will also notice that the pie graphs in Figures 5.1 and 5.2 take on a different appearance—one is flat (1-D) and the other 3-D. Throughout this chapter, we present pie graphs in 1-D and 3-D versions. The difference is partially cosmetic and is introduced here since the authors believe that adding the perspective of volume increases one's ability to think in a proportional manner. We present both models in this chapter and leave it up to the readers to decide for themselves.

---

[1]You may wish to look at Chapter 18 Section 18.2.7 for an example of a deceptive pie graph.

5.1.1 Pie Graph Showing Percentages

Figure 5.1 is an example of a pie graph that contains four slices and shows percentages. This pie graph depicts the result of one question in a survey of 37 statistics students. The students were asked to predict the grade they would earn in the class: A, B, C, D, or F. The data collected for this survey question is discrete since it is measured at the nominal level (SPSS designation).

The question about this survey item concerns the development of a clear picture of the proportion of students predicting the various grades. An example of such a question might be—What proportion of students predicted they would earn the letter grade of C? To answer this question, we build an image of the classes' predicted grades by creating a pie chart. The pie chart enables us to answer this question while also answering questions about the prediction of the other grades by the 37 students.

We see that the exploded slice in Figure 5.1 represents the 32.43% of the students predicting that they would earn a C in the class. Exactly the same percentage of students predicted that they would earn a grade of B. We also see that 29.73% of the students predicted an A in the class. Finally, we observe that 5.41% predicted a grade of D. Also notice that SPSS does not assign a slice of the pie to the F category (look at the legend) because no student predicted that they would fail in the class. To check if we have all the categories represented, we add the percentages shown in all pie slices (categories) with the result of 100%.

Figure 5.1   Exploded Pie Graph Example: Students' Predicted Grade

5.1.2 Pie Graph Showing Labels, Counts, and Percentages

The pie graph in Figure 5.2 was built using the database consisting of 1,050 intermediate-level statistics students. It presents the grades earned by these 1,050 students and the percentages and numbers of students for each of the five categories of A, B, C, D, and F.

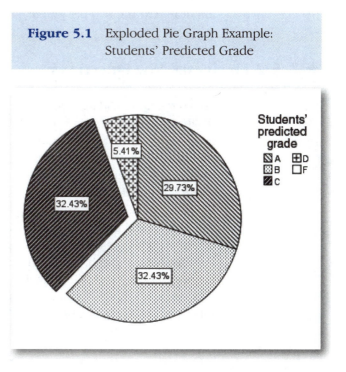

Figure 5.2   Pie Graph Showing Names, Numbers, and Percentags for Each Slice

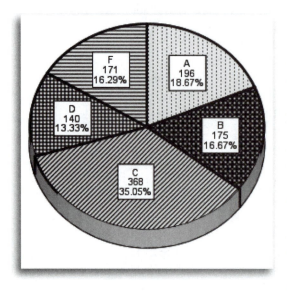

In other words, it summarizes the grading history for 11 years of teaching statistics at a major university.

As you can see, Figure 5.2 provides information beyond what was shown in Figure 5.1.

For the graph builder, the choice between these two pie styles rests with the type of questions about the database. Another consideration would be the size of the slices and the length of the slice name. Small slices (few cases) and long names generally don't mix well, and SPSS will not always display the label on the finished graph. For variables with long category names and few cases per slice, you will most likey not delete the legend as is demonstrated in Figure 5.2. Long names are not a problem for data used in Figure 5.2 as the category names are simply letter grades of A, B, C, D, and F. An alternative to displaying the legend is to insert the data labels and simply click and drag the label to a point outside the graph. In the following sections, we present several types of questions applicable to the two pie graphs just discussed.

★   5.2 DATABASES AND QUESTIONS

For your graph-building experience, in this chapter, you will use two different databases both found in the SPSS Sample file. The first, **poll_cs_sample .sav**, is used to build a pie graph showing percentages only. These are hypothetical data containing a sample of voters and are made of 9,449 cases and 14 variables. You will build this pie graph using the discrete variable named *county* and labeled *County*. This variable has five categories: Eastern, Central, Western, Northern, and Southern.

The second pie style uses **credit_card.sav**, which are also hypothetical data representing a database of 26,280 individuals measured on 11 variables. For this style pie graph, you use the discrete variable named *card* and labeled *Primary credit card*. This variable has five categories: American Express, Visa, MasterCard, Discover, and Other. Below are questions associated with these two styles of pie graphs.

5.2.1 Questions for the Pie Graph Showing Percentages

1. What percentage of the 9,449 survey respondents live in the Eastern part of the county?
2. Which county region has the largest percentage of respondents?
3. Which county region has the smallest percentage of respondents?
4. What are the ranks (from the least to most respondents) for the five different regions?

5.2.2 Questions for the Pie Graph Showing Labels, Counts, and Percentages

1. Which credit card is in use by the highest percentage of people, and how many people does this percentage represent?
2. Which of the five card categories represent the fewest card users, and what is the number and percentage of individuals in this category?
3. What are the ranks of the credit cards in terms of their number and percentage of users from the most to the least popular?

5.3 USING SPSS TO BUILD THE PIE GRAPH   ★

In this section, you build two pie graphs. The first displays data labels telling the user what percentage of cases are represented by each slice. The second provides the reader data labels that show the slice name, number of cases, and the percentage of the total represented by each slice.

5.3.1 Building the Pie Graph Showing Percentages

Open **poll_cs_sample.sav** and follow the bullets to build the pie graph that will provide the information required to answer the questions about this database.

- Open the **poll_cs_sample.sav** (found in the SPSS Sample file).
- Click **Graphs**, then click **Chart Builder**.
- Click **Pie/Polar** in the *Choose from:* list.
- Click and drag the **Pie Graph icon** to the large panel at the top right of the window.
- Click and drag **County** (found in the *Variables:* panel) to the *X-Axis* (the *slice by* box).

- In the *Statistics* Section of the *Element Properties* window, click the **black arrow** to the right of *Count*, then click **Percentage (?)**.
- Click **Apply**.
- Click **OK** (*Output Viewer* displays Figure 5.3).

The SPSS *Output Viewer* should now display the pie graph exactly (except for its color) as shown in Figure 5.3. The procedures given below show how to embellish this basic pie graph with additional information required to answer our questions about the *county* variable.

You next use the *Chart Editor* to improve the ability of the basic pie graph to directly answer our questions about the data.

Before making improvements to the basic graph by using the *Chart Editor*, we offer a couple of explanations concerning what you will accomplish and why. You will change the pie graph from a flat 1-D picture to a 3-D representation partially for reasons of appearance. However, the 3-D pie increases the reader's ability to visualize proportions by adding the appearance of volume to the graph. You will also separate a slice from all others to emphasize a particular category that may be important to the study.

Figure 5.3 Basic Pie Graph With *No* Embellishments: County Regions

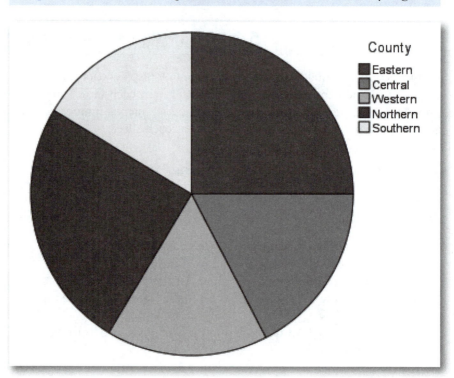

This procedure is simply known as "exploding" a slice. You will also change the slice colors to unique patterns since most books and scientific articles are not published in color.

Follow the procedures given below to make several changes in the basic pie graph that is shown in Figure 5.3.

- Double click the **graph** as it appears in the *Output Viewer* (The *Chart Editor* opens).
- Click the **small box** to the left of **Eastern** and a faint yellow border appears around the slice that represents the Eastern region (the word Eastern is found in the upper-right corner of the graph, and this area is referred to as the *legend* area of your graph).
- Click on the **Explode Slice icon,** which is the last icon in the *Chart Editor* (if the icon is not present, click on the **Elements** menu choice in the top of the *Chart Editor*, then click **Explode Slice**).

- Click the **Data Label Mode icon** (the one that resembles a target), then click on each **Slice of the Pie** in the graph to insert the percentage.
- Click the **Data Label Mode icon** to turn it off.
- Click on the **circular line** that encloses the whole pie (you select the whole pie).
- In the *Properties* window, click on the **Depth & Angle tab** (see Figure 5.4).
- In the *Effect* panel, click the **small circle to the left of 3-D**.
- In the *Angle* panel, click and drag the **slide** to adjust the angle of the pie to **negative 35** (you can select your own preference for the angle of the pie by selecting a different number).
- Click **Apply** as shown in Figure 5.4.
- In the *Properties* window, click the **Fill & Border tab**.
- Click the **small box** to the left of the county region of **Eastern** (a faint frame appears around the box and the corresponding slice in the graph).

Figure 5.4   *Properties* Window With *Depth & Angle* Tab Highlighted

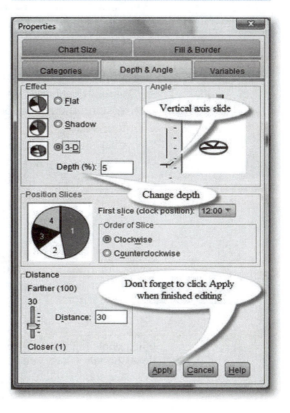

- In the *Color* section, click the **white rectangular box** in the top row of available colors.
- Click the **black arrow** beneath *Pattern*, then click the **second pattern** in the **first** row.
- Click **Apply**.
- Click the **box** to the left of the county region of **Central**.
- Click the **white rectangular box**, click the **black arrow** beneath *Pattern*, then click the **third pattern** in the **first** row and click **Apply**.
- Click the **box** to the left of **Western**.
- Click the **white rectangular box**, click the **black arrow** beneath *Pattern*, and then click the **first pattern** in the **second** row and click **Apply**.
- Click the small **box** to the left of **Northern**.
- Click the **white rectangular box**, click the **black arrow** beneath *Pattern*, and then click the **second pattern** in the **second** row and click **Apply**.
- Click the small **box** to the left of **Southern**.
- Click the **white rectangular box**, click the **black arrow** beneath *Pattern*, and click the **second pattern** in the **fourth** row and click **Apply**.
- Click directly above the small box of **Eastern** (the mouse pointer should be lower than the word County) (a yellow rectangular frame with little squares on it surrounds the entire legend).
- Position the mouse pointer in any of the little squares until you get a four-sided pointer.
- Click and drag the **rectangular frame** closer to the graph to improve the graph appearance once it is complete.
- Click the **X** in the **box** in the top right-hand corner of the *Chart Editor* (the finished graph now appears in the *Output Viewer* exactly as shown in Figure 5.5).

You just created a pie graph containing the information needed to answer our questions about the five different regions of the county.[2] In Section 5.4.1, we examine how the graph in Figure 5.5 accomplishes this task.

---

[2]Some people that have looked at this particular pie have expressed the idea that it does not only answers questions about the data but it also looks good enough to be eaten.

Figure 5.5   Final Pie Graph for County Regions Including Embellishments

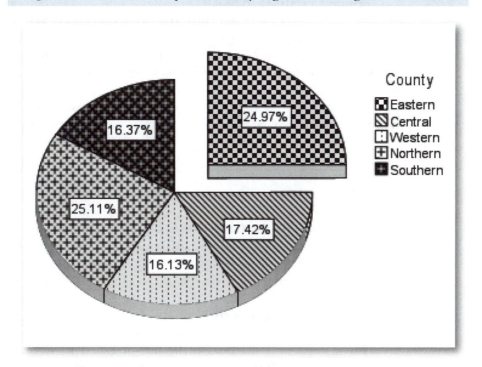

5.3.2 Building the Pie Graph Showing
Labels, Counts, and Percentages

Open **credit_card.sav** and follow the bullets to build the pie graph that will provide the information required to answer the questions about this database.

- Open the **credit_card.sav** (found in the SPSS Sample file).
- Click **Graphs**, then click **Chart Builder**.
- Click **Pie/Polar** in the *Choose from:* list.
- Click and drag the **Pie Graph icon** to the large panel at the top right of the window (*Chart preview* panel).
- Click and drag **Primary credit card** (found in the *Variables* list) to the *X-Axis* (the *Slice by?* box).
- Click **OK** (*Output Viewer* opens showing the basic graph).
- Double click the **graph** (*Chart Editor* opens).
- Click **Show Data Labels** (second icon from the left in the bottom row) (data labels appear on slices of the pie showing percentages).

- In the *Properties* window (with the *Data Value Labels* highlighted), click **Primary credit card** found in the *Not Displayed:* section of the *Label* panel, then click the **upward pointing green arrow** found to the right (moves the *Primary credit card* to *Displayed*).
- Click **Count** in the *Not Displayed* section, then click the **upward pointing green arrow** (*Percent*, *Primary credit card*, and *Count* should now be in the *Displayed:* section).
- Click **Percent**, then double click the **downward pointing black arrow** (this arrow is found to the right) (by double clicking the arrow, you move *Percent* to the lowest position of the three items: *Primary credit card*, *Count*, and *Percent*).
- Click **Apply**.
- Click **below** *Other* in the *legend* (found in the upper right-hand corner of the graph) and a frame surrounding the entire legend appears, then *right* click **within the frame**, and finally, *left* click **delete** (in the drop-down menu), and the *legend* disappears (the legend is not needed as labels show this information within the pie).
- Click the **Pie** remembering to avoid the labels (a frame surrounds the entire pie).
- Click the **American Express slice** (avoid clicking the label).
- In the *Properties* window (with the *Fill & Border* tab highlighted) and in the *Color* panel, click the **box to the left of Fill**, then click the **white rectangular box**, next click the **black arrow** beneath *Pattern*, and click **third pattern** in the **third** row.
- Click **Apply**.
- Click the **Visa slice** (avoid clicking the label).
- In the *Properties* window (with the *Fill & Border* tab highlighted) and in the *Color* panel, click the **box to the left of Fill**, then click the **white rectangular box** next click the **black arrow** beneath *Pattern* and finally click the **second pattern** in the **second** row.
- Click **Apply**.
- Click the **MasterCard slice** (avoid clicking the label).
- In the *Properties* window (with the *Fill & Border* tab highlighted) and in the *Color* panel, click the **box to the left of Fill**, then click the **white rectangular box**, next click the **black arrow** beneath *Pattern*, and finally click the **second pattern** in the **fourth** row.
- Click **Apply**.
- Click the **Discover slice** (avoid clicking the label).
- In the *Properties* window (with the *Fill & Border* tab highlighted) and in the *Color* panel, click the **box to the left of Fill**, then click the **white rectangular box**, next click the **black arrow** beneath *Pattern*, and

finally, click the **sixth pattern** in the **second** row.
- Click **Apply**.
- Click the **Other slice** (avoid clicking the label).
- In the *Properties* window (with the *Fill & Border* tab highlighted) and in the *Color* panel, click the **box to the left of Fill**, then click the **white rectangular box**, next click the **black arrow** beneath *Pattern*, and finally, click the **first pattern** in the **third** row.
- Click **Apply**.
- In the *Properties* window, click the **Depth & Angle tab**, and in the *Effect* panel, click **3-D** then change *Depth (%)* from **5** to **10**.
- In the *Angle* panel, click the **vertical axis slide** and set to **negative 40** (see Figure 5.4).
- Click **Apply**.
- Click the **X** in the upper right-hand corner of the *Chart Editor* (*Chart Editor* closes and the graph shown in Figure 5.6 appears in the *Output Viewer*).

Figure 5.6 Pie Graph Displaying Category Names, Numbers of Cases, and Percentages

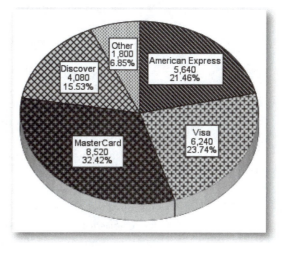

5.4 INTERPRETATION OF THE PIE GRAPH ★

In this section, we show how the graphs you produced in Figures 5.5 and 5.6 provide the information needed to answer the questions.

5.4.1 Questions and Answers for the Pie Graph Showing Percentages

The answers to the following questions are provided by the graph in Figure 5.5.

1. What percentage of the 9,449 survey respondents live in the Eastern part of the county?

The slice representing the Eastern region of the county shows that 24.97% of the respondents live in this part of the county.

2. Which county region has the largest percentage of respondents?

The Northern region has the highest percentage of respondents (25.11%). We can see that the slice that represents this region is proportionally larger than the other slices.

3. Which county region has the smallest percentage of respondents?

The Western part of the county has the smallest percentage of respondents (16.13%). The slice is smaller than all other slices of the pie.

4. What are the ranks (from the fewest to most respondents) for the five different regions?

The smaller slice of the pie is the one that represents the Western region (16.13%), followed by that of the Southern region at 16.37%. Next is the slice representing the Central region (17.42%), followed by the Eastern region at 24.97%. Finally, we have the slice that represents the Northern region, indicating that 25.11% chose this part of the county as a place to live.

Figure 5.5 gave us the information we needed to compare the different regions of the county with the whole county and with each other. We did this, in a proportional way, by visually comparing the size of the slices and by looking at the percentages displayed inside each slice.

5.4.2 Questions and Answers for the Pie Graph Showing Labels, Counts, and Percentages

The answers to the following questions are provided by the graph in Figure 5.6.

1. Which credit card is in use by the highest percentage of people, and how many people does this percentage represent?

The MasterCard has the highest percentage of users at 32.42%, which represents 8,520 individuals.

2. Which of the five card categories represent the fewest card users, and what is the number and percentage of individuals in this category?

The Other category represents the smallest category of card users at 6.85%, representing 1,800 individuals.

3. What are the ranks of the credit cards in terms of their number and percentage of users from the most to the least popular?

Most used credit card is the MasterCard (8,520 or 32.42%), followed by Visa (6,240 or 23.74%), American Express (5,640 or 21.46%), Discover (4,080 or 15.53%), and Other (1,800 or 6.85%).

5.5 REVIEW EXERCISES   ★

1. Open the SPSS Sample file titled **workprog.sav**, and select the discrete variable labeled *Level of education* and called *ed*. You will also change the graph to read percentage. Build the pie graph shown in Figure 5.7.

Questions: (a) What percentage of people have a high school degree? (b) What is the category of education that has the highest percentage of people? (c) What is the category of education that has the lowest percentage of people? (d) What are the ranks of the educational categories from the highest to the lowest? (e) Why does the graphed pie have just three slices when the variable we used to build it has four categories?

Figure 5.7   Review Exercise: Pie Graph for Level of Education

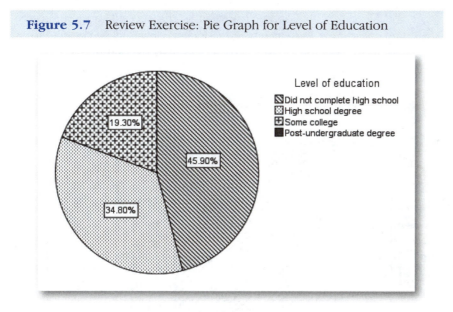

2. Open SPSS Sample file **satisf.sav**, and select the discrete variable named *agecat* and labeled *Age category* to build a pie graph. Build the pie graph as shown in Figure 5.8, displaying the names of the categories, the numbers of observations, and the percentages of total for the slices.

Figure 5.8   Review Exercise: Pie Graph for Age Category

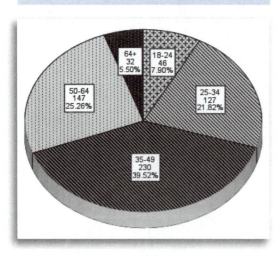

Questions: (a) What percentage of people are 18 to 24 years old? (b) How many individuals are 50 to 64 years old? (c) What is the largest age category? (d) What is the quantity and its respective percentage for the individuals who are 25 to 34 years old? (e) What is the quantity and its respective percentage for the smallest category?

3. Open **customer_dbase.sav**, and select the discrete variable named *inccat* and labeled *Income category in thousands*. In the *Element Properties* window, be sure to select *Percentage (?)*. Build the pie graph as shown in Figure 5.9.

Questions: (a) What is the largest income category, and what percentage of the whole does it represent? (b) What is the percentage of individuals who are in the highest income category? (c) What is the second most populated income category, and what is its percentage? (d) Is it true that over half the respondents earns less than $49,000, and what is that percentage?

Figure 5.9   Review Exercise: Pie Graph for Income Category in Thousands

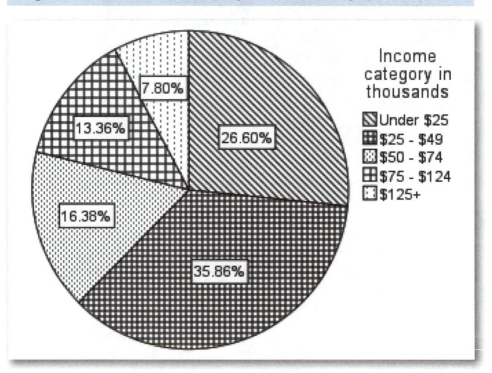

4. Open **dmdata3.sav**, select the discrete variable named *Region*, and build a pie graph as shown in Figure 5.10. Embellish the graph to display the names of the categories, the numbers of observations, and the percentages of total for the slices to answer the following questions.

Questions: (a) What is the largest region and what percentage of the total respondents does it represent? (b) Which region is the smallest, and how many individuals does it have? (c) What is the number of customers and the percentage of individuals for the *North*? (d) What is the number of customers and its respective percentage for the *West*? (e) Rank the regions from the smallest to the biggest.

5. Open **Employee data.sav** and select the variable named *jobcat* and labeled *Employment category*. Build the pie Graph as shown in Figure 5.11 and answer the following questions.

Questions: (a) What is the largest employment category, and what percentage of the total does it represent? (b) What is the second largest employment category, and what is its percentage? (c) What is the smallest category of workers and what percentage of the total does it represent?

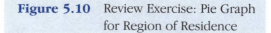

Figure 5.10 Review Exercise: Pie Graph for Region of Residence

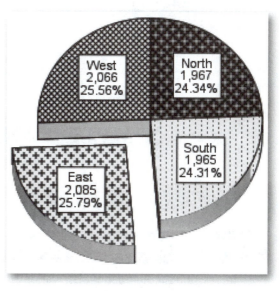

Figure 5.11 Review Exercise: Pie Graph for Employment Category

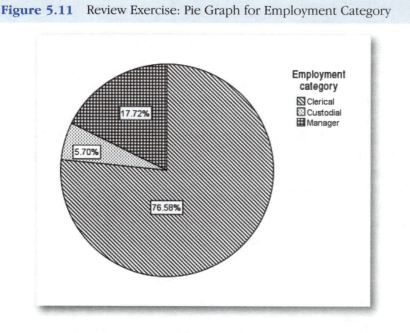

6

SIMPLE LINE GRAPH

PURPOSES OF GRAPHS YOU ARE ABOUT TO BUILD

- To describe the number of observations in each category of the discrete variable
- To describe the number of observations in the intervals of a continuous variable
- To describe the relationship between two continuous variables and explore for a trend
- To show a pre–post trend line for a continuous variable by categories of a discrete variable

★ 6.1 INTRODUCTION TO THE SIMPLE LINE GRAPH

In the previous chapter, we presented the pie graph and explained how it can be used to describe a distribution of discrete data. In the current chapter, the simple line graph is presented and we show how it can be used in various ways to describe both discrete and continuous data distributions.

The simple line graph is not as "simple" as the name might imply as it has many different uses in analyzing databases. The graph can take on many different appearances, we show many of these, but you can experiment as you become better acquainted with its use. For one thing, the information conveyed and its appearance will be drastically altered by switching the axis of the variables—try it later when you learn to build this versatile graph. It is one of the most popular graphs since it is easy to understand when used to describe a discrete or continuous variable that is placed on the x-axis.[1]

In this chapter, we discuss two uses of the simple line graph: one for *describing* data distributions and the other for searching for a *trend line*. When using the simple line graph for descriptive purposes, we are referring to describing the distribution of the categories (discrete data) or values (continuous data) of one or two variables. When used in this manner, it communicates much of the same information as the simple bar graph or histogram. You have already seen the simple bar graph in Chapter 2 and will be introduced to the histogram in Chapter 8.

When using the simple line graph in an attempt to discover a *trend line*, we are looking for a recognizable change in the values of one variable over a period of time or successive operations.[2] For instance, as an individual's age increases, does his or her income change in any identifiable manner? To take another example, as a product moves along an assembly line, does the number of production errors increase, decrease, or remain constant?

When you are graphing discrete or continuous data for descriptive purposes, the variables are placed on the x-axis and count or percent on the y-axis. If we choose to explore for a trend line, we may place a discrete or continuous variable on the x-axis and some chosen statistic, like the mean, of a continuous variable on the y-axis.

A variant of the use of the line graph for trend analysis is the *pre–post trend line graph*, which seeks to discover a trend following a specific event. An example of this application would be the graphing of the number of marijuana arrests prior to the enactment of medical marijuana legislation (the event) and the number of such arrests following the legislation. With this type of the line graph, you place a vertical reference line that rises from the x-axis at the point (time) of the event. Thus, we can then observe any change in the direction and angle of the line to the right of the vertical reference line.

---

[1]The line graph can be built with the intention of misleading the graph reader. The interested reader will find an example of such deception in Chapter 18 on deceptive uses of graphs and specifically in Figure 18.6.

[2]The concept of graphing changes over time for one variable is expanded in Chapter 7. In Chapter 7 (multiple line graphs), you will learn how to follow changes in two or more variables over a period of time. Using this multiple line approach will make it possible to observe changes in more than one variable over time, and these can be displayed on the same graph.

6.1.1 Simple Line Graph for Descriptive Purposes: Discrete Data

When using the line graph to describe a single variable, you may place either a discrete or a continuous variable on the *x*-axis. If the variable chosen is discrete, then you should choose between "count" and "percentage (?)" that are found in the *Element Properties* window. The types of questions you have about the database will influence this choice.

Figure 6.1 shows a simple line graph produced from a class survey for 37 upper-division university students. For this example, we have selected one discrete variable, which is the student's self-rated anxiety level about taking the class. The *Self-rated anxiety level* variable was moved to the *x*-axis and the *y*-axis was left in the default position of *Count*. When describing the distribution of a single discrete variable, you might also use the simple bar graph as described in Chapter 2. It really is a matter of personal preference. The question for the graph maker is which one conveys the desired information in the most efficient manner. As with many of the graphs presented in this book, it is recommended that both be produced, you look at it, and then make the choice. One of the great advantages in using SPSS *Graph Builder* is the ease with which graphs are produced—gone forever are the days of

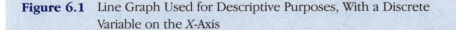

Figure 6.1   Line Graph Used for Descriptive Purposes, With a Discrete Variable on the *X*-Axis

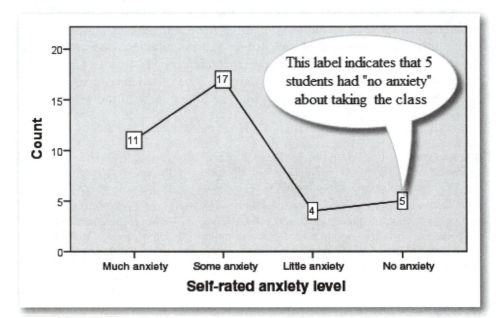

lined graph paper and a bottle of black India ink. If the line graph fails to communicate the answer to the question about your data, then it only takes minutes (sometimes seconds) to build a histogram or a bar graph.

The graph shown in Figure 6.1 immediately answers questions concerning the distribution of the four anxiety levels for these students. Next, we see what the simple line graph looks like with a continuous variable on the *x*-axis.

6.1.2 Simple Line Graph for Descriptive Purposes: Continuous Data

We next use the same database (37 students) that was used above to show a simple line graph when placing a continuous variable on the *x*-axis. This type of graph is the same as a frequency polygon or what is sometimes referred to as a smoothed histogram. The frequency polygon can be found as one of the choices in the *Chart Builder* window once histogram is chosen.

Figure 6.2 uses the number of points earned on the first exam as the continuous variable on the *x*-axis. Once again, we are using the simple line graph in the descriptive manner only. We are interested in describing the distribution of values (scores on a test) for a single variable. Since these scores are

Figure 6.2   Line Graph for Descriptive Purposes, With Continuous Variable on the *X*-Axis

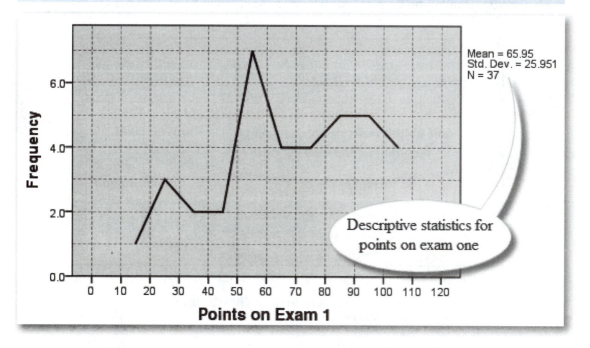

continuous data, what we see in Figure 6.2 is a "form" of a histogram. This one, however, does not use rectangular bars as is presented in a Chapter 8. The choice between the line graph and the histogram, as to which type best answers questions about the data, is up to the graph builder. However, the authors recommend the histogram, shown in Chapter 8, when describing continuous data. The histogram style uses rectangular bars that encourage a vision of proportionality not present when using the line graph.

6.1.3 Simple Line Graph for Trend Analysis: Discrete and Continuous Data

We use data collected on 1,050 students in many intermediate-level statistics classes to demonstrate the use of the simple line graph. We are looking for a trend between the hour that the class met and the mean number of semester points. The examples shown in Figures 6.3 and 6.4 use one discrete variable (hour of class) and one continuous variable of the average points earned for the entire semester. When using a discrete variable on the x-axis and continuous variable on the y-axis, SPSS automatically calculates the mean points earned for all those students in the various class hours. It then places a point on the graph that corresponds with the class hour and the mean

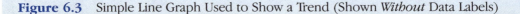

Figure 6.3   Simple Line Graph Used to Show a Trend (Shown *Without* Data Labels)

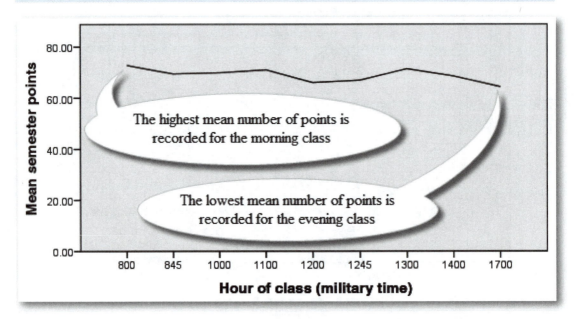

points earned by all those students enrolled in that class. Finally, it connects those points with a single line.

Figure 6.3 shows a line that slightly decreases and increases as the hour of the class progresses throughout the series of class hours. However, we may say that, on average, the overall "trend" is a slight decrease of semester points that students earn. Thus, we discovered a trend (although very slight) by simply looking at the graph.

To facilitate an understanding of the graph, we have added *data labels* in Figure 6.4, which show the mean semester points for each individual class hour shown on the *x*-axis. These labels make it easy to interpret the graph; however, in this case, they tend to hide the downward slope of the line. Whether you choose to show data labels often depends on your data questions and, perhaps, your personal preference. They are easy to add and delete, so there is no reason not to try data labels. We show you how to add and delete these data labels later in this chapter.

Figure 6.4 Simple Line Graph Used to Show a Trend (Shown *With* Data Labels)

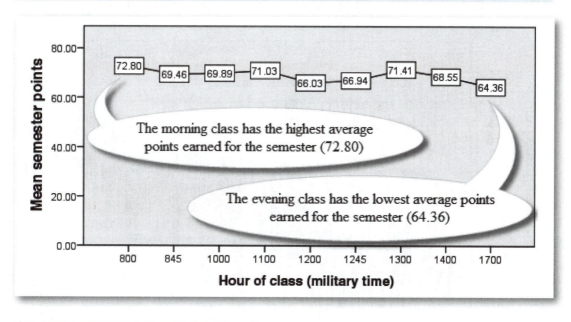

6.1.4 Simple Line Graph for Trend Analysis: Two Different Appearances

Another variation of a simple line graph results when you place a continuous variable on the *x*-axis *and* another on the *y*-axis. For this demonstration, we use the database for 1,050 statistics students. Figure 6.5 results when you use the actual data (the counts) on the *y*-axis *not* the *mean* as shown in Figure 6.6. The graph in Figure 6.5 is rather cluttered as it reports the actual scores. However, it is useful in that it does show an upward trend. The upward trend is that the higher the students score on the first exam, the more final points they earn. The trend is reflected in the graphs depicted in Figures 6.5 and 6.6.

It must be noted that to build the line graph shown in Figure 6.5, which has one continuous variable on each axis (not the mean of one on the *y*-axis), you must follow one of the following two procedures. (1) In the *Chart Builder*, you must move the variable you choose for the *x*-axis *first*. If you do not do this, SPSS automatically changes your *y*-axis variable to a *mean*. (2) The second way to remedy this is to go to the *Statistics* panel in the *Element Properties* window and change *mean* to *value* and then click **Apply**. Once you have clicked **Apply**, your *y*-axis variable returns to the

Figure 6.5   Simple Line Graph, With Continuous Variable on *X*-Axis and *Y*-Axis

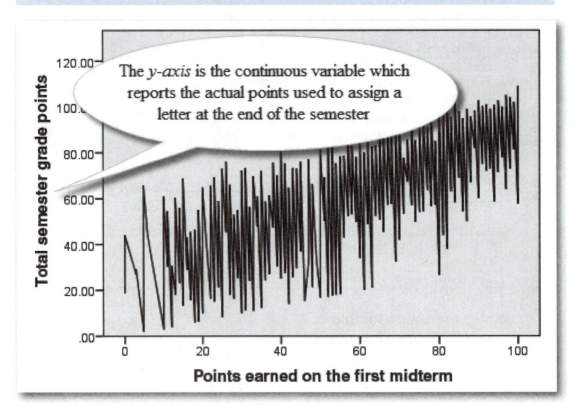

actual values—not the mean. We show you exactly how to accomplish this later in this chapter, when you actually build a graph requiring this procedure.

Let's take a closer look at Figure 6.6, which uses the same data as our previous graph (Figure 6.5). However, the *mean* of all students scoring a particular value on the first midterm is now used on the *y*-axis. In this graph, we have placed a bubble showing a particular point. This point approximately corresponds with the value of 60 on the *x*-axis (points earned on the first midterm) and the *mean* value of 55 from the *y*-axis. Thus, SPSS looks at all students that scored 60 points on the first midterm and then calculates the average points earned at the end of the semester by those students. In the case of students who earned 60 points on the first midterm, their average total semester points was 55.

Both graphs shown in Figures 6.5 and 6.6 are derived from the same data. The only difference is that Figure 6.5 uses the *actual total points earned* and Figure 6.6 uses the *mean points earned* on the *y*-axis. It is up to

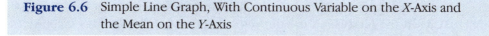

Figure 6.6   Simple Line Graph, With Continuous Variable on the *X*-Axis and the Mean on the *Y*-Axis

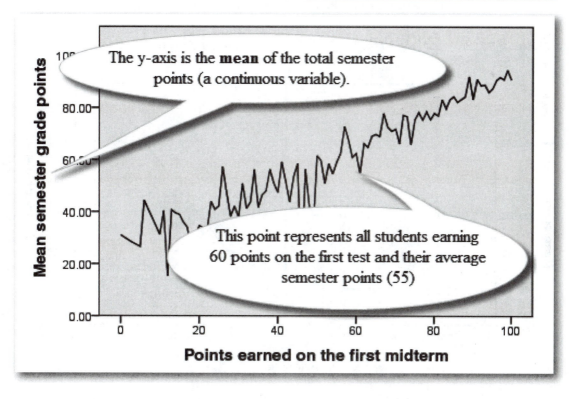

the graph maker to select the one that best answers his or her questions about the data.

6.1.5 Pre–Post Trend Line Graph

A variation of the simple line graph is when we wish to visualize the effect of an event (considered to be the independent variable) on the value of a second (the dependent) variable. For instance, we may wish to determine the number of ounces of gold sold prior to and during a government-declared economic recession. The event would be the recession, which is the discrete/independent variable. It is placed on the x-axis and is measured in units of time—years for this example. The y-axis records the continuous and dependent variable, which is the ounces of gold sold in a particular year. In this example, the "event" is the onset of the recession. Therefore, the pre-event time period is the condition of normal economic times, while the postevent period is the years of recession.

By looking at Figure 6.7, we can easily visualize the pre- and post-recession changes in the sale of gold. We must remember that other variables must be examined before we can say we have strong evidence that the recession caused the increase in the ounces of gold sold. However, this graph does provide enough evidence to warrant further research.

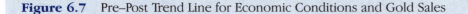

Figure 6.7   Pre–Post Trend Line for Economic Conditions and Gold Sales

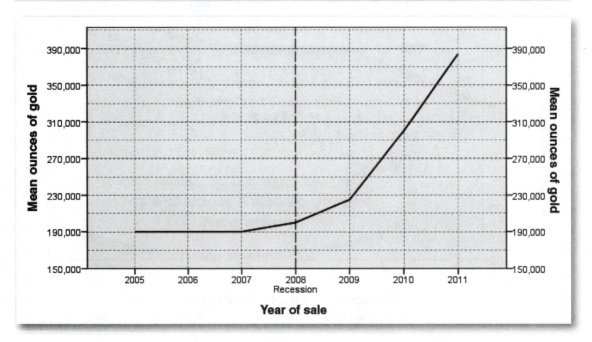

6.2 DATABASES AND QUESTIONS ★

In this section, we once again use the **customer_dbase.sav** to build the first three graphs. Recall that this database consists of 5,000 cases that are measured on 132 variables. You should open the database now and locate the variables that are used to build the various simple line graphs. For this exercise, we use the discrete variable called *Level of education*, which separates education level into five unique categories. We also use the continuous variables of *Years of education* and *Household income*.

The fourth graph built is constructed from data found in the **catalog_seasfac.sav** database. For the *x*-axis variable, you use the variable named *MONTH_* and labeled *Month, period 12*. For the *y*-axis, you use the variable named *jewel* and labeled *Sales of jewelry*.

The following questions represent just a few of the questions that could be answered by producing SPSS graphs from these data.

6.2.1 Questions: Line Graph
Showing Counts and Percentages

1. How many customers are in each of the five categories of the educational variable?

2. What are the percentages of customers in each of the five educational categories?

3. What are the relative ranks of the five educational categories?

6.2.2 Questions: Line Graph for
Describing Continuous Data

1. How are the years of education distributed around their mean value?

2. Are the ages distributed skewed right, left, or are they normal?

3. How many individuals were reported to have the mean years of education?

6.2.3 Questions: Line Graph for
Two Continuous Variables (Trend)

1. Is there a trend when looking at years of education and mean household income?

2. What is the mean household income for someone with 19 years of education?

3. How many years of education mark the point of a steady upward increase in household income, and what are the income amounts?

6.2.4 Questions: Pre–Post Trend Line Graph

1. In the months preceding and including October, is there any consistent trend in the sales of jewelry?

2. What happened to the sales of jewelry following October, and what is a reasonable explanation?

3. Can you offer some explanation for the spike in sales during the month of May?

In the following section, you build several of the line graphs to answer the questions presented in the previous four subsections.

★   ## 6.3 USING SPSS TO BUILD THE SIMPLE LINE GRAPH

In this section, you build line graphs very similar to those discussed at the beginning of this chapter. One places discrete data on the x-axis and labels the y-axis as *Count* (an example is given in Section 6.3.1). Another graph uses continuous data on the x-axis and labels the y-axis as *Frequency* (see Section 6.3.2). Yet another graph places discrete data on the x-axis and the mean of a continuous variable on the y-axis (Section 6.3.3). The final graph uses discrete data on the x-axis and continuous on the y-axis and places a reference line to separate the line into two parts. The trend line on the left side of the reference line represents the pre-event time period. The trend line to the right represents the postevent time period (Section 6.3.4).

6.3.1 Building a Line Graph to Display a Discrete Variable for Descriptive Purposes

- Open **customer_dbase.sav** (found in the SPSS Sample file).
- Click **Graphs**, then click **Chart Builder** to open *Chart Builder* window.
- Click **Line** in the *Choose from:* panel, then click and drag the **Simple Line icon** to the *Chart preview* panel.
- Click and drag **Level of Education** to the *X-Axis* box.

- Click **OK** (the basic graph now appears in the *Output Viewer*).
- If desired, you can change the size of the graph at this time.
- Double click the **graph** to open the *Chart Editor*.
- Click the **Data Label icon** (looks like a target and is found just above and to the left of the graph in the *Chart Editor*.
- Place the mouse pointer (now the target icon) on the beginning of the line and click the **line** (data labels should appear at all five points along the line).
- Click the **Data Label icon** to turn it off.
- Click the **X** in the box in the upper right-hand corner of the window (Figure 6.8 appears in the *Output Viewer*).

Figure 6.8   Line Graph of Discrete Data, Including Data Labels Showing Counts

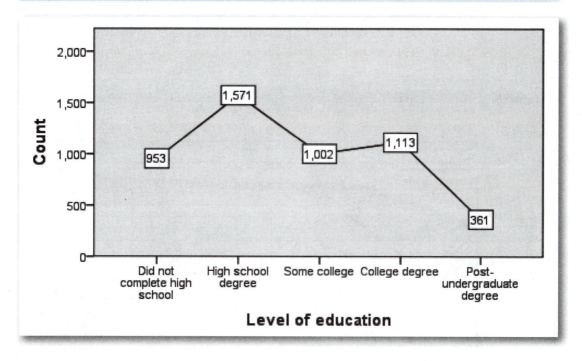

You have changed *data labels* from counts to percentages in previous chapters (see Figures 2.2 and 2.3), but let's go through the process once again. At the risk of being redundant, we repeat the procedures given above while inserting three additional steps (5, 6, and 7) that are needed to change actual counts to the desired percentages.

- Open **customer_dbase.sav** (found in the SPSS Sample files).
- Click **Graphs**, then click **Chart Builder** to open *Chart Builder* window.
- Click **Line**, click and drag the **Simple Line icon** to the *Chart Preview* panel.
- Click and drag **Level of Education** to the *X-Axis* box.
- If the *Element Properties* window is not open, click the **Element Properties button** found in the *Chart Builder* window.
- Click the **black arrow** to the right of the word *Count* that is located in the *Statistics* panel.
- From the drop-down list, click **Percentage (?)**, then click **Apply**.
- Click **OK** (the basic graph now appears in the *Output Viewer*).
- If you desire, you should change the size of the graph at this time.
- Double click the **graph** to open the *Chart Editor*.
- Click the **Show Data Labels icon** (looks like a bar graph and is found just above and to the left of the graph in the *Chart Editor*) (data labels should appear at all points along the line).
- Click the **X** in the box found in the upper right-hand corner (Figure 6.9 appears in the *Output Viewer*).

Figure 6.9   Line Graph of Discrete Data, Including Data labels Showing Percentages

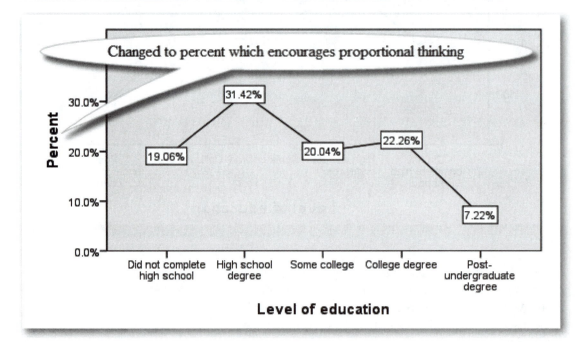

Once finished, your graph should look exactly as the one shown in Figure 6.9. It now displays percentages rather than counts, which encourages proportional thinking. Examine both graphs and notice how each will provide different information required to answer our questions. This aspect is covered in greater detail in the interpretation section of this chapter.

6.3.2 Building a Line Graph to Display One Continuous Variable for Descriptive Purposes

There are occasions when you may wish to display a continuous variable as a simple line graph. The authors are not particularly fond of graphing continuous data in this manner, but there are occasions when it is useful.

- Open **customer_dbase.sav** (found in the SPSS Sample files).
- Click **Graphs**, then click **Chart Builder** to open the *Chart Builder* window.
- Click **Line**, click and drag the **Simple Line icon** to the *Chart Preview* panel.
- Click and drag **Years of education** to the *X-Axis* box.
- Click **OK** (the basic graph now appears in the *Output Viewer*).
- If you desire, you can change the size of the graph at this time.
- Double click the **graph** to open the *Chart Editor*.
- Click **any number** on the *x*-axis.
- In the *Properties* window, click the **Scale tab**, and in the *Range* panel change the *Major Increment* to **2**, then click **Apply**.
- Click the **Show Grid Lines icon**.
- In the *Properties* window, click the **Lines tab**, and in the *Lines* panel, click the **black arrow** beneath *Weight* and then click **0.5**, next click the **black arrow** beneath *Style* and click the **first dotted line**, and finally, click **Apply**.
- Click **any number** on the *y*-axis.
- Click **Show Grid Lines icon**.
- In the *Properties* window, click the **Grid Lines tab**, then click the **small circle** to the left of *Both major and minor ticks*, and click **Apply**.
- Click **any y-axis grid line**, and in the *Lines* panel of the *Properties* window, click the **black arrow** beneath *Weight* and then click **0.5**, next click the **black arrow** beneath *Style*, and click the **first dotted line**, and finally, click **Apply**.
- Click the **X** in the box found in the upper right-hand corner (Figure 6.10 appears in the *Output Viewer*).

Figure 6.10 is helpful when you wish to summarize a single continuous variable. It should be noted that the *y*-axis is showing *Frequency* but could just as well display *Percent* by opening the *Element Properties* window and changing the *y*-axis label of *Histogram* to *Percent* [found as *Percentage (?)*] in the *Statistics* panel. You have performed this operation previously, so bullets are not given regarding details of this procedure. Whether you choose *Frequency* or *Percent*, the shape of the graph is the same. When the *y*-axis is labeled as a percentage, proportional thinking is encouraged. Your choice between count and frequency is contingent on the questions you are seeking to answer about the data.

Figure 6.10   Line Graph for Continuous Data

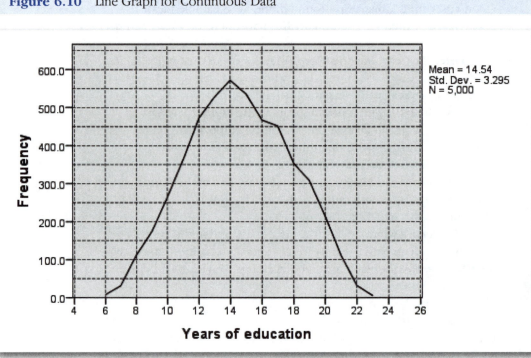

6.3.3 Building a Line Graph to Display Two Continuous Variables (Trend Line)

In this exercise, you will build a simple line graph to answer questions about a possible relationship between two continuous variables. The *x*-axis variable is *Years of education*, while the *y*-axis will use the mean of the *Household income in thousands* variable.

- Open **customer_dbase.sav** (found in the SPSS Sample files).
- Click **Graphs**, then click **Chart Builder** to open the *Chart Builder* window.
- Click **Line**, click and drag the **Simple Line icon** to the *Chart Preview* panel.
- Click and drag **Years of education** to the *X-Axis* box.
- Click and drag **Household income in thousands** to the *Y-Axis* box.
- If *Element Properties* window is not open, then click the **Element Properties button** found in the *Chart Builder* window.
- Click the **black arrow** to the right of *Value* found in the *Statistic* panel.
- Click **Mean**, then click **Apply**.
- Click **OK** (basic graph appears in the *Output Viewer*).
- Double click the **graph** (*Chart Editor* opens).
- Click the **Y-Axis title**, click the **title** a second time and type **Mean household income (in thousands)**.
- Click **any number** on the *y*-axis.
- Click the **Scale tab** in the *Properties* window, then in the *Range* panel, change *Major Increment* from **20** to **10**, then change *Origin* from **0** to **20**, and finally, click **Apply**.
- Click **Show Grid Lines icon** (fifth from the right side of the menu).
- In the *Properties* window, click the **Lines tab**, and in the *Lines* panel, click the **black arrow** beneath *Weight* and click **0.5**, then click the **black arrow** beneath *Style*, and click the **first dotted line**, and finally, click **Apply**.
- Click **any number** on the *x*-axis.
- Click the **Scale tab** in the *Properties* window, then in the *Range* panel, change *Major Increment* from **5** to **1**, click **Apply**.
- Click **Show Grid Lines icon** (the fifth icon from the right side of the menu).
- In the *Properties* window, click the **Lines tab**, and in the *Lines* panel, click the **black arrow** beneath *Weight* and click **0.5**, then click the **black arrow** beneath *Style*, and click the **first dotted line**, and finally, click **Apply**.
- Click **X** in the **box** found in the upper right-hand corner (*Output Viewer* opens with finished graph shown in Figure 6.11).

Figure 6.11   Line Graph of Continuous Data and the Mean of a Second Continuous Variable

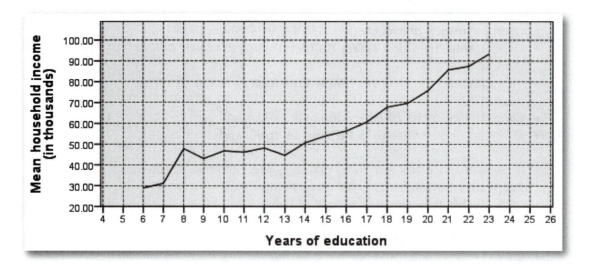

6.3.4 Building a Pre–Post Trend Line Graph

- Open **catalog_seasfac.sav** (found in the SPSS Sample files).
- Click **Graphs**, then click **Chart Builder** to open *Chart Builder* window.
- Click **Line**, click and drag the **Simple Line icon** to the *Chart Preview* panel.
- Click and drag **Month, period 12** to the *X-Axis* box.
- Click and drag **Sales of jewelry** to the *Y-Axis* box.
- Click **OK** (the basic graph now appears in the *Output Viewer*).
- Double click the **graph** (*Chart Editor* opens).
- Click **any number** on the *y*-axis.
- If the *Properties* window does not open, click the **Show Properties Window icon**.
- In the *Properties* window, click the **Number Format tab**, and in the *Decimal Places* box, change **12** to **0**, then click **Apply**.
- Still in the *Properties* window, click the **Scale tab**, and in the *Range* panel, change *Minimum* to **10000**, *Major Increment* to **5000**, and *Origin* to **10000**, then click **Apply**.
- Click the **Show Grid Lines icon**, and in the *Properties* window, click the **small circle** to the left of *Both major and minor ticks*, then click **Apply**.
- Click any **Grid line** (all grid lines should be highlighted).
- In the *Properties* window, click the **Lines tab**, and in the *Lines* panel, click the **black arrow** beneath *Weight*, then click **0.25**, next click the

black arrow beneath *Style*, and click the **first dotted line**, and finally, click **Apply**.

- Click the **Y-Axis title**, click the **title** again and change it to read **Mean sales of jewelry in dollars**.
- Click the **number 1** on the *x*-axis, then click **it** a second time and delete **1** and type **Jan**.
- Click the **number 2** on the *x*-axis, then click **it** a second time and delete **2** and type **Feb**.
- Click the **number 3** on the *x*-axis, then click **it** a second time and delete **3** and type **Mar**.
- Click the **number 4** on the *x*-axis, then click **it** a second time and delete **4** and type **Apr**.
- Click the **number 5** on the *x*-axis, then click **it** a second time and delete **5** and type **May**.
- Click the **number 6** on the *x*-axis, then click **it** a second time and delete **6** and type **Jun**.
- Click the **number 7** on the *x*-axis, then click **it** a second time and delete **7** and type **Jul**.
- Click the **number 8** on the *x*-axis, then click **it** a second time and delete **8** and type **Aug**.
- Click the **number 9** on the *x*-axis, then click **it** a second time and delete **9** and type **Sep**.
- Click the **number 10** on the *x*-axis, then click **it** a second time and delete **10** and type **Oct**.
- Click the **number 11** on the *x*-axis, then click **it** a second time and delete **11** and type **Nov**.
- Click the **number 12** on the *x*-axis, then click **it** a second time and delete **12** and type **Dec**.
- Click the **X-Axis title** and change it to read **Month**.
- Click **Jan** on the *x*-axis, then click the **Show Grid Lines icon**.
- In the *Properties* window, click the **Lines tab**, and in the *Lines*, panel click the **black arrow** beneath *Weight*, then click **0.25**, next click the **black arrow** beneath *Style*, and click the **first dotted line**, and finally, click **Apply**.
- Click **any open space** on the graph (this click activates the *Show Derived Axis* icon).
- Click the **Show Derived Axis icon** (fourth from the right), then click the **right-sided Y-Axis title**, then click the **title** a second time, and change it to read **Mean sales of jewelry in dollars.**
- Click **any open space** on the graph.
- Click the **Add a reference line to the X-axis icon** (the 11th icon from the left) (a highlighted vertical line rising upward from the *x*-axis now appears).

- In the *Properties* window in the *Category Axis* panel, click the **black arrow** to the right of *Position*, then click **10:Oct**, then click **Apply**.
- Still in the *Properties* window, click the **Lines tab**, and in the *Lines* panel, click the **black arrow** beneath *Weight*, then click **1.5**, then click the **black arrow** beneath *Style*, and click the **sixth line** (dashed), finally, click **Apply**.
- Click anywhere on the **trend line** (the solid line).
- In the *Properties* window (with the *Lines tab* highlighted) in the *Lines* panel, click the **black arrow** beneath *Weight*, then click **2**, finally, click **Apply**.
- Click **X** in the **box** found in the upper right-hand corner (*Output Viewer* opens with finished graph shown in Figure 6.12)
- If you desire, you can change the size of the graph at this time.

Figure 6.12   Pre–Post Trend Line Graph for Month and Jewelry Sales

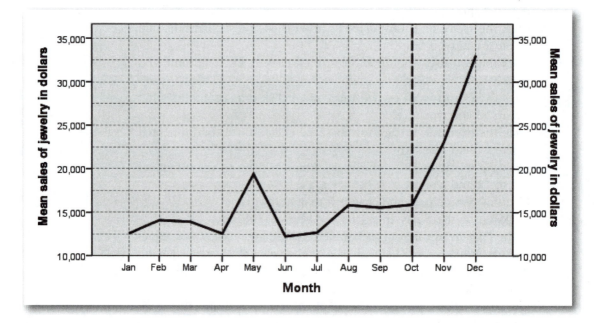

★   6.4 Interpretation of the Simple Line Graph

Did we make the mass of data more understandable? Let's look at our original questions and see how the graphs answered the questions.

6.4.1 Questions and Answers: Line Graph Showing Counts and Percentages

Answer the following questions using Figures 6.8 and 6.9.

1. How many customers are in each of the five categories of the educational variable?

Figure 6.8, the simple line graph with labels, shows that 953 customers did not complete high school; 1,571 earned a high school degree; 1,002 had some college education; 1,113 earned a college degree; and 361 earned a post-undergraduate degree.

2. What are the percentages of customers in each of the five educational categories?

Figure 6.9, another simple line graph but with the *Data Labels* showing percentages, indicates that 19.06% of the customers did not complete high school; 31.42% earned a high school degree; 20.04% had some college education; 22.26% earned the college degree; and 7.22% earned a post-undergraduate degree.

3. What are the relative ranks of the five educational categories?

Ranking from the largest to smallest category, we find that 1,571 or 31.42% of the customers earned a high school degree; 1,113 or 22.26% earned a college degree; 1,002 or 20.04% had some college education; 953 or 19.06% did not complete high school; and 361 or 7.22% earned a post-undergraduate degree.

6.4.2 Questions and Answers: Line Graph for Describing Continuous Data

Answer the following questions using Figure 6.10.

1. How are the years of education distributed around their mean value?

The line graph shows a mean of 14.54 and standard deviation of 3.295 with the approximate shape of a normal distribution.

2. Are the ages distributed skewed right, left, or are they normal?

The graph shows a distribution that approximates normality; it is neither skewed right nor left.

3. How many individuals were reported to have the mean years of education?

Approximately 560 individuals reported as having the mean of 14.54 years of education.

6.4.3 Questions and Answers: Line Graph for Two Continuous Variables (Trend)

Answer the following questions using Figure 6.11.

1. Is there a trend when looking at years of education and mean household income?

The graph indicates that as years of education increases, the mean household income increases as well. There is a definite upward trend when these two variables are compared.

2. What is the mean household income for someone with 19 years of education?

For 19 years of education, the mean household income is $70,000.

3. How many years of education mark the point of a steady upward increase in household income, and what are the income amounts?

Once the 13th year of education has been reached, there is a steady increase in the mean household income. At 13 years of education, the mean income is $45,000, and at 23 years, it is $92,000.

6.4.4 Questions and Answers: Pre–Post Trend Line Graph

Answer the following questions using Figure 6.12.

1. In the months preceding and including October, is there any consistent trend in the sales of jewelry?

The months up to and including October indicates that the amount of money spent on jewelry fluctuated, with the average trend indicating an increase in sales from January to October. There was also a spike in sales from $5,000 to $19,000 in the month of May.

2. What happened to the sales of jewelry following October, and what is a reasonable explanation?

Following the month of October, the sale of jewelry increased from $16,000 to $33,000. The reasonable explanation is that this represents the onset of the Christmas season.

3. Can you offer some explanation for the spike in sales during the month of May?

The large increase of jewelry sales ($5,000 to $19,000) during the month of May could be attributed to many couples selecting June as their traditional wedding time.

6.5 REVIEW EXERCISES   ★

1. Open **satisf.sav** found in the SPSS Sample file. Select the discrete variable labeled *Primary department* and named *dept*. Build a line graph as in Figure 6.13 that shows value labels at each node of the seven departments.

Questions: (a) Which department had the most visits? (b) Which department had the second-most visits? (c) Which two ranked lowest of all departments? (d) What is the rank order of the departments when ordered from the least to the most number of visitors?

Figure 6.13   Review Exercises: Simple Line Graph for Primary Department Visits

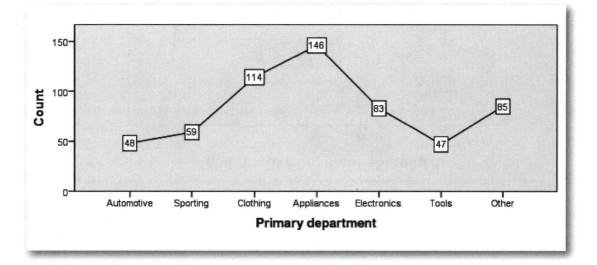

2. Open SPSS Sample file called **world95.sav**. Select the continuous (scale) variable labeled as *Average male life expectancy* and named *life-expm*. Build a simple line graph as in Figure 6.14 and answer the following questions.

Questions: (a) Is there a trend between the years of 60 and 68 years of age? (b) What happens to the frequency of death as the age of 74 is reached? (c) What is the approximate year when the males lifespan peaks (highest frequency)? (d) What is the mean, standard deviation, and number of observations for this variable.

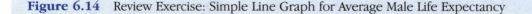

Figure 6.14 Review Exercise: Simple Line Graph for Average Male Life Expectancy

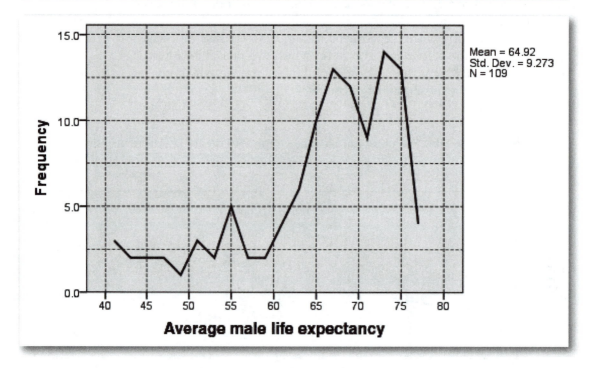

3. Open SPSS Sample file called **world95.sav**. Select two continuous (scale) variables. The first one (x-axis variable) is labeled *Daily calorie intake* and named *calories*. The second one is labeled *Infant mortality* (deaths per 1,000 live births) and named *babymort*. Build a simple line graph as in Figure 6.15 and answer the following questions.

Questions: (a) What happens to the mortality rates when daily calorie intake increases to 2,400 per day? (b) What happens to the mortality when calories reach about 3,400 per day? (c) How would you describe the overall trend when daily calorie intake is compared with infant mortality?

Figure 6.15 Review Exercise: Simple Line Graph for Infant Mortality and Daily Calorie Intake

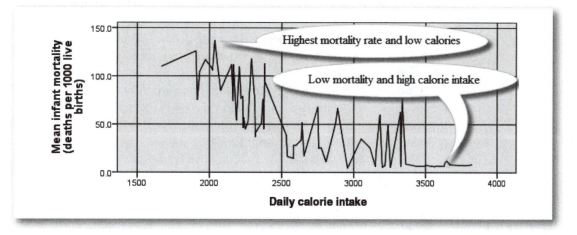

4. Open **satisf.sav** and select the continuous variable named *distance* and labeled *Distance from home* as the single continuous variable to be placed on the *x*-axis. The *y*-axis should record percentages. Build a simple line graph as in Figure 6.16 to answer the following questions.

Questions: (a) What percentage of the people live the greatest distance from the store? (b) What is the percentage of people who live 30 or more miles from the store? (c) Once the peak distance of 1 to 5 miles from the store is reached, can you describe a trend? (d) What percentage of customers live 1 mile or less from the store? (e) What percentage of the customers live more than 1 mile from the store?

Figure 6.16 Review Exercise: Simple Line Graph for Distance From Home

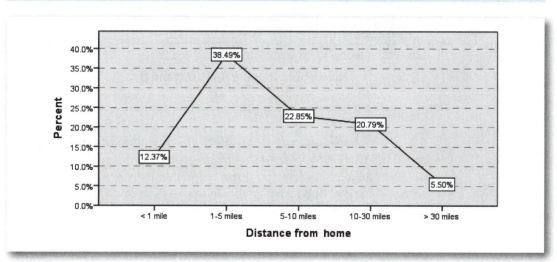

5. Open **customer_dbase.sav** and select the continuous variable named *income* and labeled *Household income in thousands* for placement on the *x*-axis. For the *y*-axis, select the continuous variable named *creddebt* and labeled as *Credit card debt*. In the *Statistics* panel of the *Element Properties* window, change the *y*-axis to the *Mean*. Build a line graph as shown in Figure 6.17 using these two continuous variables and answer the following questions.

Questions: (a) What was the most credit card debt, and what was the income less than or more than 1 million? (b) Was there an identifiable pattern for credit card debt when income surpassed $575,000, and if so, describe it? (c) Between $0 and $250,000 income, what is the highest amount of credit crad debt? (d) Estimate the credit card debt for someone earning $440,000.

Figure 6.17   Review Exercises: Simple Line Graph for Household Income and Credit Card Debt

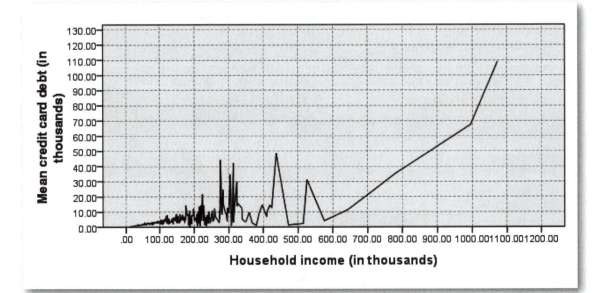

6. Open **bankloan.sav**, and select the continuous variable named *income* and labeled *Household income in thousands* for placement on the *y*-axis. For the *x*-axis, select the discrete variable named *ed* and labeled as *Level of education*. Build a line graph shown in Figure 6.18 using these variables and answer the following questions.

Questions: (a) What is the overall trend for education and household income prior to earning the college degree? (b) What happens to the trend line once the college degree is earned? (c) What does the trend line show once a post-undergraduate degree is earned? (d) What is the overall average trend for the relationship between all levels of education and mean household income?

Figure 6.18   Review Exercises: Pre–Post Trend Line for Educational Level and Income

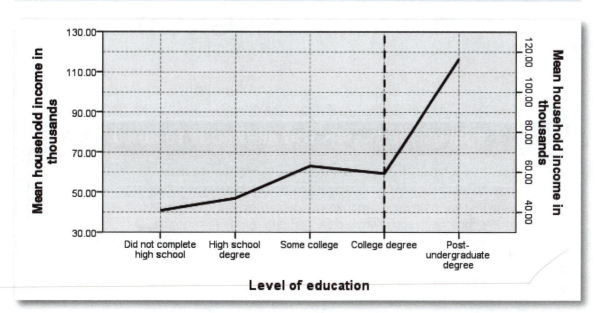

7

MULTIPLE LINE GRAPH

PURPOSE OF GRAPHS YOU ARE ABOUT TO BUILD

- To show an interaction for two discrete and one continuous variable
- To show no interaction for two discrete and one continuous variable
- To compare two continuous variables categorized by a discrete variable
- To explore for a trend with two discrete and one continuous variable

★ ## 7.1 INTRODUCTION TO THE MULTIPLE LINE GRAPH

In the previous chapter, you used the simple line graph to describe both discrete and continuous data distributions. You also used the simple line graph to explore for trend lines when you have various combinations of discrete and continuous data. In this chapter, you have an opportunity to expand on the usefulness of the line graph by using multiple lines to plot the values of two or more variables.

Multiple line (multiline) graphs can answer a variety of questions concerning databases. The lines in this type of graph can represent individual variables or variable categories. Multiple line graphs are useful in describing situations where you have multiple independent variables.[1] It can be used to investigate whether two independent variables work together (interaction effect) to influence the value of the dependent variable. The multiline graph can be used to visually compare categories of one variable within another variable. It can be used to identify a trend line for changes in one or more variables over time. Multiline graphs will also show the relative change between two or more variables.

The multiline graph can be built using various combinations of discrete and continuous data, resulting in many useful variations. You will learn to build and interpret these graphs in the following pages. The graph-building methods in this chapter do not describe the ways in which SPSS can produce these multiline graphs as part of a larger analysis. By this, we mean that sometimes SPSS performs certain statistical procedures that give the analyst the option to produce these graphs, which it refers to as *plots*. Usually these plots (graphs) are produced with a single click of the mouse. The techniques learned in this chapter will provide you with insights into the many uses of the multiline graph, which includes the production of plots during statistical analysis. The following sections provide many of the applications of the multiline graph in the quest to better understand data.

7.1.1 Multiline Graph: Two Discrete and One Continuous Variable (Interaction)

The data used to build the multiline graph in this section were obtained from the survey of 37 students. The graph provides a visual picture that will help us determine if two independent variables may act together to influence the value of a dependent variable. This is referred to as an *interaction* effect. The multiline graph provides some evidence (not conclusive) of an interaction when the two lines, representing the independent variables, cross one another. This effect is illustrated in Figure 7.1 when the independent variables of *gender* and *time of class* are graphed along with the dependent variable of mean points on Exam 1. It is important to remember that lines do not

---

[1]In this chapter, we often use independent variable as a descriptive term for those variables thought to influence change in the dependent variable of a posteriori probability-type study. In this context, the terms independent and dependent are not limited to experiments but may include correlational and predictive research models.

Figure 7.1   Multiline Graph Showing a Possible Interaction Between Class Time and Gender

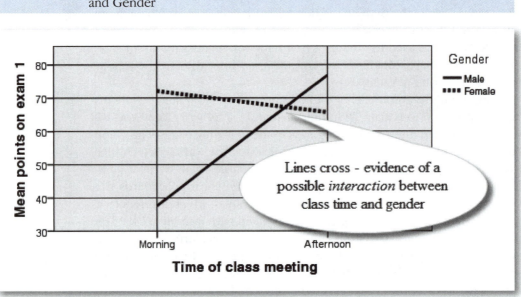

indicate that the interaction is significant as further evidence must be obtained for confirmation.[2]

The intersection of the lines in Figure 7.1 informs us that *time of class* and *gender* may interact in some undefined way to influence the number of points earned on the first exam. If this effect is confirmed (see Footnote 2), we can place little importance on the *individual* effects of gender and class time on the number of points earned. An interaction would provide some evidence that these two variables work together to significantly change the points earned.

In addition to the possible interaction effect, what can we learn by looking at the graph? For one thing, we can say that in the morning class the females averaged 72 points, while males earned 38 for a difference of 34 points. In the afternoon class, females earned, on average, 66 points with males earning 77, a difference of 11 points. We will leave the development of plausible explanations for these observations as a fun project for the reader.

---

[2]SPSS general linear model (GLM) univariate analysis of variance was conducted to confirm or deny the interaction. The interaction of gender and time of class was found to be significant at the .013 level.

7.1.2 Multiline Graph: Two Discrete and One Continuous Variable (No Interaction)

We next illustrate the appearance of the multiline graph when the lines are approximately parallel. This situation provides evidence that there is *no* interaction between the two variables. We use the same database as above but substitute *dichotomized anxiety* for *class time*. Therefore, we now have *anxiety level* and *gender* as the two independent-like variables. The dependent variable remains as in the previous example as points earned on the first exam. The graph in Figure 7.2 indicates that it is unlikely that *gender* and *anxiety level* interact in a manner that influences the score on the first exam. More specifically, we can say that it is unlikely that the variables of *dichotomized anxiety* and *gender* act together to influence the mean points earned on Exam 1.[3]

What else can we say about the data used to build this multiple line graph? Those males with anxiety averaged 55 earned points, while females

Figure 7.2   Multiline Showing *No* Interaction Between Anxiety and Gender

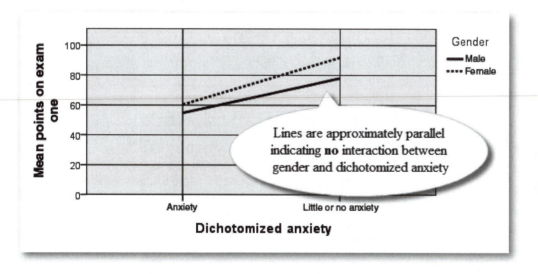

[3]SPSS GLM univariate analysis of variance was used to confirm or deny the information presented in the graph. The GLM test confirmed (significance level of .694) that there was no interaction for gender and anxiety.

averaged 60—a difference of 5 points. Males with little or no anxiety averaged 78 points, while females averaged 92—a difference of 14 points. The important thing to notice is that gender and anxiety level did not appear to interact in a manner that influenced performance on the first exam. From a statistical point of view, we could now consider if each of the impendent-like variables influenced performance of the exam.

7.1.3 Multiline Graph: Two Continuous and One Discrete Variable

We next present an example of the multiline graph with the intention of comparing the performance of males and females on two different tests. For this example, we rely on data for the 1,050 statistics students. In this application of the multiline graph, we summarize two continuous variables (first- and second-midterm exams) by instructing SPSS to calculate separate means for males and females on the two tests. Therefore, we have two categories of the *gender* variable. Simply stated, SPSS first determines the mean score for all males on the first- and second-midterm exams and then does the same for the female category.

In Figure 7.3, the solid line represents the first midterm exam. We see that males earned an average of 65.5 points on the first midterm exam (solid line),

Figure 7.3   Multiline Comparing Gender and Performance on Two Midterms

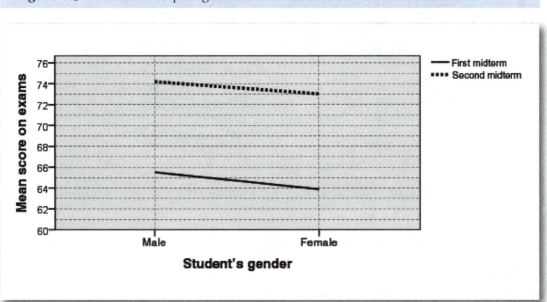

while females earned 64. The pattern with females earning slightly fewer points than males continued for the second midterm exam. The dotted line (second exam) shows males earning 74.2 points, with females at 73. Both males and females improved their test scores from the first to the second exams. There appears to be no practical gender effect on test performance. Gender differences are extremely unlikely in that both males and females earned approximately nine additional points when taking the second midterm.

7.1.4 Multiline Graph: Trend Exploration

You may recall that in Sections 6.1.3 and 6.1.4 of the previous chapter, we presented four examples of trend analysis when using the simple line graph. We now demonstrate the use of multiple lines to represent a discrete variable having two categories. You could have more categories, but we are confident that two lines will effectively make our point.

In this section, Figure 7.4 displays multiple lines that represent the two categories of the discrete variable of gender. The solid line represents the category for males, and the dotted line represents the female category. Each of these gender categories are separately measured by SPSS to determine the average points earned (our continuous variable) for a particular year (our second discrete variable). The graph will answer many questions about male and female performance over a period of 11 years.

Figure 7.4 Multiline Graph: Gendered Average Semester Points by Year of Class

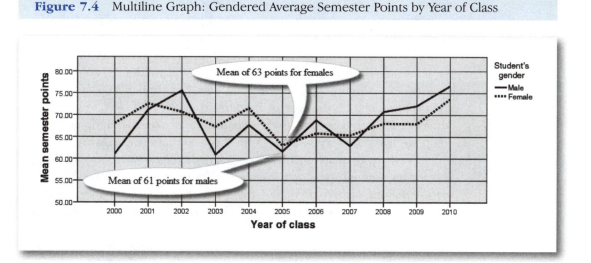

The bubbles in Figure 7.4 show one of the many comparisons between the three variables made possible by this multiline graph. The bubbles bring attention to the year 2005 where females earned an average of 63 points while males earned 61. This comparison can be made for each of the 11 years. Another question might be concerned with whether this pattern persisted over a significant number of years.[4] The overall trend for this 11-year history of classes is another interesting question to investigate. An example might be to note the initial values for males (61) and females (67) in the year 2000 and then do the same for the final year 2010. In 2010, males earned more average points (76) than females (74). This represents a reversal of the beginning where females scored higher than males. The one trend we see on the graph is that average points earned by both males and females increased over the data collection period. We recognize an overall upward trend for points earned when looking at the entire 11-year period.

There are many interesting questions associated with this type of graph. In the next section, you will see additional questions that can be answered by the multiline graphs that you will soon build.

★   7.2 DATABASES AND QUESTIONS

The first graph built in this chapter uses **customer_dbase.sav**. From this database, you will use the two discrete variables of *age* (for the *x*-axis) and *gender* for the *legend* variable. On the *y*-axis, you will place the continuous variable that recorded "*other debt*" in thousands of dollars. Therefore, the questions about these variables center on the identification of possible relationships between *age*, *gender*, and the *amount of debt*.

The second graph built also uses the **customer_dbase.sav** SPSS database and the same discrete variables placed in the same location in the *Chart Builder*, but a different continuous variable is selected for the *y*-axis. The *y*-axis variable is the dollar amount spent on the respondent's *primary credit card*. We are attempting to identify any relationship between *age*, *gender*, and *expenditures* on the primary credit card.

The third graph once again uses **customer_dbase.sav**. In this graph, you will place two continuous variables on the *y*-axis, and two separate lines will represent the two variables. The amount spent on the *primary* credit card is the first and the amount spent on the *secondary* credit card is the second. You also use the discrete variable of *gender*. The questions for these variables center on differences in the amount spent on these two credit cards by males and females.

---

[4]One such test could be a one-way chi-square test to compare the number of years and their various outcomes in terms of female versus male performance.

The fourth graph uses **credit_card.sav**, a large database consisting of 26,280 cases. For this multiline graph, you will use the amount spent as the *y*-axis continuous variable. The *x*-axis discrete variable is the month of the expenditure and the legend variable is once again gender. This graph will produce a line for males and another for females and plot the amount spent every month (the second discrete variable) over 1 year. The questions will center on the identification of the trend lines for males and females on a month-by-month basis.

7.2.1 Questions When Graphing Two Discrete and One Continuous Variable (Interaction)

1. What is the age interval for those having the most debt?
2. What is the age interval for those having the least amount of debt?
3. At what age interval are the spending differences between genders the greatest?
4. Is there a possible interaction between age and gender?
5. What is the dollar amount recorded for the highest debt?

7.2.2 Questions When Graphing Two Discrete and One Continuous Variable (No Interaction)

1. What is the age interval for those having the most primary card debt?
2. What is the highest recorded monthly primary card expenditure?
3. At what age interval(s) would you estimate that the gender differences are the greatest?
4. Is there a possibility that there is an interaction between age and gender when looking at expenditures on the primary credit card?
5. Do males or females spend more for the primary credit card?

7.2.3 Questions When Graphing Two Continuous and One Discrete Variable

1. What are the mean dollar amounts for males on their secondary and primary credit cards?
2. What are the mean dollar amounts for females on their secondary and primary credit cards?

3. What does the downward slope for the primary card (solid line) tell us?

4. What does the downward slope for the secondary card (dotted line) tell us?

5. When the slopes for both credit cards are the same (parallel lines), does this provide any useful information?

7.2.4 Questions When Graphing for Trend Exploration

1. What were the credit card expenditures for males and females in January?

2. In how many months did the females outspend the males?

3. Which month recorded the highest expenditure for males?

4. What can you say about the overall pattern of expenditures for males and females?

5. What were the highest and the lowest monthly expenditures regardless of gender?

★ 7.3 USING SPSS TO BUILD THE MULTIPLE LINE GRAPH

The first three of the following multiline graphs are built using **customer_dbase.sav**. This database has 132 variables and 5,000 cases and is found in the SPSS Sample file. The database **credit_card.sav** measures 26,280 individuals on 11 different variables and is used to build the fourth and final multiline graph.

Various discrete and continuous variables are selected for study in four separate examples. The first presents a graph showing a possible interaction. The second shows no interaction, while the third graph compares two continuous distributions. Finally, the fourth graph presents a continuous variable split by a discrete variable, and then both the distributions are presented together on one graph. Sounds challenging and can we say, interesting? Let's build some SPSS graphs.

7.3.1 Building the Multiline Graph: Two Discrete and One Continuous Variable (Interaction)

The discrete variables used to build this graph are named *agecat* and labeled *Age Category* and *gender* and labeled *Gender*. The continuous variable is named *othhdebt* and labeled as *Other debt in thousands*. The finished graph will depict two lines that intersect providing some evidence that age and gender interact to influence the amount of "Other" debt. This aspect was discussed in Section 7.1.1.

- Open **customer_dbase.sav**.
- Click **Graphs**, then click **Chart Builder**.
- Click **Line** in the *Choose from* list, then click and drag **Multiple Line icon** to the *Chart preview* panel.
- Click and drag the **Age category** variable to the *X-Axis* box.
- Click and drag **Other debt in thousands** to the *Y-Axis* box.
- Click and drag **Gender** to the *Set color* box.
- Click **OK** (*Chart Builder* closes and *Output Viewer* opens showing the basic graph).
- Click the **graph** (a frame appears), grab the lower right **black square** (when the double-headed arrow appears), and drag it to the midpoint of the vertical line and release the mouse button to adjust the graph size (see Section 4.3.3 for more sizing details if needed).

The following procedures will embellish the basic graph so that it takes on the appearance shown in Figure 7.5.

- Double click the **graph** to open the *Chart Editor*.
- Click the **short line** to the left of *Male* in the graph's legend (upper right-hand side) (the line representing males in the graph is now highlighted).
- In the *Properties* window (with the *Lines* tab highlighted) and in the *Lines* panel, click the **black arrow** beneath *Weight*, then click **2**, and in the *Color* panel, click the **black rectangular box**.
- Click **Apply**.
- Click the **short line** to the left of *Female* in the graph's legend (upper right-hand side).
- In the *Properties* window with the *Lines* tab highlighted and in the *Lines* panel, click the **black arrow** beneath *Weight*, then click **2.5** and click the **black arrow** beneath *Style* then click the **first dotted line**. In the *Color* panel, click the **black rectangular box**.
- Click **Apply**.
- Click **any number** on the *x*-axis, then click the **Categories tab** in the *Properties* window.
- In the *Categories* panel, click **<18**, then click the **red X** found just to the right.
- In the *Categories* panel, click **no response**, then click the **red X** found just to the right.
- Click **Apply** (this will delete the empty categories of *<18* and *no response*).
- Click **any number** on the *x*-axis.

- Click the **Show Grid Lines icon**.
- In the *Properties* window, click the **Lines tab**, and in the *Lines* panel, click the **black arrow** beneath *Weight* and click **0.5**, then click the **black arrow** beneath *Style* and click the **first dotted line**, and finally, click **Apply**.
- Click the **Y-Axis** title, click the **title** a second time and edit it to read **Mean other debt (in thousands)**.
- Click **any number** on the *y*-axis.
- Click the **Show Grid Lines icon**.
- In the *Properties* window with the *Grid Lines* tab highlighted, click the **small circle** to the left of *Both major and minor ticks*, then click **Apply**.
- Click **any of the grid lines** for the *y*-axis.
- Click the **Lines tab** in the *Properties* window, then in the *Lines* panel, click the **black arrow** beneath *Weight* and click **0.5**, then click the **black arrow** beneath *Style* and click the **first dotted line**, and finally, click **Apply**.
- Click **X** found at the upper right-hand corner of the *Chart Editor*.
- If *Output Viewer* does not open, then click **Output** found on the task bar at the bottom of your computer's screen (Figure 7.5 will appear).

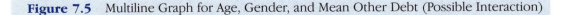

Figure 7.5   Multiline Graph for Age, Gender, and Mean Other Debt (Possible Interaction)

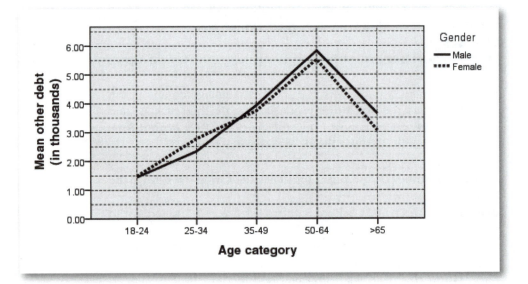

Explanation for this graph is detailed in the interpretation section. In the next section, you build a multiline graph once again exploring for relationship between three variables.

7.3.2 Building the Multiline Graph: Two Discrete and One Continuous Variable (No Interaction)

The discrete variables used to build this graph are *agecat* (*Age Category*) and *gender* (*Gender*). The continuous variable is *cardspent* and is labeled *Amount spent on primary card last month*. The finished graph will depict two lines that do not intersect, providing some evidence that age and gender do not act together to influence amount spent on the credit card. This aspect of the line graph was discussed in Section 7.1.2.

- Open **customer_dbase.sav**.
- Click **Graphs**, then click **Chart Builder**.
- Click **Line**, then click and drag **Multiple Line icon** to the *Chart preview* panel.
- Click and drag the **Age Category** variable to the *x*-axis.
- Click and drag **Amount spent on primary card last month** to the *y*-axis.
- Click and drag the **Gender** variable to the *Set color* box.
- Click **OK** (*Output Viewer* opens showing the basic multiple line graph).
- Click the **graph**, click and drag (when the double-headed arrow appears) the **small black square** at the lower right-hand side of the frame to the **black square** immediately above the one just clicked (release the mouse button and the graph is now resized).
- Double click the resized **graph** to open the *Chart Editor*.
- Click on the **short line** to the left of *Male* in the upper right-hand portion of the graph.
- If *Properties* window is not open, click **Properties icon** (third from the left on the menu).
- Click the **Lines tab** if not highlighted.
- In the *Lines* panel, click the **black arrow** beneath *Weight*, then click **2**.
- In the *Color* panel, click the **black rectangular box**.

- Click **Apply**.
- Click the **short line** to the left of *Female* found in the legend.
- In the *Properties* window and in the *Lines* panel, click the **black arrow** beneath *Weight*, then click **2.5**.
- In the *Lines* panel, click the **black arrow** beneath *Style*, and click the **first dotted line**.
- In the *Color* panel, click the **black rectangular box**, click **Apply**.
- Click **any number** on the *x*-axis, then click **Categories tab** in the *Properties* window.
- In the *Categories* panel, click **<18**, then click the **red X** found just to the right.
- In the *Categories* panel, click **No response**, then click the **red X** to the right.
- Click **Apply**.
- Click **any number** on the *x*-axis.
- Click the **Show Grid Lines icon**.
- In the *Properties* window, click the **Lines tab**, and in the *Lines* panel, click the **black arrow** beneath *Weight* then click **0.25**, click the **black arrow** beneath *Style* and click the **first dotted line**, then click **Apply**.
- Click the **Y-Axis title** (a frame appears around it), click the **title** again and it moves to the horizontal position and is ready for editing. Type: **Mean amount spent on primary card last month**.
- Click **any number** on the *y*-axis.
- In the *Properties* window, click the **Scale tab**, and in the *Range* panel, change the *Minimum* to **200**, *Maximum* to **450**, *Major Increment* to **40**, and *Origin* to **200**.
- Click **Apply**.
- Click **Show Grid Lines icon**.
- In the *Properties* window with the *Grid Lines* tab highlighted, click the **small circle** to the left of *Both Major and minor ticks*, then click **Apply**.
- Click **any of the grid lines** for the *y*-axis.
- In the *Properties* window, click the **Lines tab**, and in the *Lines* panel, click the **black arrow** beneath *Weight* then click **0.25**, click the **black arrow** beneath *Style* and click the **first dotted line**, then click **Apply**.
- Click the **X** in the upper right-hand corner to close the *Chart Editor* and open the *Output Viewer* (you should see Figure 7.6).

Figure 7.6 Multiline Graph for Age, Gender, and Primary Credit Card Expenditures

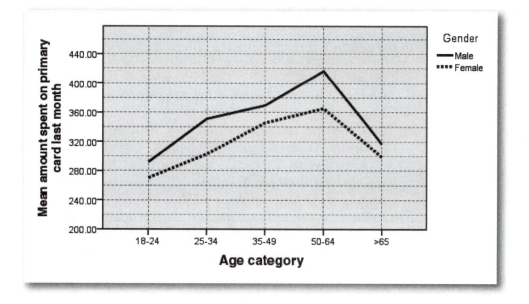

In the following section, you produce a multiple line graph using two continuous and one discrete variable.

7.3.3 Building the Multiline Graph for Comparing Two Continuous and One Discrete Variable

In this section, you build a multiline graph using the two continuous variables of *cardspent* (*Amount spent on primary card last month*) and *card-2spent*, which is labeled *Amount spent on secondary card last month*, and a single discrete variable of *gender*.

- Open **customer_dbase.sav**.
- Click **Graphs**, click **Chart Builder**, then click **Line** in the *Choose from* panel.
- Click and drag the **Multiple line icon** to the *Chart preview* panel.
- Click and drag **Amount spent on primary card last month** to the *y*-axis.

- Click and drag **Amount spent on secondary card last month** to the *y*-axis (Important note: To drag this second variable to the *y*-axis, you must hover the mouse pointer at the top of the box on the *y*-axis. A small box with a red plus sign will appear—this is where you must drop the second variable).
- Once you drop the second variable, *Create Summary Group* window opens, click **OK**.
- On the *x*-axis **SPSS inserted INDEX**, click and drag **INDEX** to the *Set color* box.
- Click and drag the **Gender** variable to the *x*-axis, click **OK** (*Output Viewer* opens showing the basic graph as output).
- Click the **graph**, click and drag (when the double-headed arrow appears) the **small black square** at the lower right-hand side of the frame to the **black square** immediately above the one just clicked (release the mouse button and the graph is now resized).
- The following procedures opens the *Chart Editor*, which is used to modify the basic graph to build the multiline graph as shown in Figure 7.7.
- Double click the **graph** (*Chart Editor* opens).
- Click the **short line** to the left of *Amount spent on primary card last month* found in the legend at the upper right-hand side of the graph.
- Click **Show Properties Window icon**.
- In *Properties* window, click the **Lines tab**, in the *Lines* panel, click the **black arrow** beneath *Weight* and click **2**.
- In the *Colors* panel, click the **black rectangular box**, then click **Apply**.
- Click the **short line** to the left of *Amount spent on secondary card last month* found in the legend at the upper right-hand side of the graph.
- In the *Properties* window, click the **Lines tab**, in the *Lines* panel, click the **black arrow** beneath *Weight*, then click **2.5**.
- Click the **black arrow** beneath the *Style*, click the **first dotted line**.
- In the *Color* panel, click the **black rectangular box**, click **Apply**.
- Click **Mean** on the *y*-axis (a frame appears), click it again (the title *Mean* moves to the horizontal position and is ready to edit), type **Mean amount spent**.
- Click **Male** or **Female** label on the *x*-axis.
- Click **Show Grid Lines icon** (the fifth icon from the right end of the menu bar).
- Click **any number** on the *y*-axis.
- In the *Properties* window, click the **Scale tab**, and in the *Range* panel, change *Minimum* to **100**, *Major Increment* to **50**, and *Origin* to **100**.
- Click **Apply**.
- Click the **Show Grid Lines icon**.

- Click **one of the vertical grid** lines rising upward from male or female (all grids should now be highlighted, if not, click at any intersection of the grid lines).
- In the *Properties* window, click the **Lines tab**, then in the *Lines* panel, click the **black arrow** beneath *Weight* and click **0.5**, next click the **black arrow** beneath *Style* and click the **first dotted line**, and finally, click **Apply** (all grids should become dotted lines).
- Click the **X** in the box found in the upper right-hand corner of the *Chart Editor*, and the *Output Viewer* opens to show the graph in Figure 7.7.

Figure 7.7   Multiline Graph: Two Continuous and One Discrete Variable

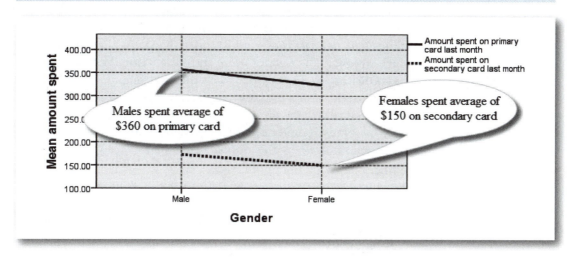

The two lines representing these two variables are found to be approximately parallel (they do not cross), indicating that an interaction between the two variables is unlikely. A more detailed meaning of the Figure 7.7 is explained later in this chapter when specific questions about the data are answered in the interpretation section.

7.3.4 Building the Multiline Graph for Trend Exploration

In this section, you build a multiline graph using two discrete and one continuous variable. One of the uses of this type of graph is to answer questions about any trend in expenditures (continuous variable) over a period of 12 months (discrete variable) for males and females (discrete variable). You might find the finished graph just a bit more interesting than those built in the previous sections since we now have an *x*-axis variable with 12 categories. Prior multiline graphs only placed two categories on the *x*-axis for a discrete variable.

For this project, you use **credit_card.sav** from the SPSS Sample files. This SPSS Sample file has 11 variables and 26,280 cases. SPSS does not provide documentation concerning the source of this database, so we assume it is hypothetical. We use the discrete variables of *gender* labeled *Gender* and *month* labeled as *Month*. The continuous variable for this graph-building exercise is named *spent* and labeled *Amount spent*.

- Open **credit_card.sav**.
- Click **Graphs**, click **Chart Builder**, then click **Line** in the *Choose from* panel.
- Click and drag the **Multiple Line icon** to the *Chart preview* panel.
- Click and drag **Month** to the *x*-axis.
- Click and drag **Amount spent** to the *y*-axis.
- Click and drag **Gender** to the *Set color* box.
- In the *Element Properties* window and in the *Statistics* panel, click the **black arrow** to the right of *Value* and click **Mean**, then click **Apply**.
- Click **OK** (*Output Viewer* opens with the basic graph).
- Next adjust the size of the basic graph (you have done this before, but let's quickly review the process), click the *graph* and a frame appears, place the mouse pointer on the lower right **black square** found on the frame, and when the *double-headed arrow* appears, drag it upward and to the right until you approximate the graph size shown in Figure 7.8, release the mouse button and the graph is resized.
- Double click the **graph** (*Chart Editor* opens).
- Click the **short line** to the left of male found in the legend at the upper right-hand side of the graph (a frame appears around the line that represents males).
- In the *Properties* window (with the *Lines* tab highlighted) and in the *Lines* panel, click the **black arrow** beneath *Weight* and click **2**, then click the **black rectangular box**.
- Click **Apply**.
- Click the **short line** to the left of *Female* found in the legend (upper right-hand side of the graph).
- In *Properties* window with the **Lines** tab highlighted, click the **black arrow** beneath *Weight* and click **2.5**, then click the **black arrow** beneath *Style*, click the **first dotted line** then click the **black rectangular box** found in the *Color* panel.
- Click **Apply**.
- Click the **x-axis title**, then click the **title** a second time and type: Month of expenditure (1 = *January*, 2 = *February*, etc.) (it is not necessary to type all months—etc. is enough).
- Click **any number** on the *x*-axis.

- In the *Properties* window, click the **Scale tab**, in the *Range* panel, change *Minimum value*, *Major Increment*, and *Origin* all to the value of **1**, then click **Apply**.
- Click the **Show Grid Lines icon**.
- Click **any number** on the *y*-axis.
- In the *Properties* window, click the **Scale tab**, and in the *Range* panel, change *Major Increment* from **10** to **5**.
- Click **Apply**.
- Click **Show Grid Lines icon** (the fifth icon from the right), grid lines appear on the graph.
- In the *Properties* window (with the *Grid Lines* tab highlighted), click the **small circle** to the left of *Both major and minor ticks*, then click **Apply**.
- Click the **X** in the upper right-hand corner of the *Chart Editor* window, the edited graph is then moved to the *Output Viewer* (if *Output Viewer* does not open, click **Output** on the task bar at the lower portion of the computer screen).
- The finished multiline graph should appear as in Figure 7.8—minus the bubbles.

Figure 7.8   Multiline Graph for Gender, Month of Expenditure, and the Amount Spent

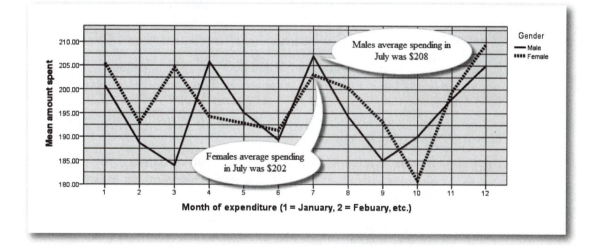

In the following section, we show how the above graphs answer the questions presented earlier.

★   **7.4 Interpretation of the Multiple Line Graph**

The following sections provide answers for our original questions about the databases used to build our graphs. It is these answers that make our data more understandable.

7.4.1 Questions and Answers: Two Discrete and One Continuous Variable (Interaction)

The information needed to answer the following questions is found in Figure 7.5.

1. What is the age interval for those having the most debt?

Looking at the graph, we see that the separate lines for males and females both are the tallest in the 50 to 64 age group. We may also note that there is little difference (perhaps $150) for males and females at this age interval.

2. What is the age interval for those having the least amount of debt?

Examine Figure 7.5, and you will quickly notice that the age category with the lowest recorded expenditure was 18 to 24. Also, you can see that for this age category, males and females spend the same amount on their primary credit card, approximately $1,200.00 per month.

3. At what age interval are the spending differences between genders the greatest?

The graph reveals that the two lines representing males and females are the farthest apart in the category for 65 and older group. The males spend about $3,500, while the females spend $3,000—a difference of $500.00.

4. Is there a possible interaction between age and gender?

It is possible that there is an interaction between age category and gender since the graph shows that the lines for gender and age intersect. However, one must conduct the appropriate test to provide additional evidence of such a relationship.[5]

5. What is the dollar amount recorded for the highest debt?

The multiline graph shows $5,900 as the highest debt. This high point was for males aged 50 to 64.

-----

[5]The authors did a GLM univariate analysis of variance and found that the interaction was *not* significant ($p = .264$). This finding illustrates the caution required when attempting to interpret the intersection of lines in a multiline graph. Significance ($p = .000$) was only established for the age categorical variable. One should remember that when using SPSS that $p = .000$ means that the probability was not necessarily zero but less than .001.

7.4.2 Questions and Answers: Two Discrete and One Continuous Variable (No Interaction)

The information needed to answer the following questions is found in Figure 7.6.

1. What is the age interval for those having the most primary card debt?
The graph shows that the age interval 50 to 64 contains those who have the most primary credit card debt.

2. What is the highest recorded monthly primary card expenditure?
The graph shows that the highest recorded monthly primary credit card debt was $420.00. This amount represented males aged 50 to 64.

3. At what age interval(s) would you estimate that the gender differences are the greatest?
The graph indicates that it is reasonable to assume that the age intervals of 25 to 34 and 50 to 64 are very close to equal in terms of expenditures and represent the greatest differences.

4. Is there a possibility that there is an interaction between age and gender when looking at expenditures on the primary credit card?
The graph in Figure 7.6 shows that the lines representing males and females are approximately parallel. This finding strongly suggests that there is no interaction between age and gender.[6]

5. Do males or females spend more for the primary credit card?
Looking at the graph reveals that the solid line, representing males, indicates that for all age categories males outspend females on the primary credit card. The solid line for males is higher, relevant to the y-axis, than the dotted line representing females.

7.4.3 Questions and Answers: Two Continuous and One Discrete Variable

The information needed to answer the following questions is found in Figure 7.7.

1. What are the mean dollar amounts for males on their secondary and primary credit cards?

---

[6]We confirmed this using the GLM univariate analysis of variance finding of a p of .376. This large *p value* provides evidence that age category and gender did not interact in a manner that would change the amount spent variable.

For this question, read the graph and direct your attention to x-axis male category. Follow the line upward and read where the dotted line (secondary card) intersects and find $180. Continue upward to where the sold line (primary card) intersects and find $360.

2. What are the mean dollar amounts for females on their secondary and primary credit cards?

For this question, read the graph and direct your attention to x-axis female category. Follow the line upward and read where the dotted line (secondary card) intersects and find $150. Continue upward to where the sold line (primary card) intersects and find $320.

3. What does the downward slope for the primary card (solid line) tell us?

The downward slope of the solid line (primary card) in the graph indicates that males spend more for the primary credit card than females.

4. What does the downward slope for the secondary card (dotted line) tell us?

The downward slope of the dotted line (secondary card) in the graph indicates that males spend more for the secondary credit card than females.

5. When the slopes for both credit cards are the same (parallel lines), does this provide any useful information?

The lines for both credit cards are parallel, which informs the graph reader that the gender pattern is the same for both credit cards. Females are found to spend less than males for both primary and secondary credit cards. It also informs us an interaction between credit card type and gender, which influences the amount spent.

7.4.4 Questions and Answers: Trend Exploration

The information needed to answer the following questions is found in Figure 7.8.

1. What were the credit card expenditures for males and females in January?

The graph shows that for the month of January, females spent $205, while males spent less at $201.

2. In how many months did the females outspend the males?

Counting the number of months on the x-axis in the graph where the dotted line is higher than the solid line (males), we count 8 of the 12 months where females outspent males.

3. Which month recorded the highest expenditure for males?

The graph informs us that Month 7 (July) represented the highest expenditure for males.

4. What can you say about the overall pattern of expenditures for males and females?

The multiline graph indicates that at the end of the year (12 months), both males and females spent slightly more on the credit card than at the beginning of the year. Females continued to outspend males by a very slight amount. No real trend can be detected since the data would have to be adjusted for seasonal spending, there is always increased spending during Christmas time.

5. What were the highest and the lowest monthly expenditures regardless of gender?

The x-axis on the graph reveals that the highest expenditure of $209 was for females during the 12th month (December). Females also spent the least at $181 during the 10th month.

In the final section of this chapter, we offer some review exercises designed to reinforce your multiline graph-building skills.

7.5 REVIEW EXERCISES ★

1. Open the **adl.sav** database found in the SPSS Sample file. Select the following variables to build the multiline graph in Figure 7.9. First select the *psd (post-stroke depression)* variable for the *set color* variable, then choose *age (Pt. age)* for y-axis and *hypertns (Hypertensive)* for the x-axis variable. Hint: As you build this graph, you must use the *Properties* windows to change the y-axis scale as follows: *Properties > scale tab >* then change *Minimum* to **71**, *Major Increments* to **0.1**, and *Origin* to **71**.

Questions: (a) What is the mean patient age for those suffering from post-stroke depression and are hypertensive? (b) What is the mean patient age for those suffering from post-stroke depression and are *not* hypertensive? (c) What is the mean patient age for those not suffering from post-stroke depression and are hypertensive? (d) What is the mean patient age for those not suffering from post-stroke depression and are *not* hypertensive? (e) Does there appear (by looking at the graph) to be a relationship between age and whether the patient has hypertension and post-stroke depression? (f) Could the patient's age be used to improve the prediction of whether someone has hypertension and post-stroke depression?

Figure 7.9   Review Exercise: Multiline Graph for Hypertension, Age, and Depression

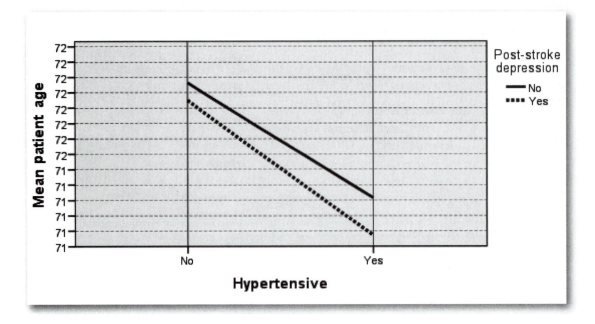

2.   Open the **adl.sav** database found in the SPSS Sample file. Select the following variables to build the multiline graph shown in Figure 7.10. Select the *psd* (*post-stroke depression*) variable for the *color* variable, then *age* (*Pt. age*) for *y*-axis, and finally, *diabetic* (*Diabetes mellitus*) for the *x*-axis variable. Hint: as you build this graph, you must use the *Properties* windows to change the *y*-axis scale as follows: *Properties > scale tab >* then change *Minimum* to **70.5**, *Major Increment* to **0.2**, and *Origin* to **70.5**.

Questions: (a) What is the mean patient age for those suffering from post-stroke depression and diabetes mellitus? (b) What is the mean patient age for those suffering from post-stroke depression and are *not* diabetic? (c) What is the mean patient age for those free of post-stroke depression and are diabetic? (d) What is the mean patient age for those free of post-stroke depression and are *not* diabetic? (e) Does there appear (by looking at the graph) to be a relationship between age and whether the patient has diabetes and post-stroke depression? (f) Could the patient's age be used to improve the prediction if someone has diabetes and post-stroke depression?

Figure 7.10   Review Exercises: Multiline Graph for Age, Diabetes Mellitus, and Depression

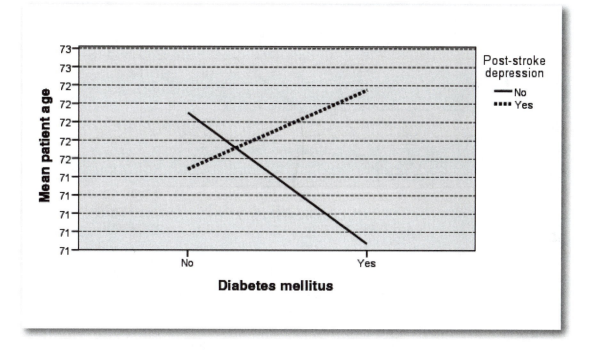

3. Open the **AMLsurvival.sav** database found in the SPSS Sample file. Select the following variables to build the multiline graph in Figure 7.11. Select *chemo* (chemotherapy) for the *x*-axis variable, then *Status* for the *color* variable, and *time* [*Time (weeks)*] for the *y*-axis variable. Note: Think of *censored* as meaning that the patient is disease free.

Questions: (a) Is there a difference for survival time for those receiving chemotherapy? (b) For those patients suffering from a disease relapse, what is the difference (in weeks) of survival for those who had and those who did not have chemotherapy? (c) For those censored patients, what is the difference (in weeks) of survival for those who had and those who did not have chemotherapy? (d) If these data were scientifically correct, what would you do regarding the decision for chemotherapy?

Figure 7.11   Review Exercises: Multiline Graph for Weeks, Chemotherapy, and Status

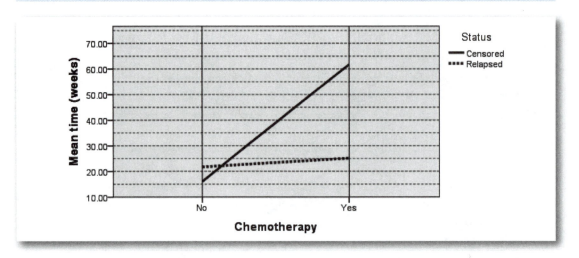

4. Open **customer_dbase.com** and select the discrete variable named *ed* and labeled *Level of education* for placement on the *x*-axis. For the *Set Color* discrete variable use *gender*, and for the *y*-axis, use the continuous variable named *income* and labeled *Household income in thousands*. Build the multi-line graph in Figure 7.12 and answer the following questions.

Questions: (a) What are the mean household incomes for males and females who have a post-undergraduate degree? (b) At what level of education are male and female mean incomes the closest? (c) What is the overall trend for level of education and mean household income? (d) What is the category having the lowest household income, and what is that amount?

Figure 7.12   Review exercises: Multiline Graph for Income, Education, and Gender

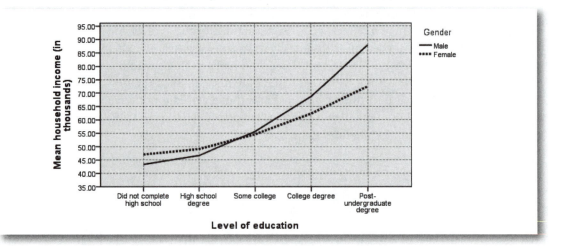

5. Open **customer_dbase.com** and select the discrete variable named *empcat* and labeled *Years with the current employer* for the *x*-axis. For the *Set Color* discrete variable use *gender*, and for the *y*-axis use the continuous variable named *income* and labeled *Household income in thousands*. Build the multiline graph in Figure 7.13 and answer the following questions.

Questions: (a) What can you say about the overall trend for males and females? (b) Which category for years with employer shows the greatest gender difference? (c) Do female employees working for an employer for more than 15 years earn more than males?

Figure 7.13   Review Exercises: Multiline Graph for Income, Years With Employer, and Gender

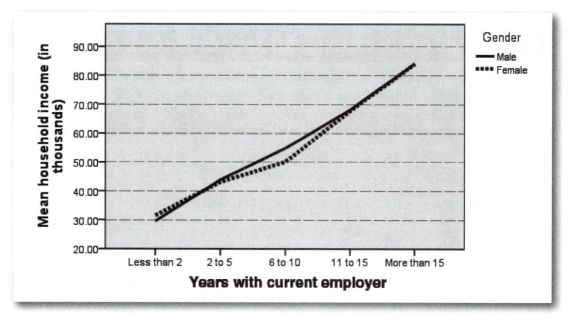

8

SIMPLE HISTOGRAM

PURPOSE OF GRAPHS YOU ARE ABOUT TO BUILD

- To show a normally distributed continuous variable
- To show a non-normally distributed continuous variable
- To describe data by adding the number of observations in each successive interval

★ **8.1 INTRODUCTION TO THE SIMPLE HISTOGRAM**

In the previous chapter on the multiple line graph, we covered various data questions dealing with both continuous and discrete data. We explored and examined relationships between various combinations of continuous and discrete variables by building a graph that used lines to represent the data. In this chapter, we present a graphing technique that draws a picture of a single continuous variable by using rectangular bars. The simple histogram looks much like the simple bar graph; however, there are no spaces between the bars. The lack of space between bars is because the histogram represents continuous data, not separate categories as with the bar graph.

The bars of the histogram provide a convenient way to record the frequency of data that occur within specified intervals of continuous data.[1] As with the bar graph, the height of each bar represents the frequency or percentage within its respective interval.

Like the bar and pie graphs, the histogram is used to analyze a single variable but only with variables measured at the continuous level. The histogram differs from the bar or pie graph in that computing power of SPSS is used to construct intervals that permit the counting of observations within these intervals. Thus, we can use the power of the *Chart Builder* to provide a convenient way to visualize proportions of observations within intervals.

In a histogram, the *x*-axis specifies the values that are observed (what was measured), while the *y*-axis represents the number of times (or percentage) that the values were observed. For example, consider the speed interval of 85 to 90 miles per hour to be the *x*-axis value, and if speeds in this interval occurred 12 times, then the *y*-axis records this value. When looking at the histogram (or any graph), it is important to carefully note the values specified on both the *x*-axis and the *y*-axis.

Some examples of the measurements recorded on the *x*-axis of a histogram are as follows: scores on a test, miles per hour, weight of a newborn baby, height of a mountain, depth of the ocean, length of a hike, and inches of rainfall. The *y*-axis of the histogram most often displays the frequency or percent; however, we show in this chapter how cumulative percent on the *y*-axis can provide useful information.

The default setting for the *Chart Builder* labels the *y*-axis as frequency; however, it is easy to change this to percent, which will then report the percentage of the total cases contained within each interval on the *x*-axis. When the research question seeks the percentages of cases within intervals, the *Chart Builder* can be used to display percentages rather than frequencies.

The shape of the histogram tells us how the data are distributed. There are many shapes that the histogram can follow; in this introduction, we present three basic shapes. First, we show the histogram for a normal distribution (resembles the shape of a bell). Next, we have the histogram that is skewed to the left (negatively skewed). And third, we have the histogram that is

---

[1]The reader may ask himself or herself about the differences between a category (discrete) and interval—definitely a legitimate question. This question deals with the disciplines dealing with the theory of measurement and physics and whether the universe is discrete or continuous. Many mathematicians and physicists feel that the universe is mainly discrete and that continuous data are dependent on individual points; therefore, basically it is categorical or discrete. This being said—for practical reasons, we proceed (as do most statistics and research texts) without a detailed explanation of how and why SPSS programmers construct *x*-axis intervals for continuous data.

skewed to the right (positively skewed). In Section 8.3.2, you will build a histogram that is neither normally distributed nor negatively or positively skewed, but one that is called unstable.

The bars of a histogram are of the same width (automatically selected by SPSS) and the height of the bars are determined by the number (or percentage) of observations contained in each bar (interval). Taller bars indicate higher values on the y-axis, while the shorter bars indicate smaller values. The tallest bar(s) of the histogram represents the values that were observed most frequently.

By default, SPSS produces basic statistics that will assist you in the interpretation of the data and of the histogram itself. These basic statistics are included with the graph and are the mean, standard deviation, and the number of observations. These statistics are printed in the upper right-hand corner of the graph in the legend region. This information is important when attempting to interpret continuous data graphed as a histogram.

When a population has been sampled in a random manner, then we can assume that the histogram is a true representation (with certain limitations) of the larger population.[2] Thus, we can use the simple histogram as a representation of the unknown population. When used in this manner, we are within the realm of *inferential* statistics. If the sample was not collected in a random manner, then we can use our graph as a descriptive statistic of the sample and no more. This is the *descriptive* branch of statistical analysis. There are many instances where the simple histogram provides answers to inferential- and descriptive-type questions about a database.

We also discuss when it is useful to build a modified simple histogram by changing the y-axis to "cumulative percent." There is another set of questions that can be readily answered by building just such a cumulative histogram.

The cumulative histogram can also be built with an eye toward deception. For an example of how the cumulative histogram can mislead, look at Figure 18.5 in the chapter on deception. In the following sections, we show and discuss different appearances of the histogram.

---

[2]In statistical terminology, the limits we refer to are known as "confidence limits." Basically, we statistically construct an interval that we can be confident to a certain degree, say 95%, that repeated sampling would produce, approximately, the same distribution. Thus, we can use our sample's distribution to model the unknown population. It is especially good news for the statistician when data are found to be "normally" distributed. The test for the normality is the one sample nonparametric Kolmogorov–Smirov, available in SPSS (Analyze > Non-Paramertric Tests > One-Sample).

8.1.1 Histogram: Normally Distributed Data

Figure 8.1 shows a histogram built from a hypothetical database consisting of 250 students in a mathematics class. Test scores (the measurement) were created as the continuous variable then placed on the *x*-axis specifically to demonstrate the appearance of a normal distribution.

The data used to build the histogram shown in Figure 8.1 is indeed "normally" shaped as it takes on a beautiful symmetry that is pleasing to the eye. In a histogram of a normal distribution, most values (68%) are clustered around the center of the graph.[3] The farther the bars are from the center of the histogram, the fewer the values those bars contain. The data represented in the normal histogram are symmetrical; the values of the data are equally distributed above and below the mean of the data. Therefore, one half of the histogram is a reflection of the other half.

The legend in the right side of Figure 8.1 shows a mean of 50, standard deviation of 20.04, and the number of observations as 250.

Figure 8.1   Simple Histogram Showing Normally Distributed Data

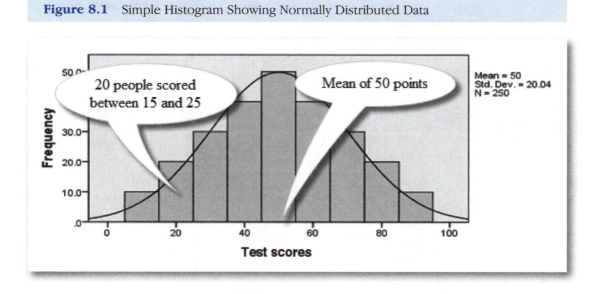

---

[3]The normal curve is mathematically constructed so that 68.26% of the total area under the curve is within the area bounded by ±1 standard deviation from the mean; ±2 standard deviations cover 95.44% of the area, while 3 standard deviations contain 99.74% of the area from the mean. How this percentage information is used to solve many statistical problems dealing with probability theory is not the subject of this book. We refer the interested reader to any introductory statistical textbook for information on this topic.

In the following section, we contrast this normally proportioned data with one where the bell-shaped curve is missing and the data present an entirely different picture.

8.1.2 Histogram: Negatively Skewed Data

Figure 8.2 presents hypothetical data for the speeds of 170 automobiles. The speeds of the automobiles were recorded on the x-axis, with the frequencies of those speeds on the y-axis. The histogram in Figure 8.2 presents data for the speeds of automobiles, but this time, the graph shows a nonsymmetrical distribution. When we say that a distribution of values is nonsymmetrical, we simply mean that the occurrences of the values are not evenly distributed on both sides of the mean. In nonstatistical language, we could say that we have a lopsided distribution, meaning that one side of the mean of the histogram is not the reflection of the other. We say the data shown in Figure 8.2 are skewed to the left. A histogram is skewed to the left when the left tail (which is made of lower speeds) is longer than the right tail. In this kind of histogram, most values are bunched up away from the y-axis and at the high end of the x-axis scale. The taller bars that represent more values are found on the right in this histogram.

Figure 8.2 also informs the graph maker that the data has a mean of 82.17, a standard deviation of 11.144, and the number of observations is 170.

Figure 8.2   Simple Histogram Showing Negatively Skewed Data

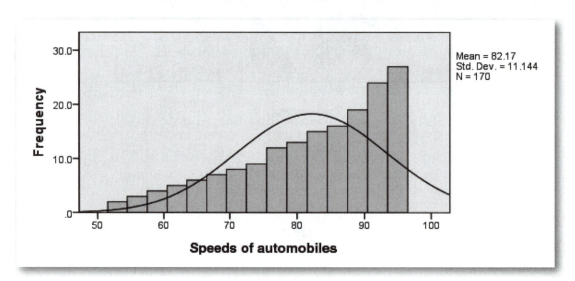

8.1.3 Histogram: Positively Skewed Data

To build the histogram in Figure 8.3, a hypothetical database consisting of 170 children was created. The children's weight (in pounds) is the continuous variable placed on the x-axis.

Figure 8.3 is an example of a nonsymmetrical distribution that is skewed to the right. A histogram is skewed to the right when the right tail is longer than the left tail. In this kind of histogram, most values are on the left tail; therefore, the bars that are closer to the y-axis are taller (more children who weigh less were observed) than the bars that are away from the y-axis. A histogram of this shape is also called a positively skewed histogram. Children's weights were at the lower end of the x-axis scale. In the distribution of children's weights, it is found that there are more lighter than heavier children.

The data used to build the histogram shown in Figure 8.3 has a mean of 114.65, a standard deviation of 3.769, and the number of observations is 170.

Figure 8.3   Histogram Showing Positively Skewed Data

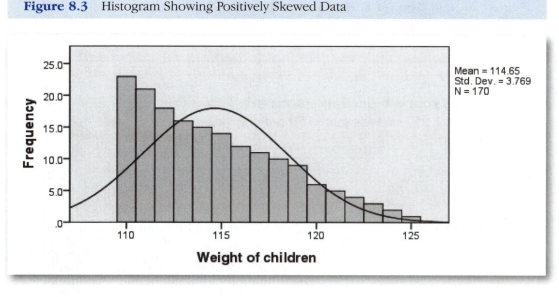

8.1.4 Cumulative Histogram

The data used to build the graph depicted in Figure 8.4 was obtained from 1,050 statistics students. It is used to illustrate a particular style of the simple histogram called a "cumulative histogram." This graph is especially useful with this database if one wishes to divide the percentage of students earning various scores into groups. It is also used to answer what are generally known as "percentile" questions. What is the percentile value for a score of 40 points? The percentile value for a test score of 40 is 20%, which is found on the *y*-axis. This graph answers some important questions. What was the test score that was surpassed by 80% of the students? (40). What was the highest score earned by the lowest 20% of the students? (40). What percentage of students scored at least 82 points? (70%). If you are able to understand these questions and answers, you will have demonstrated your understanding of the cumulative histogram and how it is related to percentile-type questions.

The bubble in Figure 8.4 will give you information about the interpretation of this useful graphic. In the following section, we present the databases used to construct the simple histogram and its cumulative cousin. You are also given questions about these databases that will be answered by the graphs that you soon build.

Figure 8.4   Cumulative Histogram for Scores on First Midterm

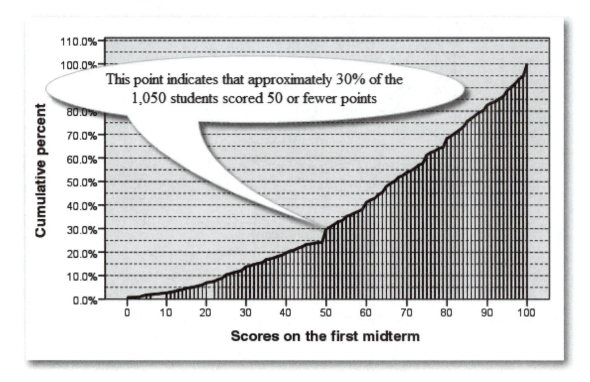

8.2 DATABASES AND QUESTIONS   ★

In this section, you build a histogram that resembles the bell-shaped curve as in Figure 8.1 (presented at the beginning of this chapter). You also build a histogram that displays data that are not normally distributed. Finally, you build a cumulative histogram similar to Figure 8.4.

For the normal and cumulative graphs, you will use the continuous variable *Years of education* as the *x*-axis variable in the **customer_dbase.sav** database. The variable labeled *Years of education* reports the number of years of education completed by the study participants. The non-normally distributed histogram is built using data from the **ceramics.sav** database. The *x*-axis variable is named *temp* and labeled *Degrees centigrade*. Both databases are found in the SPSS Sample file.

We build these three simple histograms to answer several questions about these databases.

8.2.1 Questions for the Simple Histogram (Data Are Normally Distributed)

1. Is the data skewed to the right, skewed to the left, or normal?

2. What are the mean, the standard deviation, and the number of observations in the database?

3. In this database, how many years of education did most of the people complete?

4. In this database, how many years of education did the fewest number of people complete?

8.2.2 Questions for the Simple Histogram (Data Are Not Normally Distributed)

1. Just by looking at the graph, would you say the data are normally distributed?

2. How frequently was the temperature interval of 1,504 to 1,512 observed?

3. What was the temperature interval and the frequency observed the most frequently?

4. What was the temperature interval and frequency of the least observed value in this study?

8.2.3 Questions for the Cumulative Histogram

1. How many years of education mark the middle point of the distribution (the 50th percentile)? This is the point where 50% fall above and 50% fall below this value.

2. Forty percent of the population exceeded how many years of education? (60th percentile)?

3. What are the lower and upper values for the middle 20% (40th to 60th percentile)?

4. A particular employment position required the applicant to have completed 16 years of education. Approximately, what percent of the people would meet this requirement? What is the percentile?

In the following section, you build histograms that provide information needed to answer the above questions concerning our database.

★   **8.3 USING SPSS TO BUILD THE SIMPLE HISTOGRAM**

You may recall that when you built the line graph in Chapter 6 as a way to describe continuous data, we mentioned that a histogram made a more informative graph. Let's build one and see if you agree with our contention.

8.3.1 Building the Simple Histogram (Data Are Normally Distributed)

- Open **customer_dbase.sav** (found in the SPSS Sample files).
- Click **Graphs**, then click **Chart Builder** to open *Chart Builder* window.
- Click **Histogram**, click and drag the **Simple Histogram icon** (the first icon) to the *Chart Preview* panel.
- Click and drag **Years of education** to the *X-Axis* box.
- Click **Display normal curve** in the *Elements Properties* window.
- Click **Apply**.
- Click **OK** (the basic graph now appears in the *Output Viewer*).
- Double click the **graph** to open the *Chart Editor*.
- Click **any number** on the *x*-axis (this click highlights all digits on the *x*-axis).
- In the *Properties* window, click the **Scale tab**, and in the *Range* panel, change *Major Increments* from **5** to **1**.
- Click **Apply**.

- Click the **X** in the upper right-hand box of the *Chart Editor* (the graph is moved to the *Output Viewer*).
- Click the **graph** (a frame appears around the graph), and then click and grab the **lower right corner** of the frame (marked by a small black square), hover the mouse pointer until you see a *double-headed arrow* and move it diagonally up and to the left to reach the approximate size of the graph in Figure 8.5.

Figure 8.5   Histogram for Years of Education (Data Are Normally Distributed)

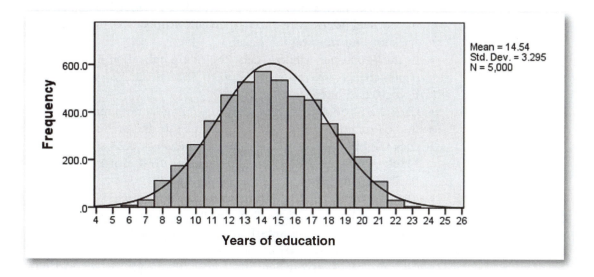

In the following section, you will construct a histogram from data that are not normally distributed.

8.3.2 Building the Simple Histogram (Data Are Not Normally Distributed)

In this section, you build another simple histogram, but this time, it displays data that are not normally distributed.[4]

- Open **ceramics.sav** (found in the SPSS Sample files).
- Click **Graphs**, then click **Chart Builder** to open *Chart Builder* window.

---

[4]We determined that the data failed to meet the specifications of a normal distribution by using SPSS to conduct the Kolmogorov–Smirnov nonparametric one-sample test.

- Click **Histogram**, click and drag the **Simple Histogram icon** (the first icon) to the *Chart Preview* panel.
- Click and drag **Degrees Centigrade** to the *X-Axis* box.
- Click **OK** (*Output Viewer* opens showing the basic graph).
- Double click the basic **graph** in the *Output Viewer*, which opens the *Chart Builder*.
- Click **any number** on the *x*-axis.
- In the *Properties* window, click the **Scale tab**, and in the *Range* panel, change *Major Increments* from **20** to **8**.
- Click **Apply**.
- In the *Properties* window, click the **Number Format tab** and change the decimal places from **2** to **0**, then click **Apply**.
- Click **any number** on the *y*-axis.
- In the *Properties* window, click the **Scale tab**, then in the *Range* panel, change *Maximum* from **60** to **55** and the *Major Increment* from **10** to **5**, then click **Apply**.
- Click the **Show Grid Lines icon** (the fifth icon from the right).
- In the *Properties* window, click the **Lines tab**, and in the *Lines* panel, click the **black arrow** beneath *Weight* then click **0.25**, next click the **black arrow** beneath *Style* and click the **first dotted line**, and finally, click **Apply**.
- Click **any bar of the histogram** (all bars are framed with a faint outline).
- In the *Properties* window, click the **Fill & Border tab**, and in the *Color* panel, click the **small box** to the left of *Fill*, then click the **white rectangular box** to the right.
- Click the **black arrow** beneath *Pattern*, then click the **second pattern** in the **fifth** row.
- Click **Apply**.
- Click the **X** in the upper right-hand corner of the *Chart Editor* (*Chart Editor* closes, and graph is moved to the *Output Viewer*).
- Click the **graph** (a frame appears around the graph) and then click and grab the **lower right corner** of the frame (marked by a small black square), hover the mouse pointer until you see a *double-headed arrow*, and move it diagonally up and to the left to reach the approximate size of the graph in Figure 8.6.
- Double click the **graph** to return to the *Chart Editor*.
- Click **below the legend** (a frame appears), move the mouse pointer over the frame until you see a four-sided arrow, then **drag the legend** into the graph as shown in Figure 8.6.
- Click the **X** in the upper right-hand corner of the *Chart Editor* (*Chart Editor* closes and the finished graph is moved to the *Output Viewer*).

Figure 8.6   Histogram for Degrees Centigrade (Data Are Not Normally Distributed)

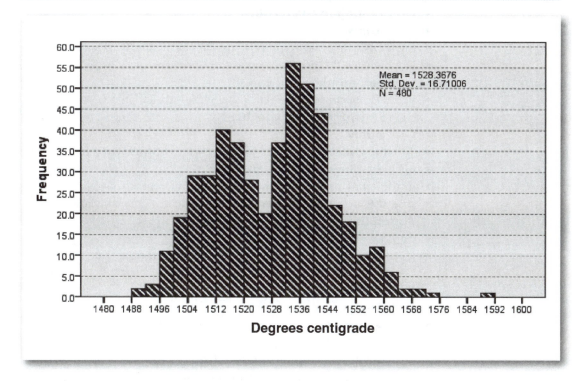

We will soon use this histogram to answer questions about the database.

8.3.3 Building the Cumulative Histogram

We next build the cumulative histogram by following the procedures below. This type of graph is especially useful when the questions about the database seek to divide the measurements into proportional units.

- Open **customer_dbase.sav** (found in the SPSS Sample files).
- Click **Graphs**, then click **Chart Builder** to open the *Chart Builder* window.
- Click **Histogram**, click and drag **Simple Histogram icon** to the *Chart Preview* panel.
- Click and drag **Years of education** to the *x*-axis.

- Click the **black arrow** next to **histogram** in the *Statistics* Panel of the *Element Properties* window.
- Click **Cumulative Percentage**.
- Click **Apply**.
- Click **OK** (the basic graph now appears in the *Output Viewer*).
- Double click the **graph** to open the *Chart Editor*.
- Click **any number** on the *y*-axis.
- In the *Properties* window, click the **Scale tab**, and in the *Range* panel, change *Major Increment* to **10**.
- Click **Apply**.
- With the *y*-axis numbers still framed, click the **Show Grid Lines icon**.
- Click the **Lines tab** in the *Properties* window.
- In the *Lines* panel, click the **black arrow** beneath *Weight* and then click **0.5**, next click the **black arrow** beneath *Style* and click the **first dotted line**, and finally, click **Apply**.
- Click **any number** on the *x*-axis.
- In the *Properties* window, click the **Scale tab**, and in the *Range* panel, change *Minimum* to **6**, *Maximum* to **23**, and *Major Increment* to **1**.
- Click **Apply**.
- Click **any place** on the **graph** to activate the *icons* and *Properties* window.
- Click the **Add interpolation line icon** (the seventh icon in the third row of menu items, or click **Elements** and then click **Interpolation line**).
- In the *Properties* window, click the **Lines tab**, and in the *Lines* panel, click the **black arrow** beneath *Weight* and click **2**.
- Click **Apply** (the interpolation line becomes thicker following this click).
- Click the **X** in the upper right-hand portion of the *Chart Editor* window (Figure 8.7 appears in the *Output Viewer*).
- Click the **graph** (a frame appears around the graph), and then click and grab the **lower right-hand corner** of the frame (marked by a small black square), hover the mouse pointer until you see a *double-headed arrow*, and move it diagonally up and to the left to reach the approximate size of the graph in Figure 8.7.

We explain the interpretation of this particular histogram in the final section when answering the questions about the distribution of years of education.

Figure 8.7   Cumulative Histogram for Years of Education

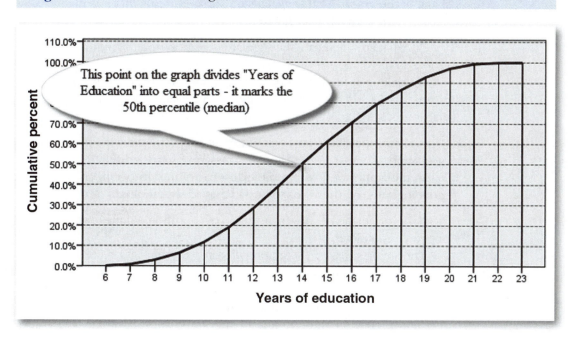

Years of education

8.4 INTERPRETATION OF THE SIMPLE AND CUMULATIVE HISTOGRAMS ★

In this section, we once again see if we were able to make the data more understandable by building the histograms. Let's look at our original questions and see if the histograms provided the information required to answer them.

8.4.1 Questions and Answers: Simple Histogram (Data Are Normally Distributed)

The information needed to answer the following questions is found in Figure 8.5.

1. Are the data skewed to the right, skewed to the left, or normal?
    By looking at the graph, we see that the shape of the graph closely resembles the shape of a bell. The bar in the middle of the graph is the tallest bar, followed by the bars right next to it (on both sides) that gradually diminish in height. The right and left side of the graph are not exactly the same,

but the difference between them is so small that it does not affect the basic shape of the graph. All these characteristics inform us that it is highly likely that we have normally distributed data.[5]

2. What are the mean, the standard deviation, and the number of observations in the database?

By looking at the legend of the graph, we see that the distribution has a mean of 14.54 and a standard deviation of 3.295 and that the number of participants is 5,000.

3. In this database, how many years of education did most of the people complete?

In the graph, we observe the tallest bar of the histogram and its corresponding value on the x-axis to be 14 years of education.

4. In this database, how many years of education did the fewest number of people complete?

The smallest bar of the graph is located on the right half of the histogram. It reveals that the least number of people have 23 years of education. Notice that the bar is very difficult to see as very few attained this level of education, but we could estimate not more than 10.[6] You might also notice that on the left side of the graph there is a bar that is just slightly taller. This second bar represents those individuals who have 6 years of education. The low frequencies of such extreme values are typical of the normal distribution.

8.4.2 Questions and Answers: Simple Histogram (Data Are Not Normally Distributed)

The information needed to answer the following questions is found in Figure 8.6.

1. Just by looking at the graph, would you say that the data are normally distributed?

Most people would say that the data are not normally distributed as it is not a bell-shaped curve.

---

[5]Recall that Kolmogorov–Smirnov is the nonparametric one-sample test to ascertain whether the observed distribution deviates from the normal more than would be expected by chance.

[6]If you required an exact count for such intervals, the easiest solution would be to have SPSS run a frequency count (Analyze>Descriptive>Frequencies).

2. How frequently was the temperature interval of 1,504 to 1,512 observed?

The interval of 1,504 to 1,512 was observed 58 times in this experiment.

3. What were the temperature interval and the frequency that were observed the most?

The interval of 1,532 to 1,536 degrees centigrade was the most frequently observed at 56 times.

4. What were the temperature interval and frequency of the least observed value in this study?

The least observed temperature interval was 1,588 to 1,592, which was observed one time.

8.4.3 Questions and Answers: Cumulative Histogram

The information needed to answer the following questions is found in Figure 8.7.

1. How many years of education mark the middle point of the distribution (the 50th percentile)?

Look at the y-axis value for 50% in the graph and follow the grid line horizontally to the right to the point where it intersects the curve. You then follow the vertical line (parallel to the y-axis) that intersects the curve and follow it down to the value of 14 years of education. This is the 50th percentile, which is the point in the distribution where half fall above it and half fall below it.

2. Forty percent of the population exceeded how many years of education? (60th percentile)?

In Figure 8.7, locate 60% on the y-axis and follow the grid line to the right to the point where it intersects the curve. Follow the vertical line that intersects the horizontal line at the curve downward to the x-axis and read the value of 15 years of education.

3. What are the lower and upper values for the middle 20% (40th to 60th percentile)?

For this question, look at the graph and follow the horizontal lines for 40% and 60% to the curve, read the vertical lines downward to find that the lower value is 13 and the upper is 15.

4. A particular employment position required the applicant to have completed 16 years of education. Approximately what percentage of the people would meet this requirement? What is the percentile?

In the graph, locate 16 years of education, trace the line upward to the curve, then follow the horizontal line to the left, and read 70%. This value informs us that 70% of the people had less than or equal to 16 years of education. We could then state that approximately 30% of the people had 16 years of education. The percentile is the 70th.

★   **8.5 REVIEW EXERCISES**

1. Open the **telco.sav** database found in the SPSS Sample file, select the variable named *Age*, and build the simple histogram in Figure 8.8.

Questions: (a) Is the distribution normal? (b) What are the mean, standard deviation, and number of cases for this distribution? (c) What was the age of approximately 71 people? (d) How many people were aged between 25 and 35? (e) How many in this database were aged 65 and older?

Figure 8.8   Review Exercises: Simple Histogram Age in Years

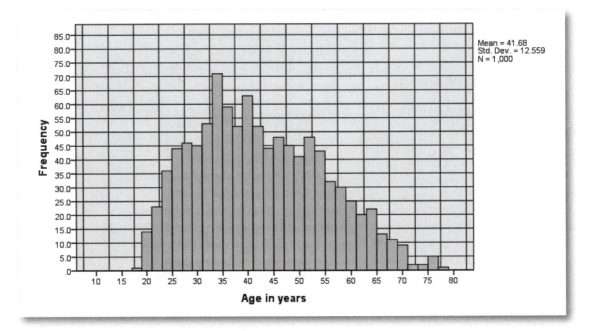

2. Open **customer_dbase.sav** found in the SPSS Sample file, select the variable named *commutetime*, and build the cumulative histogram in Figure 8.9 and answer the following questions.

Questions: (a) What is the range of the commute time for 50% of the individuals? (b) What percentage of the people commuted for 35 to 45 minutes? (c) Ninety percent of the people commuted at least how many minutes? (d) What were the upper and lower limits for the middle 20% (40% to 60%)?

Figure 8.9   Review Exercise: Cumulative Histogram for Time Measured in Minutes

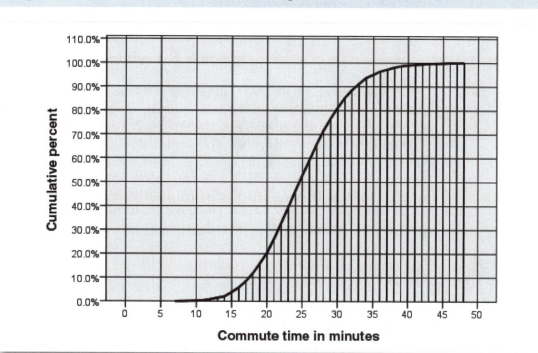

3. Open **autoaccidents.sav** found in the SPSS Sample file, select the variable named *accident* and labeled *Number of accidents* in the past 5 years, and build the simple histogram in Figure 8.10.

Questions: (a) Are the data skewed to the right, skewed to the left, or normal? (b) What are the average number of accidents for this group? (c) How many of this group reported one accident? (d) How many people had four accidents? (e) Of the 500 people in this group, how many had no accidents? (f) How many people had 3 accidents?

Figure 8.10   Review Exercises: Simple Histogram for Number of Accidents

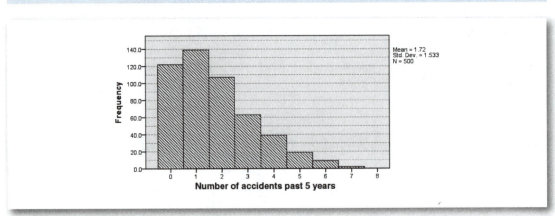

4. Open **autoaccidents.sav** found in the SPSS Sample file, select the variable named *accident* and labeled *Number of accidents past 5 years*, and build the cumulative histogram in Figure 8.11.

Questions (a) Approximately what percentage of people had one or zero accidents? (b) Approximately what percentage of people had three or less than three accidents? (c) How many accidents did the top 25% of the people have? (d) How many accidents did the top 90% of people have? (e) A particular company sells automobile insurance only to those individuals who had two accidents or less. Approximately what percentages of individuals qualify to buy the insurance?

Figure 8.11   Review Exercise: Cumulative Histogram for Accidents in the Past 5 Years

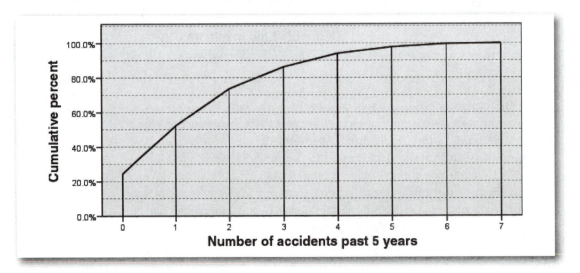

5. Open **broadband_1.sav** found in the SPSS Sample file, select the variable named *Market_1* and labeled *Subscribers for Market 1*, and build the simple histogram in Figure 8.12.

Questions (a) Do the data appear to be normally distributed? (b) What are the mean, the standard deviation, and the number of observations in the database? (c) What is the frequency for the categories between 4,000 and 6,000 subscribers? (d) What is the frequency for the categories between 6,000 and 8,000 subscribers? (e) What is the lowest frequency for the subscribers?

Figure 8.12   Review Exercises: Simple Histogram for Subscribers for Market 1

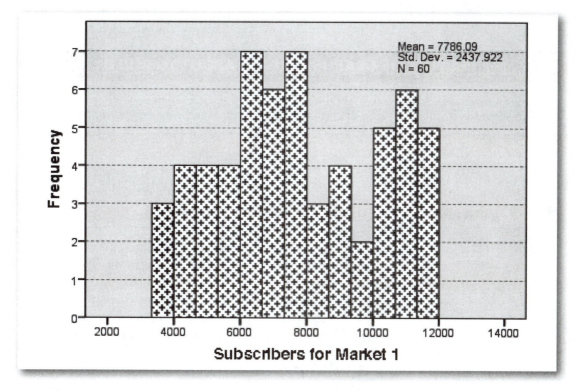

9

POPULATION PYRAMID

PURPOSE OF GRAPHS YOU ARE ABOUT TO BUILD

- To show the distributions of a continuous variable split by a discrete variable
- To show the distributions of a discrete variable split by a second discrete variable

★ 9.1 INTRODUCTION TO THE POPULATION PYRAMID

In the previous chapter, you built and interpreted histograms to display a single continuous variable. The histograms were used to visually describe a distribution of one variable. The description then provided the graph maker with a way to answer questions about the data. In the current chapter, we expand the use of the histogram by adding several dimensions. In the first case, we use the population pyramid to split a single continuous distribution into two separate distributions. The variable used to split the one continuous distribution must be discrete, preferably with two categories, but SPSS can process more than two. This graph will then answer questions about the comparability of the two distributions. An example is provided below that looks at average points earned by students and then splits the distribution of points earned by gender. The graph then provides a visual representation (in mirror imagery) of the two new distributions, making it convenient to visually compare male and female test performance.

Another use of the population pyramid is when you wish to split a discrete distribution into two parts. In the example below, you will see a graph that was built using a discrete variable that has the five grade categories of A, B, C, D, and F. This grade distribution is then split into the two categories consisting of males and females. The graph that is built then answers questions concerning the numbers of males and females earning the various grades.

In this book's Preface, we mentioned certain programming problems when using SPSS Version 20 when building various graphs. The problems become evident in this chapter when attempting to insert different patterns for categories of discrete variables. This feature was available in earlier versions of SPSS. We therefore show graphs built using Version 18 or 19, which result in graphs that we feel present a better picture of the data. However, when the reader builds graphs in Section 3, we use Version 20, which does not permit the selective application of different patterns. We place footnotes throughout this chapter to inform the reader when the various versions are to be used in building these population pyramid graphs.

9.1.1 Continuous Variable Split by a Discrete Variable Into Two Separate Distributions

In this example, we show how the population pyramid can be used to display two continuous distributions in one graph. In other words, the population pyramid provides for a direct visual comparison of two continuous distributions. The two distributions result when a single distribution of values is "split" into two parts. An example would be a single distribution consisting of the total points earned by each of the 1,050 statistics students. It would be possible to easily build a simple histogram, as in the previous chapter, which described the distribution of the total semester points earned by these 1,050 students. With the population pyramid, we can take it a step further and divide the 1,050 cases into two distributions and then compare the two new distributions. Since gender was recorded for these students, we can build a population pyramid showing a distribution describing male students and another for females. These two distributions are placed on the same graph as shown in Figure 9.1. One advantage of having both male and female students on the same graph is that differences can be quickly visualized. Figure 9.1 shows some differences; however, the overall impression is that they are much the same.

It should be noted that the splitting variable (*gender*) was made from a database consisting of 756 (72%) females and 294 (28%) males. When using

Figure 9.1 Population Pyramid for Average Semester Points Split on Gender for 1,050 Students: Horizontal Axis Shows Percentage, Making Distributions Directly Comparable[1]

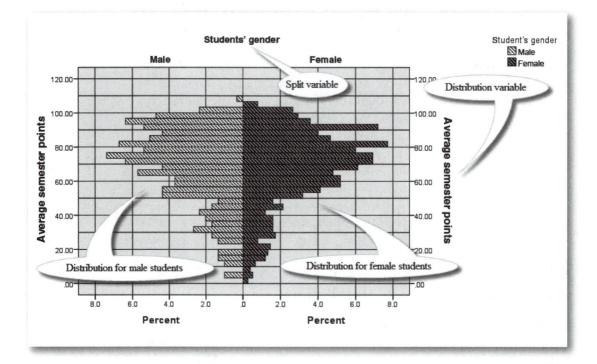

the population pyramid, caution must be exercised when attempting to make a direct comparison between the distributions of the splitting variable. If "frequency" on the horizontal axis (Figure 9.2) had not been changed to percent (Figure 9.1), the graph would be very misleading. If the values of the discrete variable used to split the distribution are not equal, then you will obtain a graph like the one shown in Figure 9.2. If the purpose of building the graph is to simply contrast the differences in the number of cases in the intervals of the continuous variable, then a population pyramid showing frequency most certainly should be used. For instance, by reading Figure 9.2, we could say that there were 20 males scoring 82 average points, while there were 58 females earning this same grade. The value of this information is limited because the

---

[1]Figure 9.1 can be built using versions 18 or 19. Version 20 will not allow the addition of unique patterns for the male and female distributions.

Figure 9.2   Population Pyramid for Average Semester Points Split on Gender of 1,050 Students: Horizontal Axis Shows the Actual Frequency, Making It Unwise to Compare These Distributions[2]

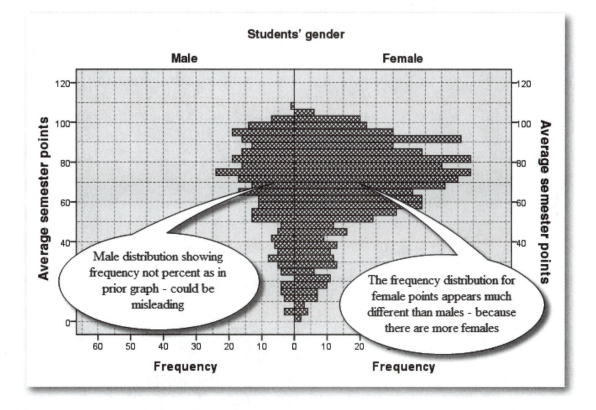

original distribution also recorded many more female students (72% females vs. 28% males). The lesson is that in many cases, you will want to change the *x*-axis to percent to make the data more directly comparable.

9.1.2 Discrete Variable Split Into Two Distributions by a Second Discrete Variable

In this section, we show how the population pyramid can be used to display the values of a discrete variable that has been split into two parts by a second discrete variable. We use another database and select a discrete variable as

[2]Version 20 was used to build this graph resulting in the same pattern for male and female distributions.

the "distribution" variable.[3] The discrete variable has five grade categories of A, B, C, D, and F. These grades represent the final letter grade each student predicts that he or she will earn in the class. This single variable of predicted grade is then split into two parts by the gender variable.

Figure 9.3 shows a graph that permits us to directly observe both gender and the numbers of individuals predicting various grades. You may notice that there are only four categories on the vertical axis. This resulted because no student predicated a grade of F. Another thing to notice is that adding all the data labels results in 37, which is the total number of students participating in the survey. The purpose of building the graph was to determine the number of males and females who predicted various grades. Remember that

Figure 9.3   Population Pyramid for Two Discrete Variables: Gender Is the "Split" Variable and Student's Predicted Grade is the "Distribution" Variable[4]

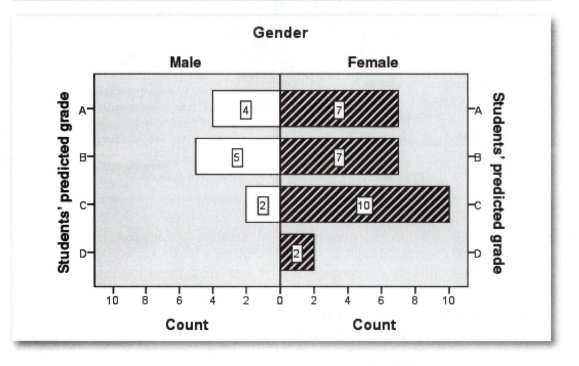

[3]In this sentence, we have placed the word distribution in quotes to bring attention to the fact that this is the terminology used by SPSS in the *Chart Builder*. When you build this graph later in this chapter, you will be required to identify the "distribution" and the "split" variable during the graph-building process.

[4]Version 20 was used to build this graph.

we cannot compare, in a proportional sense, gender differences because the original database did not consist of an equal number of males and females. There were 11 males and 26 females providing answers for this survey.

The graph in Figure 9.3 could be used to mislead the reader of the graph. An example of a misleading statement might go something like this: "The survey indicated that seven female students predicted a grade of "A," while only four males predicted this same grade." Whether the statement was made intentionally or not is of little consequence since the outcome is the same. The lesson is that caution must be exercised when the variable used to split the distribution is not equally divided.

9.2 DATABASES AND QUESTIONS ★

You use two databases to build two types of population pyramids. The first graph built uses data from the **University of Florida graduate salaries.sav** database found in the SPSS Sample files. It is made up of 1,100 cases, each being measured on six variables. There is little known about this database as it is not shown in the SPSS Sample file list.[5] We assume that it is hypothetical data. For building this first population pyramid, we use the continuous variable labeled *Starting salaries* and named *salary*. This is the "distribution" variable. We also use the *Gender* for the discrete variable. This is the "split" variable.

The second population pyramid built uses data from **workprog.sav** consisting of eight variables measured on 1,000 cases. The data are hypothetical and is concerned with government work programs designed to assist the disadvantaged get better jobs. You use two discrete variables from this database to build this graph. The distribution variable is *Level of education* (three categories), while the variable used to split the distribution is *Marital status* (two categories).

9.2.1 Questions: Continuous
Variable Split by a Discrete Variable

1. In the salary range from $30,000 to $32,000, how do the males and females compare?

2. In the category of $8,000 to $10,000 (one of the lowest salary intervals), how do males and females compare?

---

[5]To obtain a more complete description (when available) of SPSS databases go to the Help > Topics > type in "sample files" > click Go > click "sample files" > look at database list.

3. What is the starting salary for exactly 5% of the male population?

4. In general, what does the graph tell us about how the various starting salaries are distributed between the females and males?

9.2.2 Questions: Discrete Variable Split by Another Discrete Variable

1. How many married and unmarried people have a high school degree?

2. Which category of education shows the most difference between married and unmarried?

3. Which category of education contains the most people?

4. Does the population as a whole seem to be well educated?

5. What does the graph tell us about a possible relationship between marital status and level of education?

We now build the graphs that will answer these questions (and others) about our databases and those variables that are the subject of our investigation.

★   ## 9.3 Using SPSS to Build the Population Pyramid

In the following two sections, you build the two types of population pyramid graphs presented in the introduction of this chapter. We begin with the graph that makes it possible to display a continuous variable that has been divided into two parts. It should also be noted that SPSS Version 20 was used to build both graphs shown in this section.

9.3.1 Building the Population Pyramid: Continuous Variable Split by a Discrete Variable

For this graph-building experience, we use the SPSS database called **University of Florida graduate salaries.sav**.

- Open **University of Florida graduate salaries.sav**.
- Click **Graphs**, then click **Chart Builder**.
- Click **Histogram**, click and drag population pyramid (the fourth icon) to the *Chart preview* panel.

- Click and drag the **Gender** variable to the *Split Variable* box.
- Click and drag **Starting Salaries** to the *Distribution Variable* box.
- Click **OK** (*Output Viewer* opens).
- Double click the **graph** (*Chart Editor* opens).

We next follow procedures to first change the horizontal axis to show percentages rather than frequencies. We do this to account for the fact that there are 43% females and 57% males in the database. If the *split variable* was evenly distributed, we could eliminate these procedures.

- Click **any number** on the axis labeled *frequency* (*Properties* window opens).
- Click the **Variables tab** in the *Properties* window.
- Click **percent**, then click the empty **box** to the right of *percent*, click **y-axis** found in the drop-down menu.
- Click **Apply** (graph should now read *Percent* on the horizontal axis).

After changing the graph to show percentages, we can make direct comparisons between the starting salary distributions for male and female university employees. We next present several procedures to enhance the graph that will answer our questions about the database.

- Click on **any number** on the *horizontal* axis.
- In the *Properties* window click the **Number Format tab** and change *Decimal Places* from **1** to **0**.
- Click **Apply**.
- Click **any number** on the **vertical axis** on the **left** side of the graph.
- In the *Properties* window click the **Scale tab** and in the *Range* panel change *Major Increment* to **10,000** and finally click **Apply.**
- Click any **number** on the **vertical axis** on the **right** side of the graph.
- In the *Properties* window, click the **Scale tab**, and in the *Range* panel, change *Major Increment* to **10,000**, and finally, click **Apply**.
- Click the **Show Grid Lines icon** (the fifth icon from the end on the *Chart Editor's* menu).
- In the *Properties* window with the *Grid Lines* tab highlighted, click the **small circle** to the left of *Both major and minor ticks*.
- Click **Apply**.
- Click any of the **Grid lines**.
- In the *Properties* window with the *Lines* tab highlighted in the *Lines* panel, click the **black arrow** beneath *Weight* and click **0.5**, then click the **black arrow** beneath *Style* and click the **first dotted line**.
- Click **Apply**.

- Click **any number** on the *horizontal* axis (Percent).
- Click the **Show Grid Lines icon**.
- In the *Properties* window, click the **Lines tab,** and in the *Lines* panel, click the **black arrow** beneath *Weight* and click **0.5**, then click the **black arrow** beneath *Style* and click the **first dotted line**.
- Click **Apply**.
- Click on any of the **histogram's bars** (a faint frame appears around all bars).
- In the *Properties* window, click the **Fill & Border tab**, and in the *Color* panel, click the **white rectangular box**, then click the **black arrow** beneath *Pattern*, and finally, click the **last pattern** in the **first** row.
- Click **Apply**.
- Click the **X** found in the upper right-hand corner of the *Chart Editor* (Figure 9.4 appears in the *Output Viewer*).

Figure 9.4   Population Pyramid: University of Florida Starting Salaries by Gender

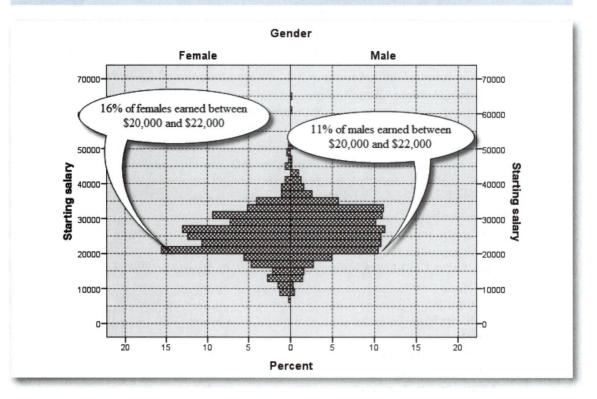

We soon use the graph shown in Figure 9.4 to answer the questions about starting salary and gender. Before doing this, we build the second population pyramid for two discrete variables.

9.3.2 Building the Population Pyramid: Discrete Variable Split by a Discrete Variable

For this graph-building project, you use the SPSS database called **workprog. sav**. There are some situations where the population pyramid is useful in providing a clear representation of two discrete variables. In this section, you build a graph showing the number of individuals in three different categories of education: (1) some college, (2) high school degree, and (3) did not complete high school. The entire distribution consists of 1,000 individuals, with each individual classified as male or female. In this graph-building project, you will use the discrete variable named *ed* and labeled *Level of education* as the *Distribution* variable and *marital* labeled as *Marital status* as the *Split* variable.

- Open **workprog.sav**.
- Click **Graphs**, then click **Chart Builder**.
- Click **Histogram**, click and drag **population pyramid** (the fourth icon) to the *Chart preview* panel.
- Click and drag the **Marital status** variable to the *Split Variable* box.
- Click and drag **Level of education** to the *Distribution Variable* box.
- Click **OK** (*Output Viewer* opens).
- Double click the **graph** (*Chart Editor* opens).
- Click **any number** on the *horizontal* axis (all numbers are highlighted).[6]
- In the *Properties* window, click the **Scale tab**, and in the *Range* panel, change *Minimum* from **50** to **0**.
- Click **Apply**.
- Click any of the **rectangular bars** in the *Unmarried* category (a frame appears around all bars in the graph). Click the **same bar** a second time (only the unmarried category remains framed).
- In the *Properties* window, click the **Fill & Border tab**, and in the *Colors* panel, click the **box** to the left of *Fill*, then click the **white rectangular box**.
- Click **Apply**.
- Click **any bar** in the *Married* category.
- In the *Properties* window with the *Fill & Border* tab highlighted, click the **box** to the left of *Fill*, then click the **white rectangular box** and click the **black arrow** beneath *Pattern*, and finally, click the **third pattern** in the **last** row.
- Click **Apply**.
- Click **any bar** on the graph.
- In the *Properties* window, click the **Categories tab**, then click the **black arrow** to the right of *Marital status* then click **Level of**

---

[6]This and the following two steps are needed when using Version 20 as Versions 18 and 19 automatically set the point of minimum correctly at zero.

education, and in the *Categories* panel, click **Post-undergraduate degree**, finally click the **red X** to the right.
- Click **Apply**.
- Click **any bar** then click **Show Data Labels icon** in the *Chart Editor*.
- Click the **X** in the upper right-hand portion of the *Chart Editor* (*Output Viewer* opens showing Figure 9.5).

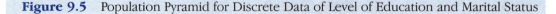

Figure 9.5   Population Pyramid for Discrete Data of Level of Education and Marital Status

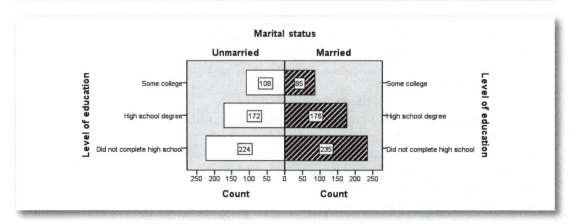

- Click the **Graph** in the *Output Viewer* and a frame appears. You can then adjust the size of your graph by using the techniques described in Section 4.3.3.

★   9.4 INTERPRETATION OF THE POPULATION PYRAMID

In this section, we answer the specific questions about the databases by referring to the just built graphs in Figures 9.4 and 9.5. The first section below answers questions about the situation where we had a continuous "distribution" variable and a discrete "split" variable.

9.4.1 Questions and Answers: Continuous Variable Split by a Discrete Variable

The answers for the questions may be obtained from the information contained in Figure 9.4.

1. In the salary range from $30,000 to $32,000, how do males and females compare?

Examine the graph and direct your attention to the rectangular box that represents the salary range from $30,000 to $32,000. You will see that approximately 11.5% of the males started at these salaries, while 9% of the females started at this same level.

2. In the category of $8,000 to $10,000 (one of the lowest salary intervals), how do males and females compare?

The $8,000 to $10,000 interval in the graph reveals that approximately 0.5% of the males started at this salary level, while 2% of the females did the same.

3. What is the starting salary for exactly 5% of the male population?

On the male side of the graph, we see that the starting salary for 5% of the male population is $18,000 to $20,000.

4. In general, what does the graph tell us about how the various starting salaries are distributed between the females and males.

A small percentage of people start with a salary less than $20,000, most people start with a salary of $20,000 to $34,000, a few start with a salary of $36,000 to $55,000. There are some outliers on the top of the graph that correspond to those who started with a salary of $60,000 or more.

9.4.2 Questions and Answers: Discrete Variable Split by a Discrete Variable

The answers for the questions may be obtained from the information contained in Figure 9.5.

1. How many married and unmarried people have a high school degree?

Look at Figure 9.5 and determine that there are 172 unmarried and 176 married individuals in this database who have earned a high school degree.

2. Which category of education shows the most difference between married and unmarried?

Figure 9.5 shows that the greatest difference between the married and unmarried is in the educational category of "Some college." There were 108 unmarried and 85 married (a difference of 23) in the "Some college" category.

3. Which category of education contains the most people?

The graph in Figure 9.5 shows that the length of the bars for the "Did not complete high school" category is the longest. There are 459 unmarried and married individuals in this category.

4. Does the population as a whole seem to be well educated?

The answer to the previous question provides evidence that the population surveyed is not well educated. Figure 9.5 indicates that almost half (224 + 235 = 459) of the 1,000 individuals did not finish high school. The answer that they are not well educated is contingent on the respondents' place of origin.

5. What does the graph tells us about a possible relationship between marital status and level of education?

Looking at Figure 9.5 and thinking in a proportional manner, we see that there is little difference between levels of education and marital status.[7] We might even say that we strongly suspect that there is no relationship between one's marital status and one's level of education. Looking at marital status by itself would not help in attempting to predicate level of education.

★   **9.5 REVIEW EXERCISES**

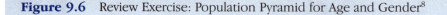

1. Open **1991 U.S. General Social Survey.sav** and select *Respondents sex* as the *split* variable and *age* as the *distribution* variable. Build the population pyramid in Figure 9.6 to compare the continuous variable of *age* split into two groups of *males* and *females*. Hint: Be sure to read the footnote on Figure 9.6 before building this graph.

Questions: (a) What age interval contained the most females? (b) What age interval contained the most males? (c) By looking at the graph, can you estimate

Figure 9.6   Review Exercise: Population Pyramid for Age and Gender[8]

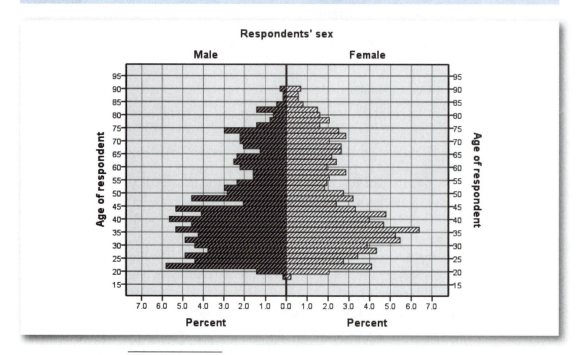

_____

[7]It would be wise to confirm this initial estimate that being married or unmarried is not related to one's level of education by conducting a chi-square test. We conducted the test and found no statistically significant relationship between the two variables.

[8]Version 18 or 19 will produce this graph with the different patterns for the male and female categories as shown in this figure, version 20 will not.

if there is a significant difference between the ages of males and females? (d) What is the gender of those in the oldest and youngest age categories? (e) How would you describe the shape of the distribution of female and male ages?

2. Open **workprog.sav** and select "prog" (Program status) for the split variable and "ed" (Level of education) as the distribution variable. Build the population pyramid in Figure 9.7 to compare these discrete variables split into two groups of program status of *0* and *1*. It has been determined that the categories of *0* and *1* are approximately equal; therefore, these distributions can be directly compared. Hint: Remember to use the *Scale* tab in the *Properties* window to change the *Minimum* to zero if using Version 20.

Questions: (a) By looking at the graph does it appear that program status and level of education are related? (b) Which of the six categories contains the most observations? (c) Which category has the least number of observations?

Figure 9.7 Review Exercise: Population Pyramid for Education and Program Status[9]

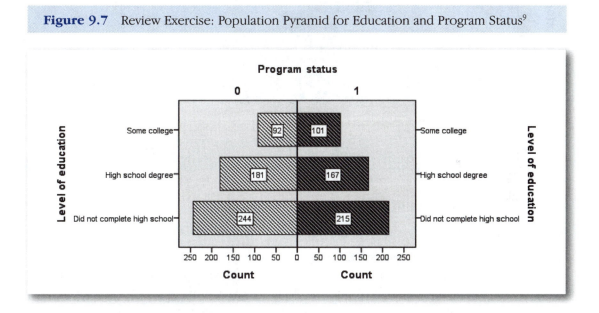

3. Open **customer_dbase.sav** to build the population pyramid in Figure 9.8. Select the continuous variable named *ed* and labeled *Years of education* (Variable 8), and move it to the distribution variable box. Select the discrete variable named *marital* and labeled *Marital status* (Variable 25), and move it to *split* variable. Hint: Version 18 or 19 will produce the graph shown in Figure 9.8.

Questions: (a) What is the most frequently occurring year of education interval for unmarried people? (b) What is the most frequently occurring year of

---

[9]Made using Version 20.

education interval for married people? (c) How many unmarried people have had 9.5 to 10.5 years of education? (d) How many married people have 7.5 to 8.5 years of education? (e) How many unmarried people have 15.5 to 16.5 years of education? (f) By looking at the graph, can you estimate if there is a significant difference between the years of education completed by married and unmarried people?

Figure 9.8   Review Exercise: Population Pyramid for Education and Marital Status[10]

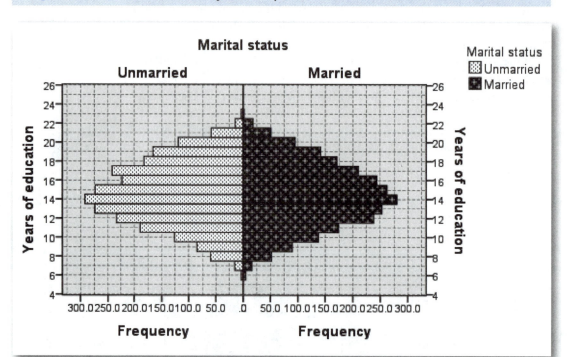

4. Open **satisf.sav** to build the population pyramid in Figure 9.9. Select the discrete variable named *overall* and labeled *Overall satisfaction* (Variable 18), and move it to the distribution variable box. Select the discrete variable named *contact* and labeled *Contact with employee* (Variable 12), and move it to the *Split Variable* box. Hint: Remember to use the *Scale* tab in the *Properties* window to change the *Minimum* to zero if using Version 20.

Questions: (a) How many customers who did not have contact with employee are strongly satisfied? (b) How many customers who had contact with employee are neutral? (c) How do most customers who did not have

---

[10]Version 18 or 19 will produce this graph with the different patterns for the married and unmarried categories.

contact with employee feel? (d) How do most customers who had contact with employee feel? (e) In which satisfaction category is the largest difference? (f) Does the graph suggest that there is a significant difference between the customers who had contact with employee and those who did not?

Figure 9.9   Review Exercise: Population Pyramid for Satisfaction and Employee Contact[11]

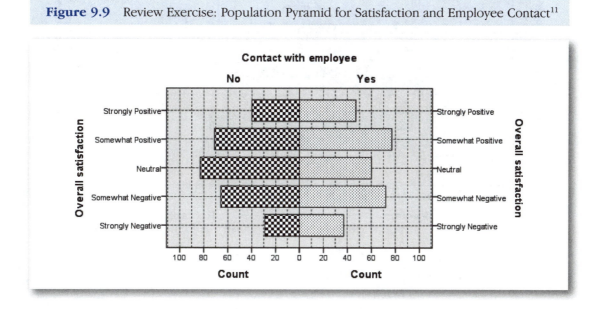

5. Open **workprog.sav** to build the population pyramid in Figure 9.10. Select the continuous variable named *incbef* and labeled *Income before the program* (Variable 4), and move it to the *distribution* variable box. Select the discrete variable named *gender* and labeled *Gender* (Variable 6), and move it to the *split* variable.

Questions: (a) What is the most frequent income for females? (b) What is the most frequently income for males? (c) What percentage of females had an income that ranges from 9.5 to 10.5? (d) What percentage of males had an income that ranges 12.5 to 13.5? (e) Fifteen percent of males had an income of? (f) By looking at the graph can you estimate if there is a significant difference between the income of females and males?

----

[11]Version 20 was used to build this graph.

Figure 9.10   Review Exercise: Population Pyramid for Satisfaction and Employee Contact[12]

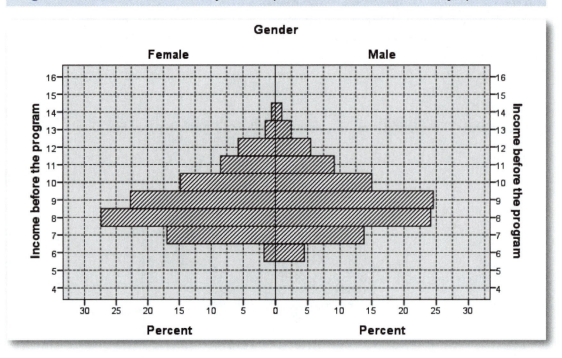

[12]Version 20 was used to build this graph.

10

1-D Boxplot

10.1 Introduction to the 1-D Boxplot ★

In the previous two chapters, which covered the histogram and population pyramid, you built and interpreted graphs that displayed continuous variables. The histograms were used to visually describe a distribution (including some basic statistics) and answer questions about a single variable. The population pyramid described a single continuous variable that was divided into parts by a second discrete variable. We begin this chapter by first describing the type of information conveyed by a boxplot and then comparing it with the histogram. The boxplot and the histogram use different approaches when attempting to decipher a mass of continuous data. The boxplot places an emphasis on variability of the data as measured by various ranges.

10.1.1 1-D Boxplot: Normally Distributed Data

You may recall that in Chapter 8 we presented three histograms (Figures 8.1, 8.2, and 8.3). These graphs were based on hypothetical data created to show the appearance of histograms when data was normally distributed (not skewed) and negatively and positively skewed. In this section, we use these same data to answer questions about the databases but will use the boxplot, not the histogram, to communicate this information. Let's start with the test scores data that were normally distributed. Figure 10.1 shows the appearance of the same data used to build the histogram in Figure 8.1, but this time, the data are displayed as a boxplot.

Figure 10.1 shows the appearance of normally distributed data. The most common axis orientation for the boxplot is to place the x-axis on the vertical where the y-axis is usually found. Figure 10.1 transposes axis orientation to facilitate the visual comparison with the histogram in Figure 8.1. We switch the axis (y to x) frequently in our three boxplot chapters as we believe that it facilitates one's ability to visualize and therefore better understand the data. The test scores that are placed on the horizontal axis in Figure 10.1 are more commonly shown as the vertical axis when using the boxplot. You may wish to jump ahead and look at Figure 10.4 to see the appearance of the boxplot when the measurement is displayed on the y-axis.

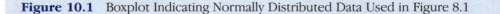

Figure 10.1   Boxplot Indicating Normally Distributed Data Used in Figure 8.1

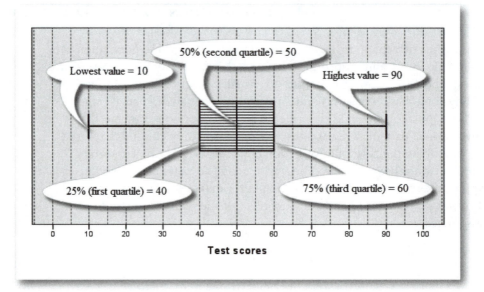

Visualize the histogram in Figure 8.1 as being placed in front of the boxplot in Figure 10.1, and you can get a good idea as to the information conveyed by the boxplot's central box and whiskers. Think of the tails of the normal curve in terms of the whiskers and the interquartile range as being related to standard deviation units. Also remember that the boxplot uses the median as the measure of central tendency rather than the mean as does the histogram. The position of the median is shown in Figure 10.1 and is the middle of the distribution. We see that a test score of 50 occupies the median position. The median is often referred to as the 50th percentile (P_{50}) or the second quartile. The overall appearance of the graph conveys the same "beautiful" picture as the histogram in Figure 8.1. It presents a picture of a well-balanced (symmetrical) distribution of scores. It represents an accurate summary of the hypothetical test scores.

The boxplot is built using the various ranges of the data. Remember that the range is simply the highest value minus the lowest value in the distribution. The central rectangular box, filled with dots, represents the middle 50% of the cases and is known as the interquartile range. The length of this box is the difference between the 25th and 75th percentiles. The size of the box conveys the amount of variability (spread) present in the data. The longer the length of the box, the more the data spreads out from the median. The whiskers that extend out from the end of the box to a perpendicular line represent the highest and the lowest values that are *not* outliers or extreme values.[1]

Before leaving this boxplot, let's consider another bit of information provided by the graph. Look at Figure 10.1 and compare the units of measurement on both sides of the median in terms of their range of the test scores. For instance, we observe that the range of the whisker on the left is 30 (40 − 10), while the range of the right whisker is also 30 (90 − 60). The ranges of the second and third quartiles are identical at 10 units. This observation tells us that we have a well-balanced distribution of values with 40 units of measurement (test scores) on each side of the median.

In summary, we say that a boxplot having equal size boxes on both sides of the median and equal whisker lengths is symmetrical and represents normally distributed data. Of course, this finding is most often happy news for the analyst who is trying to understand the data.

---

[1]*Outliers* are cases that have values between 1.5 and 3 box-lengths beyond the 25th percentile or the 75th percentile. *Extreme* cases represent values that are more than 3 box-lengths beyond the 25th or 75th percentile. If *Outliers* and *extreme* cases are present in the data, they are marked and displayed when using SPSS to build the boxplot. You will see examples of both *outliers* and *extremes* later in this chapter.

10.1.2 1-D Boxplot: Negatively Skewed Data

Figure 10.2 presents an example of data that has a negative skew. This boxplot presents the same "speed of automobiles" data displayed in Figure 8.2 of the histogram chapter. Look at the histogram (Figure 8.2) and picture it as in front of the boxplot shown in Figure 10.2. The uneven boxes on each side of the median, as well as the uneven whiskers, represent a nonsymmetrical distribution of speeds. Furthermore, the fact that the whisker and box on the left are longer indicates that we have a negatively skewed distribution. The negative skew simply means that more cars were travelling at higher rather than at lower speeds. The wider box and longer tail are the same as the longer tail shown on the histogram. When you have the long whisker and/or box to the left of the median, it means that the variability or spread of the data is greater at the lower than at the higher end of the x-axis scale. The shorter whisker and box indicate a high concentration of speeds.

Look at the mathematical differences in the ranges on both sides of the median for the speeds shown in Figure 10.2. The range of the left whisker is 21 (74 − 53), while the right whisker has a range of 3 (95 − 92). The range of the second quartile is 12 (86 − 74), and the range of the third quartile is 6 (92 − 86). We add 21 + 12 = 33 for the range of speeds at the lower end of the scale (left of the median). Repeat this for the right side of the median (higher speeds) and add 3 + 6 = 9. Thus, we have data much more variable for the lower speeds than for the higher speeds. The value of 33 represents

Figure 10.2   Boxplot Indicating Negatively Skewed Data Shown in Figure 8.2

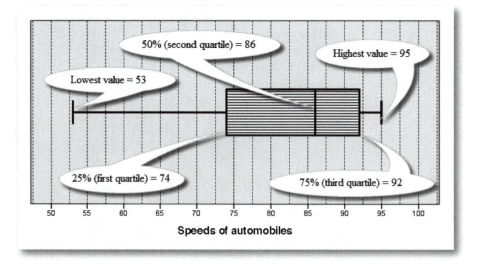

the long tail of a distribution, while the value of 6 indicates a shorter tail representing a high concentration of higher speeds.

Let's summarize the information about the speeds of these automobiles using the boxplot in Figure 10.2. Twenty-five percent of the cars were travelling at speeds between 53 and 74 miles per hour (mph), and 25% were travelling at speeds between 74 and 86 mph. The median value of 86 indicates that 50% of all cars were going between 53 and 86 mph. To the right of the median, we see that 25% of the cars were going faster than 86 up to 92 mph and another 25% were travelling faster than 92 up to 95 mph. We can say that 50% of the recorded speeds fell between 53 and 86 mph and 50% were greater than 86 and up to 95 mph. We can say that more automobiles in this database were going slower than faster. We have a distribution of speeds that is negatively skewed.

10.1.3 1-D Boxplot: Positively Skewed Data

A boxplot as shown in Figure 10.3 represents our hypothetical data for weights of children and is observed to be positively skewed. Figure 10.3 displays the same data shown in Figure 8.3 in the histogram chapter. More values are concentrated at the lower weights. For the histogram (Figure 8.3), this means taller bars on the left, for the boxplot, it means shorter whiskers and/or a shorter box to the left of the median. Once again, the shorter whisker and box represent a higher concentration of values, while the longer box and whisker represent more spread out values.

The visual picture and mathematical differences in the ranges on both sides of the median for children's weights indicate that we have a nonsymmetrical distribution. The range of the left whisker is 1 (111 − 110), while the right whisker has a range of 8 (125 − 117). The ranges of the second quartile is 3 (114 − 111), and the range of the third quartile is 3 (117 − 114). We add 1 + 3 = 4 for the range of weights at the lower end of the scale (left of the median). Repeat this for the right side of the median (higher weights) and add 8 + 3 = 11. Thus, the data indicate that there are more cases of lower weights than higher weights. The value of 11 represents the long tail of a distribution, while the value of 4 indicates a shorter tail representing a high concentration of lower weights.

The boxplot in Figure 10.3 informs us that 25% of the children weigh between 110 and 111 pounds and 25% weigh between 111 and 114 pounds. The median value of 114 indicates that 50% of all children weigh between 110 and 114. To the right of the median, we see that 25% of the children weigh between 114 and 117 and another 25% weigh between 117 and 125 pounds. We can say that we have a distribution of weights that is positively skewed. The boxplot communicated that the children's weights were concentrated at the lighter weights.

Figure 10.3   Boxplot Indicating Positively Skewed Data as Shown in Figure 8.3

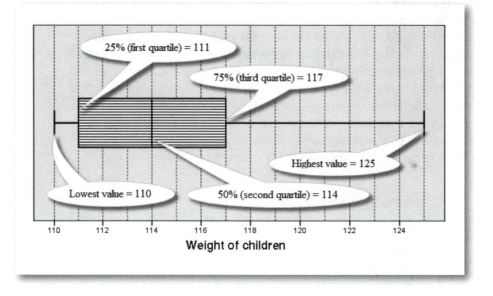

10.1.4 1-D Boxplot: Vertical Orientation

Figure 10.4 presents the final exam scores for 1,050 students. The vertical orientation places the measured variable on the x-axis, differing from the three previous graphs. The orientation for the first three graphs resulted when we instructed SPSS to transpose the axis during the editing process.

   The graph in Figure 10.4 depicts the boxplot with the measured variable on the vertical axis. This is the orientation used by SPSS and many publications. We show it here, so you can see the boxplot's more usual presentation. We prefer the horizontal orientation when using the 1-D Boxplot as we feel that it produces a more familiar picture of the data distribution's shape. To obtain the view we presented in the three preceding graphs, we simply moved the top of the graph 90° clockwise. Later, in this chapter, when you build the boxplot, you may wish to try both horizontal and vertical orientations for the boxplot. In reality, the choice is up to the graph builder as there is no "correct" orientation for the boxplot.

   Of course, the orientation does not influence the amount of information presented, just how it is presented. With our knowledge of the boxplot, we see that the distribution of grades in Figure 10.4 shows a minimum score of zero and a maximum of 115. We also observe that the first quartile is at 45, second quartile (median) is 68, and the third quartile

Figure 10.4   Vertical Orientation for Final Exam Score: SPSS Output Viewer Default Setting

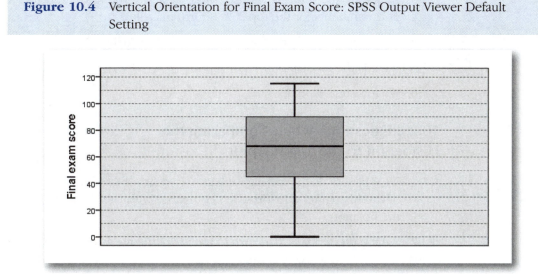

is 90. It also appears to deviate from the normal curve, but further testing would be required to confirm whether or not it is representative of normally distributed data.[2]

10.2 DATABASE AND QUESTIONS ★

You once again use the SPSS Sample file called **workprog.sav**. This database consists of 1,000 cases measured on eight variables. To build the boxplot and answer the questions given below, you use the variable labeled *Income before the program* and named *incbef*. The following questions deal with the distribution of hourly wages recorded for this variable.

10.2.1 Questions for the 1-D Boxplot

1. What are the lower and upper limits, in dollars per hour, for the middle 50% (interquartile values) of this population? And what is the value of the interquartile range?

2. What are the lower and upper limits, in dollars per hour, for the first 25% (first quartile) of the population?

---

[2]The Kolmogorov–Smirnov one-sample nonparametric test told us that the weights are not distributed according to the normal distribution.

3. Excluding the *outliers* and *extremes*, what are the lower and upper dollar amounts for the top 25% (fourth quartile)?

4. Are there any outliers, if so, then what do they tell you?

5. What is the median of the distribution?

6. What is the shape of the distribution?

10.2.2 Questions When Comparing the Histogram to the 1-D Boxplot

1. What pattern do the rectangular bars to the right of the mean (8.9 hours) of the histogram take on when compared with the right whisker of the boxplot?

2. What pattern do the bars take to the left of the mean when compared with the left whisker of the boxplot?

3. What are the measures of central tendency used with the boxplot and histogram?

4. What are the measures of variability for the boxplot and histogram?

5. What advantage of using the boxplot can you identify by looking at these two graphs?

Let's next build a boxplot and histogram and see if we can answer these questions about the income of these respondents and how both graphs convey the needed information.

★   10.3 Using SPSS to Build the 1-D Boxplot

In this section, you build two graphs (boxplot and histogram) using the same database. This process deviates slightly from the normal flow of our book as we are returning to the subject matter of a previous chapter—the histogram. Our purpose is to provide a way for you to more directly and visually compare the information communicated by these two important graphing procedures. Let's start with the boxplot.

10.3.1 Building the 1-D Boxplot

We first build the boxplot shown in Figure 10.5 by following the procedures given next.

- Open **workprog.sav** (found in the SPSS Sample files).
- Click **Graphs**, then click **Chart Builder** to open *Chart Builder* window.
- Click **Boxplot**, click and drag the **1-D Boxplot icon** (the third icon) to the *Chart Preview* panel.
- Click and drag **Income Before the Program** to the *X-Axis* box (remember, that for this type graph, SPSS places the *x*-axis on the vertical line).
- Click **OK** (the basic graph now appears in the *Output Viewer*).
- Double click the **graph** to open the *Chart Editor*.
- Click the **Transpose chart coordinate system icon** (the second icon from the right end of the top menu bar).
- Click the **Show Grid Lines icon** (the fifth icon from the right).
- In the *Properties* window, click the **Lines tab**, and in the *Lines* panel, click the **black arrow** beneath *Weight* and click **0.25**, then click the **black arrow** beneath *Style* and click the **first dotted line**.
- Click **Apply**.
- Click **any whisker** of the boxplot (a faint line appears around both whiskers).
- If the *Properties* window is not open, click the **Properties window icon** (the third icon from the left).
- In the *Properties* window, click **Lines tab** if not already highlighted.
- In the *Lines* panel, click the **black arrow** beneath *Weight*, click **2**, then click **Apply**.
- Click **any number** on the *x*-axis.
- In the *Properties* window, click the **Scale tab**, then change *Major Increment* to **1**.
- Click **Apply**.
- Click the **interquartile range box** (*Properties* window opens with *Fill & Border* tab highlighted).
- In the *Color* panel, click the **white rectangular box**.
- Click the **black arrow** beneath *Pattern*, then click the **first pattern** in the **second** row.
- Click **Apply**.
- Click the **title** (a faint frame appears around the title), click the **title** a second time and edit it to read **Income before the program (dollars per hour)**.
- Click the **X** in the upper right-hand corner of the *Chart Editor* (graph is moved to the *Output Viewer*).
- Click the **graph** (a frame appears around the graph) and then click and grab the **lower right corner** of the frame (marked by a small black square), hover the mouse pointer until you see a *double-headed arrow* and move it diagonally up and to the left to reach the approximate size of the graph in Figure 10.5.

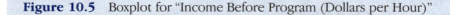

Figure 10.5   Boxplot for "Income Before Program (Dollars per Hour)"

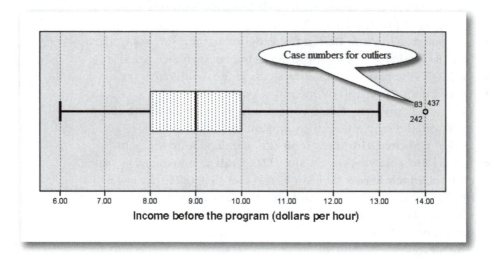

We soon use this boxplot to address the questions and provide answers in the interpretation section.

10.3.2 Building a Histogram to Compare With the 1-D Boxplot

At this point, we deviate slightly from the normal pattern of the book. You build a histogram using the same data as above to emphasize the comparability of these two important graphing procedures.

- Open **workprog.sav** (found in the SPSS Sample files).
- Click **Graphs**, then click **Chart Builder** to open *Chart Builder* window.
- Click **Histogram**, click and drag the **Simple Histogram icon** to the *Chart Preview* panel.
- Click and drag **Income before the program** to the *X-Axis* box.
- Click **OK** (the basic graph now appears in the *Output Viewer*).
- Double click the **graph** to open the *Chart Editor*.
- Click the **title** (a faint frame appears around the title), click the **title** a second time and change it to read **Income before the program (dollars per hour)**.
- Click **any number** on the *x*-axis.

- In the *Properties* window, click the **Scale tab**, then change *Major Increment* to **1**.
- Click **Apply**.
- Click **anywhere** on the **graph** (this removes frames from the *x*-axis numbers).
- Click the **Show Grid Lines icon** (*Major ticks only* is the SPSS default setting).
- Click **any of the bars** (a faint frame appears around all bars in the histogram).
- In the *Properties* window, click the **Fill & Border tab**.
- In the *Color* panel, click the **white rectangular box**.
- Click the **black arrow** beneath *Pattern*, then click the **first pattern** in the **second** row.
- Click **Apply**.
- Click **below the legend** (a frame appears around it), then hit the delete key on your computer keyboard to delete the *legend*.
- Click the **X** in the upper right-hand corner of the *Chart Editor*, this click closes the *Chart Editor* and the graph is moved to the *Output Viewer*.
- Click the **graph** (a frame appears around the graph), and then click and grab the **lower right corner** of the frame (marked by a small black square), hover the mouse pointer until you see a *double-headed arrow* and move it diagonally up and to the left to reach the approximate size of the graph in Figure 10.6.

Figure 10.6   Histogram Made to Compare With Previous Figure

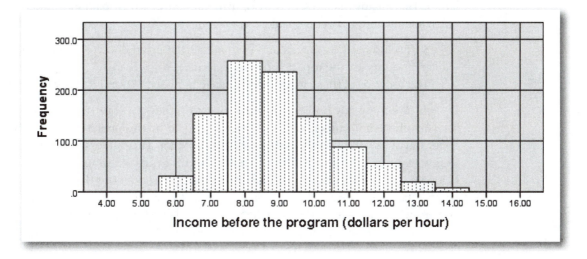

Examine Figures 10.5 and 10.6 and compare the information that is communicated by both. Take special notice of the whiskers as related to the tails of the histogram.

Let's now see if we can answer our questions concerning the many values that make up this continuous variable.

★   10.4 INTERPRETATION OF THE 1-D BOXPLOT

We next answer our original questions by looking at the two graphs just built.

10.4.1 Questions and Answers: 1-D Boxplot

Information to answer the following questions may be found in Figure 10.5.

1. What are the lower and upper limits, in dollars per hour, for the middle 50% (interquartile values) of this population? And what is the value of the interquartile range?

The graph informs us that the middle 50% of this population earned between $8 and $10 per hour. The value of the interquartile range is $10 − 8 = \$2$ per hour.

2. What are the lower and upper limits, in dollars per hour, for the first 25% (first quartile) of the population?

The lowest wage is $6 per hour; the highest for this first quartile is $8 per hour. This means that 25% of the population and the lowest paid individuals earn somewhere between $6 and $8 per hour.

3. Excluding the *outliers* and *extremes*, what are the lower and upper dollar amounts for the top 25% (fourth quartile)?

The top 25% of these wage earners make between $10 and $13 per hour.

4. Are there any outliers, if so then what do they tell you?

Yes there are outliers and extremes as shown by the presence of numbers and one symbol on the right side of the boxplot. The outliers report that a few workers earn more than 1.5 times the interquartile range, which is $3 (2 × 1.5). For these data, this means that they earned more than $13 per hour. The extremes result when cases exceed three times the interquartile range, which in this study is $6 (2 × 3). The data show that we had one extreme case of an individual earning in excess of $19 (13 + 6) per hour.

5. What is the median of the distribution?

The median for these wages is $9 per hour. This means that 50% of the population earn $9 or less, while the other 50% earn more than $9 per hour. This point in the distribution is also known as the 50th percentile (P_{50}) and also the second quartile.

6. What is the shape of the distribution?

This distribution deviates, more than would be expected by chance, from what is considered as normally distributed data. Looking at Figure 10.5, one can easily spot the long whisker on the right, which would suggest that a test for normality would be wise.

10.4.2 Questions and Answers: Comparing the Histogram to the 1-D Boxplot

Information to answer the following questions may be found in Figure 10.6.

1. What pattern do the rectangular bars to the right of the mean (8.9 hours) of the histogram take on when compared with the right whisker of the boxplot?

The rectangular bars slowly and systematically decrease in height when going outward and to the right from the mean. This differs from the other side of the mean, which actually increases in height then drops a small amount. This indicates that the tail of this distribution is long on the right side, which corresponds with the long whisker. We have a positively skewed distribution with many values bunched up toward the vertical axis.

2. What pattern do the bars take to the left of the mean when compared with the left whisker of the boxplot?

To the left of the mean, the height of the bars in the histogram increases slightly then rapidly drops to the x-axis. This observation informs us that we have a short tail for the normal curve and a short whisker for the boxplot.

3. What are the measures of central tendency used with the boxplot and histogram?

The boxplot uses the median, while the histogram uses the mean as measures of central tendency.

4. What are the measures of variability for the boxplot and histogram?

The boxplot uses ranges to measure variability, while the histogram uses standard deviations.

5. What advantage of using the boxplot can you identify by looking at these two graphs?

The boxplot identifies any outliers and extremes that the histogram does not. Knowing your outliers and extremes can prove very useful in guiding further investigation on the database.

★   **10.5 REVIEW EXERCISES**

1. Open SPSS Sample file **autoaccidents.sav** and select the variable named *age* having the label of *Age of insured*. Build the 1-D boxplot in Figure 10.7 and answer the following questions.

Questions: (a) What are the minimum and maximum ages, excluding outliers and extremes? (b) What is the age of the outlier? (c) What are the limits of the interquartile range? (d) What is the interquartile range for this age distribution? (e) What is the median value? (f) Does the graph depict normally distributed data or perhaps a negative or positive skew?

Figure 10.7   Review Exercise: 1-D Boxplot for Age of Insured Driver

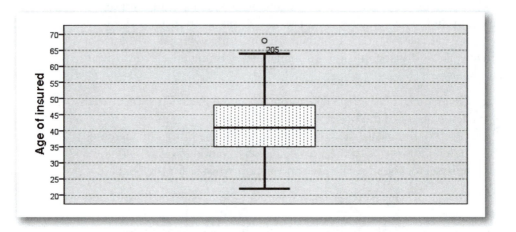

2. Open **contacts.sav** found in the SPSS Sample file and select *Amount of last sale* (named *sale*) and build the 1-D boxplot shown in Figure 10.8 to answer the following questions.

Questions: (a) What are the minimum and maximum amounts spent, excluding outliers and extremes? (b) How much was the sale for the most extreme case?? (c) What are the limits of the interquartile range? (d) What is the interquartile range for this distribution? (e) What is the median value? (f) Does the graph depict a normally distributed data or perhaps a negative or positive skew?

Figure 10.8   Review Exercise: 1-D Boxplot for Amount of Last Sale

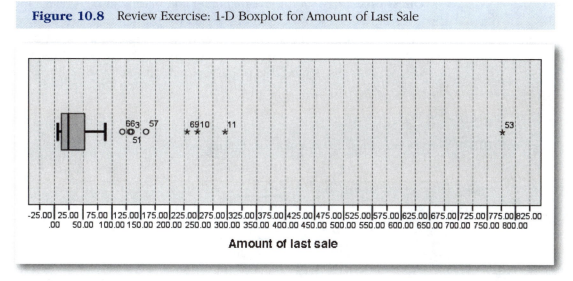

3. Open **contacts.sav** found in the SPSS Sample file and select *Time since last sale* (named *time*) and build the 1-D boxplot shown in Figure 10.9 to answer the following questions.

Questions: (a) What are the minimum and maximum amount of time passing since the last sale? (b) What are the limits of the interquartile range? (c) What is the interquartile range for this distribution? (d) What is the median value? (e) Does the graph depict a normally distributed data or perhaps a negative or positive skew?

Figure 10.9   Review Exercise: 1-D Boxplot for Time Since Last Sale

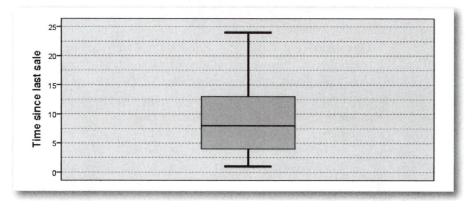

4. Open **stocks2004.sav** and select the continuous variable named *High* for the vertical variable (now called the *x*-axis by SPSS). Build the 1-D boxplot as in Figure 10.10 and answer the following questions.

Questions: (a) What are the minimum and maximum high values for the price of this stock? (b) What are the limits of the interquartile range for this stock's high price? (c) What is the interquartile range for this distribution? (d) What is the median value for the selected stock? (e) Does the graph depict a normally distributed data or perhaps a negative or positive skew?

Figure 10.10   Review Exercises: 1-D Boxplot for the High Variable

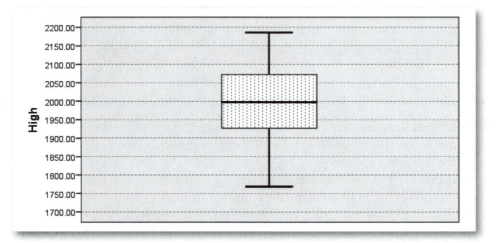

5. Open **Employee data.sav** and select the continuous variable named *salbegin* and labeled *Beginning salary* for the vertical variable (now called the *x*-axis by SPSS). Build the 1-D boxplot in Figure 10.11 and answer the following questions.

Questions: (a) What are the minimum and maximum dollar values for the beginning salaries when outliers are omitted? (b) What are the limits of the interquartile range for this salary data? (c) What is the interquartile range for this distribution? (d) What is the median value for the salaries? (e) What is the dollar amount of the most extreme salary?

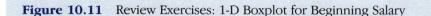

Figure 10.11   Review Exercises: 1-D Boxplot for Beginning Salary

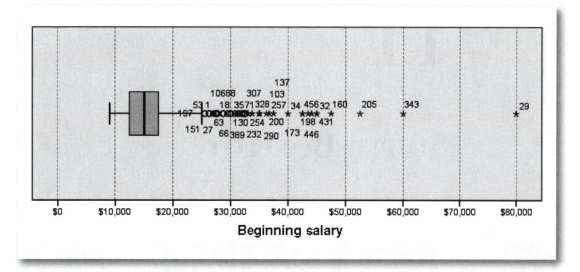

11

SIMPLE BOXPLOT

PURPOSE OF GRAPHS YOU ARE ABOUT TO BUILD

- To compare the variability of a continuous variable categorized by a discrete variable

★ 11.1 INTRODUCTION TO THE SIMPLE BOXPLOT

First, we advise you not to be misled by what we consider to be a confusing name especially when this graph is compared with the 1-D boxplot described in the previous chapter. The simple boxplot discussed in this chapter is not as "simple" as the 1-D boxplot. The simple boxplot is not more difficult to build; however, it does convey considerably more information making it much more complex than the 1-D boxplot.

The simple boxplot displays the same five statistics as you did in the previous chapter (minimum, first quartile, median value, third quartile, and maximum value). Recall that these statistics were calculated for a single continuous variable. In that chapter, we used a single continuous variable, but the simple boxplot takes it a step beyond. The simple boxplot displays the same five statistics but separates the continuous variable into the several categories of a discrete variable. For an example of the simple boxplot, look at Figure 11.1 that uses data describing 1,050 students in terms of test performance (score on final exam) and hour of their class.

Figure 11.1 Simple Boxplot Displaying a Continuous (Scores) and Discrete (Time) Variable

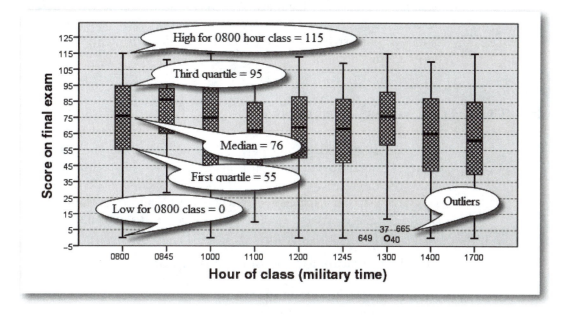

The authors have chosen the default vertical orientation for this graph. You see a discrete variable with its nine categories (hour of class) displayed on the horizontal axis. The continuous variable is score on the final exam (vertical axis), which ranges from 0 to 125. The −5 value on the vertical axis represents a graph-editing procedure to eliminate the lower whiskers from landing directly on the horizontal axis. We can assure you that the professor did not issue minus points on the exams.

Figure 11.1 shows nine separate box and whisker plots, each giving the same statistics as the 1-D boxplot in the previous chapter. In this figure, you see our information bubbles giving the values for just one of the nine categories of this variable. For the 0800 hour (8 a.m.) class students scored between 0 and 115 points. The middle 50% scored between 55 and 95 points; thus, the interquartile range is 40 points (95 − 55). The median value for the entire grade distribution of the 0800 hour class is 76. We can say that the lowest scoring 25% earned between 0 and 55 points, while the highest scoring 25% earned between 95 and 115.

Remember that the statistics given in the preceding paragraph are for only one class time. By carefully reading the graph, you have these same statistics for all nine class times. The major purpose of this graph is to permit a convenient way to visually compare *all* nine class times on these five statistics at the same time. The analyst can look for differences and then conduct further investigations to establish plausible explanations for differences. In an experimental research approach, you might specify expected differences before the analysis. Regardless of your research approach, under certain conditions, various statistical tests could be conducted to determine if differences are significant or due to chance fluctuations in the data.[1]

★   11.2 DATABASE AND QUESTIONS

For your simple boxplot-building experience, you use the **1991 U.S. General Social Survey.sav** consisting of 1,517 cases measured on 43 variables. The discrete variable is labeled *Race of respondent* and named *race*. This variable has three categories of White, Black, and Other. The continuous variable for this exercise is labeled *Age of respondent* and named *age*.

11.2.1 Questions for the Simple Boxplot

1. What are the median ages, ranked from the lowest to the highest, for the three race categories?

2. What are the race category, age, and gender of the one outlier in the graph? (Notice that you must first examine the graph and then check the database to answer this question.)

3. What are the ranks, from the lowest to the highest, for the three race categories in terms of overall ranges of ages? (Give the values for these three ranges.)

4. What are the interquartile ranges for the "White," "Black," and "Other" race categories? (Exclude the outlier from your calculations.)

5. Just by looking at the graph, what can you say about the distributions?

In the next section, you will build the simple boxplot graph that will answer questions about this variable.

---

[1]There are different statistical tests that might be used if one wished to determine if the statistics varied significantly between meeting times for these classes. For instance one may want to determine if the medians differed significantly by using the independent-samples Kruskal–Wallis test. Perhaps, you may wish to check for significant differences in variability for the nine distributions by using a chi-square test of equality.

11.3 USING SPSS TO BUILD THE SIMPLE BOXPLOT   ★

In this section, you will build the basic simple boxplot and then use the *Chart Editor* to make one similar in appearance to the graph shown in Figure 11.1.

- Open **1991 U.S. General Social Survey.sav** (found in the SPSS Sample files).
- Click **Graphs**, then click **Chart Builder** to open *Chart Builder* window.
- Click **Boxplot**, click and drag the **Simple Boxplot** (the first icon) to the *Chart preview* panel.
- Click and drag **Race of Respondent** to the *X-Axis* box.
- Click and drag **Age of Respondent** to the *Y-Axis* box.
- Click **OK** (the basic graph now appears in the *Output Viewer*).
- Double click the **graph** to open the *Chart Editor*.
- Click **any number** on the *y*-axis.
- In the *Properties* window, click the **Scale tab**, then in the *Range* panel, change *Major Increment* to **10**.
- Click **Apply**.
- Click the **Show Grid Lines icon** (the fifth icon from the right).
- In the *Properties* window, click the **Lines tab**, and in the *Lines* panel, click the **black arrow** beneath *Weight* and click **0.25**, then click the **black arrow** beneath *Style* then click the **first dotted line**.
- Click **Apply**.
- Click on **any whisker of a boxplot** (a faint line appears around all whiskers).
- If *Properties* window is not open, click the **Properties Window icon**.
- In the *Properties* window, click the **Lines tab**, and in the *Lines* panel, click the **black arrow** beneath *Weight*, then click **2**.
- Click **Apply**.
- Click **any boxplot box** (a faint frame appears around all boxes).
- In the *Properties* window, make sure that the *Fill & Border* tab is highlighted.
- In the *Color* panel, click the **white rectangular box**.
- In the *Color* panel, click the **black arrow** beneath *Pattern*, and click the **first pattern** in the **second** row.
- Click **Apply**.
- Click the **X** in the upper right-hand corner of the *Chart Editor* (graph is moved to the *Output Viewer*).

- Click the **graph** (a frame appears around the graph), and then click and grab the **lower right corner** of the frame (marked by a small black square), hover the mouse pointer until you see a *double-headed arrow*, and move it diagonally up and to the left to reach the approximate size of the graph in Figure 11.2.

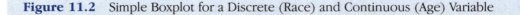

Figure 11.2 Simple Boxplot for a Discrete (Race) and Continuous (Age) Variable

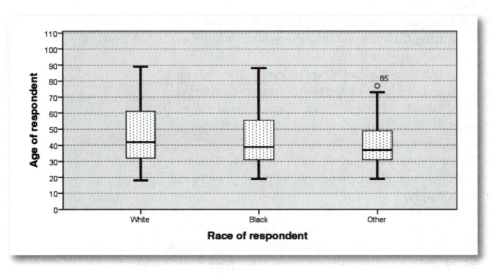

★ **11.4 INTERPRETATION OF THE SIMPLE BOXPLOT**

This section repeats those questions presented earlier (Section 11.2.1) but this time with the answers provided by the information presented in the graph just built.

11.4.1 Questions and Answers for the Simple Boxplot

The information to answer the following questions may be found in Figure 11.2.

1. What are the median ages, ranked from lowest to highest, for the three race categories?

The youngest median age of 36 years is for the "Other" race category, next is for "Black" at 39, and finally, the oldest median age is for the "White" category at 42.

2. What are the race category, age, and gender of the one outlier in the graph? (Notice that you must first examine the graph and then check the database to answer this question.)

The one outlier shown on the graph is for the "Other" race category and is labeled as Case Number 85. If the database is not open do so now, go to Case Number 85 and determine that this respondent is a female and aged 77.

3. What are the ranks, from the lowest to highest, for the three race categories in terms of overall ranges of ages? (Give the values for these three ranges.)

The lowest range for age is found in the "Other" category at 55 (73 – 18) and the next lowest is for the "Black" category at 69 (88 – 19). Those with the largest range is the white category at 71 (89 – 18).

4. What are the interquartile ranges for the "White," "Black," and "Other" race categories? (Exclude the outlier from your calculations.)

The "White" category interquartile age range is 61 (third quartile) – 32 (second quartile) = 29 years. The "Black" category has an interquartile range of 55 (third quartile) – 31 (second quartile) = 24 years. Finally, the "Other" category has an interquartile range of 49 (third quartile) – 31 (second quartile) = 18 years.

5. Just by looking at the graph, what can you say about the distributions?

The distributions appear to be roughly the same shape with all having a slight to moderate degree of positive skew.

11.5 REVIEW EXERCISES   ★

1. Open **ceramics.sav** in the SPSS Sample files. Select a discrete variable named *batch* and labeled *Alloy*. This variable has two categories, 1 = *premium* and 2 = *standard*. The continuous variable is named *temp* and labeled *Degrees centigrade*. Build the simple boxplot in Figure 11.3 and answer the following questions. (Hint: you will have to make some changes in the *Chart Editor* > *Properties* window > *Scale* tab > *Range* panel > *Minimum* = 1,486, *Maximum* = 1,592, *Major Increment* = 10, and *Origin* = 0.)

Questions: (a) What are the median heat values for both batches? (b) What are the minimum and maximum heats for the premium batch (exclude the outliers)? (c) What are the minimum and maximum temperatures for the standard batch? (d) Which of the two batch types show the more normal distribution?

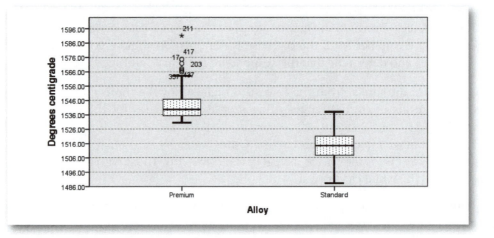

2. Open **car_sales.sav** and select the discrete variable named *type* and labeled *Vehicle type*. The continuous variable is named *resale* and labeled *4-year resale value*. Build the simple boxplot as in Figure 11.4 and answer the following questions.

   Questions: (a) Which distribution approximates the normal distribution? (b) Which of the two distributions has the highest median resale value and what is this value? (c) What are the highest resale values for trucks and automobiles when outliers and extremes are excluded? (d) What is the interquartile range for automobiles? (e) What are the minimum and maximum values for the resale value of the middle 50% of the trucks?

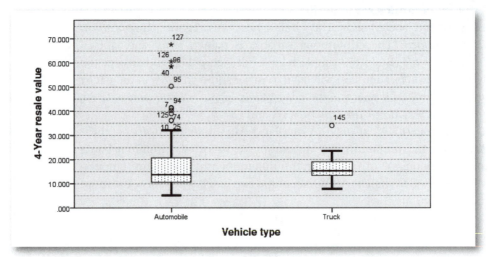

3. Open **Employee data.sav**, and select *gender* as the discrete variable. Select the continuous variable named *Salary* and labeled *Current salary*. Build the simple boxplot in Figure 11.5 and answer the following questions.

Questions: (a) What is the value of the most extreme value in the male salary distribution? (b) What is the most extreme salary for the females? (c) If you exclude the outliers and extremes, what are the highest and lowest salaries for the males? (d) Excluding the outliers and extremes, what are the high and low salaries for females? (e) What are the median salaries for males and females?

Figure 11.5 Review Exercises: Simple Boxplot for Current Salary and Gender

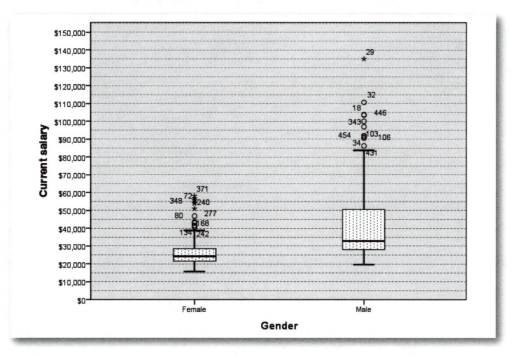

4. Open **credit_card.sav** from the SPSS Sample file, and select *Type of transaction* as the discrete variable. Select the continuous variable named *spent* and labeled *Amount spent*. Build the simple boxplot in Figure 11.6 and answer the following questions.

Questions: (a) What type of transaction has the largest interquartile range, and what is that value? (b) Which type of transaction recorded the highest expenditure as measured by the median, and what was that amount? (c) Which type of transaction recorded the highest expenditure, and what was that amount? (d) Rank from high to low the types of transactions and their maximum spent. (e) Which transaction type has the highest minimum expenditure, and what is that amount?

Figure 11.6   Review Exercise: Simple Boxplot for Amount Spent and Transaction Type

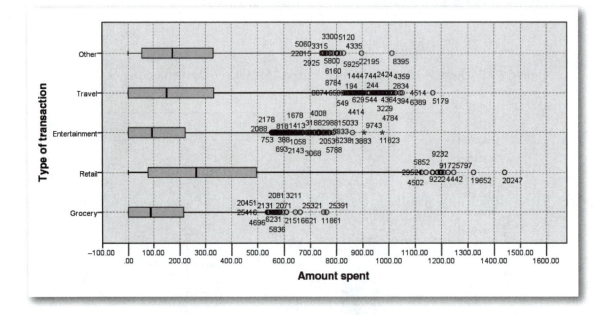

5. Open **credit_card.sav** from the SPSS Sample file, and select *gender* as the discrete variable. Select the continuous variable named *spent* and labeled *Amount spent*. Build the simple boxplot in Figure 11.7 and answer the following questions.

Questions: (a) Which gender has the largest interquartile range, and what are both these values? (b) Which gender recorded the highest expenditure as measured by the median, and what was that amount? (c) Which gender recorded the highest expenditure, and what was that amount? (d) Excluding the outliers and extreme values, which gender had the maximum expenditure and what is that amount? (e) Which gender has the highest minimum expenditure, and what is that amount?

Figure 11.7   Review Exercise: Simple Boxplot for Amount Spent and Gender

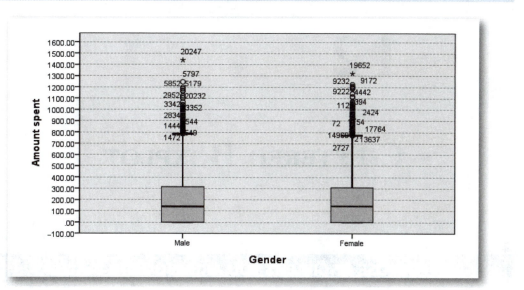

12

Clustered Boxplot

★ 12.1 Introduction to the Clustered Boxplot

In the last two chapters, we presented two types of boxplots. The first was the 1-D boxplot, which displayed the upper and lower limits, second and third quartiles, the median, and finally, the extreme and outlier cases for a single continuous variable. The second type was called the simple boxplot and was used to describe a single continuous variable but added a new twist. The continuous variable was separated into various parts by the categories of a discrete variable. For instance, you may have a continuous distribution of automobile speeds and then divide it into male and female categories by using the discrete variable of gender.

In this chapter, you will learn to use a third type of boxplot known as the clustered boxplot. It is similar to the clustered *bar* graph you built in Section 4.3.2. As with the clustered bar graph, we take a single continuous variable, divide its values using a discrete variable, and then divide the new divisions once again. It may sound complicated but is really quite straightforward. The clustered boxplot differs from the clustered *bar* graph in that you plot, and then visualize, a different set of statistics. You learn other things about the variables you are investigating. The major statistics generated while using the clustered boxplot convey information about the variability or how the data may be spread out or concentrated around a central value.

An example of this graph is shown in Figure 12.1, which uses the same data used to build the clustered bar graph shown in Figure 4.2. To get a clear picture of the information differences in these two graph types, you may wish to compare the graph depicted in Figure 12.1 with Figures 4.2 and 4.6.

The data used to build the graphs pictured in Figures 12.1 and 4.2 resulted from the records of 1,050 students. On the *x*-axis, you see the discrete variable of *dichotomized class time*, which is divided into two categories, day and evening. The other discrete variable is *gender*, which has the two categories of male and female. In *Chart Builder* terminology, gender is the *legend* or *color* variable. The single continuous variable is *score on the final exam* and is found on the *y*-axis.

When looking at Figure 12.1, you may notice that there are no grid lines. We did this to show how clean and uncluttered the graph may appear. It does, however, make its interpretation of specific values more difficult. You

Figure 12.1   Clustered Bar Graph: Two Discrete and One Continuous Variable

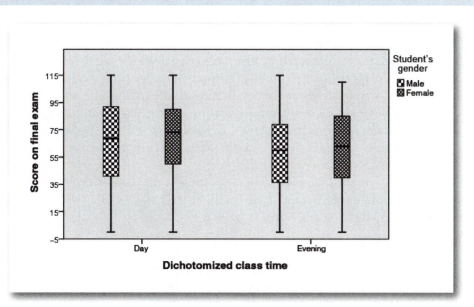

may wish to build one with grids to make it easier to locate values on the *y*-axis (as we did) and another for presentation to an audience.

When looking at Figure 12.1, you see four separate boxplots that describe four distributions created by SPSS by following directions of the graph maker. Let's look at the first box and whisker plot (left side) and examine the information it conveys. After doing this, we take it a step further and show how to make comparisons between all possible combinations of these four unique distributions.

The first plot is calculated on the distribution of scores when all students enrolled in *day* classes are divided by gender. Thus, we have a box and whisker plot that describes the performance on the final exam (scores) for male students who attended one of the day classes. What can we learn from this single boxplot? By looking at the top and bottom whiskers and the *y*-axis, we see that the male daytime students scored from 0 to 115 points on the final exam. By directing our attention to the checkered box, we see that the middle 50% scored between 97 and 41 points. If we subtract the lowest from the highest value we have the interquartile range of 56 (97 – 41). We can also say that this distribution has no outliers or extreme values. We cannot forget the important measure of central tendency—the median. The position of the median is indicated by the solid, black, horizontal line running through the checkered box, and for its value, read the *y*-axis at 68 points. Furthermore, we may say that the shape of the distribution approximates a normal curve but does have a slight negative skew as shown by the longer lower whisker. Recall that this indicates a higher concentration of scores at the higher end of the scale.

As you can see, there is a tremendous amount of information packed into one little boxplot. Of course, we could provide these identical statistics for the remaining three distributions, but we choose to leave this as an exercise for the reader. Another purpose of this graph is to provide a way to visually compare these four distributions to look for differences or similarities. There are six possible comparisons: (1) day males with day females, (2) day males with evening males, (3) day males with evening females, (4) day females with evening males, (5) day females with evening females, and (6) evening males with evening females.[1]

In the following section, we present the database you will use to build a clustered boxplot and the questions you answer using the information provided by the graph that you build.

---

[1]The significance or lack of significance between these six possible combinations can be investigated by using the nonparametric independent-samples Kruskal–Wallis test to look for differences between the medians. There are also chi-square tests that can be used to test for differences between the variability of the various groups.

12.2 DATABASE AND QUESTIONS   ★

The database used to build the clustered boxplot is named **dmdata3.sav** and can be found in the SPSS Sample files. This database consists of nine variables and 8,083 cases. These hypothetical data contain information on the demographics and purchasing behaviors of customers of a fictitious direct marketing company. One discrete variable placed on the *x*-axis is named *Income* and labeled as *Income category (thousands)*. This variable has four categories that are given in thousands of dollars, <$25, $25 to $49, $50 to $74, and $75+. The second discrete variable is *gender*, which has two categories—this is the *legend* or *color* variable. The continuous variable for the *y*-axis is named *Reside* and labeled *Years at current residence*. Next, we list some questions that can be answered about this database once you build the graph.

12.2.1 Questions for the Clustered Boxplot

1. What are the median values for the number of years living at the current residence for the 8,083 customers who make up the eight groups depicted in the clustered boxplot?

2. When outliers and extremes are excluded, which of the eight groups has the greatest range of years living at their current residence? What are the highest and the lowest numbers of years of residence for this group?

3. What are the upper and lower limits, in years of residence, for the middle 50% (interquartile values) for the females earning more than $75? And what is the value of the interquartile range?

4. What is the age and educational level of the uppermost outlier in the male category for those earning more than $75,000 per year?

5. Which income category provides evidence supportive of gender differences in the upper and lower limits for the middle 50%, and what are the values?

Let's use the power of SPSS to build a clustered boxplot and answer the questions.

12.3 USING SPSS TO BUILD THE CLUSTERED BOXPLOT   ★

For this graph-building exercise, you use **dmdata3.sav** from SPSS Sample file.

- Open **dmdata3.sav** (found in the SPSS Sample files).
- Click **Graphs**, then click **Chart Builder** to open *Chart Builder* window.

- Click **Boxplot**, click and drag the **Clustered Boxplot** (the middle icon) to the *Chart preview* panel.
- Click and drag **Income category** to the *X-Axis* box.
- Click and drag **Years at current residence** to the *Y-Axis* box.
- Click and drag **Gender** to the *Cluster on X: set color* box.
- Click **OK** (the basic graph now appears in the *Output Viewer*).
- Double click the **graph** to open the *Chart Editor*.
- Click **any number** on *y*-axis, in the *Properties* window, click the **Scale tab** if not already highlighted.
- In the *Range* panel, change *Minimum* to **−2**, *Maximum* to **22**, and *Major Increment* to **2**, then click **Apply**.
- Click **any boxplot whisker**, which will highlight all the whiskers (*Properties* window should open with the *Lines* tab highlighted, if not open, then click the **Properties** window icon and then click the **Lines tab**.
- In the *Lines* panel, click the **black arrow** beneath *Weight*, and click **1**. Click **Apply**.
- Click **inside the boxplot for males earning <25** (a faint frame appears around all boxes), click this **boxplot** a second time, and now only the male boxes have the frame.
- Click the **Properties** window icon, click the **Fill & Border tab**.
- In the *Color* panel, click the **white rectangular box**, click the **black arrow** beneath *Pattern*, then click the **second pattern** in the **first** row, then click **Apply**.
- Click in any of the **boxes for females** (a faint border appears around all boxes for females).
- In the *Color* panel, click the **white rectangular box**, click the **black arrow** beneath *Pattern*, then click the **last pattern** in the **first** row, then click **Apply**.
- Click **any number** on the *y*-axis, then click the **Show Grid Lines icon**.
- Click the **Lines tab** in the *Properties* window, and then click the **black arrow** beneath *Weight* in the *Lines* panel and click **0.25**, then click the **black arrow** beneath *Style* and click the **first dotted line**, and finally, click **Apply**.
- Click the **X** in the upper right-hand corner of the *Chart Editor* (graph is moved to the *Output Viewer*).
- Click the **graph** (a frame appears around the graph) and then click and grab the **lower right corner** of the frame (marked by a small black square), hover the mouse pointer until you see a *double-headed arrow* and move it diagonally up and to the left to reach the approximate size of the graph in Figure 12.2.

Figure 12.2   Clustered Boxplot for Income, Gender, and Years at Current Residence

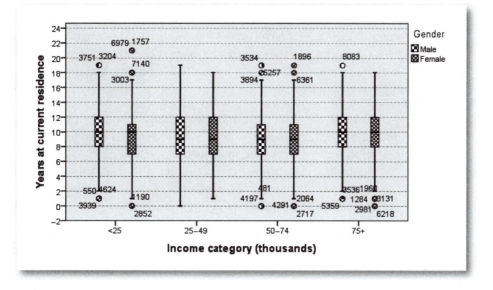

The following section provides the answers obtained from the informa-tion obtained from the graph in Figure 12.2.

12.4 INTERPRETATION OF THE CLUSTERED BOXPLOT   ★

We next answer questions about **dmdata3.sav** database by an examination of the clustered boxplot built in the previous section.

12.4.1 Questions and Answers for the Clustered Boxplot

The information needed to answer these questions can be found in Figure 12.2.

1. What are the median values for the number of years living at the cur-rent residence for the 8,083 customers who make up the eight groups depicted in the clustered boxplot?

The median values for the eight groups consisting of income categories and gender are 10, 10, 9, 9, 9, 9, 10, and 10 (from left to right in Figure 12.2).

2. When outliers and extremes are excluded, which of the eight groups has the greatest range of years living at their current residence? What are the highest and lowest numbers of years of residence for this group?

To answer this question, we look for the group having the longest whiskers in Figure 12.2. The males having an income between $25,000 and $49,000 report that they have lived at their current residence from a high of 19 years to a low of less than 1 year. Thus, we have a range for this group of approximately 20 years.

3. What are the upper and lower limits, in years of residence, for the middle 50% (interquartile values) for the females earning more than $75? And what is the value of the interquartile range?

Figure 12.2 informs us that the middle 50% in this group lived between 12 and 8 years at their current residence. Given this information, the interquartile range for this group is $12 - 8 = 4$ years.

4. What is the age and educational level of the uppermost outlier in the male category for those earning more than $75,000 per year?

To answer this question, look at Case Number 8083 in the database and determine that this outlier is aged 35 and has a college education.

5. Which income category provides evidence supportive of gender differences in the upper and lower limits for the middle 50% and what are the values?

The only income category showing gender differences in years of residence for the middle 50% is the category for those earning less than $25,000 per year. For the males in this income category, we have limits from 8 to 12 years of residence, and females show 7 to 11 years of residence. Notice that the interquartile ranges for males and females in this income category are identical ($12 - 8 = 4$ and $11 - 7 = 4$), but the limits are different.

★ 12.5 REVIEW EXERCISES

1. Open SPSS Sample file **workprog.sav**. Select the discrete variable named *marital* having the label of *Marital status* for the *x*-axis. For the *color/legend* variable, select one named *gender* and labeled *Gender*. The continuous variable for the *y*-axis is named *age* and labeled *Age in years*. Build the clustered boxplot as in Figure 12.3 and answer the following questions.

Questions: (a) What is the median age of the unmarried females? (b) Which of the four groups had the largest interquartile range and what were the upper and lower limits? (c) What is the median age for married females? (d) What is the interquartile range for the married males? (e) Which of the four groups have distributions that are positively skewed?

Figure 12.3   Review Exercise: Clustered Boxplot for Age by Marital Status and Gender

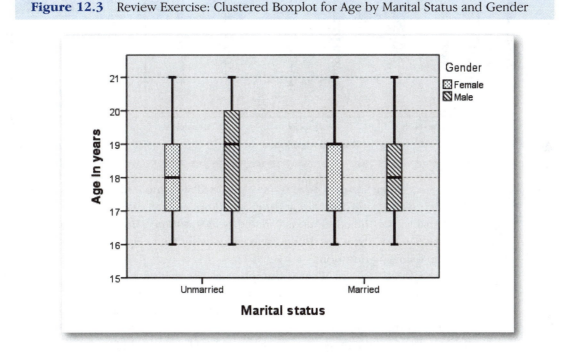

2. Open **1991 U.S. General Social Survey.sav** and select *Sex* and *Happy* (*General happiness*) as the two discrete variables. Use the *General happiness* variable on the *x*-axis and *Sex* as the *color/legend* variable. For the continuous variable, select *Age of respondent* and place it on the *y*-axis. Build the clustered boxplot shown in Figure 12.4 and answer the following questions.

Questions: (a) What is the median age for males and females that indicated they were very happy? (b) Which group had the lowest median age, and what is their happiness level? (c) What is the age range for the females who were not too happy? (d) What is the age range of the females stating that they were very happy? (e) What is the age of the outlier most distant from the median?

Figure 12.4   Review Exercises: Clustered Boxplot for Age by Happiness and Sex

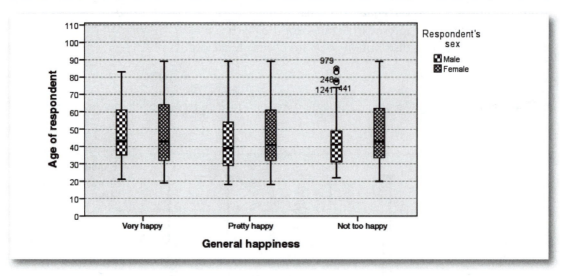

3. Open **Employee data.sav** in the SPSS Sample file. Select *gender* as the *color/legend* variable and *jobcat* (Employment category) as the *x*-axis variable. For the continuous variable, select *jobtime* (*Month since hire*) and place this on the *y*-axis. Build the boxplot as shown in Figure 12.5 and answer the following questions.

Questions: (a) What is the interquartile range for the female custodial employees? (b) Which employment category, manager or clerical, has the largest median difference between males and females in months since hire? (c) What is the interquartile range for males and females in the manager category? (d) What are the ranges of months since hire for male and female managers?

Figure 12.5   Review Exercises: Clustered Boxplot for Months by Employment Type and Gender

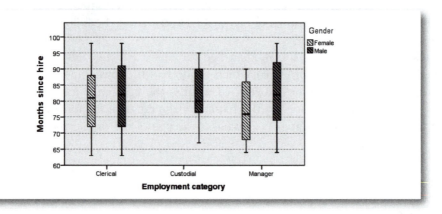

4. Open **workprog.sav** in the SPSS Sample file. Select the discrete variable named *ed* having the label of *Level of education* for the *x*-axis. For the *color/legend* variable, select one named *gender* and labeled *Gender*. The continuous variable for the *y*-axis is named *incaft* and labeled *Income after the program*. Build the clustered boxplot as in Figure 12.6 and answer the following questions.

Questions: (a) What is the median income for females with a high school degree? (b) Which of the six distributions had the largest interquartile range, and what were the upper and lower limits? (c) What is the median income for females with some college? (d) What is the interquartile range of income for males who did not complete high school? (e) Which of the six groups have the highest median income, and what is that value?

Figure 12.6   Review Exercises: Clustered Boxplot for Income by Education and Gender

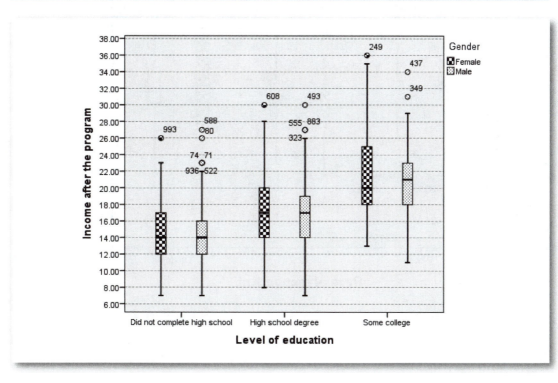

5. Open **1991 U.S. General Social Survey.sav** and select the variables named *sex* and labeled as *Respondent's sex* and *race* labeled as *Race of respondent* as the two discrete variables. Use the variable named *educ* and labeled

Highest year of school completed on the *y*-axis as the continuous variable. Use the *race* variable on the *x*-axis and *sex* as the *color/legend* variable. Build the clustered boxplot shown in Figure 12.7 and answer the following questions.

Questions: (a) What are the highest numbers of years of education completed for these three race categories? (b) Which group had the lowest median number of years of education, and what is the number of years? (c) Which group has the largest interquartile range, and what is this value? (d) What is the interquartile range for male years of completed education in the White race category? (e) Which race category has the least amount of variability between genders as measured by the interquartile range?

Figure 12.7   Review Exercises: Clustered Boxplot for School Completed by Race and Sex

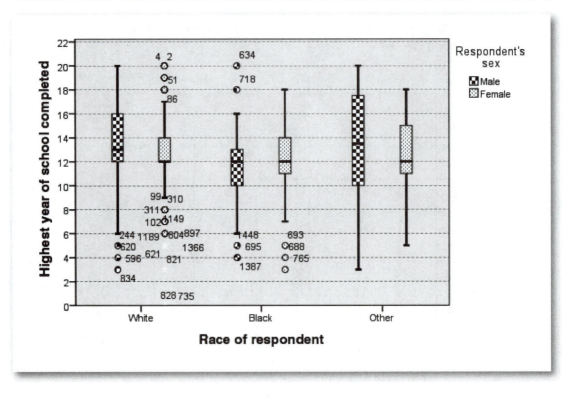

13

SIMPLE SCATTERPLOT

PURPOSE OF GRAPHS YOU ARE ABOUT TO BUILD
• To discover the strength and direction of any relationship between two continuous variables (with confidence intervals for the regression line)

13.1 INTRODUCTION TO THE SIMPLE SCATTERPLOT ★

In the preceding three chapters, we presented three different uses for the boxplot. You learned to use these graphs to show measures that displayed the "spread" (variability) of continuous data. The statistics generated by these graphs were the range of values (high and low), interquartile range (third quartile minus the second quartile), median, outliers, and also extreme values. These graphs provided an excellent picture of the variability of continuous distributions. You were also given graphing methods that allowed for the comparison of several distributions on one graph.

In this chapter, you use a graphing method that seeks to discover how two continuous variables are related. You might recall that in Chapter 7, you used the multiple line graph for this same purpose. The major difference is that with the scatterplot each of the data points represent two values, one for x and another for y. These points are referred to as *bivariate* data points because each represents two values of a continuous variable. Another way in which the scatterplot differs from the line graph is that the data points are not connected. We can, however, produce a "best fit" line or simply look for a pattern in the data points. The "best fit" line is referred to as the *regression line*. The regression line is calculated in a way that minimizes its distance from all bivariate data points on the scatterplot—think of it as an average.

In the first sentence of the previous paragraph, we stated that the scatterplot will help discover *how* two continuous variables are related. We use the scatterplots in Figures 13.1, 13.2, and 13.3 to explain how the scatterplot answers three broad relational questions about two variables.[1] When questioning how two variables are related, we usually seek information concerning the *strength*, *direction*, and *shape* of the relationship. Notice that the scatterplot does not tell us whether one variable causes the change in the other. This concept bears repeating—the scatterplot does *not* display a cause and effect–type relationship. The scatterplot informs us of an association (or lack of association) between two variables but is silent on whether one causes the change in the other.

13.1.1 Scatterplot Showing a Perfect Positive Linear Relationship

Let's begin our discussion by looking at Figure 13.1, a graph that displays a perfect (the strength), positive (the direction), and linear (the shape) relationship for two continuous variables.

Each of the black circles on the graph represent two values that were observed as occurring together. For instance, the leftmost information bubble in Figure 13.1 points to a black circle that represents an individual student who spent three hours studying and earned 70 points on the exam. The uppermost black circle on the "best fit" line represents another student studying for six hours and earning 100 points. Remember that each point on the graph represents a value for x and a value for y.

---

[1]The data used to build the graphs in Figures 13.1, 13.2, and 13.3 are hypothetical and were created to illustrate the three relational concepts of *strength*, *direction*, and *shape*.

Figure 13.1 Scatterplot for Hours of Study and Points on Exam: Showing a Strong (Perfect), Positive, and Linear Relationship Between the Two Variables

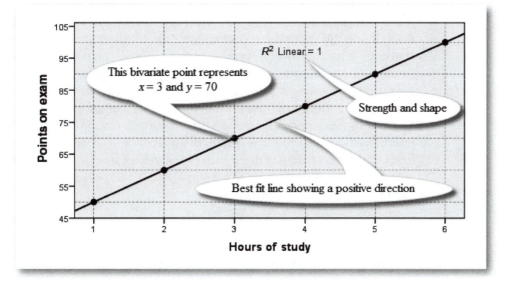

The strength of the relationship (or association) is the square root of R^2 (R squared) shown in Figure 13.1.[2] The *square root* of R^2 is known as the correlation coefficient (designated as r) and can vary from minus one (−1) to a positive one (+1). The closer the correlation coefficient is to the value of 1 (either positive or negative), the stronger the relationship. In the example

---

[2]The "R^2 linear = 1" as seen in Figures 13.1, 13.2, and 13.3 is not present in the basic scatterplot. SPSS automatically added this information when we requested the best fitting line. The R^2 is the coefficient of determination and is used with regression analysis that is beyond the purpose and scope of this textbook. For our purposes, here we say that R^2 is the proportion of variance in the dependent variable that can be explained by the independent variable. Similar to correlation coefficient, the closer R^2 is to the value of 1, the better the line fits the data. However, we must realize that we are using it here to arrive at the correlation coefficient as we are not looking for a cause–effect relationship but for an association between two variables. We use R^2 to determine the actual correlation coefficient by taking the square root of R^2. The *square root* of R^2 then answers questions concerning the *strength* of the relationship by providing us with the correlation coefficient. The *direction* (positive or negative) is then determined by looking at the graph. A line sloping upward from left to right indicates a positive relationship. If the line slopes downward from left to right you have a negative relationship.

given in Figure 13.1, we have a "perfect" relationship as shown by the R^2 value of 1. The square root of 1 is 1, which is the correlation coefficient for these data.

The sign of the correlation coefficient (positive or negative) tells us about the direction of the relationship. In this example, we do not directly see the correlation coefficient, only R^2, therefore, we must look at the best fit line to determine direction of the relationship since the square root of a number is always positive. The direction question is answered by looking at the best fit line. A line that slopes upward from the lower left to the right is indicative of data having a positive relationship. In our example, this means that for each one hour of study the points earned on the exam increase by 10 points (considered as one unit). This means that as the x variable increases by one unit, the y variable does the same. In the following section, we present a scatterplot showing a negative correlation.

13.1.2 Scatterplot Showing a Strong Negative Linear Relationship

The scatterplot in Figure 13.2 indicates that the two variables have a strong (strength) and negative (direction) linear (shape) relationship. The scatterplot informs us that as recreation time increases (1 through 6 hours), points earned on the exam decrease.[3]

The line in Figure 13.2 slopes from the upper left side to the lower right side of the graph. Scatterplots with this line orientation indicate a negative correlation between the two variables. In this example, we are not hypothesizing a causal relationship; therefore, this line can be interpreted in two ways. From the student's standpoint, it could be said that as one spends more time in recreation, test points decrease. One might also speculate that as time spent in recreation decreases, test points increase. No matter how it is stated, you still have a strong negative linear relationship. This can be determined by simply looking at the slope of the best fit

---

[3]Remember, the data used to build the scatterplot shown in Figure 13.2 are fictitious. Also remember that this is not evidence of a causal relationship as the scatterplot only demonstrates the magnitude of association between the two variables.

Figure 13.2 Scatterplot for Hours of Recreation and Points on Exam: Showing a Strong, Negative, and Linear Relationship Between the Two Variables

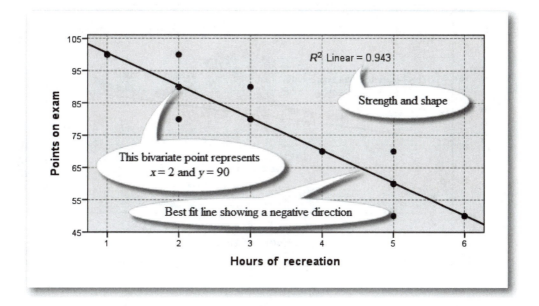

line as we did in our first example. Taking the square root of R^2 (0.943), we calculate a correlation coefficient of 0.97. We assign the minus sign to agree with the slope of the best fit line; therefore, we have, $r = -0.97$.

13.1.3 Scatterplot Showing a Very Weak Relationship Between Two Variables

The scatterplot presented in Figure 13.3 shows the appearance when two variables have a very weak correlation. The observed correlation is almost certainly a product of pure chance, and most analysts would simply conclude that there was no correlation. The graph displays an R^2 value of 0.087. Taking the square root, we find an extremely weak, correlation coefficient of 0.29. The graph indicates a slightly positive slope.

When looking at this graph, we can determine that the hours of sleep appears not to be related to the number of points earned on the exam—at least this is the case for our hypothetical data.

Figure 13.3   Scatterplot for Hours of Sleep and Points on Exam: Very Weak Correlation

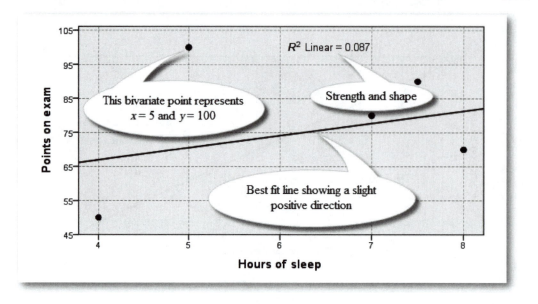

13.1.4 Scatterplot for 1,050 Students

We present the scatterplot in Figure 13.4 to give a more realistic view of a graph depicting some "real" data. In constructing Figure 13.4, we seek to discover if there is a relationship between the total points earned in the semester with the score on the final exam. By building the scatterplot, including the best fit line, we can answer the three major questions associated with this type of graph (strength, direction, and shape).

The scatterplot confirms what one might suspect about these 1,050 statistics students. On average, students who did well on the final tended to earn more total semester points. The same relationship is true for students not doing well on the final in that they earned fewer total semester points. In other words, our scatterplot provided empirical evidence in support of our idea (suspicion) that the two variables were correlated. By looking at the graph, we see that $R^2 = 0.744$. Finding the square root of 0.744, we get 0.86, indicating a correlation coefficient that tells us there is a moderate to strong linear relationship between these two variables.

By looking at the slope of the line, we also determine that the direction is positive. Given this information, we can say that if we know how someone did on the final exam we will be better able to more accurately predict their total points for the semester. On average, we say that performance on the final exam is related to the number of total semester points earned by the students. At the risk of sounding like a broken record, we remind the reader that this is not direct evidence of a cause–effect relationship—it is only an association.

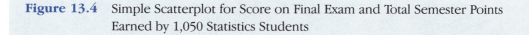

Figure 13.4 Simple Scatterplot for Score on Final Exam and Total Semester Points Earned by 1,050 Statistics Students

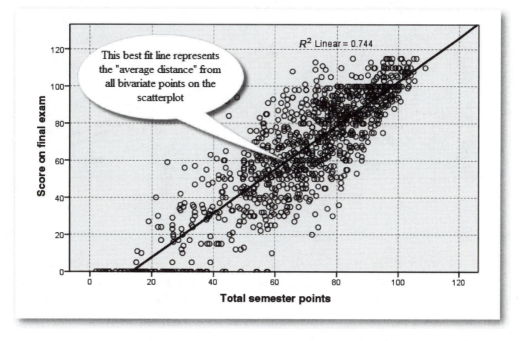

13.1.5 Scatterplot With Confidence Interval

Before using confidence intervals and a best fit line, you must make certain that the data meet several conditions. Our intention here is not to list these conditions but to show how to interpret the lines and later how to add them to the graph. The information concerning how and when such confidence intervals can be used is found in any intermediate-level statistics book.

The hypothetical data used to build the graph in Figure 13.2 are once again utilized to create a scatterplot, but we added lines that represent the 99% confidence interval for the best fit line. These upper and lower limits provide the graph user with an easy way to visualize the usefulness of the best fit line. These lines represent the percentage of samples that would result in a best fit line within the limits of the upper and lower dotted line shown in Figure 13.5.

The confidence interval (dotted lines) in Figure 13.5 provide evidence that the best fit line would be a good indicator of what one would expect if additional samples were obtained from the same population. In

Figure 13.5   Ninety-Nine Percent Confidence Interval for the Best Fit Line of a Scatterplot

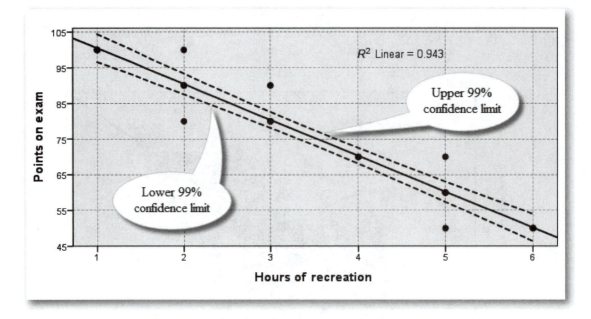

99% of the samples, the best fit line would fall within the dotted lines. However, don't forget that this is only true when the data conditions have been met.

13.1.6 Using the Best Fit Line as Part of Regression Analysis

Scatterplots are sometimes built as part of the larger analysis known as regression. The SPSS user simply requests a scatterplot during the process of conducting the regression analysis by clicking an item. One use of this application is to provide evidence that you can use linear regression to analyze the data. If the answer is in the affirmative, then the best fit line can assist one in making predictions about unknown values on the *y*-axis. In this application, regression is often used to predict the value of a dependent variable based on the knowledge of the value of the independent variable. A note of caution when interpreting the scatterplot in regression analysis is that you should *not* use the best fit line (or its equation) to make predictions beyond the range of the data.

For an example of this logic, look at Figure 13.1 and notice that six hours of study is the highest number of hours that was observed. Could we use our scatterplot, with its best fit line, to predict the number of points earned on the exam for an individual studying 10 hours? The answer is that we cannot as it is beyond the range of values observed for these data. However, we could predict the points earned on the exam for a student studying 2.5 hours even though this study time was not directly observed. One way to accomplish this is by drawing a line parallel to the *y*-axis starting on the *x*-axis at 2.5 and moving upward to a point where it intersects the best fit line. Make another line parallel to the *x*-axis that intersects with the line you just drew and the best fit line. Extend this new line leftward to the *y*-axis. Read the value of 65 earned points on the *y*-axis that tells us that a student studying 2.5 hours will, on average, earn 65 points on the exam (within certain confidence limits and at a certain confidence level). Next we examine the database and questions you will seek to answer by building a scatterplot.

13.2 DATABASE AND QUESTIONS ★

For this graph-building project, you use the SPSS Sample file named **advert .sav**. SPSS states that these are hypothetical data collected to answer questions about the relationship between spending for advertising and amount of sales. The database has 24 cases measured on two continuous variables. One variable is named *advert* and labeled *Advertising spending*. The other is named *sales* and labeled as *Detrended* sales. Once the scatterplot is built, you will answer questions about the nature of the relationship (or lack of relationship) between the amount spent on advertising and subsequent sales amounts.

13.2.1 Questions for the Simple Scatterplot

1. What does the graph tell us about the *strength*, *direction*, and *shape* of the distribution that describes the two variables of advertising expenditures and the sales amount?

2. What is the value of detrended sales if the retail store spends 2.5 on advertising?

3. What can be learned about sales amounts from the scatterplot if the retail store decides not to spend any money on advertising?

4. What is the value of detrended sales if the retail store spends 4.0 on advertising?

5. The upper confidence limit bisects which bivariate value?

In the following section, you will build the scatterplot that will answer these five questions.

★   13.3 USING SPSS TO BUILD THE SIMPLE SCATTERPLOT

For this graph-building exercise, use the data found in the SPSS Sample file named **advert.sav**. These data will provide the information needed to answer the above questions.

- Open **advert.sav** (found in the SPSS Sample files).
- Click **Graphs**, then click **Chart Builder** to open *Chart Builder* window.
- Click **Scatter/Dot**, click and drag the **Simple Scatter** (the first icon) to the *Chart preview* panel.
- Click and drag **Advertising spending** to the *X-Axis* box.
- Click and drag **Detrended sales** to the *Y-Axis* box.
- Click **OK** (basic scatterplot appears in the *Output Viewer*).
- Double click the **graph** (*Chart Editor* opens).
- Click the **Add Fit Line at Total icon** (the fifth icon from the left on the lowest menu bar). Following this click, a highlighted line appears on the graph.
- In the *Properties* window, click the **Lines tab**, in the *Lines* panel, click the **black arrow** beneath *Weight* and click **2**.
- Click **Apply**.
- In the *Properties* window, click the *Fit Line* tab, and in the *Confidence Interval* panel, click the **small circle** to the left of *Mean* and then change **95%** to **99%**.
- Click **Apply** (confidence interval lines appear on each side of the best fit line).
- Click on **one of the confidence interval lines**.
- In the *Properties* window, click the **Lines tab**, and in the *Lines* panel, click the **black arrow** beneath *Weight* and click **2**, then click the **black arrow** beneath *Style* and click the **third dotted line**.
- Click **Apply**.
- Click any of the small circles on the graph (a faint frame appears around all these *data point markers*).
- In the *Properties* window with the *Marker* tab highlighted and in the *Marker* panel, click the **black arrow** beneath *Size*, then click **8**.
- In the *Color* panel, click the **small box** to the left of *Fill*, then click the **black rectangular box**, click **Apply**.
- Click the **Show Grid Lines icon** (the fifth icon from the right on the menu bar) (the small circle to the left of *Major ticks only* should already be selected in the *Properties* window).
- In the *Properties* window, click the **Lines tab**, and in the *Lines* panel, click the **black arrow** beneath *Weight* and click **0.25** then click the **black arrow** beneath *Style* and click the **first dotted line**.

- Click **Apply**.
- Click **R² Linear = 0.839** (a frame appears around it, hover the mouse over it until you see an arrow with four points). Click and drag **R² Linear = 0.839** onto the graph.
- Click **any number** on the *y*-axis.
- In the *Properties* window, click the **Scale tab** (if *Properties* window is not open, then click its icon (the third from the left on the *Chart Editor's* menu).
- In the *Range* panel of the *Properties* window, change *Major Increment* from **2** to **1**.
- Click **Apply**.
- Click the **X** in the upper right-hand corner of the *Chart Editor* (graph is moved to the *Output Viewer*).
- Click the **graph** (a frame appears around the graph), and then click and grab the **lower right corner of the frame** (marked by a small black square). Hover the mouse pointer over the black square until you see a *double-headed arrow* and move it diagonally up and to the left to reach the approximate size of the graph in Figure 13.6.

Figure 13.6   Scatterplot for Advertising Spending and Detrended Sales

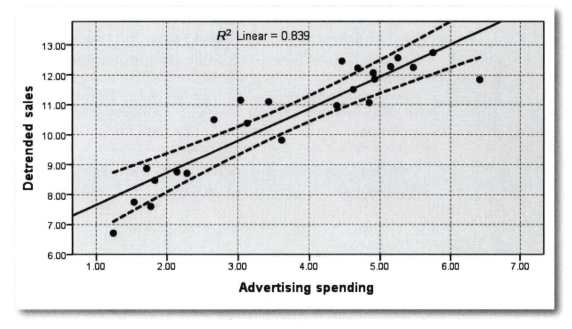

Let's now use the finished scatterplot shown in Figure 13.6 to answer our questions about this database.

★   13.4 Interpretation of the Simple Scatterplot

The information needed to answer the following questions is in Figure 13.6.

1. What does the graph tell us about the *strength*, *direction*, and *shape* of the distribution that describes the two variables of advertising expenditures and the sales amount?

Since the square root of R^2 (0.839) is 0.92, we can say that there is a strong relationship between spending for advertising and sales. By looking at the graph, we determine that the line direction is positive in that it shows spending increases for advertising are associated with increased sales. It can be said that there is a linear relationship between the two variables.

2. What is the value of detrended sales if the retail store spends 2.5 on advertising?

Draw a line parallel to the *y*-axis from the 2.5 point on the *x*-axis, upward until it intersects with the best fit line. Starting at this intersection, draw another line parallel to the *x*-axis leftward to the *y*-axis and read the value of 9.25. This is the estimated sales when spending 2.5 for advertising.

3. What can be learned about sales amounts from the scatterplot if the retail store decides not to spend any money on advertising?

The data used to build the scatterplot do not include any observations where no money was spent on advertising. Given this fact, the scatterplot would provide little empirical help in making such a prediction.

4. What is the value of detrended sales if the retail store spends 4.0 on advertising?

Draw a line parallel to the *y*-axis from the 4.0 point on the *x*-axis, upward until it intersects with the best fit line. Starting at this intersection, draw another line parallel to the *x*-axis leftward to the *y*-axis and read the value of 10.80. This is the estimated sales when spending 4.0 for advertising.

5. The upper confidence limit bisects which bivariate value?

The upper confidence limit bisects the value of $x = 3.15$ and $y = 10.30$.

★   13.5 Review Exercises

1. Open **band.sav** from the SPSS Sample file. Use the continuous variable named *sales* and labeled *Sales of CDs* on the *y*-axis of your graph. On the *x*-axis, select the variable named *web* and labeled as *Web hits with sample clip*

download. Build the simple scatterplot with a best fit line as in Figure 13.7 and answer the following questions.

Questions: (a) In one word, how would you describe the relationship between web hits and sales of CDs? (Hint: For the *y*-axis, change to read *Maximum* of 1,600 and *Major Increment* of 250. The *x*-axis should have a *Major Increment* of 25) (b) What is the estimated value of sales for 225 web hits? (c) What are the sales figures for 600 web hits? (d) Does the graph indicate a positive or negative correlation?

Figure 13.7   Review Exercise: Simple Scatterplot CD Sales and Web Hits

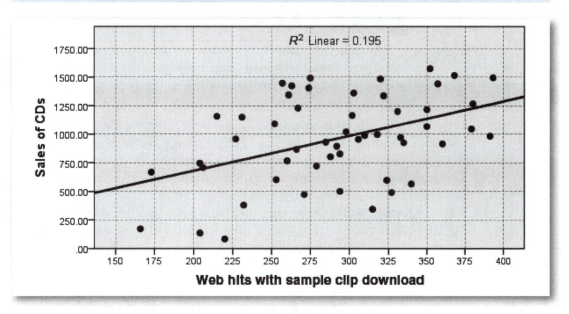

2.   Open **bankloan.sav** found in the SPSS Sample file. Choose the continuous variable named *income* and labeled *Household income in thousands* for the *x*-axis. The *y*-axis variable is named *creddebt* and labeled *Credit card debt in thousands*. Build a simple scatterplot with its best fit line as in Figure 13.8 and answer the following questions.

Questions: (a) What does the large black mass found at the bottom left-hand side of the graph indicate? (b) What are the strength and direction of the relationship between the two variables? (c) What was the highest reported salary, and how much credit card debt did they have? (d) What is the salary of the individual having the most credit card debt, and what is that amount?

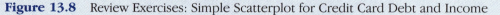

Figure 13.8   Review Exercises: Simple Scatterplot for Credit Card Debt and Income

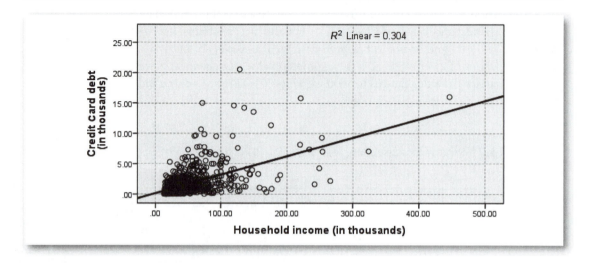

3. Open **bankloan.sav** found in the SPSS Sample file. Select the continuous variable named *age* and labeled *Age in years* for the x-axis. For the y-axis, choose the variable named *employ* and labeled as *Years with current employer*. Build the simple scatterplot with the best fit line as in Figure 13.9 to answer the following questions.

Questions: (a) On average, how many years would a 36-year-old person have been employed? (b) What are the strength and direction of the relationship? (c) What is the range of years with the employer for someone aged 55?

Figure 13.9   Review Exercises: Simple Scatterplot for Years With Employer and Age

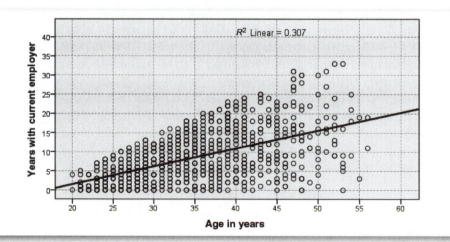

4. Open **catalog_seasfac.sav**, select the variable named *print* and labeled *Amount spent on print advertising* for the *x*-axis continuous variable. For the continuous *y*-axis variable, use *jewel* labeled as *Sales of jewelry*. Build the simple scatterplot as in Figure 13.10 and answer the following questions.

Questions: (a) On the average, spending 32,000 on print advertising would result in what amount of jewelry sales? (b) What are the strength and direction of the relationship? (c) What is the average cost of print advertising for 30,000 in jewelry sales?

Figure 13.10   Review Exercise: Simple Scatterplot Advertising and Jewelry Sales

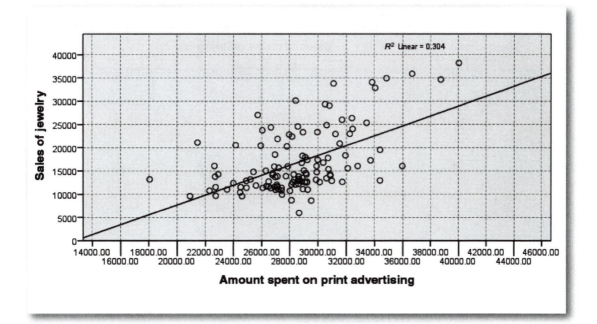

5. Open **catalog_seasfac.sav**, select the variable named *men* and labeled Sales of men's clothing for the *x*-axis continuous variable. For the continuous *y*-axis variable, use *women* that is labeled *Sales of Women's clothing*. Build the simple scatterplot as in Figure 13.11 and answer the following questions.

Questions: (a) On average, if sales of men's clothing reach 30,000 what would be the expected sales for women's clothing? (b) What are the strength and direction of the relationship? (c) What is the expected men's sales for clothing when women's sales are $30,000?

Figure 13.11   Review Exercise: Simple Scatterplot for Sales of Men's and Women's Clothing

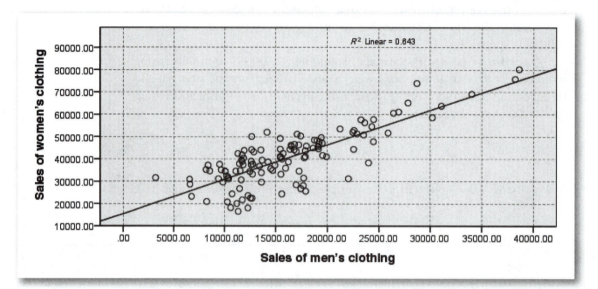

14

GROUPED SCATTERPLOT

14.1 INTRODUCTION TO THE GROUPED SCATTERPLOT ★

In the previous chapter, you were introduced to the simple scatterplot and how it is used to discover information about the relationship between two continuous variables. The specific questions we sought to answer dealt with the strength of their relationship, whether it was positive or negative, and if the shape was linear. When building and using the grouped scatterplot, we seek the same information but with an added dimension. You still use the scatterplot to describe the strength, direction, and shape of a relationship between two continuous variables but then use a discrete variable to divide the distribution of bivariate points into subgroups. The following sections present two examples of grouped scatterplots.

14.1.1 Grouped Scatterplot (First Example): 37 Students

The grouped scatterplot can be challenging to visualize, so let's examine carefully the graph pictured in Figure 14.1. The scatterplot in this figure

Figure 14.1   Grouped Scatterplot: Exams 2 and 3 Divided Into Male and Female Groups

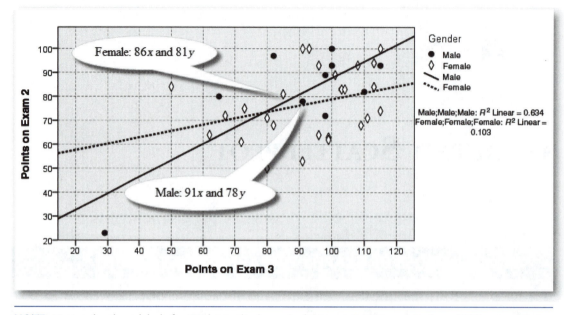

NOTE: Notice the three labels for "Male" in the legend of this graph. This results from SPSS programming and will be corrected in future versions.

depicts the points earned by 37 students on two exams, the two continuous variables, and the discrete variable of gender.

The graph takes on the appearance of the simple scatterplot built in the previous chapter in that each bivariate point represents two values for an individual. The two values in Figure 14.1 are the numbers of points earned on Exams 3 (x) and 2 (y). The difference is that you now have a legend in the upper right-hand corner of the graph, which identifies two styles of *markers*: black circles for males and diamonds for females.[1] There is also a solid black line next to male and a dotted line for females. The point markers for the data and the two line styles are found on the graph. The markers represent bivariate data points, while the lines are best fit lines.[2] SPSS was instructed to plot scores earned for Exams 2 and 3, but this time doing it separately for the subgroups of males and females.

---

[1]There is no hidden symbolism here but the female coauthor did insist on a diamond shape to represent her gender.

[2]Think of the "best fit" line as an average of the observed bivariate data points. It is used here as a convenient summary of all data points not as an inferential model for unknown and unobserved data.

In Figure 14.1, we have marked two of the bivariate points with information bubbles. One draws attention to a female that earned 86 points on Exam 3 (found on the *x*-axis) and 81 points on Exam 2 (*y*-axis variable). The other bubble shows a male who earned 91 on Exam 3 and 78 points on Exam 2.

The legend also displays information useful to determine the strength and shape of the distribution. For the males, we have an R^2 of 0.634 and the correlation coefficient is the square root of R^2 or 0.80. We can describe the bivariate male distribution as a moderate to strong positive linear relationship. The females have an R^2 of 0.103, and the correlation coefficient is the square root of R^2 or 0.32. Therefore, we describe the female distribution as having a weak positive and linear relationship.[3]

Before we leave Figure 14.1, we note one more item of interest—the outlier. Direct your attention to the lower left-hand portion of the graph, and you will see one black circle. This bivariate point represents a male who earned 29 points on Exam 3 and 21 points on Exam 2. When compared with the other 36 students, a case could be made for removing this outlier from the analysis. One of the beauties of the *Chart Builder* is that you can easily remove outliers, see how it impacts the analysis, and then make a decision. We left the outlier in the chart as it had little effect on the scatterplot. It also afforded us the opportunity to discuss outliers within the context of our grouped scatterplot.

14.1.2 Grouped Scatterplot (Second Example): 1,050 Students

We next examine an additional grouped scatterplot but this time built from the much larger database consisting of 1,050 students. Figure 14.2 once again assigns black circle markers and a solid best fit line to males and diamonds and a dotted line to females. This graph depicts the relationship between the total semester points and the final exam.

Apart from the almost identical best fit lines, you may have noticed the markers along the *x*-axis and that the *y*-axis has a minimum of −5. During the chart-building process, we changed the minimum on the *y*-axis from 0 to −5 to accommodate the diamonds and black circles. Before making this change, the horizontal line for the *x*-axis hides the markers from view. The change we made did not affect the accuracy of the graph, the markers are still centered

---

[3]The purpose of this textbook is not to comment on such findings, but we will say that a plausible explanation for these gender differences is the small sample size of 37 students. Building the same scatterplot for the 1,050 statistics students on Exams 2 and 3 resulted in nearly identical R^2 values for males at 0.320 and females of 0.327.

Figure 14.2   Grouped Scatterplot: Total Semester Points and Final Exam Points for 1,050 Students Split Into Male and Female Groups

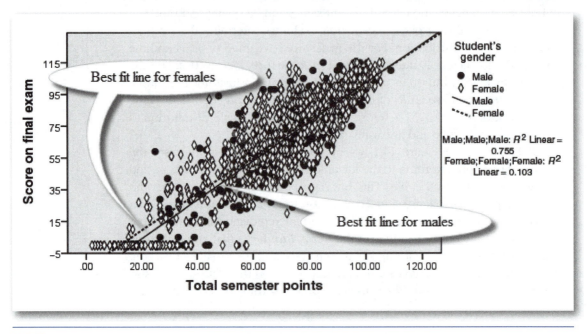

NOTE: Notice the three labels for "Male" in the legend of this graph. This results from SPSS programming and will be corrected in future versions.

on zero. In our opinion, it does, however, improve its visual appearance. These markers represent students who did poorly throughout the semester and elected not to take the final exam. In the next section, we introduce the database you use to build a grouped scatterplot and the questions you will answer once the grouped scatterplot is built.

★   **14.2 DATABASE AND QUESTIONS**

You use a database named **car_sales_unprepared.sav** from the SPSS Sample file to build the grouped scatterplot. This database has 14 variables and 157 cases. SPSS describes this database as being based on hypothetical data obtained from various online resources such as edmunds.com and various manufacturer's web pages.

The discrete variable, used as the *Set color* variable, is named *type* and labeled as *Vehicle type*. This variable has the two categories of automobile and truck. The *x*-axis variable is named *horsepow* and labeled *Horsepower*.

The *y*-axis variable is named *engine_s* and labeled *Engine size*. The chart you build will display the relationship between horsepower rating and engine size for two groups of vehicle types: autos and trucks. Let's next examine a sampling of some of the questions we hope to answer with the grouped scatterplot you produce.

14.2.1 Questions for the Grouped Scatterplot

1. What type of vehicle has the most horsepower and the largest engine, and what is its horsepower and engine size?

2. Using the correct best fit line, what is the estimated engine size for an automobile having 400 horsepower? What size would a truck engine be if it had the same horsepower rating?

3. What are the correlation coefficients for engine size and horsepower for automobiles and trucks in this study?

4. For these 157 vehicles, what is the horsepower and largest engine size for the truck category?

5. What could you say about the strength, direction, and shape of the relationship between engine size, horsepower, and type of vehicle from the information conveyed by the scatterplot?

14.3 USING SPSS TO BUILD THE GROUPED SCATTERPLOT   ★

In this section, you build a grouped scatterplot using two continuous and one discrete variable.

- Open **car_sales_unprepared.sav** (found in the SPSS Sample files).
- Click **Graphs**, then click **Chart Builder** to open *Chart Builder* window.
- Click **Scatter/Dot** found in the *Choose from* list.
- Click and drag the **second icon** in the **first** row (*Grouped Scatter*) to the *Chart preview* panel.
- Click and drag **Horsepower** to the *X-Axis* box.
- Click and drag **Engine size** to the *Y-Axis* box.
- Click and drag **Vehicle type** to the *Set color* box in the *Chart preview* panel.
- Click **OK** (*Chart Builder* closes and the graph is moved to the *Output Viewer*). If *Output Viewer* does not open, click **Output** on the task bar at the bottom of your screen.

- Double click the **graph** to open the *Chart Editor* window.
- Click the **Add Fit Lines at Subgroups icon** (the sixth icon from the left in the third row of icons).
- Click the **short line** to the **left** of *Automobile* found in the legend (the line for automobiles in the graph is now highlighted).
- In the *Properties* window, click the **Lines tab**, and in the *Color* panel, click the **box** to the left of *Line*, then click the **black rectangular box**, and finally, click **Apply**.
- Click the **short line** to the **left** of *Truck* (found in the legend).
- In the *Properties* window, click the **Lines tab**, and in the *Lines* panel, click the **black arrow** beneath *Style*, and click the **first dotted line**. In the *Color* panel, click the **box** to the **left** of *Line* then click the **black rectangular box**, and finally, click **Apply**.
- Click the **circle** to the **left** of *Automobile*, then in the *Color* panel, click the **box** to the left of *Fill*, and then click the **black rectangular box**.
- Click the **box** to the left of *Border*, next click the **black rectangular box**, and finally, click **Apply**.
- Click the **circle** to the **left** of *Truck*, then in the *Properties* window, with the *Marker* tab highlighted and in the *Marker* panel click the first *Marker* type which is the square. Next click the **black arrow** beneath *Size*, and click **6**.
- Click the **box** to the left of *Fill*, then click the **white rectangular box**. Next click the **box** to the left of *Border*, then click the **black rectangular box**, click **Apply**.
- Click the **Show Grid Lines icon** (the fifth icon from the right side of the top menu bar).
- Click **any number** on the *x*-axis, then in the *Properties* window, click the **Scale tab**, and in the *Range* panel, change the *Major Increment* to **50** and click **Apply**.
- Click **X** in the upper right-hand corner of the *Chart Editor* (*Chart Editor* closes and the graph is moved to the *Output Viewer*).
- If the *Output Viewer* is not open, do so by clicking **Output** found on the task bar at the bottom of your computer screen.
- Click the **graph** (a frame appears around the graph), and then click and grab the **lower right corner** of the frame (marked by a small black square), hover the mouse pointer until you see *a double-headed arrow* and move it diagonally up and to the left to reach the approximate size of the graph in Figure 14.3.

Figure 14.3 Grouped Scatterplot: Engine Size, Horsepower, and Vehicle Type

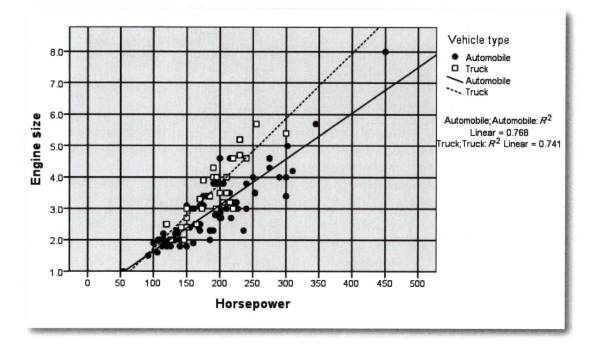

14.4 Interpretation of the Grouped Scatterplot ★

There are many questions coming from many different perspectives that one might have about the data collected on these 157 vehicles. We understand that the data was collected by SPSS for the purpose of demonstrating the capabilities of their computer program, but we (and you the reader) can hypothesize about research questions. Some of the questions and their answers provided by the grouped scatterplot that you build are obvious. An example, when looking at the graph, you see that as engine size increases so does horsepower—not exactly a startling revelation. The intent here is to demonstrate the various types of questions (and answers) made possible by building the grouped scatterplot graph. We are hopeful that you recognize the benefits of this graph and that you will use the grouped scatterplot in your future data explorations.

14.4.1 Questions and Answers: Grouped Scatterplot

The information needed to answer the following questions can be found in Figure 14.3.

1. What type of vehicle has the most horsepower and largest engine, and what is its horsepower and engine size?

    The vehicle with the largest engine and the most horsepower is an automobile with an engine size of 8.0 and a horsepower of 450.

2. Using the correct best fit line, what is the estimated engine size for an automobile having 400 horsepower? What size would a truck engine be if it had the same horsepower rating?

    An automobile that has 400 horsepower would be estimated to have an engine of size 6.0. The engine size for the truck would be 8.0.

3. What are the correlation coefficients for engine size and horsepower for automobiles and trucks in this study?

    The automobiles have a correlation coefficient of 0.88 (square root of R^2 of 0.768), while trucks have a correlation coefficient of 0.86 (square root of R^2 of 0.741).

4. For these 157 vehicles, what is the horsepower and largest engine size for the truck category?

    For the truck category, the largest engine size is 5.4 with a horsepower of 300.

5. What could you say about the strength, direction, and shape of the relationship between engine size, horsepower, and type of vehicle from the information conveyed by the scatterplot?

    Both automobiles and trucks have a strong positive correlation between engine size and horsepower. They are almost identical in strength (0.88 and 0.86) and linear in shape for both automobiles and trucks. As horsepower increases, so does the engine size, and this holds true for both trucks and automobiles.

★ 14.5 REVIEW EXERCISES

1. Open **car_sales_unprepared.sav** and select the variable named *wheelbas* and labeled as *Wheelbase* for placement on the *x*-axis. For the *y*-axis, use the variable named *price* and labeled *Price in thousands*. For the *Color set* discrete variable, select *type*, which is labeled as *Vehicle type*. Build the grouped scatterplot in Figure 14.4 and answer the following questions.

Questions: (a) Which of the vehicle types has a correlation coefficient closest to zero? (b) For the truck category, does the graph tell you that size of the truck, as measured by the wheelbase, have any influence in its price? (c) What is the correlation coefficient for the automobile category? (d) How would you describe the relationships for both automobiles and trucks in this database?

Figure 14.4   Review Exercise: Grouped Scatterplot Price, Wheelbase, and Vehicle Type

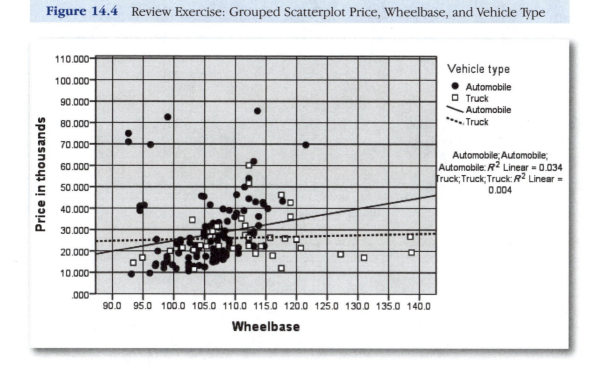

2. Open **Employee data.sav** and select the variable named *salbegin* and labeled as *Beginning salary* for use on the *x*-axis. For the *y*-axis, use the variable named *salary* and labeled *Current salary*. For the *Color set* discrete variable, select *minority*, which is labeled as *Minority classification*. Build the grouped scatterplot shown in Figure 14.5 and answer the following questions.

Questions: (a) Which of the two race classifications have the highest beginning and current salaries and what are those amounts? (b) What are the correlation coefficients between the two salaries for nonminorities and minorities? (c) How would you describe the best fit lines for minorities and nonminorities? (d) What is the estimated current salary for a minority having a beginning salary of $60,000? (e) What is the estimated current salary for a nonminority having a beginning salary of $40,000?

Figure 14.5   Review Exercises: Grouped Scatterplot Beginning and Current Salary and Minority

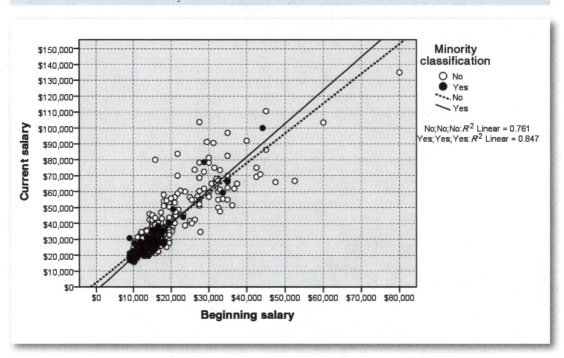

3. Open **car_sales_unprepared.sav** and select the variable named *curb_wgt* and labeled as *Curb weight* for use on the *x*-axis. For the *y*-axis, use the variable named *fuel_cap* and labeled *Fuel capacity*. For the *Color set* discrete variable, select *type*, which is labeled as *Vehicle type*. Build the grouped scatterplot shown in Figure 14.6 and answer the following questions.

Questions: (a) What type of vehicle has the greatest weight and fuel capacity? (b) What are the correlation coefficients for curb weight and fuel capacity for both automobiles and trucks? (c) How would you describe the best fit lines for automobiles and trucks? (d) What would be the estimated fuel capacity for an automobile weighing 4.500? (e) What is the estimated fuel capacity for a truck weighing 5.500?

Figure 14.6   Review Exercise: Grouped Scatterplot Fuel Capacity, Weight, and Vehicle Type

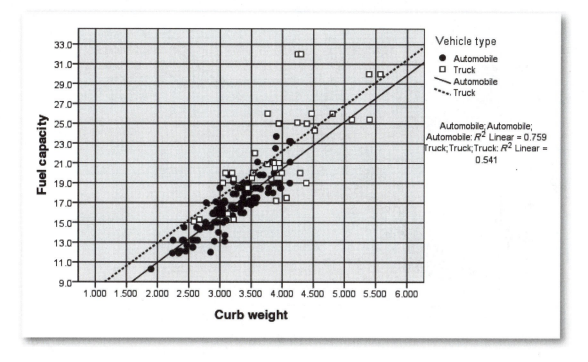

4. Open **Employee data.sav** and select the variable named *salbegin* and labeled as *Beginning salary* for use on the *x*-axis. For the *y*-axis, use the variable named *salary* and labeled *Current salary*. For the *Color set* discrete variable, select *gender*, which is labeled as *Gender*. Build the grouped scatterplot shown in Figure 14.7 and answer the following questions.

Questions: (a) Which gender has the highest beginning and current salaries and what are those amounts? (b) What are the correlation coefficients between the two salaries for females and males? (c) How would you describe the best fit lines for males and females? (d) What is the estimated current salary for a female having a beginning salary of $45,000? (e) What is the estimated current salary for a male having a beginning salary of $70,000?

Figure 14.7   Review Exercises: Grouped Scatterplot Beginning and Current Salary and Gender

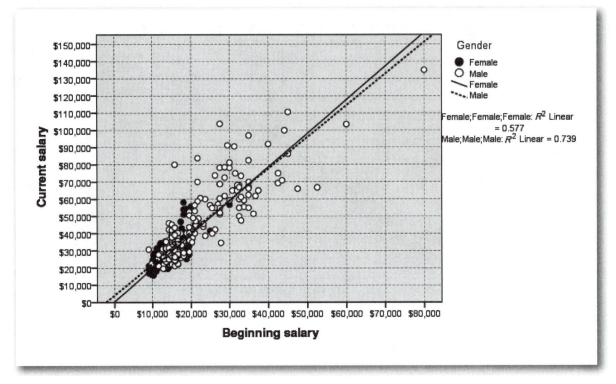

5. Open **car_sales_unprepared.sav** and select the variable named *width* and labeled as *Width* for placement on the *x*-axis. For the *y*-axis use the variable named *length* and labeled *Length*. For the *Color set* discrete variable, select *type*, which is labeled as *Vehicle type*. Build the grouped scatterplot in Figure 14.8 and answer the following questions.

Questions: (a) When measuring the correlations of width and length of automobiles and trucks, is there a great deal of difference? How does the graph answer this question? (b) If you knew the width of a truck, how much could you reduce your error in estimating its length? (c) What would you estimate the length of a truck or automobile to be, given the width was 70.0? (d) What are the correlation coefficients between the width and length of automobiles and trucks? (e) How would you describe the two correlations?

Figure 14.8   Review Exercise: Grouped Scatterplot for Length, Width, and Vehicle Type

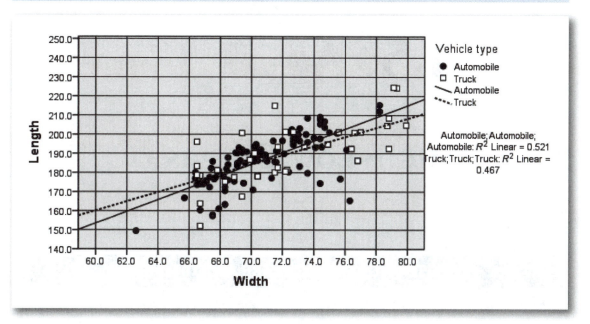

15

HIGH–LOW GRAPHS

PURPOSE OF GRAPHS YOU ARE ABOUT TO BUILD

- To show a single selected statistic for each of the three continuous variables at a specific time (the discrete variable) to observe any changes over time
- To show a single selected statistic for each of the three continuous variables, which are then categorized by a discrete variable
- To show a single selected statistic for each of the three continuous variables, which are then categorized by two discrete variables

★ **15.1 INTRODUCTION TO HIGH–LOW GRAPHS**

In the previous two chapters, you learned about the simple and grouped scatterplots as used to explore the relationship between two continuous variables. This was done by measuring an individual or object on two variables, an x and y, and then observing the strength, direction, and shape of a distribution of those bivariate xy points. In Chapters 10, 11, and 12, we graphed ranges using various boxplots to better understand the variability of a continuous variable. This chapter returns to describing variables in terms of their range of values, but now we use charts known as high–low graphs.

The value of the range is the maximum value minus the minimum value. In this chapter, we graph the maximum and minimum values in a distribution that provides for a visual picture of the range of data. This is especially useful when comparing the ranges of different variables or distributions of the same variable. For instance, we may wish to compare the range of scores on a test for females and males. This can be accomplished by graphing the two separate distributions side by side.

As with any single statistic, there are limitations on the usefulness of such information, but it can be helpful when trying to understand data. The purpose of this chapter is not to describe the limitations of the range but to present graphs, which depict the range in different ways, and to point out how they may be useful in one's quest to understand data. Therefore, we continue the theme of the book by specifying questions that may be answered by building three different styles of high–low range charts.

15.1.1 High–Low–Close Graph for Stock Value

The high–low–close graph is most often used to graph financial data dealing with securities. It is a form of time/series graph that records the changes in the price of a security, such as stock, over some period of time. Added to the standard time/series graph is the capability to show changes on a daily or even hourly basis in the stock price in terms of the maximum and minimum and the closing price for the day. The graph compiles these daily or hourly changes into a form of a line, which, when combined with many such lines, shows the overall trend in the same manner as a time/series line graph. See Figure 15.1 for an example of the high–low–close graph similar to the one you will soon build.

As you can see, the y-axis is used to display the scale that describes the dollar value of the stock. In this example, it ranges from \$1,700.00 to \$2,250.00. These are the possible ranges for the three continuous variables describing maximum, minimum, and closing daily values of the stock. The x-axis is used to display the discrete variable of date (time of observation).[1] In Figure 15.1,

---

[1]There are several different *date* formats acceptable to SPSS. SPSS will normally interpret these formats correctly. We specify date as a continuous variable when building the graph in Figure 15.1. It should also be known that when using this type of graph for tracking the value of securities, the data in the spreadsheet provides three single continuous numbers for the y-axis. These single numerical values are the maximum value, the minimum value, and the closing price for a particular time period. Notice that the last part of the y-axis title of Figure 15.1 simply states "Close." This is as it should be; however, we had to delete the word "Mean" just preceding (Close) as this is what the SPSS places in the title. When you build a similar chart later in this chapter, you will see that SPSS leaves the description of the third variable as "Mean (Close)" (see Figure 15.5). As you now know, this makes little sense since this value is based on a single value—the closing price. In the next section, we show how the graph can be used in business where it makes sense to have a mean.

Figure 15.1   High–Low–Close Graph: Stock Price Daily Changes Over a 5-Month Period

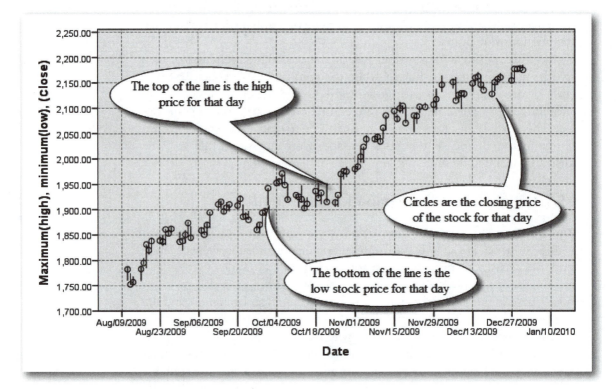

the time period covered is approximately 5 months. The information bubbles describe how the individual marks (lines and circles) describe the daily fluctuations of the stock price. Each of the vertical lines represents the range of the stock price for a particular day, while the circles represent the value when the stock market closed for the day. When you put these all vertical lines and circles together in a line, you have a trend line that is clearly visible as shown in Figure 15.1. The 5-month trend for this security is definitely upward, which can be very useful information for the financial analyst.

15.1.2 High–Low–Close Graph for Business Application

There are cases where the high–low–close graph is useful in answering questions concerning sales and marketing. Actually, the graph can be helpful in many retail or wholesale businesses where information concerning periodic movements of sale amounts can aid management's decision making. The example shown in Figure 15.2 graphs three continuous variables: the maximum sales figures for women's food purchases, the minimum for men's food purchases, and the mean for other merchandise.

Figure 15.2   High–Low–Close for Business Application

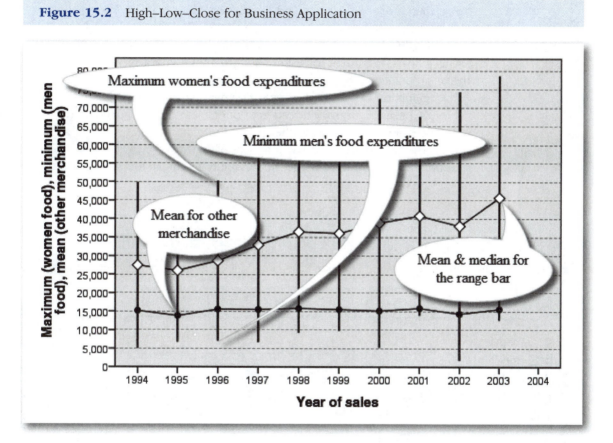

15.1.3 Simple Range Bar Graph

The simple range bar graph will show the maximum value for one variable, minimum value for another, and the mean of a third continuous variable. You can also split the three continuous variables by a single discrete variable. As with the graph shown in the previous section, the y-axis is reserved for the scale that describes the three continuous variables. The x-axis is for the discrete variable that is used to split the three continuous variables. Bars are used to describe the maximum and minimum for two of the continuous variables, while a third marker (a black circle) is used to show the mean of the third variable.

The example shown in Figure 15.3 once again uses data from 37 university students taking an intermediate-level statistics class. On the *y*-axis, you see three descriptors: maximum (points on Exam 3), minimum (points on Exam 2), and finally, mean for Exam 1. The values for these three items are presented two times on the graph, once for students expressing anxiety about taking the class and a second time for those having little or no anxiety. Thus, there are six individual and interesting data points expressed on the graph. The information bubbles in Figure 15.3 point out the values for those exhibiting little or no anxiety. The equivalent values for the anxiety group are as follows: maximum for Exam 3 is 115, minimum for Exam 2 is 23, and the mean of Exam 1 is 59.

Examination of the graph shows dissimilarities in both range and mean values. We leave it up to the reader to offer plausible explanations for the differences. Before producing the graph, there were unknown facts about the data—the simple range bar graph provided many answers. The major question that sought to compare the variability and mean for the two student anxiety groups revealed that there were differences.

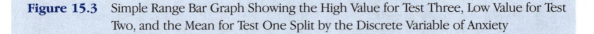

Figure 15.3   Simple Range Bar Graph Showing the High Value for Test Three, Low Value for Test Two, and the Mean for Test One Split by the Discrete Variable of Anxiety

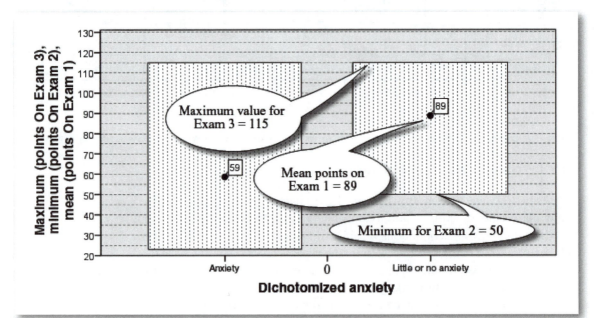

15.1.4 Clustered Range Bar Graph

There are occasions when questions may require one to split the "split" variable. Look at Figure 15.4 where the anxiety variable is split by gender as an example. When this is done, you have reason to build a clustered range bar graph. In the following graph, we will split the two anxiety groups into male and female sub-groups. Figure 15.4 splits the anxiety variable into males and females.

By looking at the graph, we can directly compare the males and females for both anxiety groups. In the anxiety group, the range of Exams 2 and 3 was larger for males $(110 - 23 = 87)$ than for females $(115 - 54 = 61)$. The females also scored slightly higher on Exam 1 having a mean of 60 versus 55 for males. For the little or no anxiety group, the range for the two exams was much less for males $(115 - 94 = 21)$ than for females $(115 - 65 = 65)$. Females did have a higher mean score (93) than males (978) on Exam 1. Comparing the anxiety and little or no anxiety groups, we say that both males and females scored higher on Exam 1 than those rated as having anxiety about the class. The differences between the two groups are such that as anxiety

Figure 15.4   Clustered Range Bar Graph: Three Tests Split by Anxiety and Gender

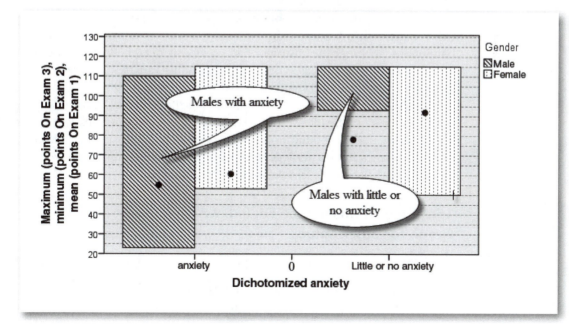

increases, the variability of test scores for males increases. For females, there is little change. The purpose here is not to speculate as to the reasons for these patterns but to show the reader the type of information these graphs communicate.

★   15.2 DATABASES AND QUESTIONS

The first graph to be built is called a high–low–close graph. It is built with data from the SPSS Sample file called **stocks2004.sav**. This database has 252 cases measured on seven variables related to the price of a stock and the dates of these observations. You will move the discrete variable (date) to the *x*-axis and three continuous variables to the *y*-axis. You build a graph to answer several questions in order to make this database more understandable.

The second high–low–close graph uses data from **catalog_seasfac.sav**. You build the same type of graph as the first one in this section, but this one takes on a totally different appearance (look at Figures 15.5 and 15.6). The different look results from the fewer range bars on the *x*-axis and the different scales on the *y*-axis. The lesson here is that data themselves and how they are scaled may change a once recognizable graph into something totally foreign. For this graph, you will place the 12 months of the year on the *x*-axis as the discrete variable. The three continuous variables relate to the dollar sales of jewelry and women's and men's clothing.

The third graph built uses **bankloan.sav** and is the simple range bar. For this project, you will once again use four variables, one discrete and three continuous. Whether the customer had previously defaulted will be the discrete variable on the *x*-axis. The three continuous variables are credit card debt, other debt, and income-to-debt ratio.

The fourth graph built is the clustered range bar and uses **bankloan.sav** database. This graph will use two discrete and three continuous variables. The customers level of education will be placed on the *x*-axis, while default history becomes the cluster/legend variable. The same continuous variables as used in the previous example are used to build this graph.

15.2.1 Questions for the High–Low–Close Graph for Stock Value

1. What was the mean price of the security on the first of January 2004?

2. How would you describe the price movement of the security during the third quarter (01-July-2004 to 01-Oct-2004)?

3. What is the change in value for this security over the four quarters recorded in the high–low–close graph?

4. Which of the three quarters exhibited the most consistent increase in value for this security?

15.2.2 Questions for the High–Low–Close Graph for Business Application

1. For the year 1995, what are the maximum sales for women's clothing and the minimum for men's?

2. What are the medians for the range (maximum to minimum) for the years 1989 and 1998? Was there an identifiable trend over the 10 years between these two values?

3. What happened to the average sales figures for jewelry over the 10-year period?

4. Which of the 10 years had the most and least variability between the maximum sales of women's clothing and the minimum for males, and what were those ranges?

15.2.3 Questions for the Simple Range Bar Graph

1. Which of the two groups (Defaulted, No and Yes) had the most variability for the maximum in other debt and the minimum for credit card debt?

2. What are the ranges (maximum other debt and the minimum credit card debt) for those defaulting and those who have not, and which is the smallest?

3. Can you identify a pattern between the two groups representing those who have defaulted and those who have not for the debt-to-income and the size of their ranges?

15.2.4 Questions for the Clustered Range Bar Graph

1. Which groups have the largest and smallest mean debt-to-income ratio?

2. What are the mean differences for all educational groupings on default history?

3. In which of the five educational categories does the default history have the least impact on the debt-to-income ratio?

4. Which of the 10 groups has the most and the least variability in the maximum other debt and minimum credit card debt?

★ 15.3 USING SPSS TO BUILD HIGH–LOW GRAPHS

In this section, you build four high–low type graphs. The first graph is a high–low–close built by tracking stock prices over a period of 252 days in 2004. The second one is also a high–low–close with a business oriented application. The third graph is a simple range bar, while the final graph is a clustered range bar.

15.3.1 Building the High–Low–Close Graph for Stock Value

For this graph, you will use **stocks2004.sav** from the SPSS Sample file. The three continuous variables are *High*, *Low*, and *Close* and the discrete variable is *Date*. There are 252 cases (dates for financial transactions) recorded in this database.

- Open **stocks2004.sav** found in the SPSS Sample file.
- Click **Graphs**, then click **Chart Builder**.
- Click **High-Low** in the *Choose from:* panel of the *Chart Builder*.
- Click and drag the **High–Low–Close icon** (the first icon) to the *Chart preview* panel.
- Click and drag the **Date** variable to the *X-Axis* box.
- Click and drag the **Close** variable to the *Close variable* box.
- Click and drag the **Low** variable to the *Low variable* box.
- Click and drag the **High** variable to the *High variable* box.
- Click **OK** (*Output Viewer* opens with the basic graph).
- Double click the **graph** to open the *Chart Editor*.
- Click **any number** on the *y*-axis.
- In the *Properties* window, click the **Scale tab**, in the *Range* panel, change *Major Increment* to **50**, then click **Apply**.
- Click the **Number Format tab**, and change the *Decimal Places* to **0** and click **Apply**.
- Click **Show Grid Lines icon** (the fifth icon from the right), click the **Lines tab** in the *Properties* window. In the *Lines* panel beneath *Weight*, click the **black arrow** and change to **0.5**, then click the **black arrow** beneath *Style* and click the **first dotted line**.
- Click **Apply**.
- Click **any number** on the *x*-axis.

- Click the **Show Grid Lines icon** (the fifth icon from the right), click **the Lines tab** in the *Properties* window. In the *Lines* panel beneath *Weight*, click the **black arrow** and click **0.5**, then click the **black arrow** beneath *Style* and click the **first dotted line**.
- Click **Apply**.
- Click the **X** in the upper right-hand corner of the *Chart Editor* (graph is now moved to the *Output Viewer*).
- Click the **graph** (a frame appears around the graph), and then click and grab the **lower right corner** of the frame (marked by a small black square), hover the mouse pointer until you see a *double-headed arrow* and move it diagonally up and to the left to reach the approximate size of the graph in Figure 15.5.

One thing you should notice about Figure 15.5 is the *y*-axis title. As discussed in Footnote 1, the word "mean" is incorrect when using the high–low–close graph to show financial data. The close variable is not a mean of anything; it represents a single value—the closing price of the stock. We left the word "mean" in Figures 15.1 and 15.5 to bring your attention to this SPSS anomaly.

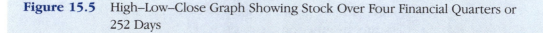

Figure 15.5   High–Low–Close Graph Showing Stock Over Four Financial Quarters or 252 Days

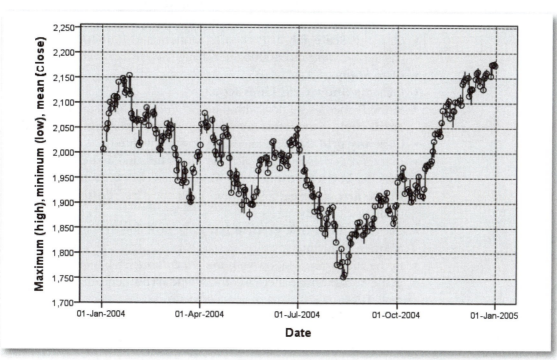

15.3.2 Building the High–Low–Close
Graph for Business Application

For building this graph, you use three continuous variables, the *x*-axis (discrete) variable records the month that the sales figures were observed. The other three continuous variables represent sales figures for jewelry and men's and women's clothing.

- Open **catalog_seasfac.sav** found in SPSS Sample file.
- Click **Graphs**, then click **Chart Builder**.
- Click **High-Low** in the *Choose from:* panel of the *Chart Builder*.
- Click and drag the **High-Low-Close icon** (the first icon) to the *Chart preview* panel.
- Click and drag the **Year, not periodic** variable to the *X-Axis* box.
- Click and drag the **Sales of jewelry** variable to the *Close variable* box.
- Click and drag the **Sales of men's clothing** variable to the *Low variable* box.
- Click and drag the **Sales of women's clothing** variable to the *High variable* box.
- Click **OK** (*Output Viewer* opens with the basic graph).
- Double click the **graph** to open the *Chart Editor* window.
- Click **any number** on the *y*-axis.
- In the *Properties* window, click the **Number Format tab** and change *Decimal Places* from **12** to **0**, then click **Apply**.
- Click the **Scale tab** in *Properties* window, and in the *Range* panel, change *Maximum* to **80000** then change *Major Increment* to **10000**.
- Click **Apply**.
- Click the **Show Grid Lines icon**.
- In the *Properties* window with the *Grid lines* tab highlighted, click the **small circle** to the **left** of *Both the major and minor ticks*, click **Apply**.
- Click **any grid line** (grid lines are now highlighted).
- In the *Properties* window, click the **Lines tab**, and in the *Lines* panel, click the **black arrow** beneath *Weight*, then click **0.25**, then click the **black arrow** beneath *Style*, and click the **first dotted line**, and finally, click **Apply**.
- Click **any high low vertical bar** while avoiding the circles (all bars are then highlighted).
- In the *Properties* window with the *Fill & Border* tab highlighted and in the *Border Style* panel, click the **black arrow** beneath *Weight*, then click **1.5**.
- Click **Apply**.

- Click **any Marker** (circle) found on each of the vertical bars.
- In the *Properties* window with the *Marker* tab highlighted and in the *Marker* panel, click the **black arrow** beneath *Size*, and then click **6**, in the *Color* panel, click the **box** to the **left** of *Fill*, then click the **black rectangular box** to its right.
- Click **Apply**.
- Click any **high low vertical bar** while avoiding clicking circles (all bars are framed).
- Click the **Add interpolation line icon** (the seventh icon from the left on the third menu bar row and two lines connecting the vertical bars appear).
- Click the **upper interpolation line** if not already highlighted.
- In the *Properties* window, click the **Lines tab**, and in the *Lines* panel, click the **black arrow** beneath *Weight* and click **1.5**, then click the **black arrow** beneath *Style* and click the **first dotted line**.
- Click **Apply**.
- With the dotted interpolation line highlighted, click the **Add Markers icon** (the fourth from the left on the third menu row).
- In the *Properties* window, click the **Marker tab**, and in the *Marker* panel, click the **black arrow** beneath *Type*, then click the **second type** in the **first** row (diamond shape), next click the **black arrow** beneath *Size* and click **8**, and in the *Color* panel, click the **box** to the **left** of *Fill*, then click the **white rectangular box**.
- Click **Apply**.
- Click the **X-Axis title**, click the **title** again and edit the title to read: **Year of sales**.
- Click the y-axis title, click the title again and edit the title to read: Maximum (women's clothing), Minimum (men's clothing), Mean (jewelry).
- **Click any** open space on the **graph** to activate the icons.
- Click the **Show Legend icon** (the third icon from the right on the *Chart Builder* menu).
- In the *Legend*, click on the uppermost **label** for the *Interpolation Line* (a frame appears around it), click this *Interpolation Line* **label** a second time and type **Median of the high low values for each year**.
- In the *Legend*, click on the lower **label** for the *Interpolation Line* (a frame appears around it), click this *Interpolation Line* **label** a second time and type **Mean amount spent for jewelry each year**.
- Click the **X** in the upper right-hand corner of the *Chart Editor* (Graph is now moved to the *Output Viewer*).
- Adjust the size of the graph to be the same as Figure 15.6.

Figure 15.6   High–Low–Close Graph for Business Application

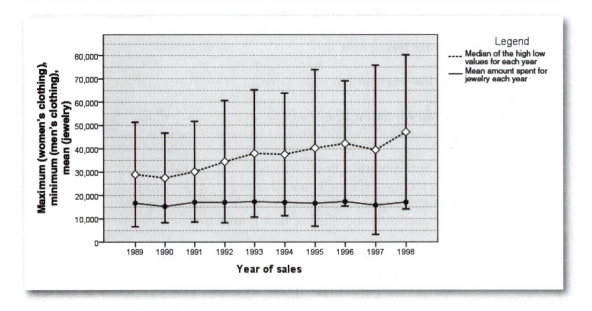

15.3.3 Building the Simple Range Bar Graph

For this graph-building project, open **bankloan.sav**. You will use three continuous and one discrete variable from this database. The first of the continuous variables is named *debtinc* and labeled *Debt to income ratio (×100)*. The next is named *creddebt* and labeled *Credit card debt in thousands*, and the final variable is named *othdebt* and labeled *Other debt in thousands*. The discrete variable placed on the *x*-axis is named *default* and labeled as *Previously defaulted*.

- Open **bankloan.sav** found in the SPSS Sample file.
- Click **Graphs**, then click **Chart Builder**.
- Click **High-Low** in the *Choose from:* panel of the *Chart Builder*.
- Click and drag the **Simple Range Bar icon** (the second icon) to the *Chart preview* panel.
- Click and drag **Previously defaulted** to the *X-Axis* box.

- Click and drag **Debt to income ratio (×100)** to the *Close variable* box.
- Click and drag **Credit card debt in thousands** to the *Low variable* box.
- Click and drag **Other debt in thousands** to the *High variable* box.
- Click **OK** (closes the *Chart Builder* and moves the basic graph to the *Output Viewer*).
- Double click the **graph** to open the *Chart Editor*.
- Click **any number** on the *y*-axis.
- In the *Properties* window, click the **Scale tab**, and in the *Range* panel, change *Minimum* to **−5**, *Major Increment* to **4**, and *Origin* to **−5**.
- Click **Apply**.
- Click **Show Grid Lines icon** (fifth icon from the right), and in the *Properties* window, click the **Lines tab**.
- In the *Lines* panel, click the **black arrow** beneath *Weight* and click **0.25**, then click the **black arrow** beneath *Style* and click the **first dotted line**, and finally, click **Apply**.
- Click **any bar** in the **graph** (both bars are framed).
- In the *Properties* window with the *Fill & Border* tab highlighted, click the **box** to the left of *Fill*, in the *Color* panel, click the **white rectangular box**.
- In the *Color* panel, click the **black arrow** beneath *Pattern*, then click the **third pattern** in the **first** row, then click **Apply**.
- Click the **circle** (*marker*) **in one of the bars**, and in the *Properties* window with the *Marker* tab highlighted and in the *Marker* panel, click the **black arrow** beneath *Size* and then click **10**.
- In the *Color* panel, click the **box** to the left of *Fill*, then click the **white rectangular box**.
- Click **Apply**.
- Click the **Data Label Mode icon**, then click **each circle** to add data labels.
- Click the **Data Label Mode icon** to turn it off.
- Click the **X** in the upper right-hand corner of the *Chart Editor* (graph is now moved to the *Output Viewer*).
- Adjust the size of the graph to be the same as Figure 15.7.

Figure 15.7   Simple Range Bar: Maximum Other Debt, Minimum Credit Card Debt, Mean of Debt-to-Income Ratio (×100), and Previously Defaulted

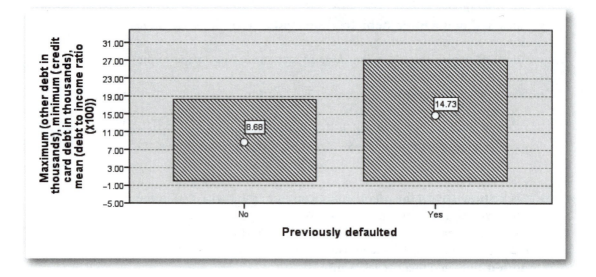

In the following section, you use the same data as above but you will add a fifth variable, level of education.

15.3.4 Building the Clustered Range Bar Graph

In the graph you are about to build, you first separate individuals into levels of education and then split those groups into those who have or have not defaulted on loans.

- Open **bankloan.sav** found in the SPSS Sample file.
- Click **Graphs**, then click **Chart Builder**.
- Click **High-Low** in the *Choose from:* panel of the *Chart Builder*.
- Click and drag the **Clustered Range Bar icon** (the third icon) to the *Chart preview* panel.
- Click and drag **Level of education** to the *X-Axis* box.
- Click and drag **Debt to income ratio (x100)** to the *Close variable* box on the *y*-axis.
- Click and drag **Credit card debt in thousands** to the *Low variable* box on the *y*-axis.
- Click and drag **Other debt in thousands** to the *High variable* box on the *y*-axis.
- Click and drag **Previously defaulted** to the *Cluster on X: set color* box.

- Click **OK** (closes the *Chart Builder* and moves the basic graph to the *Output Viewer*).
- Double click the **graph** to open the *Chart Editor* window.
- Click **any number** on the *y*-axis.
- In the *Properties* window, click the **Scale tab**, and in the *Range* panel, change *Minimum* to **−5**, *Major Increment* to **5**, and *Origin* to **−5**.
- Click **Apply**.
- Click the **Show Grid Lines icon** (the fifth icon from the right).
- In the *Properties* window with the *Grid Lines* tab highlighted, click the **small circle** to the **left** of *Both major and minor ticks*, then click **Apply**.
- Click any **grid line**.
- In the *Properties* window with the *Lines* tab highlighted and in the *Lines* panel, click the **black arrow** beneath *Weight* and click **0.25**, next click the **black arrow** beneath *Style* and click the **first dotted line**.
- Click **Apply**.
- Click **any of the labels** on the *x*-axis (e.g., "some college") (this places a frame around all labels—you will next click some of them to edit the labels as follows).
- Click the **first label** and change it to read **No high school degree**.
- Click the **fifth label**, click the **label** a second time and change it to read **Post-undergraduate**.
- Click the **small circle** to the **left** of *Minor ticks (between categories) only*.
- Click **Apply**.
- Click any **grid line** for the *x*-axis.
- In the *Properties* window with the *Lines tab* highlighted and in the *Lines* panel, click the **black arrow** beneath *Weight* and click **0.25**, next click the **black arrow** beneath *Style*, then click the **first dotted line**, and finally, click **Apply**.
- Click the **small box** to the left of *No* in the legend found in the upper right-hand corner (only the bars representing the *No* category, the blue bars in SPSS, are framed).
- In the *Properties* window with the *Fill & Border* tab highlighted, click the **box** to the **left** of *Fill*, in the *Color* panel, click the **white rectangular box**.
- In the *Color* panel, click the **black arrow** beneath *Pattern*, then click the **first pattern** in the **second** row, then click **Apply**.
- Click the **small box** to the left of *Yes* in the legend found in the upper right-hand corner (only the bars representing the *Yes* category, the green bars in SPSS, are framed).

- In the *Properties* window with the *Fill & Border* tab highlighted, and in the Color panel click the **box** to the **left** of *Fill*, then click the **white rectangular box**.
- In the *Color* panel, click the **black arrow** beneath *Pattern*, then click the **third pattern** in the **second** row, then click **Apply**.
- Click the **circle** (called a marker) **in one of the bars**, and in the *Properties* window with the *Marker* tab highlighted and in the *Marker* panel, click the **black arrow** beneath *Size* and click **8**.
- In the *Color* panel, click the **box** to the left of *Fill*, then click the **black rectangular box**.
- Click **Apply**.
- If the black circles on each bar are not framed, then click **any of them** to frame them all.
- Click the **Show Data Labels icon** (the second from the left) (adds data labels to all circles or markers).
- Click the **X** in the upper right-hand corner of the *Chart Editor* (graph is now moved to the *Output Viewer*).
- Adjust the size of the graph to be the same as Figure 15.8.

Figure 15.8   Clustered Range Bar Graph: Black Dots Represent Mean Credit Card Debt

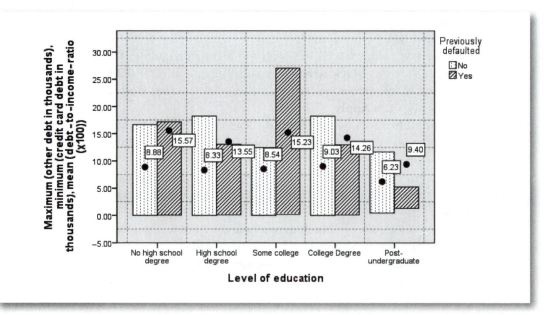

In the following three sections, we see how these four graphs answer the previously posed questions.

15.4 INTERPRETATION OF THE HIGH–LOW–CLOSE GRAPHS   ★

In this section, we see how well the graphs you built convey the information required to answer the questions about the database. What did you learn about the mass of numerical values that made up the database? Are the variables you graphed more understandable? Could the graphs assist you in making an educated decision?

15.4.1 Questions and Answers for the High–Low–Close Graph for Stock Value

The information needed to answer the following questions can be found in Figure 15.5.

1. What was the mean price of the security on the first of January 2004?

The mean price is determined by reading the y-axis value for 01-Jan-2004, which is approximately $2,010.00.

2. How would you describe the price movement of the security during the third quarter (01-July-2004 to 01-Oct-2004)?

At the beginning of the quarter, the price rapidly declines to $1,750.00, then it begins a steady increase to $1,925.00, a slight decline, and then resumes an increase in value.

3. What is the change in value for this security over the four quarters recorded in the high–low–close graph?

The value at the beginning of 2004 was $2010.00, and at the end of the year, its value was $2,175.00, an increase of $165.00.

4. Which of the three quarters exhibited the most consistent increase in value for this security?

The fourth quarter (01-Oct-2004 to 01-Jan-2004) started with a slight downturn in value but quickly recovered and changed direction for the remainder of the quarter.

15.4.2 Questions and Answers for the High–Low–Close Graph for Business Application

The information needed to answer the following questions can be found in Figure 15.6.

1. For the year 1995, what are the maximum sales for women's clothing and the minimum for men's?

The maximum sales for women's clothing is $74,000, the minimum amount for men's is $6,000.

2. What are the medians for the range (maximum to minimum) for the years 1989 and 1998? Was there an identifiable trend over the 10 years between these two values?

The median for 1989 is $29,000 and for 1998 is $47,000. During the 10 years of data collection, there was a steady increase in the median of the range except for the year 1997 when there was a slight decrease in the median value.

3. What happened to the average sales figures for jewelry over the 10-year period?

The sales figures for jewelry were steady starting in the year 1989 at $16,000 and ending in the year of 1998 slightly higher at $16,500.

4. Which of the 10 years had the most and least variability between the maximum sales of women's clothing and the minimum for men's, and what were those ranges?

In the year 1997, the maximum was $76,000 and the minimum was $3,000 for a range of $73,000. In the year 1990, the maximum was $47,000 and the minimum was $8,000 for a range of $39,000. We can say that the most variability was observed in 1997 and the least in 1990.

15.4.3 Questions and Answers for the Simple Range Bar Graph

The information needed to answer the following questions can be found in Figure 15.7.

1. Which of the two groups, those that defaulted or did not, had the most variability for the maximum in other debt and the minimum for their credit card debt?

The "yes" group that had previously defaulted had the most variability.

2. What are the ranges (maximum other debt and the minimum credit card debt) for those defaulting and those that have not, and which is the smallest?

The range for those defaulting (answered yes) is from 0 to $27,000.00 for a range of $27,000. The range for those not defaulting (answered no) is 0 to $18,000.00 for a range of $18,000. The not defaulting group has the smallest range.

3. Can you identify a pattern between the two groups representing those that have defaulted and those that have not for the debt-to-income and the size of their ranges?

Yes, the two measures increase together. As the variability increases (size of the range) so does the mean debt-to-income ratio. For those who did not default, the range is $18,000 with a mean of 8.68, while for those who had defaulted, the range is $27,000 and the mean is 14.73.

15.4.4 Questions and Answers for the Clustered Range Bar Graph

The information needed to answer the following questions can be found in Figure 15.8.

1. Which groups have the largest and smallest mean debt-to-income ratio?

Those respondents who had no high school degree and had previously defaulted have the highest ratio at 15.57. Those having the smallest debt-to-income ratio are post-undergraduates who have not previously defaulted with a ratio of 6.23.

2. What are the mean differences for all educational groupings on default history?

No high school degree $15.57 - 8.88 = 6.69$, $13.55 - 8.33 = 5.22$, $15.23 - 8.54 = 6.69$, $14.26 - 9.03 = 5.23$, and $9.40 - 6.23 = 3.17$.

3. In which of the five educational categories does the default history have the least impact on the debt-to-income ratio?

Those with post-undergraduate educational status have a debt-to-income ratio that is effected the least by their default status at 3.17.

4. Which of the 10 groups has the most and the least variability in the maximum other debt and minimum credit card debt?

The most variability goes to those who have defaulted and have some college but no degree. The smallest variability goes to the post-undergraduate group who has previously defaulted.

★   **15.5 REVIEW EXERCISES**

1. Open **catalog_seasfac.sav** and use the discrete variable named *MONTH_* and labeled as *Month, period 12* for the *x*-axis. For the *High* variable, choose the one named *women* and labeled as *Sales of women's clothing*. For the *Low* variable, select *men*, which is labeled as *Sales of men's clothing*. For the *Close* variable, choose *jewel*, which is labeled as *Sales of jewelry*. Build the high–low–close graph as shown in Figure 15.9 and answer the following questions.

Questions: (a) In which month was the highest sale of women's clothing recorded and what was that amount? (b) What direction did the mean of the range bar move between months 11 and 12? (c) What direction did the mean sales for jewelry sales take from months 1 to 12, and what were the two values? (d) Which month had the lowest median value for the range and what was that value?

Figure 15.9   Review Exercise: High–Low Graph for Men's and Women's Clothing and Month

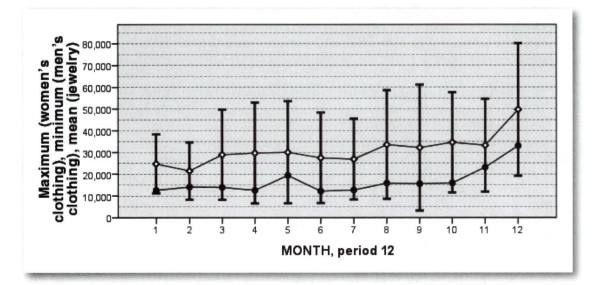

2. Open **customer_dbase.sav** and use the discrete variable named *edcat* and labeled as *Level of education* for the *x*-axis. For the legend variable, use the variable named *gender* and labeled *Gender*. For the *High* variable, use the variable named *age* and labeled as *Age in years*. The *Low* variable is named *ed* and labeled *Years of education*. The close variable is named *income* and labeled *Household income in thousands*. Build the clustered range bar graph as in Figure 15.10 and answer the following questions.

Questions: (a) What is the age of the oldest male who has a college degree? (b) What is the fewest number of years of education for the females? (c) Which category for both males and females has the most years of education and how many years do they have? (d) Which group has the highest mean income, and what is this amount? (e) What is the highest mean income for the females, and what is their level of education?

Figure 15.10   Review Exercise: Clustered Range Bar Graph for Age, Education, Income and Gender

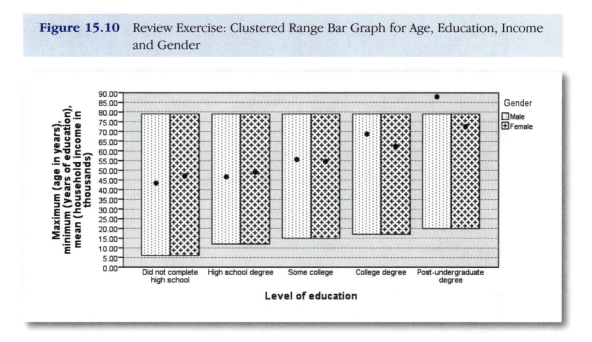

3. Open **customer_dbase.sa** and use the discrete variable named *edcat* and labeled as *Level of education* for the *x*-axis. For the *High* variable, use the variable named *age* and labeled as *Age in years*. The *Low* variable is named *ed* and labeled *Years of education*. The close variable is named *income* and labeled *Household income in thousands*. Build the simple range bar graph as in Figure 15.11 and answer the following questions.

Questions: (a) What is the age of the oldest person who has earned a college degree? (b) What is the fewest number of years of education attained by any of the respondents? (c) Which category has the most years of education, and how many years do they have? (d) Which group has the highest mean income, and what is this amount? (e) What is the mean income for those not completing high school?

Figure 15.11   Review Exercises: Simple Range Bar for Age, Education, and Income

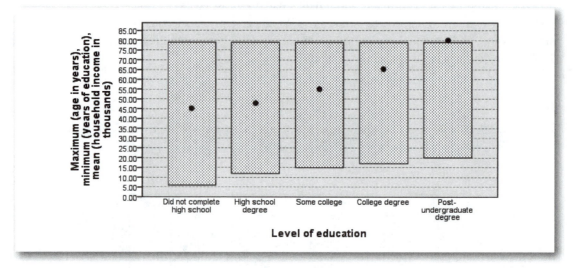

4. Open **stocks2004.sav** and use the discrete variable named *Date* for the *x*-axis. For the *High* variable, choose the one named *High*, and for the *Low* variable, select the variable named *Low*. For the *Close* variable, choose the variable named *Close*. Build the high–low–close graph as shown in Figure 15.12 and answer the following questions.

Figure 15.12   Review Exercise: High–Low–Close Stock Value by Date

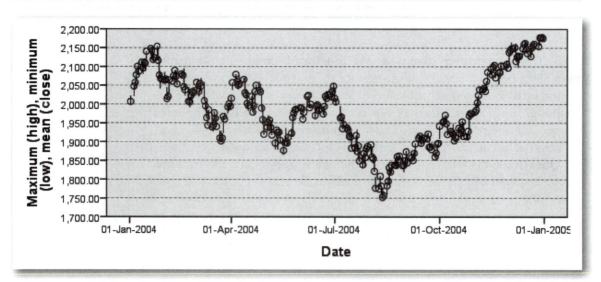

Questions: (a) What is the lowest price of the stock, and approximately when did this occur? (b) What is the highest price of the stock, and approximately when did this occur? (c) Which month for purchasing the stock would have resulted in maximum profits if it was held for 4 months? (d) If you bought the stock at the start of 2004 and sold it at the end the year, how much would you earn from its sale?

5. Open **workprog.sav** and select the discrete variable named *marital* and labeled as *Marital status* as the x-axis variable. For the *High* variable choose *incaft*, which is labeled as *Income after the program*. For the *Low* variable, select *incbef*, which is labeled as *Income before the program*. For the *Close* variable, select *age*, which is labeled as *Age in years*. Build the simple range bar as in Figure 15.13 and answer the following questions.

Questions: (a) Is there a significant difference in the ages for the married and unmarried groups? (b) What is the minimum income for unmarried individuals before the work program? (c) What is the maximum income for the married individuals after the program? (d) Which of the two groups had the most variability between maximum and minimum values?

Figure 15.13   Review Exercise: Simple Range Bar for Income Before and After the Program and Marital Status

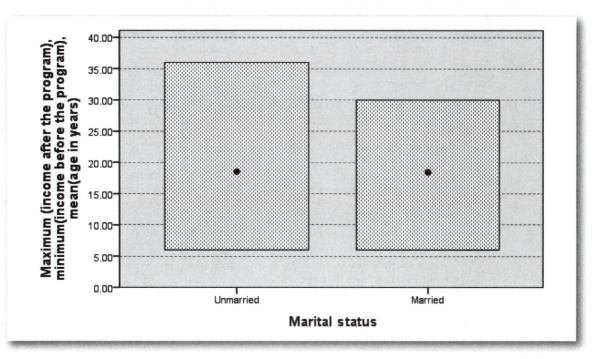

16

PANELING ON ONE DIMENSION

PURPOSE OF GRAPHS YOU ARE ABOUT TO BUILD

- To depict the relationship between the categories of two discrete variables by rows
- To depict the relationship between the categories of two discrete variables by columns
- To show a statistic of a continuous variable for the categories formed by two discrete variables
- To show one continuous variable categorized by one discrete variable

★   **16.1 INTRODUCTION TO PANELING ON ONE DIMENSION**

In this and the following chapter, we present alternative graphing techniques for several of the graphs presented in earlier chapters. The graphing methods described here are known as *paneling*. Many of the graphs you build in this chapter present the same information as the graphs already built. But you will soon see that the *paneled* format displays the data in a very different way.

When using SPSS, there are two basic ways to build paneled graphs: one dimensional and two dimensional. In this chapter, you build paneled graphs on either rows *or* columns. We choose to refer to these graphing techniques as *One Dimensional*. In Chapter 17, you build graphs based on rows *and* columns, which we designate as *Two Dimensional* panel graphing.

In this chapter, you produce several graphs while using the same data as in previous chapters. In many cases, you will be able to directly compare the graphs built in this chapter with its nonpaneled counterpart. It is often a matter of personal preference regarding the choice of styles. However, the choice should always be based on which style presents the data in the most understandable way. The final decision, to panel or not to panel, is up to the graph builder.

16.1.1 Paneling on Rows

What does a graph look like when paneled on *rows*? What type of information is conveyed when a graph is paneled by *rows*? Return to Figure 3.1 where we presented an example of a stacked bar graph. This graph presented data from 1,050 students in a way that answered questions about the percentage of males and females who earned various grades. You may recall that the *stacking* variable (x-axis) was gender and the *segment* variable was the percentage of students earning one of the five possible grades (A, B, C, D, or F). In Figure 16.1, you see a graph built using the same data and conveying identical information but presented in the paneled-by-row format.

Figure 16.1   Paneled Bar Version of Figure 3.1: Final Lecture Grade Divided by Gender (Each Panel Represents 100%)[1]

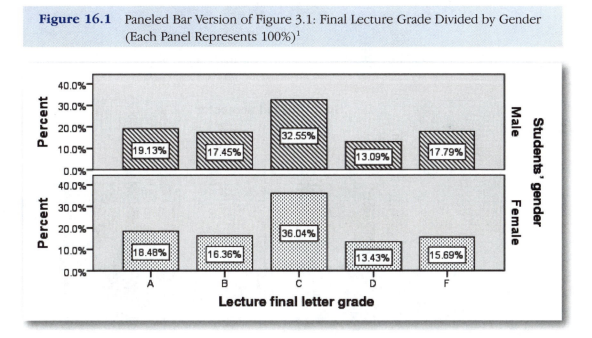

[1]You will notice that the graph depicted in Figure 16.1 has different patterns for the two rows, male and female. This graph was built using Version 18. Due to a programming problem with Version 20, you will be unable to select different patterns as we have shown in Figure 16.1. We are hopeful that by the time this book goes to press, IBM/SPSS will have fixed this problem. When building graphs, later in this chapter, we use Version 20, making it impossible to select different patterns for categories of variables.

The information conveyed in Figure 16.1 is the same as in Figure 3.1—the gender similarities and/or differences for the various earned grades by these 1,050 students. Some may feel that the paneling approach makes the data more understandable. In the authors' opinion, the stacked and paneling methods are totally acceptable as they both answer the same questions. Later in this chapter, you learn to build a paneled graph as in Figure 16.1, so the choice between stacked or paneled will ultimately be based on your personal preference.

16.1.2 Paneling on Columns

Paneling on columns results in Figure 16.2. In this example, we depicted the gender differences for the 1,050 students enrolled in all spring and fall semester classes. The first paneled column represents the gender of students attending spring semester classes, while the second column represents fall semester students. This paneled-by-column graph clearly and succinctly shows a pattern for the proportion of females and males enrolled in spring and fall semesters.

Figure 16.2   Paneled-by-Columns for Gender and Semester (Each Panel Represents 100%)[2]

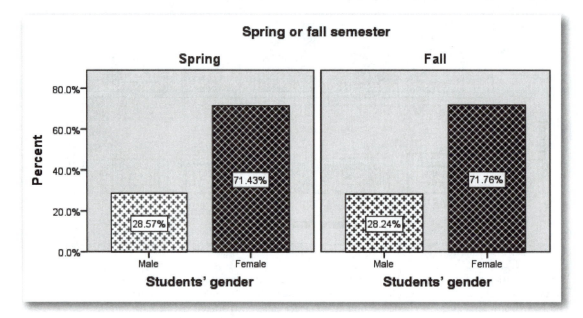

[2]See Footnote 1 regarding the patterns of this graph.

You may wish to compare the appearance of this paneled data with the stacked bar in Chapter 3 and the clustered bar presented in Chapter 4. Any of these three graphing approaches would work since they can all work with two discrete variables and percentages.

16.1.3 Paneling on Columns (Mean on the *Y*-Axis)

In this section, you see the paneled version of a multiline graph that was presented in Figure 7.4 in the chapter on multiline graphs. The graph shown in Figure 16.3 was built using the paneled-by-columns format. We used the same database (1,050 students) that was used to build the multiline graph in Figure 7.4. You may recall that the original line graph plotted the mean total semester points earned by 1,050 students over an 11-year period.

Just as in the multiline graph, we still see two separate lines representing males and females on their mean semester points over a period of 11 years.

Figure 16.3 Paneled Multiline Version of Figure 7.4: Mean Semester Points by Gender and Year

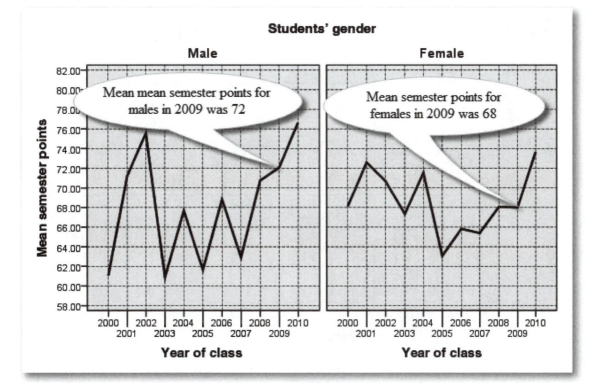

However, with the paneled format, you now have these lines on separate graphs. This may make a direct year-by-year comparison more difficult (from a direct visual aspect) as you must interpret the values on the *y*-axis. The information bubbles in Figure 16.3 show how the interpretation remains straightforward.

16.1.4 Paneling on Rows (Continuous Data on the *x*-axis)

The graph in Figure 16.4 resulted when a continuous *x*-axis variable was paneled by gender. The uppermost row displays the weights of male children as a simple histogram. The lower row shows a histogram displaying the weights of female children. This graph is rather straightforward in that SPSS simply splits the distribution of all children's weights by gender. It then constructs two histograms and places one above the other as shown in Figure 16.4. In Chapter 9, when building the population pyramid, you generated the same type of graphical information by splitting a continuous variable by using a second discrete variable. Return to Figure 9.2 for an example of what the graph would look like if you had used a population pyramid. The data used in Figure 9.2 were similar in that gender was used to split average semester points.

Figure 16.4   Paneled by Rows Using Weights of Children Split by Gender

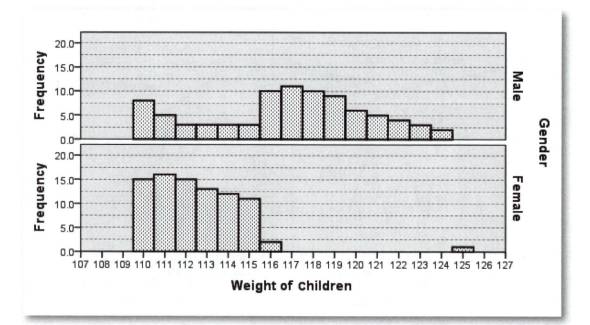

The choice between the population pyramid and the paneled graph is up to the graph builder and should be influenced by the type of audience and types of questions. You want a graph that clearly answers questions while also presenting a clear summary of your data. Given the power of the *Chart Builder*, the data used can be manipulated to make many different graphs. Therefore, you may find that a little experimentation is a good thing. You may wish to build several graphs to see which type answers the questions in the best way.

16.2 DATABASES AND QUESTIONS ★

The first graph built in this chapter uses the **customer_dbase.sav**. The variable for the *x*-axis is named *jobcat* and labeled *Job category*, and for the *legend* variable, you use *gender*. Therefore, this first paneled graph uses two discrete variables where you split various job categories by gender. We are seeking answers to questions concerning the percentages of males and females occupying different jobs by producing a graph paneled on *rows*.

The second paneled graph uses the **1911 General Social Survey.sav.** The variable for the *x*-axis is named *region* and labeled *Region of the United States*. The variable named *race* and labeled *Race of respondent* is known as the *Panel* variable when using the *Chart Builder*. This paneled graph uses two discrete variables where you split regions of the United States by the race of the respondent. We are seeking answers to questions concerning the percentages of various races that live within the three regions by producing a graph paneled on *columns*.

The third paneled graph uses **Employee data.sav**. For this graph, use the variable named *minority* and labeled *Minority classification* for the *x*-axis. For the *y*-axis, use the variable named *salary* and labeled *Current salary*. And finally, use the variable named *jobcat* and labeled *Employment category* for the panel variable. This paneled graph differs from the previous two in that we add a third continuous variable, salary. Our questions investigate the relationship between minority status, job classification, and the mean salary.

The fourth paneled graph uses **workprog.sav**. For the *x*-axis variable, use the continuous variable named *age* and labeled *Age in years*, and for the *panel* variable, use *marital*, which is labeled *Marital status*. The questions for this paneled graph will investigate the number of individuals in various age intervals and their marital status.

16.2.1 Questions for a Graph Paneled on Rows

The following questions are intended to provide information about the SPSS database called **customer_dbase.sav**. You will build a graph paneled on rows to answer these questions.

1. What job category, for males, has the highest percentage of employees?

2. What job category, for females, has the highest percentage of employees?

3. In general, what might be said about the percentages for all job categories when comparing males and females?

4. What are the job category ranks, from the highest to the lowest, for females and males, and are they the same?

16.2.2 Questions for a Graph Paneled on Columns

The following questions concern the SPSS database named **1911 General Social Survey.sav**.

1. Which region of the United States has the highest percentage of the Black race category?

2. Which region of the United States has the lowest percentage of Blacks?

3. What is the rank order (from the highest to the lowest) of the region choices for the Black race?

16.2.3 Questions for a Graph Paneled on Columns (Mean on the *Y*-Axis)

The following questions are intended to provide information about the SPSS database called **Employee data.sav**. You will build a graph paneled on columns with a mean on the *y*-axis to answer these questions.

1. Which of the three job classifications has the greatest difference in mean salaries for minority and nonminority classification?

2. Which of the three job categories has the smallest salary difference for minorities and nonminorities?

3. Which of the three job categories has the second smallest salary difference for minorities and nonminorities?

16.2.4 Questions for a Graph Paneled on Rows (Continuous Data on the *X*-Axis)

The following questions are intended to provide information about the SPSS database called **workprog.sav**. You will build a graph paneled on rows with a continuous variable placed on the *x*-axis to answer these questions.

1. How many married individuals are aged 19.5 to 20.5 years?

2. Which of the groups (married or unmarried) has the most individuals aged 20.5 to 21.5 years, and how many individuals of this age does each group contain?

3. Which of the age groups (married or unmarried) has the lowest number of individuals aged 15.5 to 16.5 years and how many individuals of this age does each group contain?

4. What is the age interval that contains the most unmarried individuals, and how many individuals does this interval contain?

5. What is the age interval that contains the most married individuals, and how many individuals does this interval contain?

16.3 USING SPSS TO BUILD THE 1-D PANELED GRAPH ★

In this section, you build four different paneled graphs using four different SPSS databases. Each will answer the specific set of questions about the database that provided the data used in their construction.

16.3.1 Building a Paneled Graph on Rows

The graph you build in this section uses the identical data and variables used to produce the clustered bar graph shown in Figure 4.4. You may wish to compare the percentages in each of the 12 jobs and gender categories with the earlier graph when you have finished building this graph.

- Open **customer_dbase.sav** (found in the SPSS Sample file).
- Click **Graphs**, then click **Chart Builder**.
- Click **Bar** in the *Choose from* list.

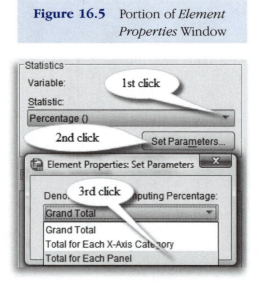

Figure 16.5 Portion of *Element Properties* Window

- Click and drag the **Simple Bar icon** (the first icon in the first row of icons) to the *Chart preview* panel.
- In the middle of the *Chart Builder* window, click the **Groups/Point ID button** and then click the **box to the left of Rows panel variable**.
- Click and drag **Job category** to the *X-Axis* box in the *Chart preview* window.
- Click and drag **Gender** to the *Panel* box on the right.
- The *Element Properties* window should be open, if not, click the **Element Properties button** in the right middle portion of the *Chart Builder* window.
- In the *Statistics* panel of the *Element Properties* window, click the **black arrow** to the **right** of *Count* (the first click as shown in Figure 16.5), then click **Percentage (?)** from the drop-down menu (notice that this menu is not shown in Figure 16.5).
- Click **Set Parameters** (the second click as shown in Figure 16.5) (*Element Properties: Set Parameters* window opens), click the **black arrow** to the right of *Grand Total,* then click **Total for Each Panel** (the third click shown in Figure 16.5).
- Click **Continue**, then click **Apply**.
- Click **OK** in the *Chart Builder* window (basic graph now moved to the *Output Viewer*—if not, open then click **Output** found on the task bar at the bottom of your screen).
- Double click the **graph**, and the *Chart Editor* opens.
- Click **any bar in the graph** (a faint frame appears around all bars).
- In the *Properties* window, click the *Fill & Border* tab, and in the *Color* panel, click the **box** to the left of *Fill*, then click the **white rectangular box**.
- Click the **black arrow** beneath *Pattern*, and click the **third pattern** in the **first** row.
- Click **Apply** (all bars now have the diagonal pattern).
- All bars should be highlighted, if not click any bar to highlight them, then click **Show Data Labels icon** (the second icon from the left).

Figure 16.6 Job Category Paneled on Rows (Each Panel Represents 100% for Each Gender)[3]

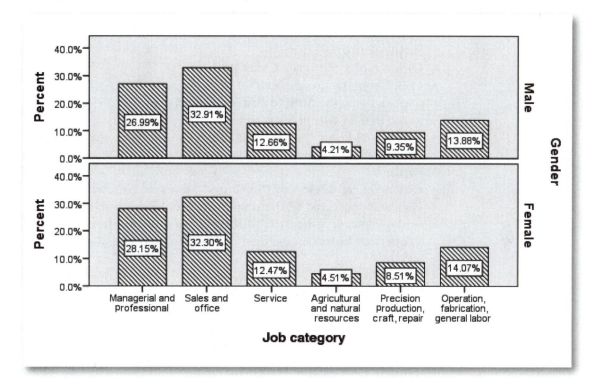

- Click the **X** in the upper right-hand corner, closing *Chart Editor* and moving the edited graph to the *Output Viewer*.
- Click the **graph** and adjust its size to approximate the graph in Figure 16.6.

16.3.2 Building a Paneled Graph on Columns

The graph you build in this section uses the identical data and variables used to produce the stacked bar graph shown in Figure 3.6. You may wish to compare

---

[3]Version 20 was used to build this graph.

the percentages in each of the nine race/region categories with the earlier graph when you have finished building this one.

- Open **1991 U.S. General Social Survey.sav** (found in the SPSS Sample file).
- Click **Graphs**, then click **Chart Builder**.
- Click **Bar** in the *Choose from* list.
- Click and drag the **Simple Bar icon** (the first icon in the first row of icons) to the *Chart preview* panel.
- In the middle of the *Chart Builder* window, click the **Groups/ Point ID button**, then click the **box** to the **left** of *Columns panel variable*.
- Click and drag **Region of the United States** to the *X-Axis* box.
- Click and drag **Race of the respondent** to the box named *Panel*.
- If the *Element Properties* window is not open, click **Element Properties button** in the right middle portion of the *Chart Builder* window.
- In the *Statistics* panel of the *Element Properties* window, click the **black arrow** to the **right** of *Count*, then click **Percentage (?)** found on the drop-down menu.
- Click **Set Parameters** (*Element Properties: Set Parameters* window opens), click the **black arrow** to the **right** of *Grand Total*, then click **Total for Each Panel**, click **Continue**, then click **Apply**.
- Click **OK** in the *Chart Builder* window (basic graph now moved to the *Output Viewer*—if not open, then click **Output** found on the task bar at the bottom of your screen).
- Double click the **graph** (*Chart Editor* opens).
- Click the **Show Data Labels icon** (inserts data labels on all bars).
- Click **any bar** in the **graph** (a faint frame appears around all bars).
- In the *Properties* window, click the **Fill & Border tab**, and in the *Color* panel, click the **box** to the **left** of **Fill** then click the **white rectangular box**.
- Click the **black arrow** beneath *Pattern,* and click the **last pattern** in the **first** row.
- Click **Apply**.
- Click the **X** in the upper right-hand corner, closing *Chart Editor* and moving the edited graph to the *Output Viewer*.
- Click the **graph** and adjust its size to approximate the graph in Figure 16.7.

Figure 16.7   Region of Residence Paneled on Race Columns (Each Panel Represents 100% for that Race)[4]

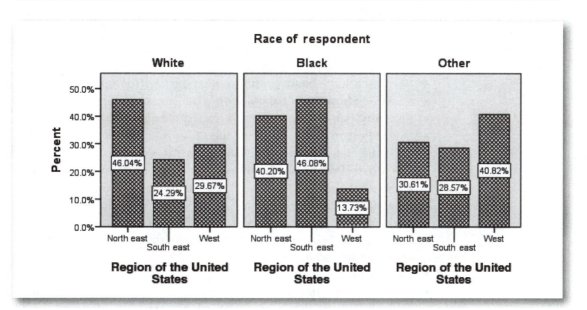

16.3.3 Building a Paneled Graph on Columns (Mean on the *Y*-Axis)

The graph built in this section is similar to the one in Figure 16.7; however, you add a continuous variable to the *y*-axis. When finished, compare the two graphs, taking special note of the different appearances of the *y*-axis. Once you build this graph as shown in Figure 16.8, you will see that patterns for the various categories are patterned in different ways. We used Version 20 to build this graph since a statistic on the *y*-axis permits the selective assignment of patterns to individual bars.

- Open **Employee data.sav** (found in the SPSS Sample file).
- Click **Graphs**, then click **Chart Builder**.
- Click **Bar** in the *Choose from* list.
- Click and drag the **Simple Bar icon** (the first icon in the first row of icons) to the *Chart preview* panel.
- In the middle of the *Chart Builder* window, click the **Groups/ Point ID button**, then click the **box** to the left of *Columns panel variable*.

---

[4]Version 20 was used to build this graph.

- Click and drag **Minority classification** to the *x*-axis.
- Click and drag **Current Salary** to the *y*-axis.
- Click and drag **Employment category** to the *Panel* box.
- Click **OK** (*Chart Builder* closes, and *Output Viewer* opens with the basic graph).
- If the *Output Viewer* is not showing, click **Output** found on the task bar at the bottom of the computer screen.
- Double click the **basic graph** to open the *Chart Editor*.
- Click the **Show Data Labels icon** (data labels appear on all bars).
- Click **any bar** (a faint frame appears around all bars).
- In the *Properties* window with the *Categories* tab highlighted, click **No**, which is found beneath *Order* in the *Categories* panel. Then click the **Move Down black arrow** found to the right, click **Apply** (changes the order of the "yes" and "no" categories on the *x*-axis of the graph).
- In the *Properties* window, click the **Fill & Border tab**, and in the *Color* panel, click the **box** to the left of *Fill*, then click the **white rectangular box** to the right.
- Click **Apply** (all bars turn white).
- Click the **first bar in left column** and click the **black arrow** beneath *Pattern*, then click the **third pattern** in the **first** row, and click **Apply**.
- Click the **second bar in the left column** and click the **black arrow** beneath *Pattern*, then click **the first pattern** in the **third** row, and click **Apply**.
- Click the **first bar in the middle column** and click the **black arrow** beneath *Pattern*, then click the **third pattern** in the **first** row, and click **Apply**.
- Click the **second bar in the middle column** and click the **black arrow** beneath *Pattern*, then click the **first pattern** in the **third** row, and click **Apply**.
- Click the **first bar in the right column** and click the **black arrow** beneath *Pattern*, then click the **third pattern** in the **first** row, and click **Apply**.
- Click the **second bar in the right column** and click the **black arrow** beneath *Pattern*, then click the **first pattern** in the **third** row, and click **Apply**.
- Click the **X** in the upper right-hand corner, closing *Chart Editor* and moving the edited graph to the *Output Viewer*.
- Click the **graph** and adjust its size to approximate the graph in Figure 16.8.

Figure 16.8 Paneled Graph With Mean on the *Y*-Axis and Discrete Variable on the *X*-Axis[5]

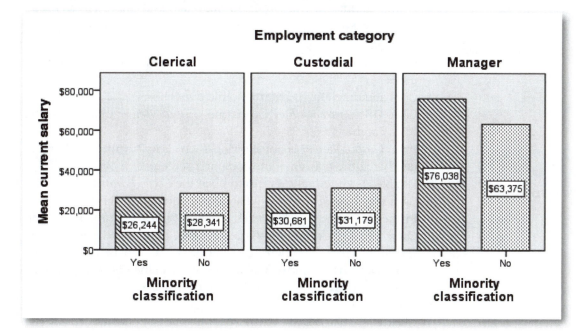

16.3.4 Building a Paneled Graph on Rows (Continuous Data on the *X*-Axis)

In this section, a continuous variable is split by a single discrete variable, having two categories, yielding two separate histograms that are stacked one on top of the other.

- Open **workprog.sav** (found in the SPSS Sample file).
- Click **Graphs**, then click **Chart Builder**.
- Click **Histogram** in the *Choose from* list.

---

[5]In contrast to Figures 16.1 and 16.2, the graph in Figure 16.8 can be built using Versions 18, 19, or 20. Version 20 will allow the graph builder to insert different patterns when using the "mean" value on the *y*-axis as in Figure 16.8.

- Click and drag the **Simple Histogram icon** (the first icon) to the *Chart preview* panel.
- In the middle of the *Chart Builder* window, click the **Groups/Point ID button**, then click the **box** to the left of the *Rows panel variable*.
- Click and drag **Age in years** to the *x*-axis in the *Chart preview* panel.
- Click and drag **Marital status** to the *panel* box.
- Click **OK** (*Chart Builder* closes and *Output Viewer* opens with the basic graph).
- If the *Output Viewer* is not showing, then click **Output** found on the task bar at the bottom of the computer screen.
- Double click the **basic graph** to open the *Chart Editor*.
- Click **any histogram bar** (a faint frame surrounds all bars).
- In the *Properties* window, click the **Fill & Border tab**, and in the *Color* panel, click the **box** to the left of *Fill* then click the **white rectangular box** to the right, click the **black arrow** beneath *Pattern* and click the **third pattern** in the **first** row, in the *Border Style* panel, click the **black arrow** beneath *Weight*, click **1.5**.
- Click **Apply**.
- Click the **Show Data Labels icon** (the second icon from the left).
- In the *Properties* window, click the **Text Style tab**, and in the *Font* panel, click the **black arrow** beneath *Preferred Size* then click **8**.
- Click **Apply**.
- Click **any number** on the *y*-axis, then click the **Scale tab** in the *Properties* window, and in the *Range* panel, change the *Major Increment* to **50**.
- Click **Apply**.
- Click **any number** on the *x*-axis.
- In the *Properties* window, click the **Scale tab**, and in the *Range* panel, change *Major Increment* to **1**.
- Click **Apply**.
- Click the **X** in the upper right-hand corner to close *Chart Editor*, which moves the edited graph to the *Output Viewer*.
- Click the **graph** and adjust its size to approximate the graph in Figure 16.9.

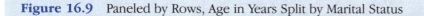

Figure 16.9   Paneled by Rows, Age in Years Split by Marital Status

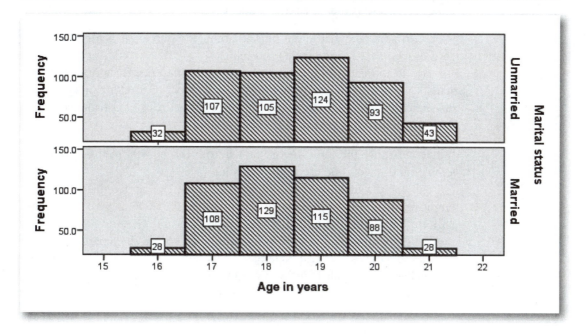

16.4 INTERPRETATION OF 1-D PANELED GRAPHS   ★

The interpretation of the four 1-D paneled graphs just built resides in the answers to the various questions posed earlier in this chapter. The following sections provide answers to these questions.

16.4.1 Questions and Answers: Graph Paneled on Rows

The information needed to answer the following questions is found in Figure 16.6.

1. What job category, for males, has the highest percentage of employees?
   The Sales and Office category has 32.91% of the male work force, making it the largest category for the males.

2. What job category, for females, has the highest percentage of employees?

The Sales and Office category has 32.30% of the female work force, making it the largest category for the females.

3. In general, what might be said about the percentages for all job categories when comparing males and females?

For all job categories, there is very little difference. It is doubtful that statistical evidence could be generated in support of the idea of significant differences. A chi-square test using the null hypothesis of equality could be used to confirm this guess.

4. What are the job category ranks, from the highest to the lowest, for females and males, and are they the same?

Sales and office have the most male (32.91%) and female (32.30%) employees, then comes Managerial and Professional at 26.99% males and 28.15% for females. The Operation, Fabrication and General Labor comes next at 13.88% males and 14.07% females, then comes the Service category with 12.66% males and 12.47% females. Precision Production, and Craft, and Repair has 9.35% males and 8.51% females, while Agricultural and Natural Resources has 4.21% males and 4.51% females.

16.4.2 Questions and Answers: Graph Paneled on Columns

The information needed to answer the following questions is found in Figure 16.7.

1. Which region of the United States has the highest percentage of the Black race category?

The South Eastern region of the United States has the highest concentration of Blacks at 46.08%.

2. Which region of the United States has the lowest percentage of Blacks?

The Western region has the lowest percentage of Blacks at 13.73%.

3. What is the rank order (from the highest to the lowest) of the region choices for the Black race?

The most popular choice of region to live in for the Black race is the South East (46.08%), then the North East (40.20%), and finally, the West at 13.73%.

16.4.3 Questions and Answers: Graph Paneled on Columns (Mean on the Y-Axis)

The information needed to answer the following questions is found in Figure 16.8.

1. Which of the three job classifications has the greatest difference in mean salaries for minority and nonminority classification?

The largest difference for the mean salary is in the manager job category with minorities earning more ($76,038) and nonminorities earning less ($63,375). The difference for this job classification is $12,663.

2. Which of the three job categories has the smallest salary difference for minorities and nonminorities?

Custodial workers have the smallest difference between mean salaries for minorities ($30,681) and nonminorities ($31,179), the difference is $498.

3. Which of the three job categories has the second smallest salary difference for minorities and nonminorities?

Clerical workers have the second smallest difference between mean salaries for minorities ($26,244) and nonminorities ($28,341), the difference is $2,097.

16.4.4 Questions and Answers: Graph Paneled on Rows (Continuous Data on the X-Axis)

The information needed to answer the following questions is found in Figure 16.9.

1. How many married individuals are aged 19.5 to 20.5 years?
There are 90 married individuals in the age interval of 19.5 to 20.5.

2. Which of the groups (married or unmarried) has the most individuals aged 20.5 to 21.5 years, and how many individuals of this age does each group contain?

The unmarried category has the most individuals for this age interval. There are 43 unmarried individuals in the age interval of 20.5 to 21.5 and there are 28 married individuals in this same age interval.

3. Which of the age groups (married or unmarried) has the lowest number of individuals aged 15.5 to 16.5 years and how many individuals of this age does each group contain?

The married group has the lowest number of individuals for this age interval. There are 28 married individuals in the age interval of 15.5 to 16.5, and there are 32 unmarried individuals for this same age interval.

4. What is the age interval that contains the most unmarried individuals, and how many individuals does this interval contain?

The tallest bar of the histogram for unmarried individuals is the bar representing those individuals who are aged 18.5 to 19.5 years. There are 124 individuals who belong to this age interval.

5. What is the age interval that contains the most married individuals and how many individuals does this interval contain?

The tallest bar for married individuals is the bar that represents those individuals who are aged 17.5 to 18.5 years. There are 129 individuals who belong to this age interval.

★   16.5 REVIEW EXERCISES

1. Open SPSS Sample file **1991 U.S. General Social Survey.sav**. Select two discrete variables—one is named *childs* and labeled *Number of children* and the other is named *race* and labeled *Race of respondent*. The graph should be paneled by rows using *Race of respondent,* and place *Number of children* on the x-axis. Set parameters to percentage of total for each panel. Build the paneled bar graph in Figure 16.10 to answer the following questions.

Questions: (a) What percentage of White respondents have no children? (b) What percentage of Black respondents have five children? (c) What percentage of respondents who belong to the Other Category have four children? (d) How many White, Black, and Other responded that they have seven children? (e) How many White, Black, and Other responded that they have two children? (f) How many White, Black, and Other responded that they have five children?

Figure 16.10   Review Exercise: Paneled Graph by Rows (Each Panel Represents 100% of that Race)

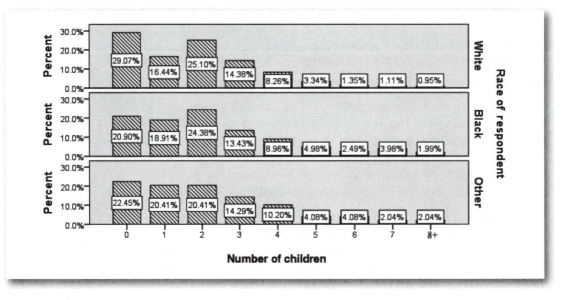

2. Open SPSS Sample file **1991 U.S. General Social Survey.sav**. Select discrete variable, named *region* and labeled as *Region of the United States* and move to the *x*-axis. Select the discrete variable named *life* and labeled *Is life exciting or dull* and use it to panel-by-column. Build the paneled bar graph shown in Figure 16.11 to answer the following questions.

Questions: (a) What percentage of those who live in the North East have an exciting life? (b) What percentage of those who live in the South East have a Routine life? (c) What percentage of those who live in the West have a Dull life? (d) What are the percentages of those who responded that they have an exciting life for the three regions (North East, South East, and West)? (e) What are the percentages of those who live in the West regarding to their outlook on life? (f) Which region has the highest percentage of people expressing that life is exiting?

Figure 16.11   Review Exercise: Paneled by Columns (Each Panel Represents 100% of Those Regions for That Particular Feeling About Life)

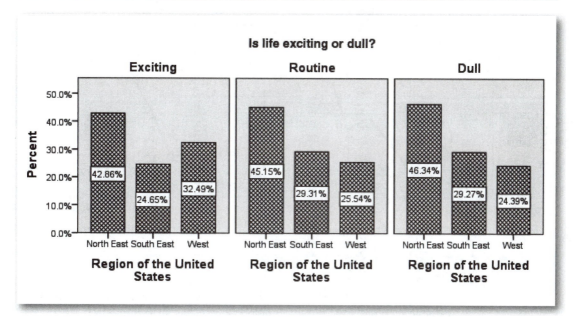

3. Open SPSS Sample file **Employee data.sav**. Select the discrete variable named *educ* and labeled *Educational level* and move it to the *x*-axis. Select the continuous variable named *salary* and labeled *Current salary* and move it to the *y*-axis. Select the discrete variable named *minority* and labeled

Minority classification and move it to the panel box. Build the paneled graph (by column) graph shown in Figure 16.12. Hint: Remember to click *Line* in the *Choose from:* list of the *Chart Builder* and move the *Simple Line icon* to the *Chart preview* to build this graph.

Questions: (a) What is the most years of education obtained by minorities and nonminorities? (b) What is the trend in earnings for the nonminority after 15 years of education? (c) What is the highest salary earned by nonminorities and minorities? (d) How would you describe the trend line for minorities after 18 years of education? (e) What is the least amount earned by minorities and nonminorities, and what are the years of education for each of those amounts?

Figure 16.12   Review Exercise: Paneled Multiline Graph With Mean on the *Y*-Axis

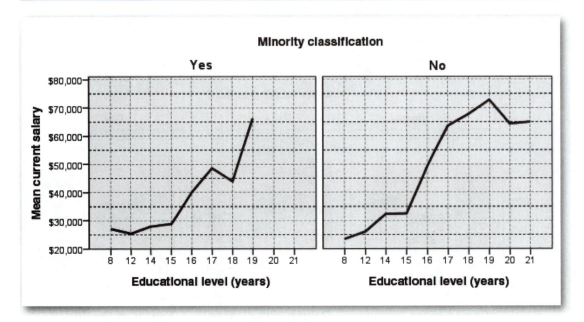

4. Open **workprog.sav** and select one discrete and one continuous variable to build a histogram paneled on rows as shown in Figure 16.13. For the *x*-axis, you use the variable named *age* and labeled *Age in years*. The discrete variable is named *ed* and labeled as *Level of education*.

Questions: (a) What is the oldest age interval for those who did not complete high school, and how many are in that interval? (b) Which age interval and level of education classification contains the largest number of individuals? (c) Which age interval and level of education classification contains the smallest number of individuals? (d) Which of the three levels of education show the greatest range of ages? (e) For those having some college education, what is the age interval containing the fewest number of individuals?

Figure 16.13   Review Exercise: Paneled on Rows Continuous Data on the *X*-Axis

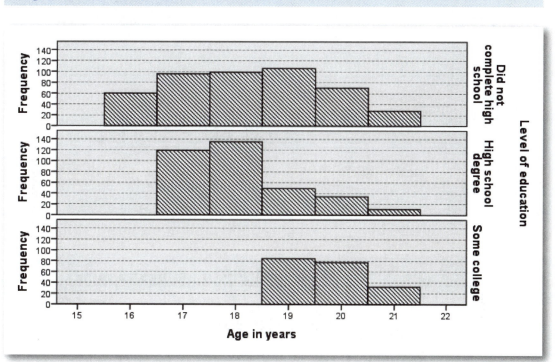

5. Open SPSS Sample file **1991 U.S. General Social Survey.sav**. Select the dicrete variable named *childs* and labeled *Number of children* for the *x*-axis. Select the discrete variable named *race* and labeled *Race of respondent* for the row paneled variable. Build the paneled graph shown in Figure 16.14. This graph shows the percentages of respondents and the number of children categorized by race. Hint: Set parameters as percentage of the grand total.

Questions: (a) What percentage of the total respondents are White and have no children? (b) What percentage are Black and have no children? (c) What percentage belongs to the Other category and have no children? (d) What is the percentage of respondents for the White race who responded to the survey? (Add percentages in the row that belong to White)? (e) What is the percentage of respondents for the Black race who responded to the survey? (f) What is the percentage of respondents for the Other race that responded to the survey? (g) Does the graph tell us that the White population in the United States has more children than the rest of the society?

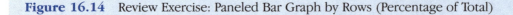

Figure 16.14   Review Exercise: Paneled Bar Graph by Rows (Percentage of Total)

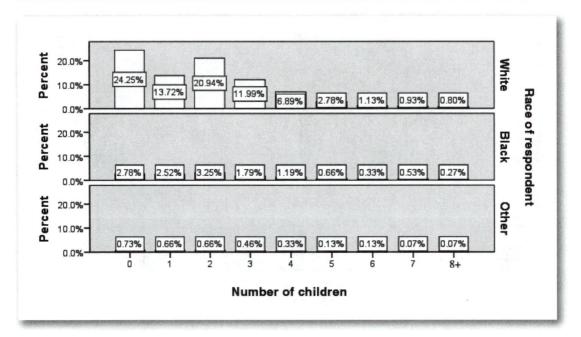

17

PANELING ON
TWO DIMENSIONS

PURPOSE OF GRAPHS YOU ARE ABOUT TO BUILD

- To show the percentage of each panel of people or objects that are contained in a group defined by the categories of three discrete variables
- To show the percentage of the total of people or objects that are contained in a group that is defined by the categories of three discrete variables
- To sort individuals or objects by the categories of three discrete variables and determine the group value for a continuous variable
- To sort individuals or objects by the categories of two discrete variables and determine the group value for a continuous variable

---

17.1 INTRODUCTION TO 2-D PANELED GRAPHS ★

In the previous chapter, alternative graphing methods were offered for many of the graphs you built in earlier chapters. This chapter continues with that theme but with an additional element added to your graph-making capabilities. In the previous chapter, you built graphs based on rows *or* columns. You now build paneled graphs based on rows *and* columns and, therefore, have a 2-D paneled graph.

When building these 2-D graphs, you utilize the same variables as in earlier chapters. Therefore, you will be able to directly observe the differences between the two unique graphing approaches.

One graphing method that is new in this chapter is building a graph depicting the relationship between three discrete and one continuous variable. We provide an example and give you the experience of building this graph. Paneling by rows and columns may sound complex but read on as we explain each of the paneling approaches used in 2-D graphing. You will find that building and understanding these paneled graphs is not difficult and possibly very useful in fulfilling your graphing needs.

17.1.1 Paneling on Rows and Columns (Percentage of Each Panel)

In this section, we demonstrate a basic graph that was paneled by rows and columns. This graph can be rather complicated, but for the right situation, it will convey useful information in a clear and efficient manner. The database used is the same as in the previous examples, so the graph presents grades earned by 1,050 students over an 11-year period. For this graph, three discrete variables are used: *Gender* (female or male), *Dichotomized class time* (day or evening), and *Semester* (spring or fall).

As seen in Figure 17.1, this graph has four separate panels, each representing four groups of students who have been categorized by gender, class time, and semester. An example of this classification system would be to look at the upper right-hand panel in Figure 17.1. Following the graph maker's instructions, the SPSS *Chart Builder* has calculated the percentage of male and female students taking day classes in the fall semesters and presented it as a simple bar graph. We can say that the graph informs us that 70.65% of the students taking day classes in the fall semesters were female and 29.35% were male.

Notice that each individual panel totals to 100%. The fact that each panel presents a unique group of students having different characteristics makes comparisons rather straightforward. There are many questions that could be answered about the data using the graph pictured in Figure 17.1. For instance, does the proportion of females to males change from panel to panel? More specifically, we might ask whether the proportion of females changes when spring semester day students are compared with fall semester evening students. The answer is yes, as the proportion of females increases from 70.37% to 74.84%. This type of paneled graph can be very useful whenever you need to categorize individuals or objects by three different discrete characteristics and then make comparisons between those groups.

Figure 17.1   Paneled by Rows and Columns Using Three Discrete Variables (Each Panel Represents 100%)[1]

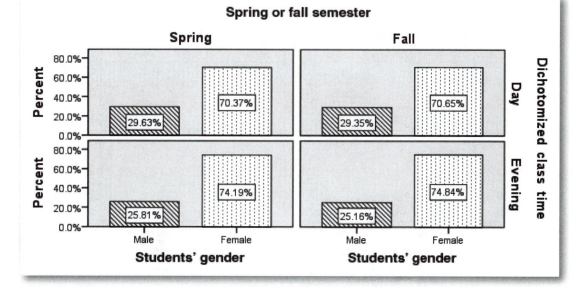

17.1.2 Paneling on Rows and Columns (Percentage of the Total)

The paneled graph in Figure 17.2 is once again based on the records of 1,050 students over a period of 11 years. The graph was produced using the three discrete variables of *Semester* (spring or fall), *Dichotomized class time* (day or evening), and *Gender* (male or female). This graph differs from the one in the previous section because the percentages presented in each bar were calculated using the total number of students (1,050). We could say, for example, that males who enrolled in evening classes during the fall semesters represented 3.81% of all students in the database. A similar statement could be made for each of the seven remaining bars. Figure 17.2 provides answers for a different set of questions than when the percentage was calculated on each individual panel as in the previous section.

---

[1]As in the previous chapter, you will notice that the graph depicted in Figure 17.1 has different patterns for one of the discrete variables, male and female. As in Chapter 16, we used SPSS Version 18 to build this graph since problems with Version 20 make it impossible to apply patterns in this fashion. Therefore, if you are using Version 20, you will not be able to select different patterns until the problem is corrected by IBM/SPSS. Versions 18 and 19 would permit you to build the graph exactly as shown in Figure 17.1.

Figure 17.2   Paneled by Rows and Columns: Three Discrete Variables (Percentage of Total)[2]

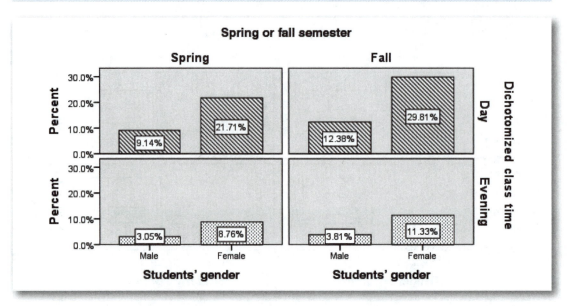

The patterns in the bars (diagonal lines and dots) were selected to bring attention to the differences between day and evening students, but any patterning scheme could have been selected. When you build this style of paneled graph (percentaged on total), the questions are different from the graph in the previous section. For example, we can say that 29.81% (313) of the students taking the class during the day in a fall semester were females. We might contrast this with females taking the evening classes. In this category, we find that 11.33% (119) of the students taking an evening class in a fall semester were females.

17.1.3 Paneling on Rows and Columns (Mean on the Y-Axis)

In this exercise, we once again show the appearance of data paneled by rows and columns, but this time we use three discrete and one continuous variable. The database used is the same as in the previous examples, the 1,050 students. For building the graph in this section, three discrete variables of *Gender* (female or male), *Dichotomized class time* (day or evening), and *Semester* (spring or fall) were used. For the paneled graph in this section, we added a continuous variable. The continuous variable measured overall performance by averaging the *Total semester points* earned by each student. Figure 17.3 presents the finished graph, which shows the relationship between these four variables.

---

[2]Please see Footnote 1 regarding the appearance of this graph.

When looking at Figure 17.3, you may tend to think of it as being rather boring. However, for the professor it is rather rewarding in that the height of the histographic bars differ only slightly. Let's take a closer look and evaluate the information presented by this paneled graph. The upper panel on the left side tells us that daytime male and female students taking the class during the spring semester differed by only 2.2 averaged semester points (68.7 – 66.48) over the 11-year period. If we examine the panel immediately to the right, we see males and females differ by less at 0.16 (70 – 69.84). It should be noted that gender differences (or lack thereof) are not the only thing reflected in these means. We must remember that SPSS calculated these values by placing all males taking spring day classes into one group and then calculated the mean score for these students. It repeated a similar process for all eight groups.

Figure 17.3 Paneled by Rows and Columns Using Four Variables (Continuous Data on Y-Axis)

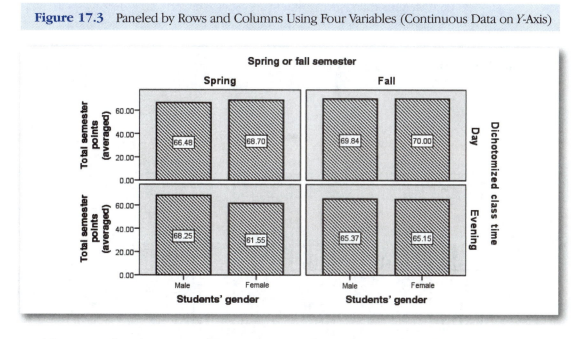

There are of course many other comparisons that could be made other than gender, we simply choose this as an example. Just by looking at the graph, one might make the judgment that there are no practical differences between the many different combinations used to calculate the group means—you would be correct.[3]

_____

[3]GLM univariate analysis revealed that there was an overall significance level of .053. However, the partial Eta squared was only .013, indicating that the value of average semester points was influenced very little by the factors of gender, time of the class meeting, and spring or fall semester.

17.1.4 Paneling on Rows and Columns (Continuous Data on the *X*-Axis)

The graph in this section once again uses the paneling by rows and columns approach but now places the continuous variable on the *x*-axis.

The data used to build the graph in Figure 17.4 is fictional and includes two discrete variables of *State* (having three categories of California, Iowa, and New York) and *Gender* (having categories of female and male). The continuous variable for the *x*-axis is the *Weight of children*. The graph therefore depicts the relationship between the three variables of *state*, *gender*, and *weight*.

Figure 17.4 permits a quick and easy visualization of six unique distributions for weights of children. For instance, we could look at New York males and estimate that their weights more closely approximated normally distributed weights than New York females. This paneled graph depicts six individual distributions in panels with the possibility of 15 unique comparisons.

Figure 17.4   Paneled Histogram by Rows and Columns With Continuous Variable on the *X*-Axis

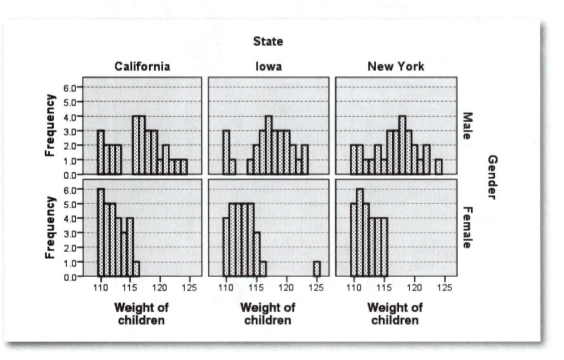

In the following section, the databases used to build these different styles of paneled graphs are discussed. Unique questions for each paneled graph styles are also presented.

17.2 DATABASES AND QUESTIONS   ★

The first graph you build uses data from **Employee data.sav**. The graph uses *Minority classification* on the *x*-axis, *Gender* as the row variable, and *Employment category* as the column variable. Percentages are calculated for each separate panel.

The second graph built also uses data from **Employee data.sav**. The same variables are also used; however, this time you only change count to percentage (on the *y*-axis) as the default setting for SPSS is to calculate percentages on the total.

The third graph once again use the SPSS Sample file called **Employee data.sav**. You will use *Minority classification* on the *x*-axis, *Gender* as the row variable, and *Employment category* as the column variable as in the previous graphs. The difference in building this paneled graph is that you add the fourth variable of *Current salary* to the *y*-axis.

The fourth graph built uses **workprog.sav** and the two discrete variables of *Gender* (row) and *Marital status* (column). Histograms are constructed by using the continuous variable of *Age* on the *x*-axis.

17.2.1 Questions for a Graph Paneled on Rows and Columns (Percentage of Each Panel)

The following questions concern the SPSS database called **Employee data .sav**. A paneled graph, that you soon build, will provide the information needed to answer the questions that follow.

1. What percentage of female managers is classified as minorities?

2. In which of the six subgroups (panels) are the differences between minority and nonminority the least and what are the percentages?

3. Which of the subgroups shows the greatest percentage difference between minority and nonminority employees?

4. What percentage of male managers is classified as nonminority?

5. What percentage of female respondents is employed as custodians?

17.2.2 Questions for a Graph Paneled on Rows and Columns (Percentage of the Total)

The SPSS database named **Employee data.sav** provides the material for the following questions that are answered when building the paneled graph.

1. Which panel reported the largest percentage of nonminority employees?

2. Which of the subgroups reports a distribution of minority and nonminority that approximates equality, and what are the percentages?

3. What percentage of the total respondent population is classified as nonminority female managers?

4. Which subgroup reports the largest percentage of minority employees?

5. What percentage of the male managers is classified as minority?

17.2.3 Questions for a Graph Paneled on Rows and Columns (Mean on the Y-Axis)

The following questions are also related to **Employee data.sav**. You will build a paneled graph, which will provide you with the information needed to answer the questions that follow.

1. What is the mean current salary for minority females who do clerical work?

2. What is the mean current salary for males who do clerical work and are not part of a minority group?

3. Which of the subgroups (panels) shows the greatest difference in salary between minority and nonminority employees, and what are the amounts?

4. Is there any difference in the mean current salary for minority and nonminority females working as custodians?

5. Which of the nine subgroups has the highest salary, and what is the amount?

7. Describe which two employment categories of males have the least difference in salary between minority and nonminority?

17.2.4 Questions for a Graph Paneled on Rows and Columns (Continuous Data on the *X*-Axis)

1. How many married males aged 15.5 to 16.5 years were enrolled in the work program?

2. Which age category has the most married females and how many are there in that category?

3. Is there an identifiable age pattern for unmarried and married females? If you can identify a pattern, describe it in terms of similarities between the two groups.

4. Which of the four groups has the fewest numbers enrolled in the work program?

5. How many unmarried females are aged 18.5 to 21.5 years?

17.3 USING SPSS TO BUILD THE 2-D PANELED GRAPH ★

In this section, you will build four different paneled graphs using two different SPSS databases. Each will answer the specific set of questions about the database that provided the data used in their construction. The finished graphs take on totally unique appearances since the percentages are calculated in different ways. We begin with a graph paneled by rows and columns, which shows the percentage of each panel.

17.3.1 Building the Paneled Graph on Rows and Columns (Percentage of Each Panel)

In this section, you will build a graph paneled on rows and columns with the percentage of each panel given as data labels on each bar. The database is called **Employee data.sav**. You use three discrete variables to build this graph that is paneled on both rows and columns. Let's get started by following the procedures given below.

- Open **Employee data.sav** (found in the SPSS Sample file).
- Click **Graphs**, then click **Chart Builder**.
- Click **Bar** in the *Choose from* list.
- Click and drag the **Simple Bar icon** (the first icon in the first row of icons) to the *Chart preview* panel.
- In the middle of the *Chart Builder* window, click the **Groups/Point ID button**, then click the **box** to the left of *Rows panel variable* and click the **box** to the left of *Columns panel variable*.
- Click and drag **Minority classification** to the x-axis in the *Chart preview* panel.
- Click and drag **Gender** to the panel on the right (this is the row panel).
- Click and drag **Employment category** to the top panel (this is the column panel).
- In the *Statistics* panel of the *Element Properties* window, click the **black arrow** to the right of *Count* and then click **Percentage (?)**, then click **Set Parameters**.
- Click the **black arrow** to the right of *Grand Total*, and then click **Total for Each Panel**.
- Click **Continue**, click **Apply**.
- Click **OK** (*Chart Builder* closes and *Output Viewer* opens with the basic graph).
- If the *Output Viewer* is not showing, then click **Output** found on the task bar at the bottom of the computer screen.
- Double click the **basic graph** to open the *Chart Editor* window.
- Click the **Show Data Labels icon**.
- Click **any bar** (a faint frame appears around all bars).
- In the *Properties* window, click the **Fill & Border tab**, and in the *Color* panel, click the **box** to the left of *Fill* then click the **white rectangular box** to the right, next click the **black arrow** beneath *Pattern*, then click the **third** pattern in the **second** row.
- Click **Apply**.
- Click **any number** on the y-axis.
- In the *Properties* window, click the **Scale tab**, and in the *Range* panel, change *Major Increment* to **40**, then click **Apply**.
- Click the **X** in the upper right-hand corner closing *Chart Editor* and moving the edited graph to the *Output Viewer*.
- Click the **graph** and adjust its size to approximate the graph in Figure 17.5.

Figure 17.5   Graph Paneled on Rows and Columns (Each Panel Represents 100% or 0%)

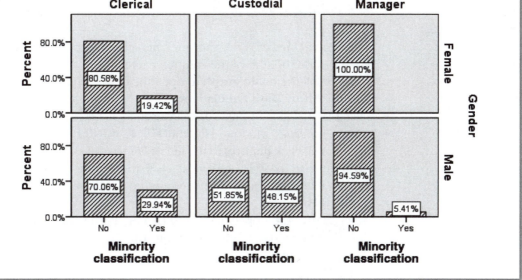

17.3.2 Building the Paneled Graph on Rows and Columns (Percentage of the Total)

This graph uses the same database (**Employee data.sav**) and same variables as the graph built in Section 17.3.1. The steps are almost identical except that *Set parameters* and changing the *Major Increment* are not needed for this graph.

- Open **Employee data.sav** (found in the SPSS Sample file).
- Click **Graphs**, then click **Chart Builder**.
- Click **Bar** in the *Choose from* list.
- Click and drag the **Simple Bar icon** (the first icon in the first row of icons) to the *Chart preview* panel.
- In the middle of the *Chart Builder* window, click the **Groups/Point ID button**, then click the **box** to the left of *Rows panel variable* and click the **box** to the left of *Columns panel variable*.
- Click and drag **Minority classification** to the *x*-axis in the *Chart preview* panel.

- Click and drag **Gender** to the panel on the right (this is the row panel).
- Click and drag **Employment category** to the top panel (this is the column panel).
- In the *Statistics* panel of the *Element Properties* window, click the **black arrow** to the right of *Count* and then click **Percentage (?)** then click **Apply**.
- Click **OK** (*Chart Builder* closes and *Output Viewer* opens with the basic graph).
- If the *Output Viewer* is not showing, then click **Output** found on the task bar at the bottom of the computer screen.
- Double click the **basic graph** to open the *Chart Editor* window.
- Click the **Show Data Labels icon**.
- Click **any bar** (a faint frame appears around all bars).
- In the *Properties* window, click the **Fill & Border tab**, and in the *Color* panel, click the **box** to the left of *Fill* then click the **white rectangular box** to the right, next click the **black arrow** beneath *Pattern*, then click the **third** pattern in the **first** row.
- Click **Apply**.
- Click the **X** in the upper right-hand corner closing *Chart Editor* and moving the edited graph to the *Output Viewer*.
- Click the **graph** and adjust its size to approximate the graph in Figure 17.6.

Figure 17.6   Graph Paneled on Rows and Columns Showing the Percentage of the Total

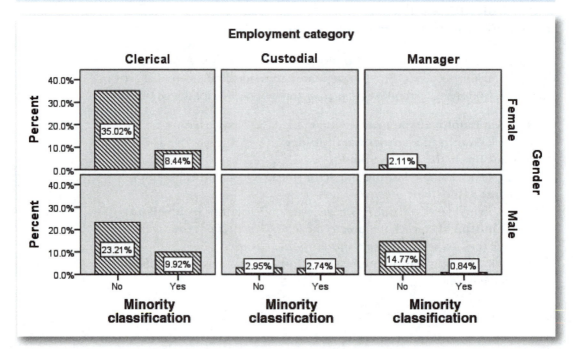

17.3.3 Building the Paneled Graph on Rows and Columns (Mean on the *Y*-Axis)

Once again you use **Employee data.sav** to build a graph paneled on rows and columns. You will use the same three discrete variables from the previous section to build this graph (*Minority classification*, *Gender*, and *Employment category*). In addition, you will use one continuous variable (*Current salary*) on the *y*-axis. Notice that when building this paneled graph, you place a statistic (in this case the mean) on the *y*-axis. SPSS Version 20 permits the selective use of patterns.

- Open **Employee data.sav** (found in the SPSS Sample file).
- Click **Graphs**, then click **Chart Builder**.
- Click **Bar** in the *Choose from* list.
- Click and drag the **Simple Bar icon** (the first icon in the first row of icons) to the *Chart preview* panel.
- In the middle of the *Chart Builder* window, click the **Groups/Point ID button**, then click the **box** to the left of *Rows panel variable*, and click the **box** to the left of *Columns panel variable*.
- Click and drag **Minority classification** to the *x*-axis.
- Click and drag **Gender** to the *Panel* on the right (this is the row panel).
- Click and drag **Employment category** to the top *Panel* (this is the column panel).
- Click and drag **Current salary** to the *y*-axis (box named *Count*).
- Click **OK** (*Chart Builder* closes and *Output Viewer* opens with the basic graph).
- If the *Output Viewer* is not showing, then click **Output** found on the task bar at the bottom of the computer screen.
- Double click the **basic graph** to open the *Chart Editor*.
- Click **Show Data Labels**.
- Click **any bar** (a faint frame appears around all bars).
- In the *Properties* window with the *Categories* tab highlighted, click the word **No** beneath *Order* in the *Categories* panel. Then click the **Move Down black arrow** to the right.
- Click **Apply**.
- In the *Properties* window, click the **Fill & Border tab**, and in the Color panel, click the **box** to the left of *Fill* then click the **white rectangular box** to the right.
- Click **Apply** (all bars turn white).
- Click the **left bar in the upper left panel**, then click the **black arrow** beneath *Pattern*, and click the **second pattern** in the **second** row and click **Apply**.
- Click the **right bar in the upper left panel**, then click the **black arrow** beneath *Pattern*, and click **the second pattern** in the **fifth** row, and click **Apply**.

- Click the **bar in the upper right panel**, click the **black arrow** beneath *Pattern*, and click the **second pattern** in the **fifth** row, then click **Apply**.
- Click the **left bar in the lower left panel**, then click the **black arrow** beneath *Pattern*, and click the **second pattern** in the **second** row, and click **Apply**.
- Click the **right bar in the lower left panel**, then click the **black arrow** beneath *Pattern*, and click **the second pattern** in the **fifth** row, and click **Apply**.
- Click the **left bar in the lower middle panel**, then click the **black arrow** beneath *Pattern*, and click the **second pattern** in the **second** row, and click **Apply**.
- Click the **right bar in the lower middle panel**, then click the **black arrow** beneath *Pattern*, and click the **second pattern** in the **fifth** row, and click **Apply**.
- Click the **left bar in the lower right panel**, then click the **black arrow** beneath *Pattern*, and click the **second pattern** in the **second** row, and click **Apply**.
- Click the **right bar in the lower right panel**, then click the **black arrow** beneath *Pattern*, and click **the second pattern** in the **fifth** row, and click **Apply**.
- Click the **X** in the upper right-hand corner to close *Chart Editor* and move the edited graph to the *Output Viewer*.
- Click the **graph** and adjust its size to approximate the graph in Figure 17.7.

Figure 17.7   Graph Paneled on Rows and Columns Showing the Mean on the *Y*-Axis[4]

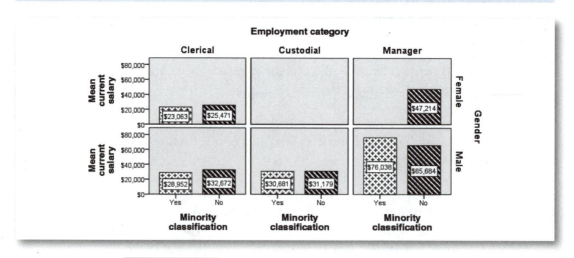

----

[4]SPSS Version 20 can be used to build this graph. Remember that selective use of patterns is possible when you have a statistic on the *y*-axis.

17.3.4 Building the Paneled Graph on Rows and Columns (Continuous Data on the *X*-Axis)

For building the paneled histogram in this section, open the **workprog.sav** database and use the continuous variable named *age* and labeled *Age in years*. Place *Age in years* on the *x*-axis and use the two discrete variables of *Gender* (rows) and *Marital status* (columns) for paneling.

- Open **workprog.sav** (found in the SPSS Sample file).
- Click **Graphs**, then click **Chart Builder**.
- Click **Histogram** in the *Choose from* list.
- Click and drag the **Simple Histogram icon** (the first icon) to the *Chart preview* panel.
- In the middle of the *Chart Builder* window, click the **Groups/Point ID button**, then click the **box** to the left of *Rows panel variable*, and click the **box** to the left of *Columns panel variable*.
- Click and drag **Age in Years** to the *x*-axis.
- Click and drag **Gender** to the *Panel* on the right (this is the row panel).
- Click and drag **Marital Status** to the top *Panel* (this is the column panel).
- Click **OK** (*Chart Builder* closes and *Output Viewer* opens with the basic graph).
- If the *Output Viewer* is not showing, then click **Output** found on the task bar at the bottom of the computer screen.
- Double click the **basic graph** to open the *Chart Editor* window.
- Click any **histogram bar** (a faint frame surrounds all bars).
- Click the **Fill & Border tab** in the *Properties* window, and in the *Color* panel, click the **box** to the left of *Fill*, then click the **white rectangular box** to the right, click the **black arrow** beneath *Pattern*, and click the **third pattern** in the **first** row (diagonal lines).
- Click **Apply**.
- Click **any number** on the *y*-axis.
- In the *Properties* window, click the **Scale tab**, and in the *Range* panel, change *Major Increment* to **10**, then click **Apply**.
- Click **Show Grid Lines icon** (the fifth icon from the right side of the menu).
- In the *Properties* window with the *Grid Lines* tab highlighted, click the **small circle** to the left of *Both major and minor ticks*, click **Apply**.
- Click any of the **grid lines** (all grid lines become highlighted).
- In the *Properties* window with the *Lines* tab highlighted and in the *Lines* panel, click the **black arrow** beneath *Weight*, then click **0.5**.
- Under *Style*, click the **black arrow** and click the **first dotted line**, then click **Apply**.

- Click the very **center of the graph** between the panels (a frame should appear around all panels), then click the **Panels tab** in the *Properties* window.
- In the *Level Options* panel, click the **black arrow** to the right of *Level*, and click **Marital status**, then change *Panel spacing (%)* to **3**, and finally, click **Apply**.
- Click the **black arrow** to the right of *Level*, and click **Gender** (from the drop-down menu), and change *Panel spacing (%)* to **3**, and then click **Apply**.
- Click **any number** on the *x*-axis.
- In the *Properties* window, click the **Scale tab**, and in the *Range* panel, change *Major Increment* to **1**, then click **Apply**.
- Click the **X** in the upper right-hand corner to close *Chart Editor* and to move the edited graph to the *Output Viewer*.
- Click the **graph** and adjust its size to approximate the graph in Figure 17.8.

Figure 17.8   Paneled Histogram by Rows and Columns With the Continuous Variable on the *X*-Axis

In the following section, we look at each of the above four paneled graphs to interpret the information they convey and then answer the questions posed earlier.

17.4 INTERPRETATION OF 2-D PANELED GRAPHS   ★

In this section, we interpret the graphs that you built so as to answer the questions stated earlier.

17.4.1 Questions and Answers: Paneled on Rows and Columns (Percentage of Each Panel)

The information needed to answer the following questions is found in Figure 17.5.

1. What percentage of female managers is classified as minorities?
There were no female managers responding to this survey; therefore, the answer is 0%.

2. In which of the six subgroups (panels) are the differences between minority and nonminority the least, and what are the percentages?
The custodial job category for males has 51.85% nonminority and 48.15% minority, making it the most balanced group.

3. Which of the subgroups shows the greatest percentage difference between minority and nonminority employees?
In the female manager subgroup, 100% are classified as nonminority, making it the panel showing the largest discrepancy between these two classifications.

4. What percentage of male managers is classified as nonminority?
The panel for male managers indicates that 94.59% of male managers are classified as nonminority.

5. What percentage of female respondents is employed as custodians?
There were no female custodians in the survey.

17.4.2 Questions and Answers: Paneled on Rows and Columns (Percentage of the Total)

The information needed to answer the following questions is found in Figure 17.6.

1. Which panel reported the largest percentage of nonminority females employees?

There were 35.05% of all respondents who were classified as nonminority and working as clerks. This was the largest subgroup in this database.

2. Which of the subgroups reports a distribution of minority and nonminority that approximates equality, and what are the percentages?

The male custodial panel reports that the percentage of nonminority employees is 2.95%, while minority employees is 2.74%, making this subgroup the most equal.

3. What percentage of the total respondent population is classified as nonminority female managers?

Female nonminority managers make up 2.11% of the employees.

4. Which subgroup reports the largest percentage of minority employees?

The subgroup of male clerical workers reports that 9.92% are classified as minority, making this the largest group.

5. What percentage of the male managers is classified as minority?

Less than 1% or 0.84% of the respondents were reported as being a minority and in a managerial position.

17.4.3 Questions and Answers: Paneled on Rows and Columns (Mean on the Y-Axis)

The information needed to answer the following questions is found in Figure 17.7.

1. What is the mean current salary for minority females who do clerical work?

If we look at the first bar on the upper left panel we see that minority females who do clerical work have a mean current salary of $23,063.

2. What is the mean current salary for males who do clerical work and are not part of a minority group?

By looking at the second bar in the lower left panel, we conclude that the mean current salary for males who do clerical work and who are not part of a minority group is $32,672.

3. Which of the subgroups (panels) shows the greatest difference in salary between minority and nonminority employees, and what are the amounts?

Males who do managerial work have the greatest minority status salary differential, with minorities earning $76,038 and nonminorities earning $65,684.

4. Is there any difference in the mean current salary for minority and nonminority females working as custodians?

There are no female custodial workers in this study.

5. Which of the nine subgroups has the highest salary, and what is the amount?

Male managers who are part of a minority group have the highest salary at $76,038.

6. Do nonminority male and female managers have the same mean salary, and what are the amounts?

No, female managers earned less than males as females earned $47,214 while males earned $65,684.

7. Describe which two employment categories of males have the least difference in salary between minority and nonminority?

The height of the bars for both minority and nonminority custodial employees are as follows: minority = $30,681 and nonminority = $31,179 for a difference of $498. For the second employment category, we have clerical workers as follows: minority = $28,952 and nonminority = $32,672 for a difference of $3,720.

17.4.4 Questions and Answers: Paneled on Rows and Columns (Continuous Data on the X-Axis)

The information needed to answer the following questions is found in Figure 17.8.

1. How many married males aged 15.5 to 16.5 years were enrolled in the work program?

By looking at the x-axis and y-axis of the lower right-hand panel, we determine that there are 15 married males between the ages of 15.5 and 16.5 years.

2. Which age category has the most married females, and how many are there in that category?

The upper right-hand panel (married females) indicates that the highest bar presents 66 females who are aged between 18.5 and 19.5 years.

3. Is there an identifiable age pattern for unmarried and married females? If you can identify a pattern, describe it in terms of similarities between the two groups.

There is a pattern for the age intervals of 16.5 to 17.5, 17.5 to 18.5, and 18.5 to 19.5. In both the unmarried and married groups, the number of females increases in each interval as age increases.

4. Which of the four groups has the fewest numbers enrolled in the work program?

Just by looking at the four histograms, you might guess that married males make up the group having the fewest members in the work program—you would be correct. The unmarried females group has 250, married females have 257, and unmarried males have 254, while the married males group has 239 individuals.

5. How many unmarried females are aged between 18.5 and 21.5 years?

By looking at the upper left-hand panel for this age group, we add 63 + 38 + 21 = 122 for the number of unmarried females.

★   17.5 REVIEW EXERCISES

1. Open SPSS Sample file **poll_cs_sample.sav**. Select the discrete variable named *county* and labeled *County* and move it to the *x*-axis. Select the discrete variable named *gender* and labeled *Gender* as the row paneled variable. Select the discrete variable named *votelast* and labeled *Voted in last election* for the column panel. Build the paneled graph shown in Figure 17.9 that shows the percentages of respondents in the various categories. Hint: Set parameters as a percentage for each panel. Note: In order to make the exact graph depicted in Figure 17.9, you must use Version 18 or 19. As mentioned in Footnote 1 of this chapter, there are programming problems with Version 20, so you will be unable to selectively use patterns as shown in this graph.

Questions: (a) What percentage of males who voted in the last election live in the Northern region? (b) What percentage of females who voted in the last election live in the Northern region? (c) Which region has the smallest percentage of female voters, and what is the percentage? (d) In the Western region, do males or females have the highest percentage of voters, and what is the percentage? (e) Which region has the highest percentage of voters, and what is the gender of those voters? (f) What percentage of the males who did not vote live in the Western region?

Figure 17.9 Review Exercise: Paneled Bar Graph by Rows and Columns (Each Panel Represents 100% of That Panel)[5]

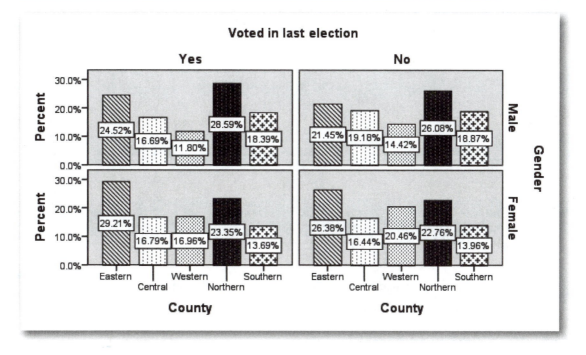

2. Open SPSS Sample file **poll_cs_sample.sav**. Select the discrete variable named *county* and labeled *County* and move it to the *x*-axis. Select the discrete variable named *gender* and labeled *Gender* as the row paneled variable. Select the discrete variable named *votelast* and labeled *Voted in last election* for the column panel. Build the paneled graph in Figure 17.10. Hint: Set parameters as a percentage of the total.

Questions: (a) What percentage of the total respondents live in the Eastern region, are females, and did not vote in last election? (b) What percentage of the total respondents live in the Central region, are males, and voted in last election? (c) What percentage of the total respondents live in the Northern region, are female, and vote in last election? (d) What is the percentage for all the male respondents who voted in last election? (Add the percentages in the row for males who voted) (e) What is the percentage for all the female respondents who did not vote in last election? (Add the percentages in the row for females who did not vote) (f) Which region had the highest percentage of nonvoting males, and what is the percentage? (g) Which regions have the highest percentage of voting for males and for females?

---

[5]SPSS Version 18 was used to build this graph.

Figure 17.10   Review Exercise: Paneled Bar Graph by Rows and Columns (Percentage of Total)

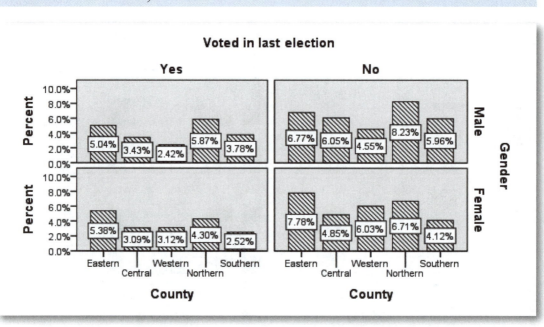

3. Open SPSS Sample file **1991 U.S. General Social Survey.sav**. Select the three discrete variables of *Race of respondent* (*race*), *Region of the United States* (*region*), and *General happiness* (*happy*). Also, select the continuous variable *Age of respondent* (*age*). Use *Region of the United States* in the column panel, *General happiness* in the row panel, *Race of respondents* on the *x*-axis, and *Age of respondent* on the *y*-axis. Build the paneled bar graph shown in Figure 17.11 to answer the following questions.

Questions: (a) What is the mean age for those respondents who said that they are White, live in the North East, and are very happy? (b) What is the mean of those who said that they belong to the Other category, live in the West, and are very happy? (c) What is the mean of those who said that they live in the South East, are Black, and are not too happy? (d) What is the mean of those who are White, live in the South East, and are pretty happy? (e) Which of the three regions has the lowest mean age of people who are not too happy? (f) Within the North East region, which race has the highest percentage of very happy people?

Figure 17.11 Review Exercise: Paneled by Rows and Columns (Mean on the *y*-axis)

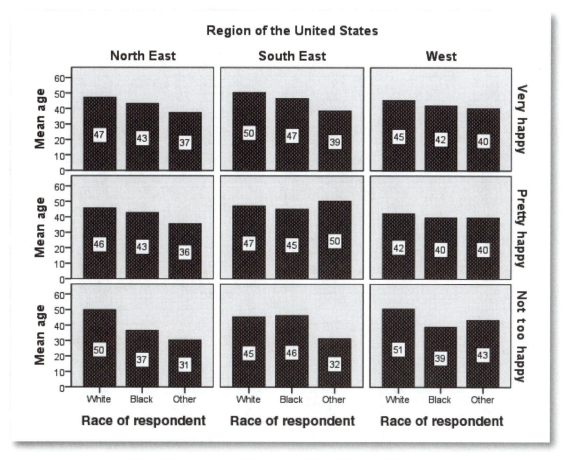

4. Open **workprog.sav** and select two discrete and one continuous variable to build a histogram paneled on both columns and rows. For the *x*-axis, you use the variable labeled as *Age in years* and named *age*. The discrete variable named *marital* and labeled as *Marital status* will be the column paneled variable. The row paneled variable is named *ed* and labeled as *Level of education*. Build the graph shown in Figure 17.12 to answer the following questions.

Questions: (a) Just by looking at the graph, identify which of the row panels (*Level of education*) contains the most people? (b) Which of the six groups has the most participants in the age interval 17.5 to 18.5 years, and how many participants are there in that group? (c) Which group has a distribution of ages that most closely resembled a normal distribution? (d) What is the shape of the distribution for unmarried individuals with high school degree?

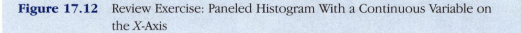

Figure 17.12   Review Exercise: Paneled Histogram With a Continuous Variable on the *X*-Axis

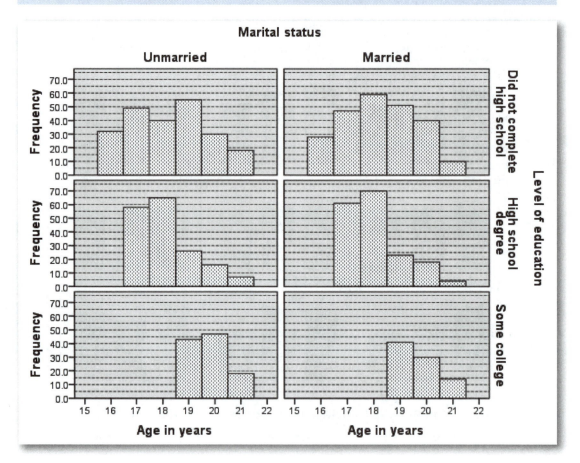

5.   Open SPSS Sample file **satisf.sav**. Select the discrete variable named *reason2* and labeled *Regular reason* and move it to the *x*-axis. Select the discrete variable named *gender* and labeled *Gender* as the row paneled variable. Select the discrete variable named *contact* and labeled *Contact with employee* for the column panel. Build the paneled graph shown in Figure 17.13 that shows the percentages of respondents in the various categories for each panel. Note: In order to make the exact graph depicted in Figure 17.13, you must use SPSS Version 18 or 19. See Footnote 1 in this chapter for more information.

Questions: (a) What percentage of the males who had contact with the employee visited the store for price reasons? (b) What percentage of females who had contact with the employee visited the store for price reasons? (c) What percentage of females who did not have contact with the employee visited the store for reasons of convenience? (d) Which group, males or females, who did not have contact with the employee and visited the store for convenience reasons, had the higher percentage, and what are the percentages for both females and males? (e) Which group, males or females, who had contact with the employee and visited the store for service reasons, had the lower percentage and what are the percentages for both females and males?

Figure 17.13   Review Exercise: Paneled Graph for Rows and Columns (Each Panel Represents 100%)

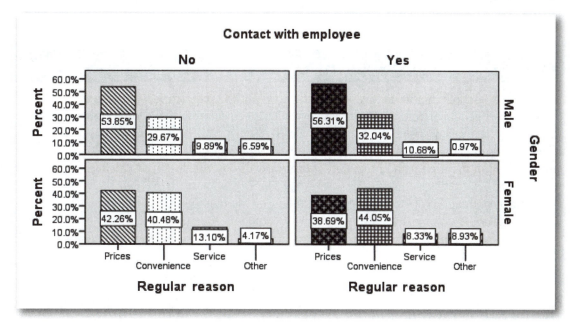

18

Deceptive Graphing Examples

PURPOSE OF GRAPHS YOU ARE ABOUT TO BUILD

- To alert people that visual distortion results from using the incorrect statistic
- To alert people of potential for visual distortion by calculating the incorrect percentages and selectively choosing data
- To inform people of the danger of using the incorrect graph
- To inform the graph readers of deception by exclusion or inclusion of carefully selected data
- To make the graph reader aware of deception by the manipulation of the axis scales
- To make the graph reader aware of how 3-D graphs can be deceptive

★ **18.1 Introduction to Deception**

The purpose of this chapter is to show how graphs can be used to deceive the graph reader. Unfortunately, graphs are sometimes used dishonestly to add a measure of mathematical support for one's particular position. A graph can be a powerful device to support one's position—whether it is truthful or deceitful. Our intention here is not to show how to build dishonest graphs but to give you the knowledge needed to recognize many of the graphing techniques used to deceive. A word of caution is that we are not aware of all the deceitful graphing techniques, so consider this chapter as an "introduction to dishonest graphing." You must be alert to other types of graphing frauds perpetrated on the data consumer. One should always pay special attention to the axis titles, labels, and numerical values prior to drawing conclusions from viewing the proportionality and relational aspects presented in the graph.

This chapter's format differs from previous chapters in several ways. Using various databases, we build graphs that present data with the intention of deceiving the graph reader. This is followed with a graph presenting the same data in a truthful manner. However, as in other chapters, you will not build graphs by following bullet points although you may enjoy using the skills obtained from earlier chapters to build similar deceitful graphs from data of your choosing.

Let's list some of the ways graphs can be used to mis-represent data:

- By deliberately changing values or codes in the data in a manner that supports a particular viewpoint
- By graphing the incorrect statistic (Section 18.2.1)
- By calculating incorrect percentages and selectively choosing data (Section 18.2.2)
- By using the incorrect graph (Section 18.2.3)
- By omission or inclusion of carefully selected data (Section 18.2.4)
- By manipulation of the axis scales (Section 18.2.5)
- By using 3-D bar graphs to conceal certain categorical response values (Section 18.2.6)
- By using a combination of deliberate slice rotation, angle, and color of the 3-D pie graph (Section 18.2.7).

The first deceitful practice listed as the first bullet above is beyond our control. To uncover this type of deception, one needs to have access to the original raw data. Obtaining these data can be difficult and expensive, especially when those perpetrating the deception refuse to provide the data. The deceptive graphing methods subject to more immediate scrutiny (as listed above) are presented in the following section.

18.2 TYPES OF DECEPTIVE GRAPHING PRACTICES   ★

The following sections present those techniques, listed in the above bulleted points, that might be used when graphing data with the intention of misleading the graph reader. The authors do not profess to be "experts" in building deceptive graphs, and the reader should be alert for other trickery that might be used by unscrupulous individuals. One of the key points to remember, when you finish reading this chapter, is to carefully read the axis labels and values on any graph that you are attempting to interpret.

18.2.1 Graphing the Incorrect Statistic

In this example, you see how the presentation of an incorrect statistic in a graph can be used for deceptive purposes. In this example, the investigator is vested in the belief that females enrolled in an intermediate-level statistics class are "smarter" than their male counterparts. He produced the simple bar graph, shown in Figure 18.1, to support his "smartness" theory. Basically, the question might go something like this: Are males or females "smarter" as measured by the number of points earned on the final exam in these statistics classes? He selected a descriptive statistic (the sum of all test points for each gender) and then built the simple bar graph in Figure 18.1.

As is evident, the females earned more points than their male counterparts. If one casually looks at the graph, neglecting the *y*-axis title, and agrees with the definition of "smartness," then one could conclude that females are indeed smarter.

Most likely, you have already observed the fallacy of Figure 18.1. Examine the *y*-axis and take note of the statistics recorded on this axis—the sum. The obvious question is what proportion of the students were males and females.

Figure 18.1 Deceptive Simple Bar Graph for Final Exam Showing Total Points Earned by Gender

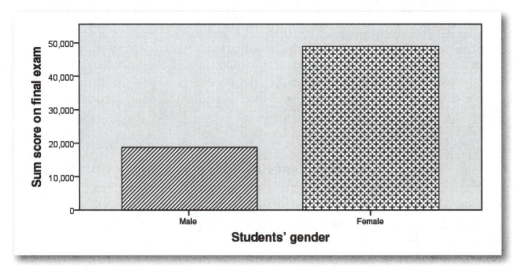

In fact, there were approximately 30% males and 70% females, which is certainly a plausible explanation for more total female points (and the larger rectangular bar) shown in the graph. The deceptive graph in Figure 18.1 serves as an important reminder to carefully read the axis titles and labels and to not judge a graph solely on proportional visualization.

Let's graph the test score data once again, but this time using the mean that is the more appropriate statistic when summarizing test performance by gender. The question remains approximately the same: Are males or females "smarter" as measured by the *mean* number of points earned on the final exam in these statistics classes?

Figure 18.2 presents the truthful representation of the data in that the influence of different proportions of female and male is greatly minimized by using the mean. As can be seen, the difference in males and females is minimal.[1] It would be difficult (if not impossible) to use this graph in support of the belief that females are the "smartest" gender in the statistic class. If one looks at the graph and agrees with the definition of "smartness," then the answer to the question is that there is no (or very little) difference between the sexes.

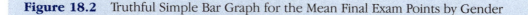

Figure 18.2 Truthful Simple Bar Graph for the Mean Final Exam Points by Gender

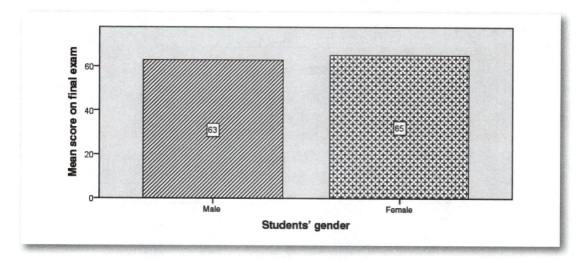

[1]The authors tested the null hypothesis of no difference using an independent samples *t* test and confirmed that there was no statistically significant difference between average points earned for males and females.

18.2.2 Calculating Incorrect Percentages and Selectively Choosing Data

The stacked bar graph shown in this section uses the same database that was used to build the graphs shown in Figures 18.1 and 18.2. However, this time, in addition to gender, we use the categories of another variable called *grade earned*. We have selectively graphed only the categories of A and B for male and female students. In this scenario, those students having earned either an A or a B will be permitted to apply for graduate school. Does the high proportion of females earning As and Bs, as shown in Figure 18.3, communicate that females are better prepared for graduate school than males?

Figure 18.3 seems to support the idea that the graduate school should be prepared to receive a large proportion of females. Just by casually looking at the A category, it is evident that the upper segment (representing females) is much larger that the male segment. The percentage of females earning the A grade is much higher than males, but what does this mean?

Figure 18.3 Deceptive Stacked Bar Graph for Letter Grade by Gender: Percentage of Total

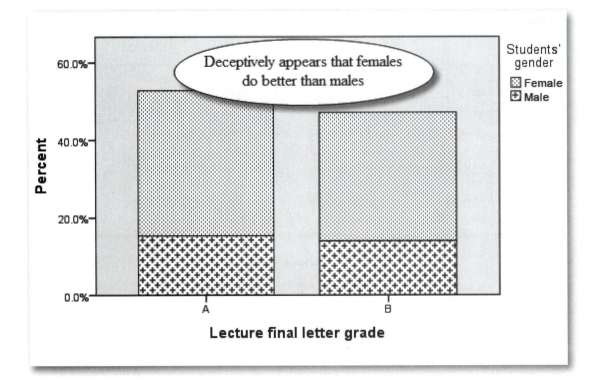

It might only mean that there were many more females enrolled in the class—which happens to be the case.

Another aspect of the graph in Figure 18.3 that contributes to its deceptive nature is that the percentages were calculated on the *total* of five grade categories. The percentages of students earning the C, D, or F were omitted. If the graph reader had the data for the C, D, and F categories, he or she would see that females earn more of these grades as well. A careful reader of a graph that shows all grade categories would realize that females earn more of all grades (good and bad). This observation would lead to the conclusion that there might be a higher percentage of females taking the classes, not that females do better than males.

With the stacked bar graph, it is important that the graph reader understands how the percentages were calculated and if any categories were omitted. Looking at the graph in Figure 18.3 communicates the idea that females earned more As and Bs than their male counterparts. Let's graph the data in a more truthful way.

Figure 18.4 Truthful Stacked Bar Graph for Letter Grade by Gender: Percentage by Gender

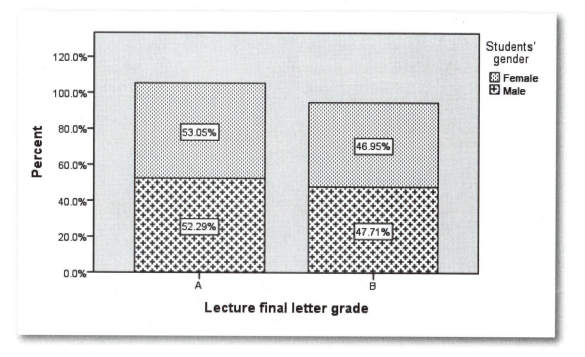

Figure 18.4 shows the truthful representation where the males and females are approximately equal in the percentages of As and Bs earned. Given this information, the graduate school should be prepared to consider an equal number of males and females for their advanced program. This truthful graph was produced by instructing SPSS to calculate percentages based on gender. One should notice that Figure 18.4 only considers the two grade categories when calculating percentages. For instance, 53.05% + 46.95% = 100%, which represents all female students earning either an A or a B. The same holds true for the males with 52.29% earning As and 47.71% earning Bs. It is important to see that there is no deception in Figure 18.4 since the percentages were calculated on all data that were chosen to build the graph.

18.2.3 Using the Incorrect Graph

The graphs in Figures 18.5 and 18.6 were built with the intention of providing visual evidence that single malt scotch whiskey sales steadily increased over an 11-year period. A young woman was interested in purchasing the liquor store where the sales were recorded. The question for the young woman interested in purchasing the liquor store was: What is the sales history for scotch for the past 11 years? The unscrupulous owner sought to mislead the potential buyer with the deceptive graphs. She was shown the graphs in Figures 18.5 and 18.6 in an attempt to prove that whiskey sales were steadily

Figure 18.5   Deceptive Cumulative Histogram Showing Dollars Spent on Single Malt Scotch

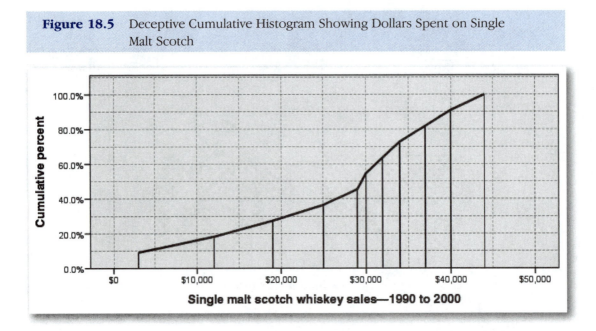

increasing. Indeed the upward lines in both graphs communicate the idea of increasing sales over the 11-year period. Let's examine each graph separately and identify the fallacy perpetrated by using these incorrect graphs.

To begin with, the cumulative histogram was incorrectly selected to graph the sales data. Using this type of graph, the sales for a set time period (could be any period) are added to the sales amounts for each successive time period. Therefore, the line, as shown in Figure 18.5, will always slope upward even if the sales in successive time periods are less than previous years. The line could only go horizontal (flat) and that would indicate no increase in sales over some unknown time period. The line for the cumulative histogram cannot slope downward.

Another clue that the graph is meant to deceive is that the axis does not record any time period. Time is only mentioned in the *x*-axis title as 1900 to 2000. If the graph was truly intended to represent scotch sales over time, then both variables would be on the graph.

The graph shown in Figure 18.6 (below) is another variation of the deception perpetrated by the cumulative histogram. This time, a simple line graph was built by instructing SPSS to calculate the cumulative percentage on the *y*-axis. The same criticisms that we made of the cumulative histogram apply to the cumulative line graph—this line graph is just another form of the same deception.

Figure 18.6 Deceptive Cumulative Line Graph Showing Dollars Spent on Single Malt Scotch

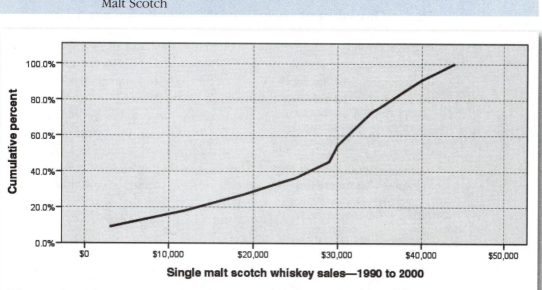

The graph below, shown in Figure 18.7, represents the truthful picture of scotch sales over the 11-year period. It correctly reports the rather large fluctuation in the yearly sales of scotch whiskey and that the differences between good and bad years are becoming greater. The false impression given by the previous two cumulative graphs is immediately discovered when viewing Figure 18.7.

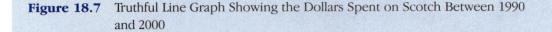

Figure 18.7   Truthful Line Graph Showing the Dollars Spent on Scotch Between 1990 and 2000

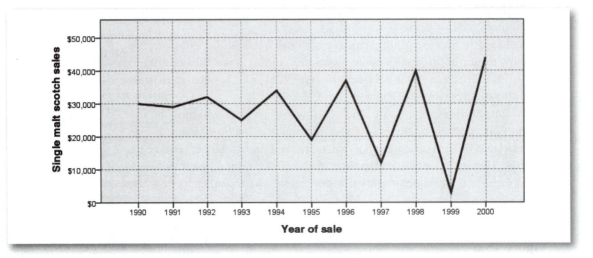

18.2.4 Omission or Inclusion of Carefully Selected Data

In this section, we use the same scotch sales data, but this time, the deception is based on how the data are selected when building the graph. We demonstrate how the omission of carefully selected data changes the graph from a truthful to a deceitful description of the data.

The graph in Figure 18.8 purports to show a steady and continual rise in the sales of scotch whiskey. The potential buyer of the liquor store where these sales were recorded believed that the sale of scotch was a strong predictor of overall sales potential. The seller of the liquor store built the graph in Figure 18.8 in an effort to provide a positive picture of scotch sales.

To some graph readers, it may seem obvious that years were omitted and that the labels for years (on the *x*-axis) were obviously designed to deceive. However, the labels could be justified by explaining that the period of time between data points always recorded an upward (increasing sales) slope. Thus, sales are increasing over every time period—the graph reader is unable to see the sales in the odd years that happen to show decreases in scotch sales. It should also be remembered, some potential buyers only *see* only what they want to *see* especially when they are anxious to purchase the store. There are unscrupulous individuals who will take advantage of this character trait, and a visual graph is an excellent way to provide "pseudo-scientific" support for the deception.

Figure 18.8   Deception by Selective Use of the Attributes of the Variable: Years Omitted

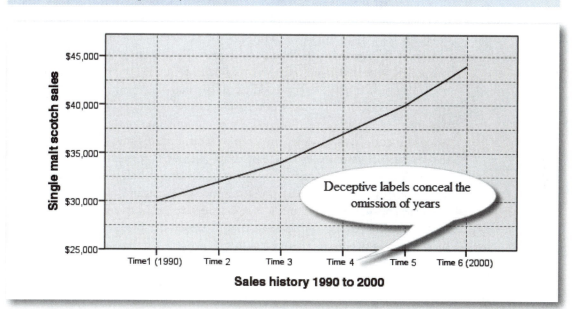

The graph in Figure 18.9 presents a truthful representation of the sales data presented in Figures 18.7 and 18.8. Figure 18.9 shows the same graph as presented in Figure 18.7 to make the direct comparison more easily.

Figure 18.9   Truthful Graph Showing Dollars Spent on Single Malt Scotch

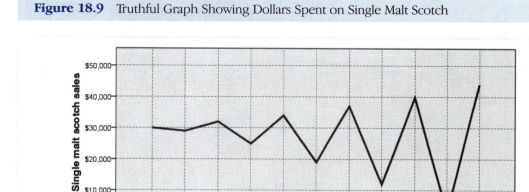

18.2.5 Manipulation of the Axis Scales

In this chapter, the first example of deceptive graphing presented a scenario where the investigator believed that female students had performed at a higher intellectual level than males. The investigator used Figure 18.1 to support the deception. In this section, we continue with that theme, but this time, the deception is based on a manipulation of the *y*-axis scale. The graph presented in Figure 18.10 is another way to present the same data in a dishonest manner.

Look at Figure 18.10 while paying special attention to the scale on the *y*-axis. The scale has been greatly compressed to record the range from 63 to 65.5. Also notice that the correct descriptive statistic (mean) was chosen for the *y*-axis. This time the distortion results not from the incorrect statistic, as was the case in Figure 18.1, but from the manipulation of the *y*-axis scale. By using the compressed scale, the graph communicates that there are major differences between males and females for average points earned on the final exam. The rectangular bar for females is much larger than the one for males. Therefore, the females must possess more of the trait being measured— correct? This may be true, but it is the deceptive proportionality that results from the compression of the *y*-axis that results in the picture showing major differences between males and females. Compressing the *y*-axis values from 63 to 65.5 ignores the zero point and the actual range of data which causes the distortion.

Figure 18.10   Deceptive Bar Graph for Final Exam Points and Gender: Compressed *Y*-Axis

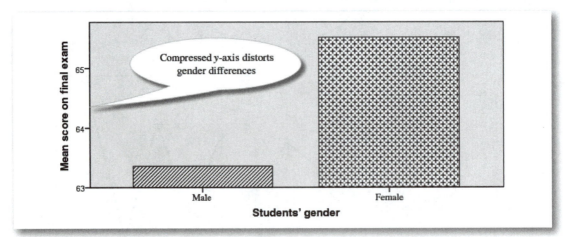

The graph in Figure 18.11 uses the same data as in Figure 18.10. It is the same graph that appears in Figure 18.2. We show it here to emphasize that a simple change of the *y*-axis scale can drastically alter the graph's appearance. The truthful graph shown in Figure 18.11 has a *y*-axis scale of 0 to 70. The result of this "honest" scale is that we now have an accurate description of the differences by depicting the entire range of values.

Figure 18.11   Truthful Bar Graph for Final Exam Points and Gender: Correct *Y*-Axis Scale

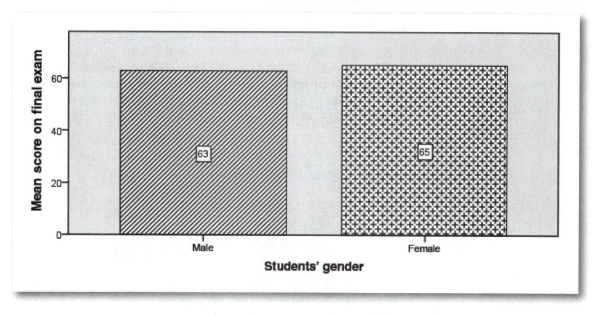

In the final section of this chapter, we present a deception made possible by plotting data on a 3-D graph.

18.2.6 Using 3-D Bar Graphs

When viewing a 3-D graph, the reader should be especially alert to deceptive practices. In the earlier chapters of this book, we chose to show 3-D techniques only in the chapters on the simple bar and pie. The 3-D effect that was demonstrated was intended to encourage proportional thinking by adding *volume* to the rectangular bars or the slices of the pie. In this section, the third dimension goes beyond the simple visual effect of adding volume in that a variable is added to a third dimension. This additional dimension is referred to as the *z*-axis. With this type of 3-D graph, you have *x*-axis, *y*-axis, and *z*-axis variables. In this section, we show one of the ways in which this 3-D graph can be used to deceive.

The 3-D graph can be used to deceive by many of the ways mentioned earlier such as manipulation of the axis scales and by using the incorrect graph and/or statistic. In this section, we introduce a deception unique to the 3-D graph: hiding categories. This deceptive practice can be easily accomplished by the manipulation of the orientation of the 3-D graph during the graph-building process. We next propose a scenario where an unscrupulous political consultant sought to mislead the public into believing that female incumbent candidates for state offices are less beholding to lobbyists than males. This conclusion was based on data showing the median number of lobbyists that contributed to male and female campaigns.

Figure 18.12 was built with truthful data that were collected by a respected government watchdog organization. The *x*-axis shows the government level (federal, state, and county), the *y*-axis was used for the median number of registered lobbyists, and finally, the *z*-axis recorded the candidates' gender

Figure 18.12   Three-Dimensional Bar Graph With Hidden Categories

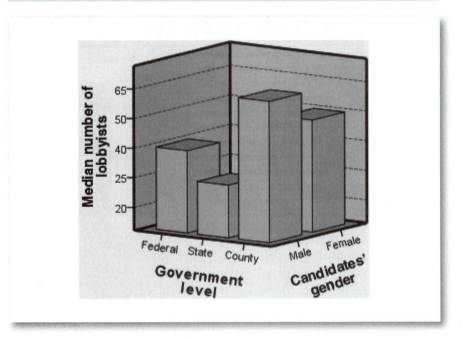

(male or female). The dishonest political consultant wished to present a "picture" showing that incumbent female candidates for state offices had fewer lobbyists contributing to their campaigns than male politicians. Looking at the political consultant's graph, one might easily conclude that male candidates for state offices had more lobbyist contributors than females. The graph shows that males have a median of 25 lobbyists, while females have many less, some graph readers may even interpret the graph to show that females have no lobbyists at both the state and federal level. Let's look at the graph shown in Figure 18.13 that honestly portrays the data used to build the graph shown in Figure 18.12.

Figure 18.13 was built using the same data and process steps as the graph earlier. The only difference was that the graph depicted here was rotated using a feature available in the *Chart Builder*. The *Rotating the 3-D chart* icon permits the graph builder to rotate the graph in 3-D space to either hide or make visible certain categories. The graph reader should always be suspicious of a 3-D graph that hides values for certain categories.

The graph in Figure 18.13 presents the data in a way that reveals the values (median number of lobbyists) for all categories. The following graph, shown in Figure 18.14, presents the clustered bar graph as an alternative to

Figure 18.13 Three-Dimensional Bar Graph Rotated to Show All Categories

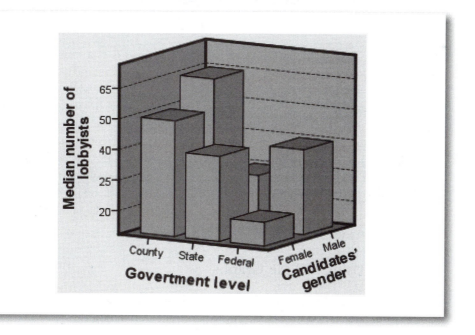

Figure 18.14 Clustered Bar Graph Displaying the Same Data as the Previous Two 3-D Graphs

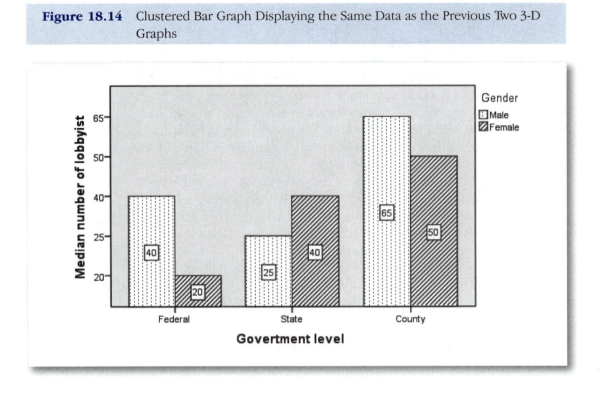

the 3-D. We feel that the 2-D clustered bar graph is the most truthful and should be used to present the data in the most understandable manner.

The clustered bar graph as shown in Figure 18.14, with its data labels, makes answering questions about the number of lobbyists for the three government levels and gender very clear. Recall that the dishonest political consultant wished to present the picture that female candidates for state offices had fewer lobbyists contributors than males. The clustered bar graph in Figure 18.14 clearly shows that this is not what the data show. Females had a median of 40 lobbyists' contributors, while males had 25. The graph does show that such contributors favored males when candidates were seeking federal and county offices.

18.2.7 Using 3-D Pie Graphs

The three-dimensional pie graph is also susceptible to being used in a deceptive manner. This can be accomplished by manipulating the rotation, angle,

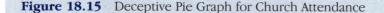

Figure 18.15 Deceptive Pie Graph for Church Attendance

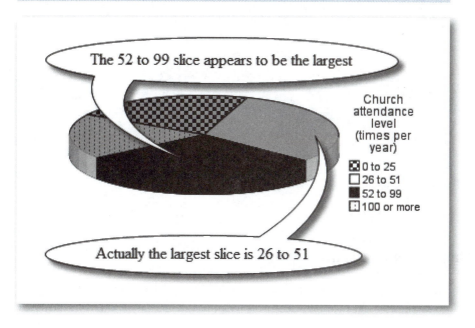

depth, and color of the slices. The combination of these graph-building techniques and the omission of data labels can result in a deceptive graph. Such a deceptive graph is shown in Figure 18.15.

Figure 18.15 presents fictitious survey data for parishioners' attendance at a large church. We designed the pie graph to convince the reader that most people attended church between 52 and 99 times during the survey year. When building this pie graph, we rotated the slice orientation to place the slice representing 52 to 99 times per year at the 6 o'clock position, gave it a dark color, and also set the angle and depth to increase its volume's appearance. As indicated by the information bubbles, many people viewing this graph believe that most people attended church between 52 to 99 times per year. Actually, most people attended between 26 to 51 times per year. Figure 18.16 represents a truthful representation of the church attendance observations.

The addition of data labels in Figure 18.16 informs the graph user of the true proportions while also presenting a succinct picture of the proportions for all categories. The largest category has also been rotated to the 6 o'clock position; this and the darker pattern for this slice present a more truthful representation of the church attendance data.

Figure 18.16   Truthful Pie Graph for Church Attendance

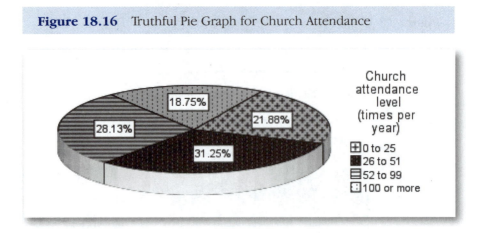

★   **18.3 DECEPTION SUMMARY**

There are many opportunities for deception under the guise of a "scientific" presentation when graphs are used to summarize a large mass of numbers. Most people give graphs an undeserved belief that they always represent the truth. This mental attitude is probably grounded in the old phrase "a picture does not lie." Combine the attitude that "a picture does not lie" with a façade of science, and you have a situation ripe for fraud.

In this chapter, we presented several methods that can be used (intentionally or perhaps accidently), which mislead the graph reader. The graphics user should be aware of the methods used in this chapter, as the purpose of graphing is to truthfully answer questions about data that have the goal of making the database more understandable.

19

Summary

This book is about extracting useful information from data that have already been collected. If one sets about collecting data, one usually has a reason in mind. This book bypasses the step in any research where you first decide what information you need to answer a set of research questions. We don't apologize for this approach but only mention it here to reinforce the fact that an essential step in the scientific investigation of phenomena is to determine what questions need to be answered and what data will provide the answers. Most of the data used to construct the graphs in this book were hypothetical (created by SPSS programmers) and were created for the demonstration of various statistical techniques and for building graphs.

In the introduction of each chapter, where specific graph types were shown, we did use actual data. Questions most often associated with exploratory and/or descriptive research were presented to demonstrate how the various graphs can provide useful answers. We often left it up to the reader to speculate about any possible discoveries that might be made when producing the graphs based on these nonfictional data.

Our intention in this book was to first provide the reader with the knowledge and skills to build and interpret graphs. The ultimate purpose was to then use the graphs to make the data more understandable. Making the data more understandable involved answering questions about certain variables contained in the databases. Thus, we presented both questions and answers about the many databases used in this book.

★   19.2 SELECTING THE APPROPRIATE GRAPH

We began this book with a brief description of the intent and purpose of building graphs. Throughout the chapters, we have attempted to demonstrate how graphical representations of data can provide useful information. The principal method used to demonstrate the usefulness of graphs was by asking questions about selected variables and then building a graph that answered those questions. Answers to the questions would then provide valid information that could then be used to make informed (educated) decisions.

Throughout this book, as often as possible, we attempted to emphasize the importance of proportional thinking when building and interpreting graphs. It was shown that thinking in terms of proportions was not only useful in inferential statistics but was also a valuable tool when exploring and/or describing data. The book's major intent was not to cover graphs used in inferential statistics; however, there were some occasions where these techniques were described. For the major part of the book, we used descriptive-type questions associated with the graphs that were built. For instance, we demonstrated how it was possible to determine the proportion of unmarried males aged 45 to 65 in a larger population just by looking at a bar graph.

Time was spent on providing the reader with the knowledge required to select the correct graph that would answer questions about various types of data. You may recall that in the first chapter, we presented four important considerations that the graph maker should think about prior to building the graph. Let's take another quick look at the considerations for the graph builder.

1. How was the data measured? An explanation of different methods used to measure data and the appropriate graph for each was given in the introductory chapter. In every chapter, following the introduction, the concept of when to use specific graphs for discrete and continuous data was discussed. No graphs were built without first describing how the data were measured and whether it should be considered as discrete or continuous. On completion of this book, the reader will be thoroughly grounded in the knowledge of which graph is appropriate for different data types.

2. It was pointed out that the second consideration for the graph maker revolves around the types of questions one has about the data. Are we seeking descriptive information about a single variable such as the shape of its distribution or perhaps the number or percentage of cases that fall in various categories? Or perhaps, we are seeking answers as to how two or more

variables are related to one another. In this regard, we demonstrated bivariate and multivariate graphs. How the value of variables may change over time was yet another possibility when selecting the appropriate graph. How to use graphs to show an interaction or lack of interaction was also illustrated. Note: These first two considerations for the graph maker are supported by additional information found in Appendix D (Graph Selection: Type and Purpose).

3. The level of statistical knowledge of readers was also discussed as part of the graph-building process.

4. The intended use of the graph was also discussed within the context of whether the basic graph made by SPSS should be embellished. The many uses of the *Chart Editor* to make improvements on the basic graph were presented throughout the book. It was also noted that such embellishments are sometimes unnecessary if you only build the graph for the purpose of guiding one in the selection of the appropriate approaches for further statistical analysis.

In the introduction of each chapter, graph examples were provided in a manner that supported those concepts as outlined above. The examples gave the reader grounding in the types of and the uses of the graphs that were presented in each chapter. Following the examples of the types of graphs to be built, specific questions were presented about databases. The databases were then used by the reader to build the specific graphs that would provide the information needed to answer the questions.

19.3 USING SPSS TO BUILD THE GRAPHS ★

SPSS has three basic ways to produce graphs: (1) the *Legacy Dialogs*, (2) *Graphboard Template Chooser*, and (3) the *Chart Builder*. The subject of this book is the most recent, and by far the most efficient, of the three methods—the *Chart Builder*. The introductory chapter gave a quick review of how to use the *Chart Builder* and discussed many of its useful features. However, the vast majority of information required for the best use of the *Chart Builder* for high quality graph building was presented in all the chapters. The idea was that the reader would learn to build a graph using many different features of the *Chart Builder*. The result of each of the graph-building exercises would produce graphs that both answered the questions and yielded a professional appearance. The reader sees the finished graph and then produces one exactly as the one shown in the book by using those features specified in each graph-building project. Once this is accomplished, the reader can and should experiment with the features and vary both the content and appearance of the graph to suit his or her personal needs. Not every possible use of every feature was discussed or demonstrated as there are hundreds of permutations for each graph-building exercise. As the reader becomes better acquainted with the *Chart Builder*, the many different possible applications will become apparent. We feel strongly that if the reader builds the graphs in this book, he or she will have the skills required to produce informative and beautiful graphs that surpass those presented in these pages.

★   19.4 FINAL REMARKS

The investigation of data may seem like a routine task; however, it can be a fascinating journey into the unknown. SPSS has vastly improved its graph-making capabilities, which opens the journey in a manner that provides many different paths to explore. Analysis of large amounts of data is often considered a mundane, even boring, task. However, possessing a bit of knowledge and the power of the *Chart Builder*, data analysis can be an exciting exploration into the unknown. The excitement of a new discovery as it emerges before your very eyes as you make that final click of the mouse button can be overwhelming. As we all know, sometimes the result of that final click can be disappointing either because of the data or the approach we used in graphing the data. Such a disappointing outcome doesn't matter when using the power of the *Chart Builder* as it is easy to back off and try another approach.

May your journeys into the unknown be as exciting as ours was when creating the many graphs that went into writing this book. We thank you for reading our work.

APPENDIX A

SPSS BASIC INFORMATION

A.1 INTRODUCTION ★

The purpose of this appendix is to provide the reader with basic information about the operation of the Statistical Package for the Social Sciences (SPSS). The first part of this appendix explains how to start (open) the program and the second discusses how variables and data are inputted into the program. The information about data and variable input are important if the reader of the book desires to graph actual data that he or she may have collected. This textbook utilizes existing databases and does not require the variable and data entry procedures given below. This information is provided for those wishing to input and graph their own research data. The information given here will give you the basics; much more can be obtained by using the SPSS tutorial, which is part of each installed SPSS package.

A.2 OPENING SPSS ★

Once SPSS is installed on your computer, you most often click the **SPSS icon** found on the desktop screen to open (start) the program. If there is no icon, then click **Start** found in the lower left-hand portion of the screen, then click **All Programs**. Scroll through the program list, click **SPSSInc**, then click **SPSS 20** or whatever version is installed on the computer.

An SPSS window either opens or will be shown at the bottom of the computer screen (on the task bar) that offers several options, close this window. A second SPSS choice presented on the task bar is called *Untitled [DataSet]* . . ., click on this and the *Data Editor Spreadsheet* opens. We next briefly describe the SPSS *Data Editor*.

★ **A.3 DATA EDITOR WINDOWS (VARIABLE VIEW AND DATA VIEW)**

There are two spreadsheet windows that you must be familiar with when entering data into SPSS. One is the *Variable View* and the other is the *Data View*. These two windows are used when you wish to directly enter variable information *and* data into SPSS.[1] The two windows are activated by clicking one of the two tabs at the bottom of the *Data Editor*. Let's start with the *Variable View* window that normally opens with the program. If it is not open at this time, click the **Variable View tab**.

A.3.1 Variable View Window

The *Variable View* screen has rows and 11 columns. The rows contain information about each of the variables that you intend to input into the program. You input the variable name and the characteristics on each row. Therefore, if you have five variables, you will have five rows completed in the *Variable View* window. The upper portion of the *Variable View* screen, showing the entry of just one variable called "Speed", is given in Figure A.1.

Our intention here is not to specify how to complete each of the 11 columns, as this can be accomplished by either trial and error or by using the help and tutoring functions that are part of every installed SPSS program.[2] However, we briefly describe four of the most important and used columns.

Figure A.1 Upper Portion of the Variable View Window

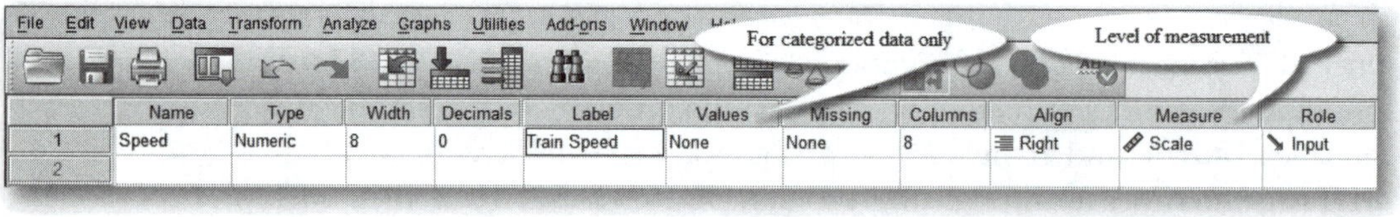

[1]This textbook utilizes existing databases and does not require the variable and data entry procedures given next. This information is provided for those wishing to input and graph their own research data.

[2]For additional detailed information, one might wish to consult *Using SPSS: An Interactive Hands-On Approach* by Cunningham and Aldrich.

The column titled *Type* is where you specify whether you have a variable recorded in numbers (numeric) or starting with alphabetic characters (string). The *Label* column is where you can give a more descriptive name for your variable than in the first column titled *Name*. The *Label* you give your variable appears on graphs and other output when you complete your analysis. The next column is titled *Values* and is where you enter information about categorized variables such as gender. In the *Values* column, you specify such information as $1 = male$ and $2 = female$ for a categorized variable such as *gender*. Finally, and perhaps, the most important variable characteristic is recorded in the column titled *Measure*. It is here that you specify the level of measurement for the variable. The choices are scale, ordinal, and nominal. In this textbook and when building graphs, you are instructed to consider data as either *continuous* or *discrete*. Scale is considered as continuous, while ordinal and nominal are discrete data. If you have difficulty in determining the correct level of measurement for your variables, you should return to Sections 1.3.1 and 1.5.2 or consult any introductory statistics textbook.

A.3.2 Data View Window

The *Data View* window is opened by clicking the **Data View tab** at the bottom of the screen once SPSS opens. Once the *Data View* tab is clicked, the screen looks much like the *Variable View* window except as noted in Figure A.2. In the unnumbered row where you see "Speed," you now see "var" in each of the columns in this row. "Var" is simply a place holder for additional variables. Your data are inputted in the column below the appropriate variable. In the example shown in Figure A.2, three speeds 15, 20, and 12 have been entered directly below the column titled "Speed." Each row is referred to as a "case." Therefore, in this example, we have three

Figure A.2   Upper Portion of the Data View Window

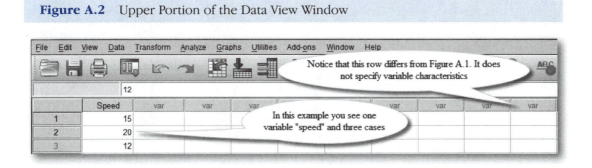

APPENDIX B

ANSWERS TO CHAPTER EXERCISES

CHAPTER 2 SIMPLE BAR GRAPH: REVIEW EXERCISES ★

1. The numbers in the five categories are 967, 1,041, 1,092, 1,014, and 886.

2. The percentages for each of the categories are 19.34%, 20.82%, 21.84%, 20.28%, and 17.72%.

3. The numbers in the two categories are Unmarried 2,559 and Married 2,441.

4. The percentages for each of the two categories are Unmarried 51.18 % and Married 48.82%.

5. The numbers of observations in each category are 2,246 (Single family), 1,554 (Multiple family), 908 (Condominium/townhouse), and 292 (Mobile home).

6. The percentages of observations in each category are 44.92% (Single family), 31.08% (Multiple family), 18.16% (Condominium/townhouse), and 5.84% (Mobile home).

7. (a) The tallest bar of the graph (the one with most individuals) is the one for high school degree. It represents 287 individuals. (b) The lower end of the error bar value is 259, and the value of the upper end of the bar is 317. (c) We can say that if repeated sampling of the larger population of customers was performed, then 95% of the samples would show that between 259 and 317 customers earned a high school degree. (d) The college degree category represents 234 individuals with the error bar showing a lower limit of 208 and an upper limit of 262.

★   CHAPTER 3 STACKED BAR GRAPH: REVIEW EXERCISES

1. Operation, Fabrication, and General Labor (male = 8.46% and female = 7.05%), Precision Production, Craft, and repair (male = 9.59% and female = 1.90%), Farming, Forest, and Fishing (male = 1.83% and female = <1%), Service (male = 4.02% and female = 10.37%), Technical, Sales, and Administrative Support (male = 8.60% and female = 23.55%), and Managerial and Professional Specialty (male = 11.28% and female = 12.62%).

2. (a) Exciting (male = 49.08% and female = 50.92%), Routine (male 39.60% and female = 60.40%), and Dull (male = 29.27% and female = 70.73%). (b) Dull category at 41.46%. (c) Exciting at 1.84%.

3. (a) Males—exciting = 50.12%. (b) Females—exciting = 39.82%. (c) Males—routine = 47.06%. (d) Females—routine = 54.95%. (e) Males—dull = 2.82%. (f) Females—dull = 5.23%. (g) There are differences but further testing such as a chi-square analysis is required to see if the differences are significant.

4. (a) 41.71%; (b) 59.50%; (c) 37.42%; (d) 61.54%; (e) 34.38%; (f) Eastern 41.71%.

5. (a) 26.47%; (b) 19.03%; (c) 27.29%; (d) 15.28%; (e) Age category: 31–45 at 29.82%; (f) Age category: 18–30 at 15.25%.

★   CHAPTER 4 CLUSTERED BAR GRAPH: REVIEW EXERCISES

1. (a) Singles (71.43%, 14.29%, and 14.29%); (b) Married (33.33%, 16.67%, and 50%); (c) Other (50%, 50%, and 0%).

2. (a) Forestry; (b) Engineering; (c) Engineering; (d) Engineering, Education, Building/Construction, and Agriculture.

3. (a) 52.94%; (b) 47.06%; (c) 48.85%; (d) 51.15%; (e) Very unlikely of any difference.

4. (a) The unmarried individuals coming from a larger hometown (>250,000) have the highest credit card debt of 2.04 ($2,040). (b) The married individuals coming from medium size towns (10,000 to 49,999) are the least in debt 1.68 ($1,680). (c) No clear pattern is shown, size of hometown and marital status appear to have little influence on the amount of credit card debt. (d) Those individuals coming from a hometown with a population of between 50,000 and 249,000 have almost identical credit card debt.

5. (a) 486. (b) The largest single group was males who had a high school degree. (c) The graph's appearance would argue for no difference but the chi-square test could be conducted to confirm this observation. (d) 5,000.

CHAPTER 5 PIE GRAPH: REVIEW EXERCISES   ★

1. (a) 34.80% of the respondents have a high school degree. (b) Did not complete high school has the highest percentage at 45.90%. (c) Post-undergraduate degree has the lowest percentage at 0%. (d) (45.90%) Did not complete high school, (34.80%) High school degree, (19.30%) Some college, and (0%) Post-undergraduate degree. (e) When a category is empty (0%), there is no slice for that category.

2. (a) 7.90%; (b) 147; (c) 35–49 years old; (d) 127, 21.82%; (e) 32, 5.50%.

3. (a) The largest income category is $25,000 to $49,000, and it represents 35.86% of all respondents. (b) 7.80% of the respondents earn $125,000 plus. (c) The second largest group is those who earn less than $25,000, and they represent 26.60% of the respondents. (d) Yes, it is true and the percentage is 62.46%.

4. (a) East, 25.79%; (b) South, 1,965; (c) 1,967, 24.34%; (d) 2,066, 25.56%; (e) South, North, West, East.

5. (a) Clerical is the largest employment category at 76.58%. (b) The second largest category is manager with 17.72% of the work force. (c) The smallest employment category is custodial at 5.70%.

CHAPTER 6 SIMPLE LINE GRAPH: REVIEW EXERCISES   ★

1. (a) Appliances; (b) Clothing; (c) Automotive and Tools; (d) All department visitor numbers ordered from least to most: Tools = 47, Automotive = 48, Sporting = 59, Electronics = 83, Other = 85, Clothing = 114, and Appliances = 146.

2. (a) Frequency steadily increases (men are dying). (b) Steady decrease in death (fewer people to die as they are already deceased). (c) Approximately 73. (d) Mean = 64.92, standard deviation = 9.273, and number of observations = 109.

3. (a) Mortality rate drops. (b) Mortality rate drops from 60 to 10 deaths per 1,000 live births. (c) As the daily calories increase, the infant mortality decreases.

4. (a) 38.49% of the respondents live 1 to 5 miles from the store. (b) About 5.5% live 30 or more miles from the store. (c) Once the peak distance is reached, the percentage of people traveling longer and longer distances declines. (d) 12.37%. (e) Approximately 88%.

5. (a) The maximum credit card debt was $110,000, and the income was well over 1 million. (b) Once income exceeds $575,000, credit card debt trends upward. (c) $21,000. (d) $50,000.

6. (a) The overall trend for mean household income and education, as expected, is a steady increase in income as education increases. (b) There is a rapid increase from approximately 62,000 to 118,000. (c) An additional degree, following the 4-year college degree, results in the most dramatic increase in household income. (d) The overall trend for all levels of education and mean household income is one of increased income with increasing levels of education.

★ CHAPTER 7 MULTIPLE LINE GRAPH: REVIEW EXERCISES

1. (a) 71.4; (b) 72.3; (c) 71.3; (d) 72.5; (e) No; (f) No.

2. (a) 72.7; (b) 71.8; (c) 71.1; (d) 72.5; (e) Yes; (f) Yes.

3. (a) Yes; (b) 25–22 weeks for 3-week difference; (c) 62–15 weeks for a 47-week difference; (d) Have chemotherapy since it seems to improve survival time.

4. (a) Mean male household income is $87,000, while female mean income is $72,000. (b) When males and females have some college, male and female incomes are separated by approximately $1,000. (c) As educational level increases so does mean household income. (d) Males who did not complete high school had the lowest household income of $44,000.

5. (a) There is very little gender difference, as years with the employer increases so does the mean household income. (b) 6–10 years show the greatest gender difference. (c) No, after 15 years they earn the same amount.

★ CHAPTER 8 SIMPLE HISTOGRAM: REVIEW EXERCISES

1. (a) When looking at the graph, one may think it is normal; however, the Kolmogorov–Smirov nonparametric test finds it is not. (b) Mean is 41.68, standard deviation is 12.559, and number of cases is 1,000. (c) 33 to 35. (d) Add the bars in this interval for a total of 254. (e) There are 33 who are 65 and older.

2. (a) 7 to 25 minutes; (b) 99% − 92% = 7%; (c) 33 minutes; (d) 23 to 26 minutes.

3. (a) Positively (right) skewed; (b) 1.72; (c) 140; (d) 40; (e) 122; (f) 63.

4. (a) 50%. (b) 85%. (c) They had from 3 to 7 accidents. (d) They had from 4 to 7 accidents. (e) 73%.

5. (a) No, the shape of the histogram does not resemble the shape of a bell. (b) Mean = 7786.09, standard deviation = 2437.922, and number of observations (N) = 60. (c) 12 (4 + 4 + 4) (d) 20 (7 + 6 + 7). (e) 2, The shorter bar corresponds to the subscribers who have a frequency of 2.

CHAPTER 9 POPULATION PYRAMID: REVIEW EXERCISES   ★

1. (a) Age interval of 35 to 37. (b) Age interval of 20.5 to 22. (c) You could be fooled here as the t test reveals a significant difference in the mean age—this is not so clear when reading the graph. (d) Both males and females with females having the larger percentage in both age intervals. (e) Both are positively skewed.

2. (a) Looking at it should strongly suggest that there are no differences between level of education and program status. This should be confirmed with a chi-square test. (b) Most of the observations are contained in the "did not complete high school" and a program status of "0"—244 individuals. (c) The least number of the observations are found in the "some college" and a program status of "0"—92 individuals.

3. (a) 13.5 to 14.5; (b) 13.5 to 14.5; (c) 125; (d) 50; (e) 225; (f) No significant difference.

4. (a) 40; (b) 60; (c) Neutral; (d) Somewhat positive; (e) Neutral; (f) No.

5. (a) 7.5 to 8.5; (b) 8.5 to 9.5; (c) 15%; (d) 2.5%; (e) 9.5 to 10.5; (f) No significant difference.

CHAPTER 10 1-D BOXPLOT: REVIEW EXERCISES   ★

1. (a) 22 and 64; (b) 68 years of age; (c) 35 and 48; (d) 48 − 35 = 13; (d) 41; (e) Not normal and has a slight positive skew (must be confirmed with the Kolmogorov–Smirnov test).

2. (a) $6 and approximately $87; (b) $776; (c) $12 to $53; (d) $53 − $12 = $41; (e) $24; (f) Not normal and has a positive skew (must be confirmed with the Kolmogorov–Smirnov test).

3. (a) 1 to 24 months (we assume the units are months); (b) 4 to 13 months; (c) 13 − 4 = 9 months; (d) 8 months; (e) Has a slight positive skew but is normal (confirmed by the Kolmogorov–Smirnov one-sample nonparametric test).

4. (a) Minimum is 1,773 and maximum is 2,185; (b) 1,925 to 2,074; (c) 2,074 − 1,925 = 149; (d) Median is 1998; (e) Has a slight negative skew but looks normal (normality was confirmed by the Kolmogorov–Smirnov one-sample nonparametric test).

5. (a) Minimum is $9,000 and maximum is $25,000; (b) $12,000 to $18,000; (c) $18,000 − $12,000 = $6,000; (d) Median is $15,000; (e) Has a positive skew and not normal (not a normal distribution was confirmed by the Kolmogorov–Smirnov one-sample nonparametric test).

★   CHAPTER 11 SIMPLE BOXPLOT: REVIEW EXERCISES

1. (a) 1539 degrees centigrade for premium and 1515 degrees centigrade for standard; (b) 1531 and 1563; (c) 1487 and 1537; (d) Standard.

2. (a) Truck; (b) Automobiles median = 14 and trucks = 16 (truck has the highest resale value); (c) Trucks = 24 and automobiles = 32; (d) Interquartile range automobiles = 10 (21 − 11); (e) Trucks minimum = 14 and maximum = 19.

3. (a) $135,000; (b) $58,125; (c) High = $84,000 and low = $25,000; (d) High = $39,000 and low = $15,000; (e) Male median = $33,000 and female median = $24,000.

4. (a) Retail has the largest interquartile range of 419 (499 − 80); (b) Retail and the value is $270.00; (c) Retail at $1,440.00; (d) Retail at $1,125, travel at $830, Other at $740, entertainment at $550, and grocery at $540; (e) Retail had the highest minimum at $90.

5. (a) Male and female have the same interquartile range of 300; (b) Male and female have identical medians of $140; (c) Males recorded the highest expenditure at $130; (d) Males at $795; (e) Males and females have the identical minimum expenditures of $0.

★   CHAPTER 12 CLUSTERED BOXPLOT: REVIEW EXERCISES

1. (a) 18. (b) Unmarried males have the highest interquartile range with the upper limits at 20 and the lower limits at 17. (c) 19 years of age. (d) 19 − 17 = 2 for the interquartile range for this group. (e) Unmarried females, married males, and married females all have distributions that are positively skewed.

2. (a) 43 years. (b) Males indicating that they were pretty happy had the lowest median age. (c) Females who are not too happy range in age from a low of 20 to a high of 90 for a range of 70. (d) From 19 to 89 for a range of 70. (e) 85 years of age.

3. (a) There are no female custodial employees. (b) Manager difference is $82 - 76 = 6$, while clerical is $83 - 81 = 2$, manager has the greatest difference. (c) Male manager range is $93 - 74 = 19$, while the females interquartile range is $86 - 67 = 19$, so the interquartile ranges are the same. (d) Range of months since hire for females is 26: high of 90 to a low of 64, while for males the range is 34: high of 98 to a low of 64.

4. (a) $17; (b) Females with some college have the highest interquartile range with the upper limits at $25 and the lower limits at $18; (c) $20; (d) $16 - 12 = 4$ is the interquartile range for this group; (e) Males who have some college have the highest median at $21.

5. (a) White = 20 years, Black = 18 years, and Other = 20 years; (b) There are four groups having the same median and the lowest number of years of school completed (12 years), they are females in all races and males in the Black race; (c) Males in the Other race category have the largest interquartile range at $17.5 - 10 = 7.5$ years; (d) $16 - 12 = 4$ is the interquartile range for this group; (e) The Black race, as the interquartile ranges are equal for males and females.

CHAPTER 13 SIMPLE SCATTERPLOT: REVIEW EXERCISES ★

1. (a) Just by looking at the graph, we see that the data points (dots) are not close to the best fit line and the square root of R^2 is 0.44 a weak correlation coefficient. In one word the relationship is weak. (b) Approximately 750.00. (c) Cannot answer this question with the information in the scatterplot as it is beyond the limits of the data. (d) Positive.

2. (a) It indicates that many of the cases in this database are concentrated with an income less than $125,000 and credit card debt of $0 to $8,000. (b) Moderate to weak since the square root of R^2 is 0.55, and it is a positive slope. (c) Income of $440,000 and credit card debt of $16,000. (d) Their salary is $125,000 and the debt is $21,500.

3. (a) 9 years; (b) Square root of 0.307, therefore, $r = .55$ (strength is moderate to weak and direction is positive); (c) 3 to 19.

4. (a) $20,000 in jewelry sales; (b) Square root of 0.304, therefore, $r = .55$ (strength is moderate to weak and positive); (c) Approximately $41,000.

5. (a) $60,000; (b) Square root of 0.643, therefore, $r = .80$ (strength is moderate positive relationship); (c) $30,000 sales in women's clothing, then men's sales are expected to be on average $9,000.

★   CHAPTER 14 GROUPED SCATTERPLOT: REVIEW EXERCISES

1. (a) The trucks have a correlation coefficient of 0.06 (square root of R^2 of 0.004). (b) These data indicate that there is no relationship between wheelbase size and price. (c) Correlation coefficient for automobiles is 0.18 (square root of R^2 of 0.034). (d) Both trucks and automobiles have very weak correlations that are slightly positive.

2. (a) Nonminority with a beginning salary of $80,000 and current salary of $135,000. (b) Correlation coefficient for nonminorities is 0.87 (square root of R^2 of 0.761) and for minorities is 0.92 (square root of R^2 of 0.847). (c) Both best fit lines indicate a strong positive linear relationship showing that as beginning salary increases so does the current salary. (d) $123,000. (e) $79,000.

3. (a) Truck. (b) Correlation coefficient for automobiles is 0.87 (square root of R^2 of 0.759) and for trucks is 0.74 (square root of R^2 of 0.541). (c) Both best fit lines indicate a strong positive linear relationship showing that as curb weight increases so does fuel capacity. (d) 23.0. (e) 29.0.

4. (a) Male with a beginning salary of $80,000 and current salary of $135,000. (b) Correlation coefficient for females is 0.75(square root of R^2 of 0.557) and for males is 0.86 (square root of R^2 of 0.739). (c) Both best fit lines indicate a strong positive linear relationship, showing that as beginning salary increases so does the current salary. (d) $85,000. (e) $132,000.

5. (a) Very little difference because the best fit lines are almost the same. (b) $R^2 = 0.467 \times 100 = 46.7\%$, which is the amount of error reduction in your estimate. (c) using both prediction lines since they cross at this point, we would estimate the length to be 185.0. (d) Correlation coefficient for automobiles is 0.72 (square root of R^2 of 0.521) and for trucks is 0.68 (square root of R^2 of 0.457). (e) Both are moderate and have a positive direction and most likely linear in shape.

CHAPTER 15 HIGH–LOW GRAPHS: REVIEW EXERCISES   ★

1. (a) Month 12 saw sales of $80,000. (b) Increased rapidly as there was an increase in variability. (c) Jewelry sales increased from $12,000 to $34,000 over this 12-month period. (d) The second month had the lowest with a value of $21,000.

2. (a) 79 years of age. (b) 6 years of education. (c) Those males and females having a post-undergraduate degree have a minimum of 20 years of education. (d) Males having a post-undergraduate degree earn a mean income of $88,000. (e) $74,000 is the highest female mean income, and this is for those who have a post-undergraduate degree.

3. (a) 79 years of age. (b) 6 years of education. (c) The group having a post-undergraduate degree has a minimum of 20 years of education. (d) Those who have a post-undergraduate degree earn a mean income of $80,000, which is the highest amount. (e) $45,000 is the mean income for those not completing high school.

4. (a) The lowest price was $1,700.00, and this occurred at the end of August or beginning of September. (b) The highest price was $2,175.00, and this occurred at the start of 2005. (c) End of August and first part of September would have been the time to purchase this stock for maximum profit if it were sold in 4 months. (d) Purchased at approximately $2,000.00 and sold at $2,175.00 for a profit of $175.00.

5. (a) There is no difference; (b) 6.00; (c) 30.00; (d) Unmarried.

CHAPTER 16 PANELING ON ONE DIMENSION: REVIEW EXERCISES   ★

1. (a) White 29.07%; (b) Black 4.98%; (c) Other 10.20%; (d) White 1.11%, Black 3.98%, Other 2.04%; (e) White 25.10%, Black 24.38%, Other 20.41%; (f) White 3.34%, Black 4.98%, Other 4.08%.

2. (a) 42.86%; (b) 29.31%; (c) 24.39%; (d) North East 42.86%, South East 24.65%, West 32.49%; (e) Exciting 32.49%, Routine 25.54%, Dull 24.39%; (f) North East region has the highest percentage of people expressing that life is exiting.

3. (a) Minorities 19 years, nonminorities 21 years. (b) Steady increase in salary until 19 years of education, which shows a slight drop and then levels off at $65,000. (c) $73,000 for nonminorities and $66,000 for minorities.

(d) Income rapidly increases from $44,000 to $66,000. (e) For minorities $26,000 (8 years of education) for nonminorities $23,000 (8 years of education).

4. (a) 20.5 to 21.5 years, 28 individuals; (b) 17.5 to 18.5 years with a high school degree, 135 individuals; (c) 20.5 to 21.5 years with a high school degree, 11 individuals; (d) Did not complete high school; (e) 20.5 to 21.5 years.

5. (a) 24.25%; (b) 2.78%; (c) 0.73%; (d) 83.43%; (e) 13.32%; (f) 3.24%; (g) No, the survey can only be used to describe the sample.

★   Chapter 17 Paneling on Two Dimensions: Review Exercises

1. (a) 28.59%; (b) 23.35%; (c) Southern, 13.69%; (d) Females, 16.96%; (e) Eastern, females 29.21%; (f) 14.42%.

2. (a) 7.78%; (b) 3.43%; (c) 4.30%; (d) 20.54%; (e) 29.49%; (f) Northern, 8.23%; (g) For males it is the Northern region (tallest bar, 5.87%) and for females the Eastern region (tallest bar, 5.38%).

3. (a) 47; (b) 40; (c) 46; (d) 47; (e) Northeast; (f) White.

4. (a) Most of the individuals in the work program did not complete high school. (b) The group with a high school education and married was the most populated having 70 individuals. (c) Of all the groups, married individuals without a high school diploma most closely resembles the normal distribution. (d) Positively skewed.

5. (a) 56.31%. (b) 38.69%. (c) 40.48%. (d) Females—40.48% and males—29.67%, therefore, females had the higher percent. (e) Females—8.33% and males—10.68%, therefore, females had the lower percent.

APPENDIX C

CHAPTERS AND SPSS DATABASES USED

Chapter	Database Used
1	accidents.sav
2	credit_card.sav, satisf.sav
3	1991 U.S. General Social Survey.sav, poll_cs_sample.sav
4	customer_dbase.sav, verd1985.sav, University of Florida graduate salaries.sav, workprog.sav
5	poll_cs_sample.sav, credit_card.sav, workprog.sav, satisf.sav, customer_dbase.sav, dmdata3.sav, Employee data.sav
6	customer_dbase.sav, catalog_seasfac.sav, satisf.sav, world95.sav, bankloan.sav
7	customer_dbase.sav, credit_card.sav, adl.sav, AMLsurvival.sav
8	customer_dbase.sav, ceramics.sav, telco.sav, autoaccidents.sav, broadband_1.sav
9	University of Florida graduate salaries.sav, workprog.sav, customer_dbase.sav, satisf.sav
10	workprog.sav, autoaccidents.sav, contacts.sav, stocks2004.sav, Employee data.sav
11	1991 U.S. General Social Survey.sav, ceramics.sav, car_sales.sav, Employee data.sav, credit_card.sav
12	dmdata3.sav, workprog.sav, 1991 U.S. General Social Survey.sav, Employee data.sav
13	advert.sav, band.sav, bankloan.sav, catalog_seasfac.sav
14	car_sales_unprepared.sav, Employee data.sav
15	stocks2004.sav, catalog_seasfac.sav, bankloan.sav, customer_dbase.sav, workprog.sav
16	customer_dbase.sav, 1991 General Social Survey.sav, Employee data.sav, workprog.sav
17	Employee data.sav, poll_cs_sample.sav, 1991 U.S. General Social Survey.sav, workprog.sav, satisf.sav
18	None
19	None

APPENDIX D

GRAPH SELECTION: TYPE AND PURPOSE

How Variables Are Measured	Graph Type	Graph's Purpose
One discrete	Simple bar graph Pie graph Simple line graph	Describe the number or percentage of observation in each category of a discrete variable
	Error bar	Visualize estimated error for discrete variables
One continuous	Simple line graph	Describes the distribution of values of a continuous variable
	Simple histogram	Describes the number of observations within intervals of the continuous variable; describes the shape of the data
	Cumulative histogram	Describes the data by adding the number of observations in each successive interval
	1-D boxplot	Describes the variability of the data by using ranges
Two discrete	Stacked bar graph Clustered bar graph Paneled bar graph on rows Paneled bar graph on columns	Depicts the relationship between the categories of two discrete variables
	Population pyramid	Compares the distribution of a discrete variable that have been split by another discrete variable
One discrete and one continuous	Simple bar graph (mean on the y-axis)	Depicts the relationship between the categories of one discrete variable and the statistics of a continuous variable
	Simple line graph for trend analysis	Shows any recognizable increase or decrease in the values of the continuous variable over time (the discrete variable)

How Variables Are Measured	Graph Type	Graph's Purpose
One discrete and one continuous (continued)	Simple line graph (pre–post trend)	Discovers changes in a trend following an event at a specific time or place
	Population pyramid	Split a continuous distribution by the categories of a discrete variable to compare these categories
	Simple boxplot	Compares the categories of a discrete variable on the ranges of a continuous variable
	Paneled graph (continuous data on the x-axis)	Split a continuous distribution by the categories of a discrete variable to compare these categories
Two continuous	Simple line graph (trend analysis)	Examine the relationship between the two variables and search for a trend
	Simple scatterplot	Seek to discover the strength and direction of any relationship between the two variables
Three discrete	Paneled graph on rows and columns	Determine the number or percentage of people or objects contained in a group that is defined by the categories of three discrete variables
Two discrete and one continuous	Multiline graph (for interaction)	Determine if the categories of two discrete variables work together to change the value of a continuous variable
	Multiline graph (for trend exploration)	Compare the values of a continuous variable for the categories of a discrete variable, while a second discrete variable seeks to analyze a trend line
	Cluster boxplot	Compares the ranges of a continuous variable categorized by two discrete variables
	Paneled graph on columns (mean on the y-axis)	Shows a statistic of a continuous variable for the categories formed by two discrete variables
	Paneled graphs on rows and columns (continuous data on the x-axis)	Sorts individuals or objects by the categories of two discrete variables and determines the group value for a continuous variable
	3-D bar graph with continuous data on the y-axis (median)	Categorize an individual or object on two discrete variables and a statistic of a continuous variable and then compare the groups
	Cluster bar graph with continuous data on the y-axis (median)	Categorize an individual or object on two discrete variables and a statistic of a continuous variable and then compare the groups

(Continued)

(Continued)

How Variables Are Measured	Graph Type	Graph's Purpose
Two continuous and one discrete	Multiline graph	Used to compare two continuous variables categorized by a discrete variable
	Grouped scatterplot	Examine the strength, direction, and shape of the relationship between two continuous variables for the categories of a third discrete variable
Three discrete and one continuous	Paneled graph on rows and columns (mean on the y-axis)	Sort individuals or objects by the categories of three discrete variables and determine the group value for a continuous variable
Three continuous and one discrete	High–low–close graphs	Show a single selected value for each of the three continuous variables at a specific time (the discrete variable) to observe changes over time
	Simple range bar graph	Shows a single selected value for each of the three continuous variables, which are then categorized by a discrete variable
Three continuous and two discrete	Cluster range bar graph	Shows a single selected value for each of the three continuous variables, which are then categorized by two discrete variables

INDEX

Note: In page references, f indicates figures.

⑤SAGE research**methods**

The Essential Online Tool for Researchers

Discover SRMO Lists— methods readings suggested by other SRMO users

The essential tool for researchers . . .

. . . from the world's leading research methods publisher

"I have never really seen anything like this product before, and I think it is really valuable."

John Creswell, University of Nebraska–Lincoln

Find exactly what you are looking for, from basic explanations to advanced discussion

Explore the Methods Map to discover links between methods

Watch video interviews with leading methodologists

Search on a newly designed taxonomy with more than 1,400 qualitative, quantitative, and mixed methods terms

Uncover more than 100,000 pages of book, journal, and reference content to support your learning

find out more at
srmo.sagepub.com